Future Education and Learning Spaces

ICT & Education in Uncertain Times

This series focuses on the possible education responses that can be implemented in uncertain times. Uncertainty could happen in times of crises or also in normal situations, where some information or actions are not known, resulting in uncertain educational scenarios. Besides, it also shows how emerging technologies, including Artificial Intelligence, Blockchain, Educational Games and Virtual Reality/Augmented Reality, will reshape the future of education to provide efficient learning/teaching experiences and assessments. Furthermore, the series discusses innovative pedagogical and learning approaches (e.g., the use of open educational practices and peer-to-peer learning) that can be applied in this rapid moving technological era to maintain education, including in uncertain times. Particularly, new instructional methods, such as game-based learning, should be designed based on the integrated technologies to provide effective learning experience, resulting in better learning outcomes. Future education should not solely focus on technology, but also on the applied instructional methods, as well as the human touch to maintain authentic and effective learning experience. The series also discusses how learning spaces can be designed to meet the growing tendency of Open and Distance Education, where thousands of learners can be taken the same course from different cultures, backgrounds and learning needs.

This series aims to establish itself, through the published books/textbooks and research, as a medium to provide guidelines and recommendations for different stakeholders, including policy makers, educational designers, teachers and students on how to enhance both learning and teaching experiences in the future for better learning outcomes, as well as how to maintain education in uncertain times. It also provides one-step ahead towards future education to prepare different stakeholders for the rapid evolution of education, even in times of uncertainty.

Mourad Abed · Dejian Liu · Ahmed Tlili
Editors

Metaverse and Artificial Intelligence in Education for a Sustainable Society

Springer

Editors
Mourad Abed
Université Polytechnique Hauts-de-France
Valenciennes, France

Dejian Liu
Smart Learning Institute
Beijing Normal University
Beijing, China

Ahmed Tlili
Smart Learning Institute
Beijing Normal University
Beijing, China

ISSN 2731-7714 ISSN 2731-7722 (electronic)
Future Education and Learning Spaces
ISBN 978-981-95-8851-0 ISBN 978-981-95-8852-7 (eBook)
https://doi.org/10.1007/978-981-95-8852-7

This Springer imprint is published by the registered company Springer Nature Singapore Pte Ltd.
The registered company address is: 152 Beach Road, #21-01/04 Gateway East, Singapore 189721, Singapore

Acknowledgements

This Proceedings of the conference is the result of the scientific contributions presented at the ICMAIE 2025 conference (International Conference on Metaverse and AI in Education for a Sustainable Society), organized within the framework of the ANR DemoES-PEIA project (Plateforme d'Expériences Immersives Apprenantes – ANR-21-DMES-0014). This project has received support from the French State as part of the "France 2030" investment programme.

We extend our sincere and deepest gratitude to the **Université Polytechnique Hauts-de-France (UPHF)** for its generous support in the publication of this Proceedings of the conference.

We also wish to thank all the authors, reviewers, members of the scientific committee, and partners whose valuable contributions have made this first edition of **Metaverse and AI in Education**.

Contents

Part III Metaverse and AI in Education

Part I
Introduction

Chapter 1
Metaverse and Artificial Intelligence in Education: A Need or an Extra Complexity

Mourad Abed, Dejian Liu, Ahmed Tlili, Hanzuore Tuxunjiang, and Mouna Denden

Abstract This chapter provides a background and a rationale of this book. It details why there is a need for more investigation related to metaverse in education.

Keywords Metaverse · Education · Simulation · AI · Sustainability

1.1 Background

Over the last few years, the idea of a metaverse has moved from science fiction to mainstream technology and policy discussions. Although the term "metaverse" combines "meta", meaning "beyond", and "verse", short for "universe" and was first introduced by Neal Stephenson in his 1992 science fiction novel Snow Crash, it has since been reinterpreted in many applied fields (Huynh-The et al., 2022).

In education, it is usually described as a persistent, multi-user digital space that combines physical reality with shared virtual environments, where learners and

M. Abed · M. Denden (✉)
Univ. Polytechnique Hauts-de-France, LAMIH, CNRS, UMR 8201, Valenciennes, France
e-mail: mona.denden@uphf.fr

INSA Hauts-de-France, Valenciennes, France

M. Abed
e-mail: Mourad.Abed@uphf.fr

D. Liu · A. Tlili
Smart Learning Institute of Beijing Normal University, Beijing, China
e-mail: liudj@bnu.edu.cn

A. Tlili
e-mail: ahmedtlili@bnu.edu.cn

H. Tuxunjiang
Academy of Future Education, Xi-an Jiaotong Liverpool University, Suzhou, China
e-mail: h.Tuxunjiang24@student.xjtlu.edu.cn

M. Abed et al. (eds.), *Metaverse and Artificial Intelligence in Education for a Sustainable Society*, Future Education and Learning Spaces,
https://doi.org/10.1007/978-981-95-8852-7_1

teachers can interact with each other in real time (Mystakidis, 2022). The metaverse is seen as an evolving ecosystem built from many emerging technologies, including big data, virtual reality (VR), augmented reality (AR), mixed reality (MR), blockchain, digital twin, artificial intelligence (AI), and so on (Lin et al., 2022). Within this ecosystem, educational implementations such as virtual labs, virtual campuses and simulation-based learning spaces provide the main environments where students can work and explore. In these environments, they can move and change objects, run experiments, or role-play professional situations that would be too expensive, risky, or hard to organize in a traditional classroom (Kye et al., 2021; Zhang et al., 2022).

Building on this spatial and experience-based foundation, the use of AI in education has pushed these trends toward more personalized and data-driven learning even further. AI tools can analyze learner data in real time, provide adaptive feedback, and create personalized content in different formats and languages, shaping how learning happens inside these virtual spaces (Hwang & Chien, 2022). For many educators and policymakers, these features promise more efficient, personalized, and inclusive learning environments, where large and diverse groups of students can receive targeted support without placing all the pressure on human teachers (Giannakos et al., 2025).

At the same time, recent reviews of metaverse and AI-powered education emphasize both the opportunities and the challenges of this development. They suggest that while immersive, data-driven environments can increase engagement, realism, and collaboration, they may also widen digital gaps, raise students' mental and emotional load, and create new concerns about data protection, dependence on commercial platforms, and reduced teacher control if they are used without careful reflection (Hwang & Chien, 2022; Kaddoura & Al Husseiny, 2023; Zhang et al., 2022). These challenges manifest at multiple levels within educational systems. On a technical level, many institutions and teachers still lack the infrastructure or digital skills needed to design and run immersive or AI-enhanced activities. From a pedagogical perspective, these tools call for new instructional models, careful alignment with learning outcomes, and ongoing professional development for teachers. Ethically and socially, questions around data privacy, equity, inclusion, and accessibility become even more urgent as more learner data is collected.

Against this background, the central question of this volume emerges: under what conditions do metaverse and AI technologies become truly necessary and clearly beneficial for education, and when do they instead add extra technical, mental, and organizational complexity to teaching and learning contexts that are already challenging?

1.2 Conclusion

Overall, the developments described above show that in some situations metaverse and AI can be genuinely needed in education. They allow teachers and students to do things that would otherwise be impossible or very hard, such as running complex simulations or connecting learners across distance. At the same time, these technologies bring real challenges and risks. It is therefore not enough to say that metaverse and AI are simply "good" or "bad"; instead, we need to understand when they are helpful and when they create extra problems.

From a technical point of view, metaverse and AI respond to clear needs when they remove barriers of time and place, and give learners access to resources, labs and learning experiences that do not exist in their local environment. From a pedagogical point of view, they are most useful when they support clear learning goals through practice, simulation, and collaboration. Socially, they can help make education more inclusive and more accessible, especially for learners with special needs or different language backgrounds. However, these same technologies become an extra layer of complexity when basic infrastructure is missing, when costs are high, or when teachers do not receive enough support to develop the necessary skills. They also create problems when they are not aligned with sound pedagogical principles and targeted learning outcomes, or when questions of data privacy, equity and power are ignored.

In this context, this volume offers both practical examples and critical reflections for educators, researchers, and decision-makers. The chapters provide frameworks and tools for designing metaverse and AI-supported learning activities, empirical studies that show how learners and teachers experience these environments, and perspectives that focus on ethical and inclusive use. Together, they aim to help readers decide when, why and how metaverse and AI should be part of their own educational practice.

Looking ahead, important challenges remain in at least three areas: building and maintaining sustainable and fair digital infrastructure, offering ongoing professional development for teachers, and managing learner data in line with clear laws and responsible governance. This volume cannot solve all of these issues, but it invites researchers, practitioners and policymakers to approach metaverse and AI with a balanced mindset: not as automatic solutions that must be adopted in every case, and not as dangers that should always be refused, but as powerful tools that need to be designed, implemented and managed with care. In this sense, the key task is not to give a final answer to whether metaverse and AI are a "need" or an "extra complexity", but to work out, in each local context, how they can support more meaningful, fair, and resilient forms of education.

References

Giannakos, M., Azevedo, R., Brusilovsky, P., Cukurova, M., Dimitriadis, Y., Hernandez-Leo, D., Järvelä, S., Mavrikis, M., & Rienties, B. (2025). The promise and challenges of generative AI in education. *Behaviour & Information Technology, 44*(11), 2518–2544.

Huynh-The, T., Pham, Q.-V., Pham, X.-Q., Nguyen, T. T., Han, Z., & Kim, D.-S. (2022). Artificial intelligence for the metaverse: A survey (Version 1).

Hwang, G.-J., & Chien, S.-Y. (2022). Definition, roles, and potential research issues of the metaverse in education: An artificial intelligence perspective. *Computers and Education: Artificial Intelligence, 3*, Article 100082.

Kaddoura, S., & Al Husseiny, F. (2023). The rising trend of Metaverse in education: Challenges, opportunities, and ethical considerations. *PeerJ Computer Science, 9*, Article e1252.

Kye, B., Han, N., Kim, E., Park, Y., & Jo, S. (2021). Educational applications of metaverse: Possibilities and limitations. *Journal of Educational Evaluation for Health Professions, 18*, 32.

Lin, H., Wan, S., Gan, W., Chen, J., & Chao, H.-C. (2022). Metaverse in education: Vision, opportunities, and challenges. In *2022 IEEE International Conference on Big Data (Big Data)* (pp. 2857–2866).

Mystakidis, S. (2022). *Metaverse. Encyclopedia, 2*(1), 486–497.

Zhang, X., Chen, Y., Hu, L., & Wang, Y. (2022). The metaverse in education: Definition, framework, features, potential applications, challenges, and future research topics. *Frontiers in Psychology, 13*, 1016300.

Part II
Design of Metaverse and AI in Education

Chapter 2
Metaverse-Enabled Instructional Design for Immersive Postgraduate Simulation Courses in Logistics: Kanban Case Study

Thi-Phuong Nguyen, Makram Mestiri, and Mourad Abed

Abstract This paper aims to advance the field of instructional design by proposing a new framework that facilitates the creation of metaverse-enabled immersive of postgraduate simulation courses. The proposed instructional design framework is mainly based on the principles of the well-known ADDIE model. Moreover, by leveraging the potential of the metaverse and related immersive technologies, we seek to address existing challenges in postgraduate logistics education and provide a pathway for future developments in immersive learning through a specific case study on the Kanban simulation game. The proposed work not only contributes to the ongoing evolution of educational practices in the rapidly changing landscape of logistics but also aims to enhance student readiness for practical industry demands.

Keywords Immersive learning · Metaverse · ADDIE model · Kanban simulation game

2.1 Introduction

The logistics industry, characterized by its dynamic nature and rapid technological advancements, demands an educational shift to meet modern needs. As logistics professionals address complex challenges in supply chain management, the efficacy of their training is crucial to their preparedness for real-world scenarios. While traditional online learning modalities are effective for delivering theoretical knowledge, they often fall short in providing the hands-on experience and practical skills such

T.-P. Nguyen (✉) · M. Abed
Laboratory LAMIH UMR CNRS 8201, Valenciennes, France
e-mail: Thi-PhuongNguyen.Nguyen@uphf.fr

M. Mestiri
Laboratory LARSH, Valenciennes, France

T.-P. Nguyen · M. Mestiri · M. Abed
Polytechnic University Hauts-de-France, Valenciennes, France

M. Abed et al. (eds.), *Metaverse and Artificial Intelligence in Education for a Sustainable Society*, Future Education and Learning Spaces,
https://doi.org/10.1007/978-981-95-8852-7_2

as operating equipment, collaborating with peers, and simulating production chains. These limitations were further exposed during the COVID-19 pandemic, as remote learning left students unable to access labs to develop practical skills.

In this landscape, the metaverse emerges as a powerful solution for education through immersive virtual environments that enhance interactivity (Mystakidis, 2022). It facilitates understanding of complex concepts via 3D visualization and manipulation while fostering practical skills through realistic simulations of logistics challenges. Current research focuses on metaverse environments design for education (Chen et al., 2023a; Han et al., 2023; Sin et al., 2023) and learning assessment in these environments (Makransky & Petersen, 2021). It lacks structured frameworks to guide instructors how to develop educational immersive contents in metaverse (Chen et al., 2023b). Existing instructional design frameworks often overlook the needs of logistics students and doesn't exploit the potential of metaverse which can lead to ineffective implementation of immersive learning experiences (Branch, 2010; Lai et al., 2024).

To address this gap, we propose a comprehensive ADDIE-based instructional design framework for creating immersive courses within the metaverse, specifically tailored to postgraduate logistics programs. The ADDIE model, comprising phases of Analysis, Design, Development, Implementation, and Evaluation, provides a systematic approach to course creation that ensures alignment with educational objectives and learner needs (Branch, 2010). Adapted for logistics education in the metaverse, this framework enhances student engagement and learning outcomes through interactive, experiential simulations. This rigorous methodology allows educators to build high-quality immersive courses that leverage the advantages of immersive technologies.

The primary contribution of this paper is the development of an instructional design framework, providing educators with a blueprint for constructing effective immersive courses in logistics. Furthermore, we present an empirical case study on designing a Kanban simulation game, which serves to illustrate the practical application of our framework in a real educational setting. Through this case study, we foster immersive simulation techniques to significantly enhance engagement and deepen understanding among logistics students.

2.2 Preliminary Background

This section introduces the essential elements, depicted in Fig. 2.1, to develop an immersive simulation course in logistics using a metaverse environment.

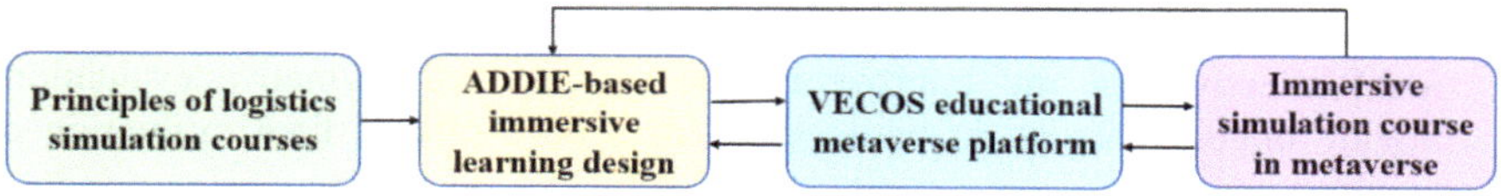

Fig. 2.1 Overview of the essential elements for designing an immersive simulation course

2.2.1 Principles of Logistics Simulation Game Courses

Simulation course principles include understanding theoretical concepts, manipulating materials, and fostering high interaction between learners and instructors. In postgraduate logistics programs, from a theoretical perspective, learners must grasp the key principles of production optimization, warehouse management, and distribution operations. From a practical perspective, students must perform various simulations related to these theoretical concepts to evaluate different scenarios and determine optimal solutions. We will illustrate these principles through a case study on the Kanban simulation game in Sect. 4.

2.2.2 ADDIE Instructional Design Model

The ADDIE model comprises five key steps (Branch, 2010), including Analysis, Design, Development, Implementation, Evaluation, whose interactions are illustrated in Fig. 2.2.

Analysis. This phase identifies learners' characteristics, needs, academic backgrounds, learning context, and desired outcomes. It determines what learners should know or be able to do after training and shows how these factors influence the Design phase.

Design. This phase involves course planning, content creation, arrangement of learning tasks, and instructional strategies. It provides a blueprint for course development.

Development. This phase involves generating instructional materials while ensuring that all learning resources align with the learning objectives and design.

Implementation. This phase is to deliver the developed course program to the learners, which makes the content accessible to the target audience.

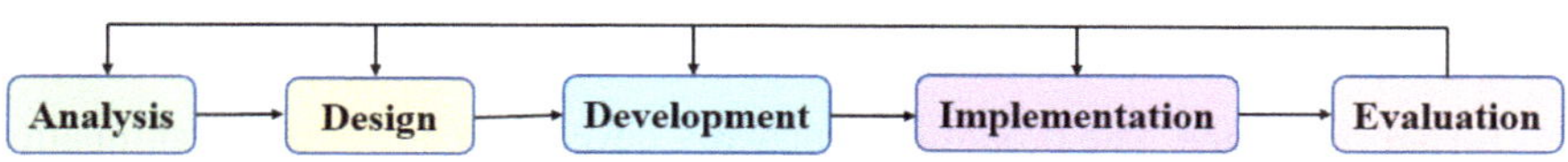

Fig. 2.2 Key steps in the classical ADDIE instructional design model

Evaluation. This includes formative and summative evaluations to assess instructional effectiveness and improve the design process. Formative evaluations provide ongoing feedback, while summative ones offer a final evaluation of learning success.

2.2.3 *VECOS Educational Metaverse Platform*

VECOS is a hybrid educational platform that combine web-based object management with a Unity-based metaverse application. It also leverages virtual reality (VR), augmented reality (AR), and artificial intelligence (AI) to provide immersive experiences. Users upload 3D models via a web platform for rendering in Unity, which allows for easy asset management and immersive interactions. VECOS features a sense of presence, interoperability, and concurrency, enabling students to learn together virtually and feel "present" despite distance (Wang et al., 2022). It is accessible on laptops, smartphones, or head-mounted displays (HMDs), with interconnections between the metaverse and the real world. Instructors and learners create avatars that reflect their physical, cultural, personal attributes and VECOS supports simultaneous multi-user access for enhanced interaction.

2.3 ADDIE-Based Immersive Instructional Design Framework

This section presents the proposed ADDIE-based immersive instructional framework for developing a postgraduate simulation course in logistics. Figure 2.3 outlines the proposed framework. The key steps (Analysis, Design, Development, Implementation, and Evaluation) should be performed sequentially, with each step starting only after the previous one is completed. Below, we explain each step and their interactions.

2.3.1 *Analysis*

This phase analyses three key elements: target audience, learning objectives, and the metaverse-based learning environment, providing essential input for the Design phase.

Target Audience. The proposed framework develops a postgraduate simulation course in logistics by analyzing the unique characteristics of students to optimize their learning experience. We first examine general factors such as age, psychological traits, attitude, and motivation, followed by specific traits like foundational

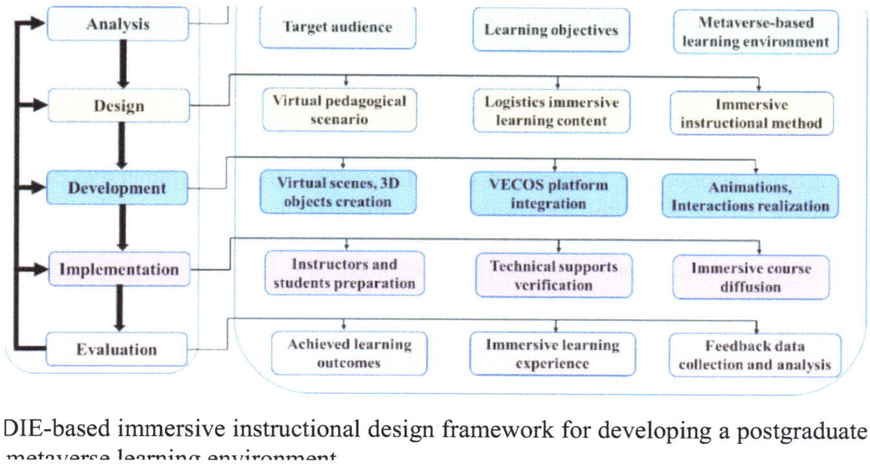

Fig. 2.3 ADDIE-based immersive instructional design framework for developing a postgraduate simulation course in a metaverse learning environment

logistics knowledge and the need for specialized subjects like production optimization and warehouse management. Most students have practical experience from internships, making them prefer applicable knowledge. Additionally, we analyze the challenges and advantages students face in the metaverse to enhance *learner-centricity*.

Learning Objectives. Based on the academic background and practical skills of the target audience, along with the requirements of the relevant postgraduate training program, we analyze the learning outcomes tailored to the course to be developed.

Metaverse-Based Learning Environment. By using 3D models and VR/AR technologies, we create digital twins of machinery, processes, and operators in the metaverse. Analyzing features like presence, interoperability, and concurrency is essential for simulating real-world logistics scenarios, enabling students to engage in course tasks (Wang et al., 2022). However, an abundance of 3D models can cause distractions and increase cognitive load, making it crucial to select relevant elements and avoid features like inappropriate lighting and sound that detract from focus and learning effectiveness (Makransky & Petersen, 2021).

2.3.2 Design

As outlined in Fig. 2.3, the Design phase focuses on three key aspects: virtual pedagogical scenario, immersive logistics content, and instructional method.

Virtual Pedagogical Scenario. Based on the analyses of the target audience and learning objectives, we determine key aspects of a pedagogical scenario for the course, including the immersive course structure, session planning (number, content, and progression), and assessment criteria. Careful planning of the time structure for each session is essential to prevent learner fatigue and overload. Each session should not exceed 30 min, with breaks incorporated to sustain focus and engagement (Kanematsu et al., 2014).

Logistics Immersive Learning Content. Creating effective immersive course content is central to the Design phase. To this end, instructors must thoroughly understand the content or closely collaborate with instructional designers to develop the course material. They must first master the learning activities required for the immersive course and then design an appropriate storyboard for those activities.

Learning activities. The learning activities can be classified into two categories: conceptual knowledge and procedural knowledge.

- *Conceptual knowledge.* This knowledge involves mental processes, including remembering, understanding, applying, analyzing, evaluating, and creating (Anderson, et al., 2001). In logistics immersive courses, conceptual knowledge focus on observing 3D scenes, exploration, analysis, and integrating prior knowledge. For example, learners may analyze a technical issue in a virtual factory and test simulations to solve logistics-related problems.
- *Procedural knowledge.* This knowledge involves following steps to complete activities (Anderson, et al., 2001). In logistics immersive courses, this may include operating an assembly line or following safety protocols before starting a virtual production line. These interrelated tasks typically require both conceptual knowledge and procedural knowledge, and classifying them helps educators identify content and activities for developing a storyboard.

Storyboard creation. After defining the content and activities, the designer creates a detailed storyboard as a production plan for all virtual scenes and immersive activities in the metaverse. In logistics, it specifies media, interactions, and activities, including object placement and durations, aligning with the pedagogical scenario. We propose a two-level storyboard structure of macro and micro designs. The macro design provides a high-level visualization of the overall scene, including its components, tools, and number of participants. It offers a general overview of the immersive logistics environment. The micro design outlines virtual scenes, detailing the manipulation of objects and learner interactions, such as operating virtual machines. Designers must carefully develop each scene, as specific storyboards enhance the user interface and streamline production in the metaverse.

Immersive Instructional Method. Choosing the right immersive instructional method is crucial during the Design phase. Although the metaverse offers innovative educational opportunities, research shows that learning in virtual environments is not always better to traditional methods (Makransky & Petersen, 2021). Misuse of immersive technologies can lead to distractions and reduced productivity. Effective immersive learning requires leveraging the metaverse's strengths while managing cognitive load to avoid overwhelming learners. We propose a hybrid instructional method that combines traditional lectures with immersive technologies like VR, AR, and XR. This approach blends the benefits of traditional lectures, delivering core content without cognitive overload, with the metaverse's interactivity, enabling dynamic visualization and exploration of complex concepts.

In logistics training, instructors can deliver lectures in a metaverse environment, such as a virtual warehouse, where students engage as avatars. Students learn about optimizing the picking process through PowerPoint presentations while performing simulations in a virtual space. The experience is further enhanced with 3D models, animations, and simulations that illustrate logistics workflows, enriching lectures, reinforcing content, and boosting learner engagement.

2.3.3 Development

This phase aims to produce educational content resources for the immersive course based on inputs from the Design phase. Development involves three key steps: creating virtual 3D objects and scenes, integrating them into the VECOS platform, and implementing animations and interactions between these objects and scenes.

Creation of Virtual 3D Objects and Scenes. As outlined in the design phase, the immersive course in the metaverse incorporates diverse learning content. Based on the storyboard and proposed hybrid instructional method, we first create an inventory of the necessary virtual 3D objects and scenes, ensuring all required resources are clearly identified. We prepare the virtual objects and scenes by downloading pre-made 3D models from online libraries like Sketchfab, creating models with tools like Blender, or scanning real-world objects to convert them into compatible formats. All 3D objects must meet the VECOS platform's technical specifications. Additionally, supplementary media like images, videos, audio files, and diagrams must be selected and prepared to enhance the learning experience.

VECOS Platform Integration. After creating 3D objects and scenes, we must integrate them into the VECOS metaverse to develop immersive learning content. Adjustments to scaling, position, orientation, and lighting are necessary to align with the storyboard. Additionally, sound, audio, videos, images, and diagrams will be tailored for the VECOS environment. Testing the accuracy of the integrated elements is essential, requiring refinements for clear visibility on all devices, including laptops, smartphones, and HMDs. This iterative testing process must be repeated to enhance the overall quality of the virtual scene.

Animations and Interactive Events Realization. To enhance interactivity in immersive courses, animations and interactive events must be integrated with virtual 3D objects on the VECOS platform. Animations and events must be tested for accuracy, relevance, and cognitive load during development. Unnecessary elements, e.g., excessive lighting or sounds, should be removed to prevent distractions. This iterative testing process ensures an optimal learning experience.

Animations of virtual 3D objects. Animations involve predefined motions or behaviors programmed into objects to enhance visual dynamics, realism, and storytelling. In logistics, they are commonly used to simulate machine operations or robot movements in warehouses. These animations can be created directly using VECOS animation tools to define object movements and other dynamic behaviors, such as opening doors.
Interactive events. Interactive events trigger animations, enabling user-driven or automated responses. The three common types of triggers are: On Click (activated as the user interacts with an object), Proximity (triggered as the user's avatar approaches), and Timed Events (occurring at preset intervals). In logistics, these events allow learners to manipulate 3D models, such as clicking objects to reveal operational details or simulating production lines.

2.3.4 Implementation

This phase focuses on delivering and deploying the instructional content and materials created in prior phases within the VECOS metaverse environment.

Preparation for Educators and Students. Before the immersive course, instructors and students must be trained to navigate the VECOS metaverse, focusing on object manipulation and simulation tasks. Course objectives should be clearly communicated with supporting video tutorials. HMD hygiene is essential, requiring cleaning before use, and breaks (e.g., every 20 min) should be scheduled to reduce motion sickness. Implementation necessitates substantial technical infrastructure and ongoing support from developers and educators to manage virtual environments and monitor learners.
Verification of Technical Supports. Adequate space must be arranged for learners to move freely. The hardware infrastructure should ensure internet connectivity and charging ports for HMDs, desktops, and smartphones. We establish VECOS user logins, avatars, access permissions, and device interoperability. Course content must align with pedagogical objectives, and technical elements like 3D assets and animations should be thoroughly tested for functionality.
Diffusion of Immersive Course with Multiple Access. For course diffusion, theoretical lessons can be delivered using presentations along with the instructor's explanations, either in a physical learning area, similar to a traditional classroom, or in the VECOS environment. However, practical skills for the course are exclusively trained on the VECOS platform. This deployment approach allows for flexibility and enhances the learning experience by leveraging the strengths of both physical and virtual environments.

2.3.5 Evaluation

The immersive course is evaluated on two criteria: achieved learning outcomes and experiences within the VECOS environment. The evaluation process includes feedback data collection and analysis. For feedback data collection, to collect feedback from learners, we can use quizzes and multiple-choice questions to assess knowledge, open-ended questions for understanding, and focus groups to gather insights on enjoyment, acceptability, and suggestions. For feedback data analysis, we use both quantitative and qualitative methods to analyze feedback data. For quantitative analysis, we apply descriptive statistics like mean, median, and standard deviation to summarize survey responses. For qualitative analysis, we use thematic analysis to identify recurring themes in focus groups and open responses.

2.4 Case Study: Results and Discussions

This section presents the case study. First, we outline the principles of the Kanban course. Next, we explain how we use the ADDIE-based instructional design framework to transform it into an immersive simulation course in VECOS metaverse platform. Finally, we discuss the results, benefits, and challenges.

2.4.1 The Kanban Simulation Game Course

The Kanban course is a role-playing simulation game where students assume positions in the production chain. They first use the push flow method and then apply the Kanban method to optimize processes (Kumar & Panneerselvam, 2007). The course helps students understand challenges in on-time product delivery and analyze causes like production inflexibility. It emphasizes push and pull production flows and requires significant interaction and collaboration, making remote teaching impractical. This course in logistics serves as a suitable case study for creating an immersive learning experience in the metaverse.

2.4.2 Developing an Immersive Kanban Simulation Game Course

Below, we outline how to apply the proposed ADDIE-based instructional framework to develop an immersive Kanban game simulation course for postgraduate logistics students.

Analysis. We analyze the learning objectives of the Kanban simulation game course, identify expected learning outcomes for postgraduate logistics students, and define the VECOS metaverse characteristics to support the course.

Target audience. Postgraduate logistics students are expected to have prior knowledge of Material Requirements Planning (MRP), net component requirements, basic Kanban principles, and the Single-Minute Exchange of Die (SMED) method. They should possess collaborative and analytical skills, effective communication, independent decision-making abilities, and strong time management. While students may demonstrate varying levels of seriousness and motivation, they generally prefer clear, engaging, and entertaining courses. However, they can quickly lose patience, become anxious when solving problems, and get bored easily, emphasizing the need for a balance between fun and effective learning.

Learning objectives of the immersive Kanban course. This course helps students understand the challenges of on-time product delivery and analyze underlying causes, such as production inflexibility and incidents. It enhances their grasp of push and pull flows through the Kanban method and emphasizes the importance of progress strategies and continuous improvement.

VECOS environment. In the Kanban simulation course, the VECOS metaverse platform offers a distinct learning experience compared to traditional classes. We create a virtual factory where students role-play various job positions. Using avatars, they navigate the factory to produce items, apply the Kanban method to optimize production, and check the warehouse. Students interact with virtual machines and 3D robots while collaborating with peers and the instructor. The metaverse enhances learning through role-playing and situated experiences, aiding knowledge retention, while minimizing unnecessary details to prevent cognitive overload.

Design. This critical phase in developing the immersive Kanban game course determines its conduct and structure, focusing on designing the scenes and course content within the metaverse.

Pedagogical scenario of the immersive Kanban course. The pedagogical scenario consists of two main phases. Phase 1 involves a push flow simulation, while Phase 2 implements a pull flow simulation using the Kanban method to optimize production. We increase the number of actions from Phase 1 to Phase 2, adding tasks like adjusting Kanban tickets, analyzing situations, and making decisions. After each simulation, the instructor conducts a debriefing with students. Each simulation lasts less than 30 min, with a 10-min break in between (Makransky & Petersen, 2021).

Content design of the immersive Kanban course. Based on various taxonomies (Anderson et al., 2001), we can classify the learning activities in the Kanban course, as shown in Table 2.1.

Using the inventory, we gain a clearer understanding of the learning activities to design the storyboard. We use the tool Storyboard. That to create both macro and micro designs for the immersive Kanban course. In the macro design,

Table 2.1 Inventory for the Kanban simulation game course learning activities

Learning activities	Description
Cognitive knowledge	
Observe	Game instructions, production procedure
Calculate	Net requirements, efficiency rate, stock, service rate
Analyze	Incidents, delivery shortage situations
Decide	Quantity, produce reference, progress
Procedural knowledge	
Manipulate	Materials, containers, 3D objects
Produce	New products
Manage	Production flow, incident, stock shortages
Write	Tracking sheets, needs calculations, progress actions
Simulate	Push flow, pull flow using Kanban method

we outline the structure of the virtual factory on the VECOS platform, which includes defining workstation positions, interactive elements, media placements, and devices needed for simulating production flows. In the micro design, we detail the activities within the factory scene. The macro design provides the information needed to develop the micro design for each scene, detailing the instructor's instructions and learners' actions during the simulation.

Instructional method for the immersive Kanban course. We apply the proposed hybrid instructional method for the theoretical content. In the VECOS learning space, the instructor and students, represented by their avatars, engage in a virtual classroom, where core concepts like MRP, SMED and Kanban methods are presented, e.g., using PPT slides. For practical simulations, students participate in activities at the virtual factory, and interact with machines. To encourage collaboration, we promote teamwork, idea exchange with the instructor, and cooperation within and between groups.

Development. This phase includes two main operations: production and testing. Using the design phase as a blueprint, we create and test immersive resources to deliver the Kanban simulation game course on the VECOS platform.

Creation of virtual 3D objects, scenes for the immersive Kanban course. We first identify the necessary elements to build the Kanban simulation game course (see Table 2.2) and then create their corresponding virtual 3D models.

VECOS metaverse platform integration. To integrate the virtual objects and scenes into VECOS, we upload all elements to the web server at hyper.VECOS.us. The Unity-based application then allows visualization and modification of the objects' dimensions, positions, and rotations.

Animation and interactive events for the immersive Kanban course. The virtual Kanban game course enhances learning by using robots, control buttons, and conveyors to simulate factory organization. In the VECOS metaverse platform,

Table 2.2 Inventory of necessary elements for creating virtual objects and scenes

Elements	Description	
3D modeling tools	Blender software	
Scripting tools	Storyboardthat.com	
Diagramming tools	Lucid.app	
Virtual objects	Tokens, Containers, Conveyors, Pallets, Robots, Kanban tickets, etc	
Virtual scene	Factory	

we develop animations and program events for production, storage, and shipping simulations. Animations specify the trajectory, position, rotation, and attributes of objects, while interactive events define conditions that trigger these animations(Fig. 2.4). This ensures that objects move in a set order based on criteria, such as one object not passing another. Additionally, students can interact with a virtual assistant through their avatars for information and assistance. Below are images of the animations and events in VECOS for the Kanban course.

Implementation. The implementation of the immersive Kanban simulation game course follows the same steps as described in Sect. 3.4.

Evaluation. The immersive Kanban simulation course can be evaluated through questionnaires and semi-structured interviews with postgraduate logistics students and instructors. The evaluation assesses learning outcomes, utility, usability, and acceptability of the course on the VECOS platform. However, the course has only been tested with a small number of participants to verify the functionalities of the developed educational content in the VECOS metaverse platform, so this evaluation phase is not yet complete.

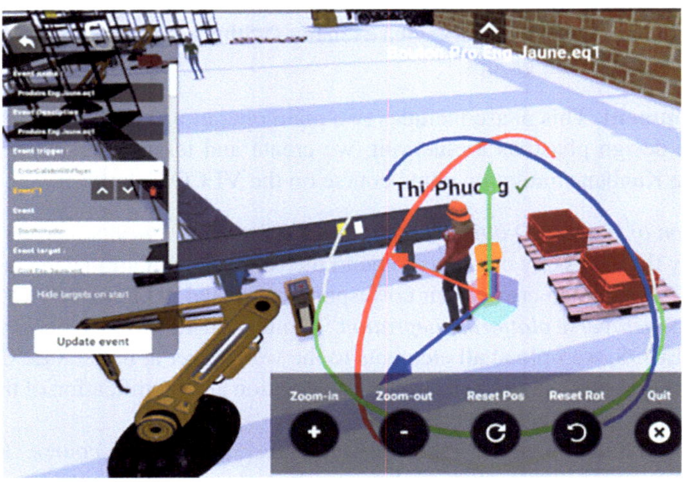

Fig. 2.4 Setting up interactive events on virtual objects in the VECOS platform

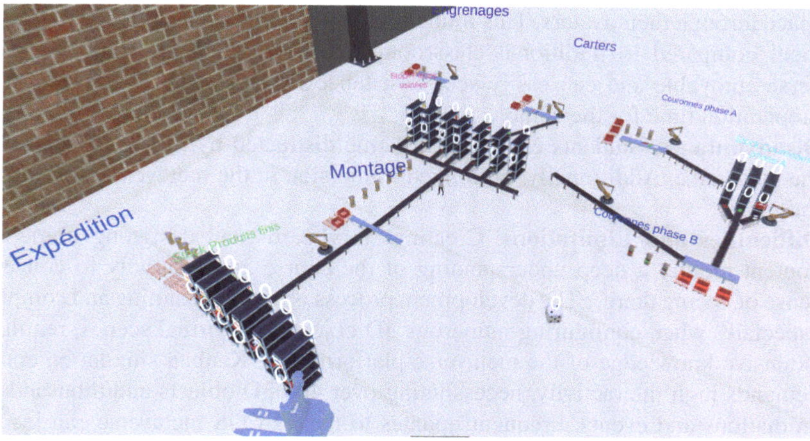

Fig. 2.5 Overview of the virtual factory scene for each participant team. Each team has five work stations (Gear station, Crankcase station, Phase A crown Station, Phase B crown station, Assembly station), and three stocks (Phase A crown stock, Machined parts stock, Final product stock)

2.4.3 Simulations with the Virtual Factory Scenes

Below, we present the virtual factory scene designed for the immersive Kanban course in the VECOS platform. Students and the instructor participate through their avatars in two teams, engaging in simulations for production and warehouse management.

Virtual Factory Scenes. The virtual factory scene accommodates two teams, each with five workstations as illustrated in Fig. 2.5. Compared to the traditional Kanban course, the VECOS metaverse creates a situated learning environment by incorporating robots, conveyors, and storage, providing students with a realistic factory practice experience.

Simulations of Production and Warehouse Management. With five workstations per team, members must collaborate to simulate the production line and decide which workstation to halt in case of problems.

2.5 Discussions

The immersive Kanban simulation game course on the VECOS metaverse platform offers advantages, disadvantages, and challenges, which are discussed below.

Advantages. The Kanban game in the metaverse allows students to access the course remotely, conduct production simulations, interact with materials, and collaborate with peers and instructors while feeling present in the same virtual space through their avatars. This immersive experience enhances student engagement compared to traditional classroom courses. Participants find the metaverse enjoyable and can easily seek assistance from a virtual assistant, saving preparation time for the game.

Disadvantages. Students can easily become distracted by the virtual scenes in the metaverse. Additionally, prolonged immersion in the metaverse may lead to fatigue.

Difficulties and Limitations. Creating storyboards and designing immersive content require a deep understanding of the course and creativity to convey a sense of "being there". The development process is time-consuming and complex, especially when configuring numerous 3D objects and virtual scenes, requiring extensive knowledge of the metaverse platform. The Kanban simulation course demands high interactivity, necessitating over 400 3D objects and thousands of animations and events. Frequent updates to the VECOS metaverse can lead to technical issues affecting functionality. Close collaboration among developers and instructors is crucial for accurately interpreting design ideas, and evaluating participant performance in the metaverse requires support from multiple stakeholders (developers, teachers, and students).

2.6 Conclusion and Perspectives

A new ADDIE-based instructional design framework has been proposed for creating immersive courses for postgraduate logistics students in the metaverse. This framework analyzes the characteristics of logistics students and provides guidelines for creating interactive course content specific to the logistics domain. As a case study, we develop an immersive Kanban simulation game course that allows users (instructors and students) to conduct simulations optimizing production flows within the VECOS metaverse platform. In the future, we will conduct user tests with a large number of postgraduate students and logistics instructors to gather and analyze feedback, evaluating the course from the perspectives of learning outcomes and immersive experiences. The results will enhance the ADDIE-based framework and the developed courses.

Acknowledgements The authors would like to express their sincere gratitude to the French National Research Agency (ANR) for its financial and institutional support through the project DemoES-PEIA (Immersive Learning Experiences Platform)—21-DMES0014. This support has been instrumental in the development, implementation, and dissemination of the research presented in this article.

References

Anderson, L., et al. (2001). *A taxonomy for learning, teaching, and assessing: A revision of Bloom's taxonomy of educational objectives*. Addison Wesley Longman, Inc.

Branch, R. (2010). *Instructional design: The ADDIE approach*. Springer.

Chen, X., Zhong, Z., & Wu, D. (2023a). Metaverse for education: Technical framework and design criteria. *IEEE Transactions on Learning Technologies, 16*(6), 1034–1044.

Chen, X., Zou, D., Xie, H., & Wang, F. (2023b). Metaverse in education: Contributors, cooperations, and research themes. *IEEE Transactions on Learning Technologies, 1*(6), 11–29.

Han, Z., Tu, Y., & Huang, C. (2023). A framework for constructing a technology—enhanced education metaverse: Learner engagement with human–machine collaboration. *IEEE Transactions on Learning Technologies, 16*(6), 1179–1189.

Kanematsu, H., Kobayashi, T., Barry, D., Fukumura, Y., Dharmawansa, A., & Ogawa, N. (2014). Virtual STEM class for nuclear safety education in metaverse. In *Procedia computer science* (pp. 1255–1261). Elsevier B.V.

Kumar, C., & Panneerselvam, R. (2007). Literature review of JIT-KANBAN system. *International Journal of Advanced Manufacturing Technology, 32*(3–4), 393–408.

Lai, L., et al. (2024). Task-driven ADDIE-twist model with a teach-study double-helix structure. *IEEE Transactions on Education, 67*(1), 1–10.

Makransky, G., & Petersen, G. (2021). The cognitive affective model of immersive learning (CAMIL): A theoretical research-based model of learning in immersive virtual reality. *Educational Psychology Review, 33*(3), 937–958.

Mystakidis, S. (2022). Metaverse. *Encyclopedia, 2*(1), 486–497.

Sin, Z., et al. (2023). Toward an edu-metaverse of knowledge: Immersive exploration of university courses. *IEEE Transactions on Learning Technologies, 16*(6), 96–110.

Wang, M., Yu, H., Bell, Z., & Chu, X. (2022). Constructing an edu-metaverse ecosystem: A new and innovative framework. *IEEE Transactions on Learning Technologies, 15*(6), 85–96.

Chapter 3
Evaluation in Metaverse: A Pilot Study in HCI Education

Yosra Mourali and Christophe Kolski

Abstract As an emerging technology, the metaverse is increasingly recognized for its potential to transform education by enabling the creation of immersive and engaging learning environments. However, its adoption remains in the early stages and is the subject of ongoing investigation. This paper presents a pilot study in which we designed and implemented a Human–Computer Interaction (HCI) course within a virtual reality environment, involving both a professor and learners. A user-centered evaluation was conducted to assess the system's usability, learners' cognitive workload, knowledge acquisition, and overall learning experience. This study leads to several perspectives.

Keywords Metaverse · Education · Evaluation · Usability · Cognitive workload · Learning experience · Avatar · Virtual reality

3.1 Introduction

The metaverse is an evolving concept that represents the convergence of physical and virtual worlds creating immersive and interactive environments where users can work, socialize, and entertain themselves through digital avatars. It is often envisioned as a decentralized, persistent, and interconnected virtual space that transcends traditional online experiences. From a scientific perspective, there is no universally agreed-upon definition of the metaverse. Ritterbusch and Teichmann conducted a systematic literature review to analyze and synthesize key characteristics from various academic sources to clarify its meaning. Their findings describe the metaverse as a "*crossword of 'meta' (meaning transcendency) and 'universe'—a (decentralized) three-dimensional online environment that is persistent and immersive, in*

Y. Mourali · C. Kolski (✉)
University Polytechnique Hauts-de-France, CNRS, UMR 8201 – LAMIH, Valenciennes, France
e-mail: Christophe.Kolski@uphf.fr

Y. Mourali
e-mail: Yosra.Mourali@uphf.fr

M. Abed et al. (eds.), *Metaverse and Artificial Intelligence in Education for a Sustainable Society*, Future Education and Learning Spaces,
https://doi.org/10.1007/978-981-95-8852-7_3

which users, represented by avatars, can participate socially and economically in a creative and collaborative manner, within virtual spaces that are independent of the physical world" (Ritterbusch & Teichmann, 2023).

The metaverse can exist in varying degrees of virtuality. Hwang and Chien suggest that it may be either entirely or partially virtual, depending on the technologies involved (Hwang & Chien, 2022). An entirely virtual metaverse is primarily experienced through Virtual Reality (VR), which allows users to achieve complete immersion via specialized headsets, making it particularly suitable for simulations, gaming, and interactive experiences (Rebbani et al., 2021; Zhao, 2009). On the other hand, a partially virtual metaverse can be facilitated through Augmented Reality (AR), which overlays digital elements onto the real world, enhancing the physical environment with additional information, graphics, or interactive content (Rebbani et al., 2021) (Dargan et al., 2023). Mixed Reality (MR), as a hybrid approach, seamlessly integrates virtual and real-world elements, allowing them to coexist and interact dynamically (Rebbani et al., 2021; Bekele et al., 2018).

The metaverse finds applications across numerous sectors: healthcare (Bansal et al., 2022), manufacturing (Doolani et al., 2020), military field (Tanwar et al., 2024), sports (Putranto et al., 2023), entertainment (Onderdijk et al., 2023), gaming (Bodzin et al., 2021), shopping (Xi & Hamari, 2021), etc.

The education sector is undergoing a profound transformation with the integration of the metaverse, reshaping both teaching and learning (Tlili et al., 2022). Virtual classrooms are breaking down geographical barriers, enabling learners from around the world to participate in the same lessons in real-time. Immersive environments, such as historical reenactments and interactive scientific simulations, offer engaging experiences that enhance understanding of complex concepts, making abstract ideas more concrete and memorable (Marougkas et al., 2023).

This paper presents a pilot study investigating the use of the metaverse, specifically virtual reality (VR), in educational settings. The study focuses on evaluating user experience and the effectiveness of a metaverse-based Human–Computer Interaction (HCI) course. The structure of the paper is as follows: Sect. 3.2 provides an overview of metaverse use in education and examines methods for evaluating user experience in such context. Section 3.3 describes the design of the HCI course developed for this study. Section 3.4 explains the evaluation methodology and presents the study's findings. Finally, Sect. 3.5 concludes with key insights and discusses future directions for metaverse-enhanced education.

3.2 Background

3.2.1 Metaverse in Education

The integration of the metaverse in education presents innovative opportunities to design immersive, interactive, engaging, and personalized learning environments. Its application has been particularly prominent in fields such as computer science, social sciences, engineering, and medicine (Al-Ansi et al., 2023). Among the various technologies, AR and VR have emerged as the most widely adopted in educational contexts (Samala et al., 2023). By combining VR, AR, MR, and/or AI, metaverse-based platforms facilitate realistic simulations, collaborative problem-solving, and experiential learning, allowing learners to construct knowledge through meaningful and contextualized experiences (Marougkas et al., 2023). In fact, AI-driven personalization is a key feature of metaverse-based education. Intelligent algorithms can adapt content and pacing to individual learner needs, providing tailored learning experiences to optimize learning outcomes (Tursunova et al., 2024).

The metaverse enables the creation of virtual classrooms and laboratories where learners can interact with digital educational content, peers and professors in real-time, transcending geographical and physical limitations. For instance, medical students can practice complex surgical procedures in risk-free virtual environments (Iwanaga et al., 2021), while engineering students can experiment with 3D models of machinery or infrastructure. According to Soliman et al., VR has positive cognitive and pedagogical benefits in engineering education, which ultimately improves the student's understanding of the subjects, performance and learning experience (Soliman et al., 2021). Furthermore, the metaverse supports gamified learning experiences, which enhance motivation and engagement by incorporating elements such as rewards and challenges (Yu et al., 2022). These environments foster critical thinking and creativity, as learners are encouraged to explore, experiment, and collaborate within dynamic, simulated settings (Rizki et al., 2024).

3.2.2 Evaluation in the Metaverse

The use of the metaverse in education is still in its early stages, with ongoing investigation and testing across various learning settings (Nguyen et al., 2024). Current studies particularly focus on its impact on learner engagement, learning outcomes, and overall learning experiences (AlGerafi et al., 2023). Evaluating these aspects in the educational metaverse requires a combination of quantitative and qualitative methods.

Engagement is measured through psycho-physiological, observational, and self-reported data. Dubovi employed psycho-physiological data streams such as facial expression, eye-tracking, and electrodermal activity sensors to evaluate learner engagement (Dubovi, 2022). However, Çelik and Baturay used the User Engagement

Scale (UES) (Çelik & Baturay, 2024). The scale consisted of 12 items and included four key dimensions: focused attention, perceived usability, aesthetic appeal, and reward factor. Responses are collected using a 5-point Likert scale ranging from strongly disagree to strongly agree. Observational methods, such as coding video recordings of learner interactions in the metaverse, also allow researchers to identify active participation behaviors, including asking questions and collaborating with peers. Learning outcomes in the metaverse are generally evaluated through performance-based assessments (Soliman et al., 2021). The overall learning experience is evaluated through interviews and questionnaires (Slavova & Mu, 2018). In our pilot study, we combine multiple methods, focusing on both learners and the professor.

3.3 Metaverse-Based HCI Course Design

The course focuses on Human–Computer Interaction (HCI). It was designed and implemented using the VECOS[1] platform (Virtual Education Collaborative System). This platform was developed as part of a project led by the Université Polytechnique Hauts-de-France in collaboration with the Université Catholique de Lille, France. Built with Unity, VECOS integrates metaverse technology and virtual reality, enabling the creation of immersive educational scenarios with interactive content. In this virtual environment, the professor and the learners are represented by their respective avatars. As suggested by Tinmaz and Singh Dhillon (2024), such representation may enhance engagement and interaction throughout the learning experience.

The course is structured into two distinct scenes: the *Virtual Classroom* and the *HCI Museum*. The learning experience begins in the *Virtual Classroom*. The classroom features educational resources on the walls, consisting of six slides and two videos as shown at top left of Fig. 3.1. At bottom left of Fig. 3.1, a slide is visible. At right of Fig. 3.1, a video is displayed (source: www.w3.org/WAI/videos/standards-and-benefits/).

The professor introduces the course and explains the first slide orally. To enhance interactivity, the professor then invites the participants to visit the second scene, the *HCI Museum* as shown in Fig. 3.2.

The *HCI Museum* offers a captivating exploration of the evolving relationship between humans and technology. Its collections include photographs, comic strips, and diverse interactive exhibits. The displayed artifacts highlight the field's richness, featuring everything from smartwatches, video games, and virtual reality headsets to printers and collaborative interactive tabletops, showcasing the various forms of Human–Computer Interaction. A dedicated section on the history of science and technology presents printers, televisions, and video games from different generations, allowing learners to trace the rapid advancement of these technologies. Additionally,

[1] https://hyper.vecos.us/users/login/.

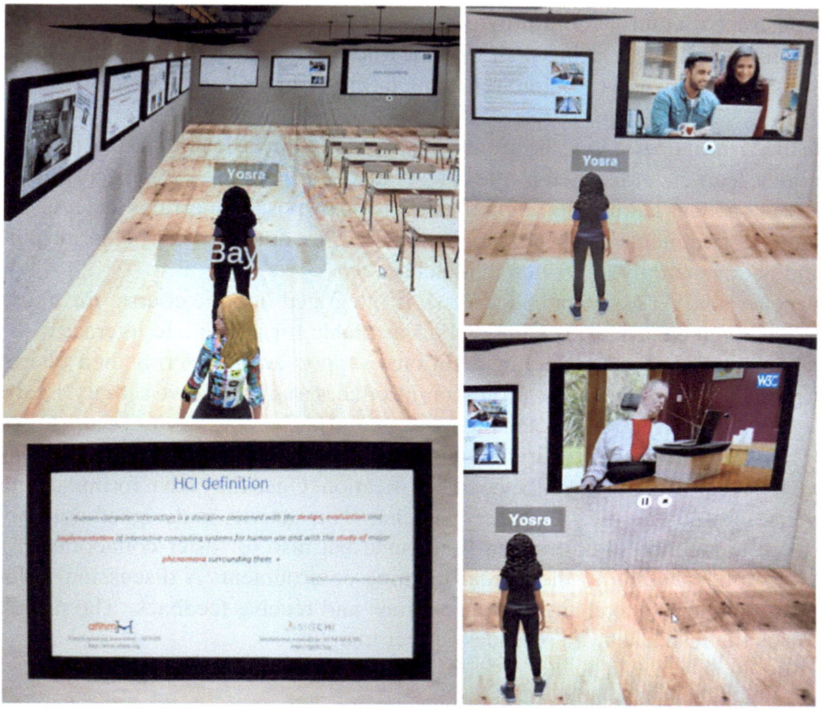

Fig. 3.1 The *Virtual Classroom* scene

Fig. 3.2 The *HCI museum* scene

a reconstructed control room provides insight into the complex interfaces used in professional settings. During their visit, learners can explore and interact with the exhibits at their own pace before returning to the *Virtual Classroom* to continue the course.

In the *Virtual Classroom*, the professor proceeds with the lecture. When presenting the slides, learners move their avatars closer to the professor to listen attentively. The professor engages learners throughout the session by posing questions and requesting opinions or comments on specific topics. The professor specifies whether responses should be given orally or written in the chat.

A generative AI assistant called *Baya* is integrated into the course. *Baya*, represented as a female avatar (see Fig. 3.1) is available for learners to interact with via private chat at any time, providing additional support and answering their queries.

At the end of the course, the professor introduces a collaborative activity. Learners engage in group discussions, exchanging ideas and perspectives as they work together to develop their responses. Throughout this process, they have the option to consult *Baya*, the AI assistant, for guidance or clarification. Once they have formulated their answers, they submit their responses via chat. This activity is designed not only to reinforce key concepts covered in the course but also to foster collaboration and problem-solving skills in the virtual learning environment. A discussion follows, allowing learners to exchange their solutions and receive feedback. The professor evaluates the responses and provides further insights.

3.4 Metaverse-Based HCI Course Evaluation

This section provides a comprehensive overview of our research methodology and evaluation process.

We begin by detailing the experimental protocol used in this pilot study, outlining the step-by-step procedure followed to evaluate the HCI course in the VECOS educational metaverse environment. Next, we describe our participant recruitment process. The third part of this section focuses on the tools and instruments used for data collection. We provide a detailed account of the quantitative and qualitative methods employed. Finally, we detail the statistical methods and qualitative analysis techniques used to interpret the collected data and draw meaningful conclusions about the effectiveness and user experience of the Metaverse-based HCI course.

3.4.1 Protocol

This section introduces the evaluation protocol for the HCI course in a metaverse environment, structured into two main phases as presented in Fig. 3.4: (1) training and (2) evaluation.

During the training phase, participants create their account and design their avatar, a process that plays a crucial role in fostering engagement and enhancing learning outcomes, as highlighted by Tinmaz and Singh Dhillon (Tinmaz & Singh Dhillon, 2024). Following this, they take part in a training session to familiarize them with the VR headset and controllers, enabling them to navigate and interact effectively within the virtual environment. The Meta Quest 3 (Oculus) technology for VR is used in this pilot study.

The evaluation phase begins with participants completing consent and image rights approval questionnaires, followed by a pre-test questionnaire to assess their prior knowledge.

Once these preliminary steps are completed, participants proceed to the course, which takes place in the two virtual scenes described in Sect. 3.3: the *Virtual Classroom* and the HCI Museum. Learners begin the course in the *Virtual Classroom*, where they listen to the professor's explanation of the first slide-based educational resource. They then move to the *HCI Museum*, where they explore interactive exhibits. After that, they return to the *Virtual Classroom* as shown in Fig. 3.3, where they continue the course with additional slides and videos. To encourage participation, the professor asks questions and invites learners to share their thoughts or comments on specific topics, specifying whether responses should be given orally or in the chat. Toward the end of the course, the professor introduces a collaborative activity, where learners submit their responses via chat. This is followed by a discussion, allowing them to exchange ideas, compare solutions, and receive feedback. The professor evaluates their answers and provides additional insights to reinforce key concepts.

After the session, learners complete a post-test and a NASA-TLX questionnaire (Hart et al., 1988). Additionally, both learners and the professor complete a SUS questionnaire (Brooke, 1996), as well as open-ended questions to assess their experience and the usability of the metaverse learning environment.

3.4.2 Participant Recruitment

Participants were recruited, using a convenience sampling method, from LAMIH UMR CNRS 8201 at the Université Polytechnique Hauts-de-France and consisted of two distinct profiles: a professor and a group of 8 learners. The professor, an expert in HCI, played a key role in designing the course that he would later deliver in the metaverse. The learners were PhD students and engineering interns specializing in computer science. Recruitment was conducted informally through word-of-mouth, with researchers specifically seeking students interested in taking part in an HCI course within the metaverse. Convenience sampling was selected due to its practicality, offering easy access to participants and minimizing time and cost, which makes it particularly appropriate for a pilot study.

Two-course sessions were organized in February–March 2025 each lasting half a day. Each session included the professor and four learners as shown in Fig. 3.5. The decision to limit the number of participants was based on observations made

Fig. 3.3 Illustrations of learning situations involving a slide or a video, alongside interactions through chat. Source of the video visible at bottom left: www.w3.org/WAI/videos/standards-and-benefits/

during the initial training session on the use of VR equipment. It was noted that a larger number of participants could cause technical issues, such as system bugs and connectivity problems, which could disrupt the learning experience.

3.4.3 Data Collection

The data collection instruments used in the evaluation study were as follows:

- Informed consent, image rights, and privacy protection: Before participation, all participants were provided with a clear and detailed explanation of the study's objectives and the experimental protocol. This ensured transparency and allowed participants to make an informed decision about their involvement. Consent was obtained voluntarily, with explicit confirmation that participants had the right to withdraw from the study at any time without facing any repercussions. As the study involved visual data collection such as photographs, it was essential to respect participants' image rights. These rights safeguard personal privacy and provide individuals with control over how their images are used. To uphold these ethical standards, we obtained explicit consent from all participants, authorizing the use of their images strictly for research, academic dissemination, and valorization purposes. By prioritizing these ethical principles, the study maintained the

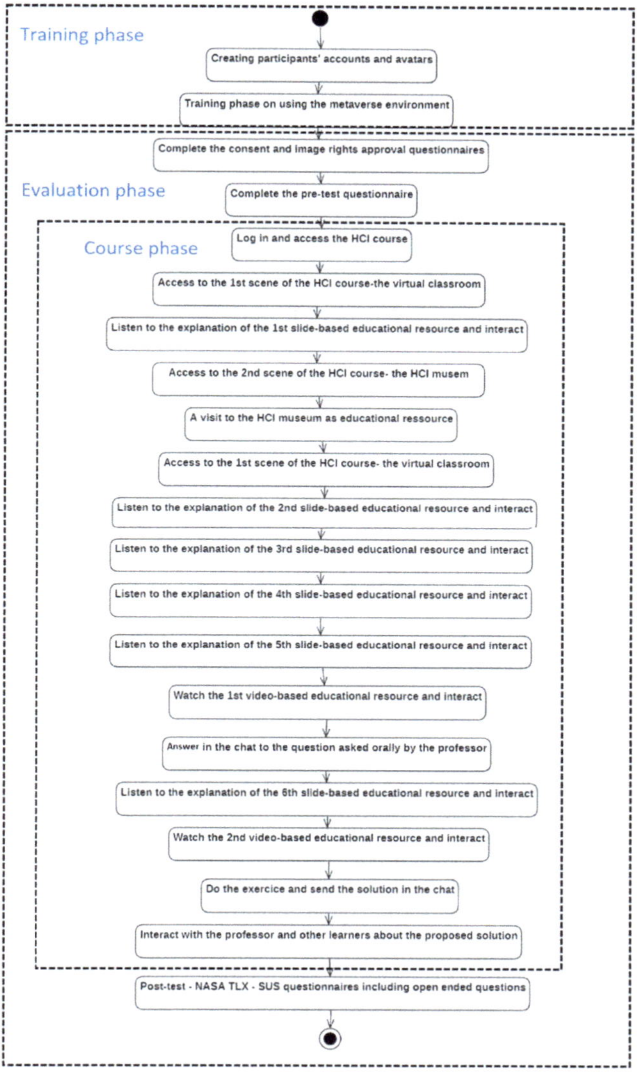

Fig. 3.4 The evaluation protocol for the HCI course in a metaverse environment

highest standards of research integrity, participant protection, and responsible data management.

- Pre-test and post-test questionnaires: They are essential assessment tools used to measure and compare participants' knowledge before and after completing the HCI course in the metaverse environment. This methodology, widely applied in various studies, such as (Chaves et al., 2015; Mortara et al., 2014; Mourali et al., 2024a), helps evaluate the effectiveness of the learning experience. To ensure

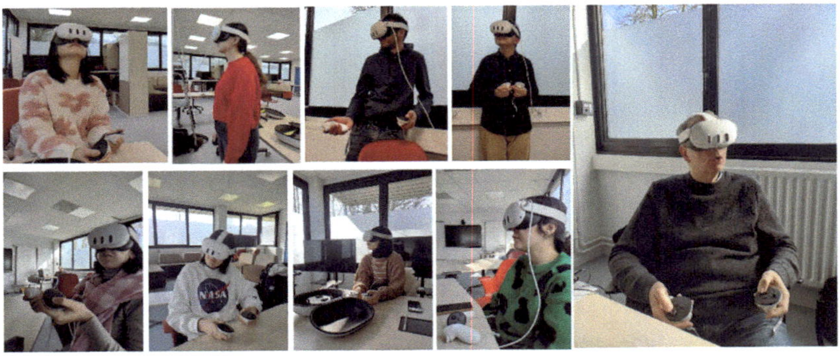

Fig. 3.5 Photos of the participants (left) and the professor (right) taken during the 2 HCI course sessions

consistency and reliability, the questions are formulated identically in both tests. In our study, each test consists of five carefully designed questions aimed at assessing key concepts covered in the course. By analyzing the differences in responses between the pre-test and the post-test, we gain insights into participants' learning progress and the overall impact of the metaverse-based educational approach.

- System Usability Scale (SUS) (Brooke, 1996) is a widely recognized tool for evaluating system usability. In our study, participants completed the SUS questionnaire after the HCI course session. They rated 10 statements on a Likert scale from 1 (strongly disagree) to 5 (strongly agree), with the final SUS score ranging from 0 to 100. To assess the overall usability of the HCI course in the VECOS metaverse environment, we calculated the average of all participant scores. This method provides a standardized measure of the system's user-friendliness, helping identify strengths and areas for improvement.
- NASA Task Load Index (NASA-TLX) (Hart et al., 1988) is a widely used subjective workload assessment tool designed to evaluate the cognitive and physical demands of a task. Developed by NASA, it measures workload across six dimensions: (1) mental demand (the level of cognitive effort required), (2) physical demand (the amount of physical effort needed), (3) temporal demand (the pressure from time constraints), (4) performance (the participant's perceived success in completing the task), (5) effort (the overall exertion required) and (6) frustration (the level of stress or annoyance experienced). Participants rate each dimension on a scale from 0 to 100, and the final workload score is calculated based on weighted averages. The NASA-TLX is commonly used in HCI, ergonomics, and usability studies to assess system complexity and user experience.
- Open-ended questions allow to obtain more details on the users' perception regarding their learning experience in the metaverse environment.

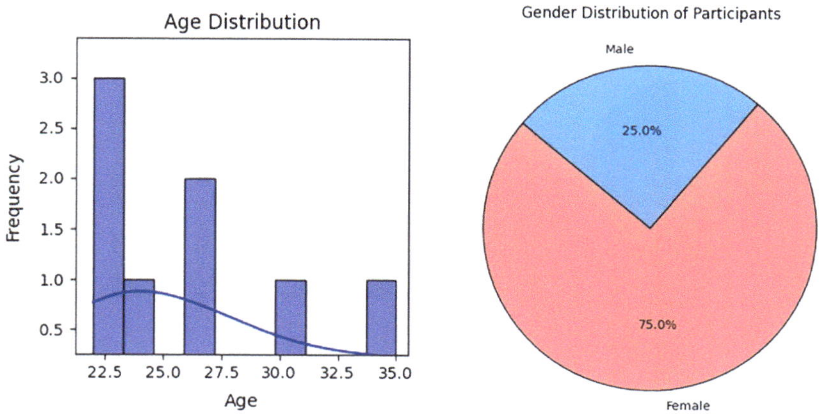

Fig. 3.6 Gender and age distribution of participants

3.4.4 Data Analysis

In this section, we focus on participants' characteristics, assessment of knowledge acquisition, usability evaluation, workload assessment, and qualitative feedback from learners.

- **Participants' Characteristics**

The study involved a total of eight learners, all of whom were either PhD students in computer science or engineering students specializing in computer science. The gender distribution among the participants showed a notable predominance of female learners (6) compared to males (2). Regarding age distribution, participants ranged from 22 to 35 years old, with a majority (predominantly between 22 and 27 years old) being in the early stages of their academic and research careers (Fig. 3.6).

- **Assessment of Knowledge Acquisition**

To evaluate the effectiveness of the metaverse-based learning environment in enhancing participants' understanding of HCI principles, pre- and post-tests were administered (see Appendix A). Analysis of the questionnaire responses revealed a significant progression in participants' comprehension of key HCI concepts (Fig. 3.7).

A pre-test score of 2.7 out of 5 revealed moderate initial knowledge. A substantial improvement was observed after course participation, with the average post-test score rising to 4.37 out of 5 representing a 61.85% enhancement in knowledge acquisition. This increase highlights the positive impact of the metaverse learning environment on HCI education and underscores its effectiveness as an interactive and immersive instructional tool. A factor in interpreting these results is the HCI background distribution among learners. The data revealed that 6 participants out of 8 had no

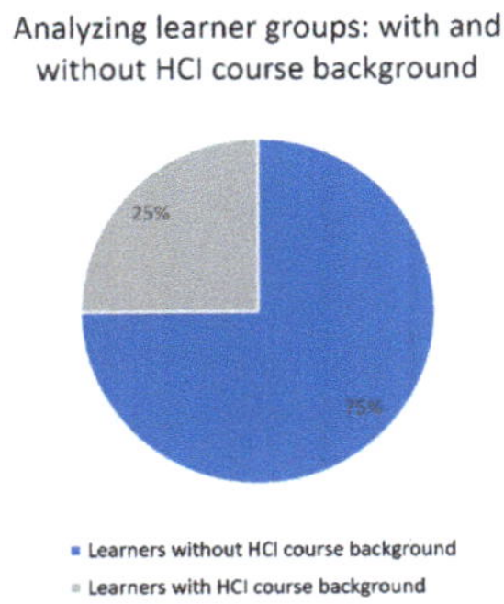

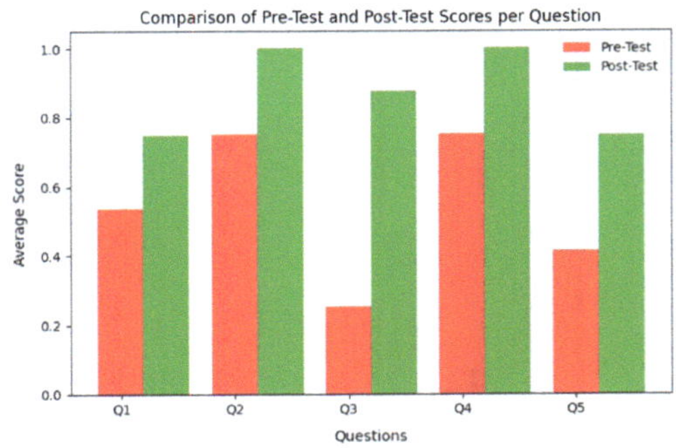

Fig. 3.7 A comparative analysis of participant responses pre- and post-HCI course participation within the metaverse environment

prior formal education in HCI, while only 2 participants out of 8 had previous exposure to HCI courses. The overall knowledge improvement is particularly promising given that the majority of learners started with a limited foundation in HCI concepts. This suggests that the metaverse-based course was effective in bridging the knowledge gap, even for those without prior exposure. Additionally, the interactive and immersive nature of the metaverse may have played a key role in facilitating an engaging learning experience, making complex HCI principles more accessible and comprehensible.

- **Usability Evaluation of the Metaverse-Based HCI Course**

The usability of the metaverse-based HCI course was evaluated from both the professor's and learners' perspectives using the SUS questionnaire. As shown in Fig. 3.8, the professor's score (57.5) and learners' score (53.75) fall within the marginal range, suggesting that while the system is functional, it requires improvements to enhance the overall experience. The professor's score reflects challenges in adapting traditional teaching methods to a virtual environment. Learners scored slightly lower at 53.75, with most being unfamiliar with VR, leading to difficulties in navigating the virtual space and adjusting to immersive learning methods. Technical issues and problems related to VR usage were prevalent among participants, raising questions about how the workload associated with these challenges might affect the overall effectiveness of such educational environment.

- **Workload Assessment with NASA-TLX**

The NASA-TLX results reveal, as shown in Fig. 3.9, valuable insights into user workload across the six dimensions during the metaverse-based HCI course. Mental demand scores ranged from 50 to 100 (median: 70), with a moderate variability in distribution, indicating that most participants perceived high cognitive strain during tasks. In contrast, physical demand exhibited significant variability (range: 10–95, median: 42.5), suggesting divergent experiences, with some participants reporting minimal exertion and others encountering substantial physical challenges. Temporal

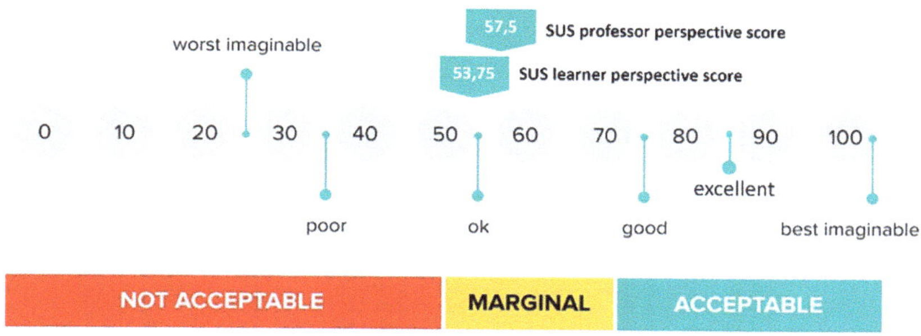

Fig. 3.8 SUS score

demand scores were moderately distributed (range: 10–70, median: 55), reflecting generally manageable time pressures. Performance scores showed high variability (range: 5–90, median: 25), with predominantly low ratings signaling widespread dissatisfaction or difficulties in achieving objectives. Effort levels were notably elevated (range: 15–100, median: 67.5), aligning with the high mental demand and underscoring the system's demanding nature. Effort levels were notably elevated (range: 15–100, median: 67.5), aligning with the high mental demand and underscoring the system's demanding nature. This heightened effort can be attributed to participants' need to divide their attention between two challenging tasks: comprehending course content and mastering unfamiliar VR technology. The cognitive load was particularly significant given that 6 participants out of 8 were first-time VR users, requiring them to simultaneously adapt to a novel user interface while absorbing academic material. Moreover, the physical discomfort reported by many participants due to wearing the VR headset added an extra layer of difficulty, potentially distracting from the learning experience and increasing the overall effort required to engage effectively with the virtual environment. Finally, frustration scores ranged widely (5–85, median: 62.5), correlating with challenges in other dimensions such as mental and physical demand.

- **Qualitative Feedback from Learners**

To complement the quantitative data, open-ended questions were posed to participants regarding the most and least engaging aspects of the metaverse-based HCI course. The most engaging aspects, as revealed by the word cloud analysis (Fig. 3.10), centered around interactive and immersive elements of the metaverse environment. Prominent features included the museum visit, chat functionality, video and image integration, voice communication, and interactions with *Baya*, the generative AI assistant. *Baya* was integrated into the learning environment to provide personalized, real-time guidance and respond to learner questions. Its effectiveness was not evaluated in this pilot study, but one participant spontaneously expressed a positive opinion of the interaction with Baya.

Participants particularly appreciated the social and interactive dimensions of the course. As one learner noted, "interaction with other learners, the professor, and

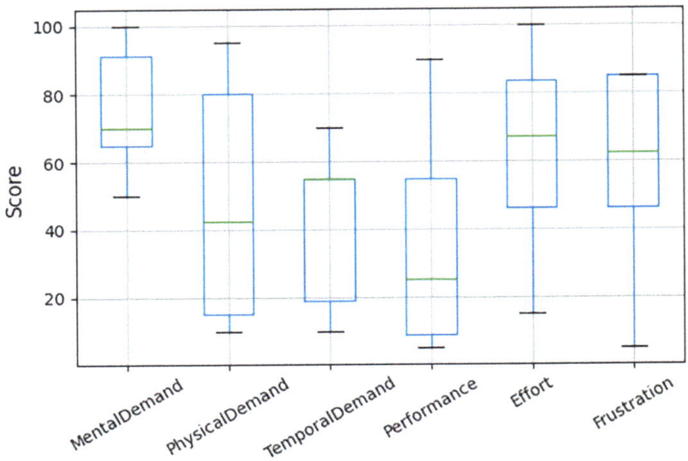

Fig. 3.9 Distribution of NASA-TLX workload dimensions

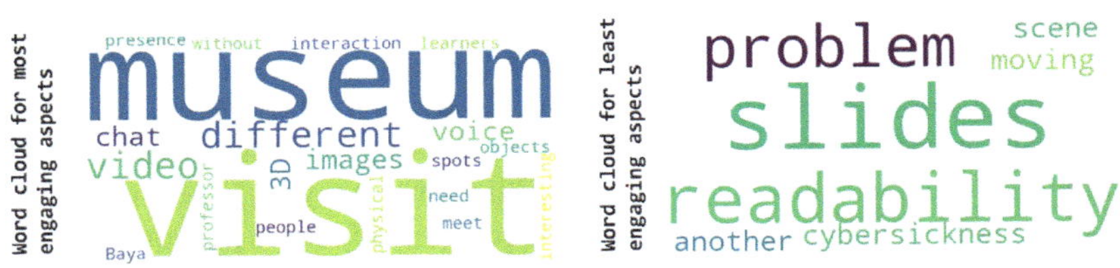

Fig. 3.10 Word clouds for most and least engaging aspects

Baya" was a highlight of their experience. Another emphasized the immersive nature of the platform, stating, that "the visit to the museum" was especially engaging. Conversely, the least engaging aspects are primarily related to usability issues and physical discomfort. The word cloud analysis highlighted concerns with slides, specifically problems with readability, as well as instances of cybersickness. These issues were reflected in participant comments, with one learner reporting, "slides: readability problem" indicating difficulties in accessing some course resources (slides). Physical discomfort was also a significant concern, as evidenced by another participant's feedback: "I felt nauseous and dizzy when moving and typing on the virtual keyboard". These qualitative insights underscore the potential of immersive, interactive elements in metaverse learning environments while also highlighting the need to address usability and comfort issues to enhance the overall learning experience.

3.5 Conclusion and Future Work

The integration of the metaverse into education is reshaping traditional learning environments by introducing immersive, interactive experiences that transcend physical boundaries. This paper presents a pilot study exploring the use of virtual reality within a metaverse-based course. The study focuses on evaluating both user experience and the educational effectiveness of this innovative approach. A dedicated HCI course was designed and delivered using the VECOS environment. As suggested by Shah et al. (Shah et al., 2024), constructivist learning theory provides a strong foundation for the design of such an immersive course. It emphasizes that students actively participate in the process of gaining new skills through experience and interaction, rather than passively receiving information. This approach is reflected in two key elements: (1) an interactive museum visit, where learners explore diverse collections including photographs, comic strips, and exhibits to discover new information autonomously; and (2) collaborative activities, in which learners work together and/or with Baya to co-construct knowledge. The HCI course impact was assessed for both learners and the professor. The results indicate that metaverse-based learning can enhance learners' engagement and understanding. Elements such as video content, interactive simulations (e.g., virtual museum visits), and real-time oral communication with the professor and peers (replicating a real classroom dynamic) contributed positively to the learning experience.

The following practical recommendations could be made to educators seeking to adopt similar metaverse-based teaching approaches: Providing an initial training session is essential to familiarize learners with the virtual environment and reduce cognitive load. Additionally, incorporating AI assistants, such as Baya, can support learner autonomy and engagement. It is also advisable to design concise and visually accessible learning materials to minimize discomfort and enhance understanding of the course. Finally, a gradual integration of immersive activities starting with short, guided sessions can help learners adapt and build confidence in navigating the metaverse.

While the study showed encouraging results, some challenges were observed, particularly among users less familiar with VR technology. These included occasional discomfort during extended use, especially following abrupt avatar movements or while reading and writing text within the virtual environment. Such issues were more noticeable among beginners and tend to diminish with increased exposure and practice. To minimize cybersickness and physical discomfort, several improvements are being considered. These include reducing session duration, incorporating regular breaks, and enhancing visual stability through higher-quality slides, clearer images, more legible text, and smoother transitions.

Furthermore, the technology can initially impose a considerable cognitive load for novice users, as attention must be shared between learning the course content and adapting to the virtual environment. Although a training session was conducted before the experiment to familiarize participants with the VR technology, it may not have been sufficient to fully mitigate the cognitive load. In future iterations, we intend to enhance this preparatory phase by extending training duration, offering guided practice scenarios, and simplifying interface interactions to further reduce dual-task interference and support more effective learning. With appropriate guidance and gradual familiarization, this cognitive effort can be reduced, supporting a smoother and more effective learning experience.

A limitation of this pilot study is the small sample size (8 learners) and the relative homogeneity of the participant profile. Although the incorporation of diversity in gender, study level, and prior knowledge of HCI, all participants were still PhD students or engineering interns in computer science. This restricts the generalizability of the findings to broader populations. Future work will address this limitation by increasing the sample size and including participants from a wider range of academic backgrounds (e.g., humanities, social sciences), different levels of education (bachelor's, master's), and technical expertise (from novice to advanced metaverse users). This approach will support a more representative evaluation of learning outcomes in metaverse-based HCI contexts. Additionally, while the findings of this pilot study provide promising insights into the potential of metaverse-based learning in HCI education, a comparative study involving a traditional teaching method would be useful to more accurately assess the specific impact of the metaverse environment on learning outcomes. Moreover, a medium-term post-test could be planned at several months (for instance 3 or 4 months) following course completion, with a long-term (for instance 9 or 12 months) post-test. These assessments would aim to evaluate both medium- and long-term knowledge retention and the sustained impact of the learning experience.

Future work will also focus on deepening the analysis of the learning experience in the metaverse by considering multiple dimensions, such as learner engagement, satisfaction, performance, and course completion (Mourali et al., 2024b). It will also aim to explore the teaching experience from the instructor's perspective. Additionally, future studies will investigate the impact of the metaverse on collaborative aspects within learning contexts. A more in-depth investigation of the role and impact of the Baya generative AI assistant should also be conducted to better understand its contribution to learner support, engagement, and autonomy in immersive environments.

Acknowledgements The authors extend their sincere gratitude to the participants who contributed to this study. We are particularly grateful to Professors Mourad Abed and Makram Mestiri for their support and for granting us access to the VECOS platform, which made this research possible. Finally, we express our warmest thanks to Khalil Jedidi, the engineer and developer of VECOS, whose expertise and technical support were essential for conducting the experiments.

Appendix A: Questions of the Pre- and Post-Tests

Tick the correct answer(s). There may be multiple correct choices.

1. Human–computer interaction is a discipline concerned with:

☐ The design of interactive computing systems
☐ The implementation of interactive computing systems
☐ The study of phenomena surrounding interactive computing systems

2. Action theory of Norman is proposed to guide the development of interactive systems by:
   ☐ The technological possibilities
   ☐ User needs
3. Ken Olsen, founder of the legendary minicomputer company DEC predicted in 1977 that everyone would have a computer:
   ☐ Yes ☐ No
4. A person with nomophobia is a person who:
   ☐ walks slowly and without attention to their surroundings because they are focused upon their smartphone
   ☐ experiences intense anxiety and fear when separated from this smartphone
5. According to ISO usability refers to
   ☐ Effectiveness
   ☐ Efficiency
   ☐ Learnability
   ☐ Satisfaction

References

Al-Ansi, A. M., Jaboob, M., Garad, A., & Al-Ansi, A. (2023). Analyzing augmented reality (AR) and virtual reality (VR) recent development in education. *Social Sciences & Humanities Open, 8*(1), Article 100532. https://doi.org/10.1016/j.ssaho.2023.100532

AlGerafi, M. A. M., Zhou, Y., Oubibi, M., & Wijaya, T. T. (2023). Unlocking the potential: A comprehensive evaluation of augmented reality and virtual reality in education. *Electronics, 12*(18), Article 18. https://doi.org/10.3390/electronics12183953

Bansal, G., Rajgopal, K., Chamola, V., Xiong, Z., & Niyato, D. (2022). Healthcare in metaverse: A survey on current metaverse applications in healthcare. *IEEE Access, 10*, 119914–119946. https://doi.org/10.1109/ACCESS.2022.3219845

Bekele, M. K., Pierdicca, R., Frontoni, E., Malinverni, E. S., & Gain, J. (2018). A survey of augmented, virtual, and mixed reality for cultural heritage. *Journal on Computing and Cultural Heritage, 11*(2), 36. https://doi.org/10.1145/3145534

Bodzin, A., Junior, R. A., Hammond, T., & Anastasio, D. (2021). Investigating engagement and flow with a placed-based immersive virtual reality game. *Journal of Science Education and Technology, 30*(3), 347–360. https://doi.org/10.1007/s10956-020-09870-4

Brooke, J. (1996). *SUS: A 'Quick and Dirty' usability scale. In usability evaluation in industry.* CRC Press.

Çelik, F., & Baturay, M. H. (2024). The effect of metaverse on L2 vocabulary learning, retention, student engagement, presence, and community feeling. *BMC Psychology, 12*(1), 58. https://doi.org/10.1186/s40359-024-01549-4

Chaves, R. O., von Wangenheim, C. G., Furtado, J. C. C., Oliveira, S. R. B., Santos, A., & Favero, E. L. (2015). Experimental evaluation of a serious game for teaching software process modeling. *IEEE Transactions on Education, 58*(4), 289–296. https://doi.org/10.1109/TE.2015.2411573

Dargan, S., Bansal, S., Kumar, M., Mittal, A., & Kumar, K. (2023). Augmented Reality: A comprehensive review. *Archives of Computational Methods in Engineering, 30*(2), 1057–1080. https://doi.org/10.1007/s11831-022-09831-7

Doolani, S., Wessels, C., Kanal, V., Sevastopoulos, C., Jaiswal, A., Nambiappan, H., & Makedon, F. (2020). A Review of Extended Reality (XR) Technologies for Manufacturing Training. *Technologies, 8*(4), Article 4. https://doi.org/10.3390/technologies8040077

Dubovi, I. (2022). Cognitive and emotional engagement while learning with VR: The perspective of multimodal methodology. *Computers & Education, 183*, Article 104495. https://doi.org/10.1016/j.compedu.2022.104495

Hart, S. G., & Staveland, L. E. (1988). Development of NASA-TLX (Task Load Index): Results of empirical and theoretical research. In P. A. Hancock & N. Meshkati (Eds.), *Human mental workload, advances in psychology, 52* (pp. 139–183). North Holland.

Hwang, G.-J., & Chien, S.-Y. (2022). Definition, roles, and potential research issues of the metaverse in education: An artificial intelligence perspective. *Computers and Education: Artificial Intelligence, 3*, Article 100082. https://doi.org/10.1016/j.caeai.2022.100082

Iwanaga, J., Kamura, Y., Nishimura, Y., Terada, S., Kishimoto, N., Tanaka, T., & Tubbs, R. S. (2021). A new option for education during surgical procedures and related clinical anatomy in a virtual reality workspace. *Clinical Anatomy, 34*(3), 496–503. https://doi.org/10.1002/ca.23724

Marougkas, A., Troussas, C., Krouska, A., & Sgouropoulou, C. (2023). Virtual reality in education: A review of learning theories, approaches and methodologies for the last decade. *Electronics, 12*(13), Article 13. https://doi.org/10.3390/electronics12132832

Mortara, M., Catalano, C. E., Fiucci, G., & Derntl, M. (2014). Evaluating the effectiveness of serious games for cultural awareness: The Icura user study. In A. De Gloria (Ed.), *Games and learning alliance* (pp. 276–289). Springer. https://doi.org/10.1007/978-3-319-12157-4_22

Mourali, Y., Barathon, B., Bourgeois Colin, M., Chaabane, S., Fassi, R., Ferrai, A., et al. (2024a). Serious game for company governance: supporting integration, prevention of professional disintegration and job retention of people with disabilities. In *Engineering Interactive Computer Systems, EICS 2023 International Workshops and Doctoral Consortium, June 26–27, 2023, Selected Papers, LNCS 14517*. Springer (pp. 41–49). https://doi.org/10.1007/978-3-031-59235-5_5

Mourali, Y., Agrebi, M., Farhat, R., Kolski, C., & Jemni, M. (2024b). Design and evaluation of online educational content: AI-informed guidelines based on machine learning analysis of learners' interactions traces. *International Journal of Human-Computer Interaction*. https://doi.org/10.1080/10447318.2024.2434765

Nguyen, A. H. D., Le, T. T., Dang, T.-Q., & Nguyen, L.-T. (2024). Understanding metaverse adoption in education: The extended UTAUMT model. *Heliyon, 10*(19), Article e38741. https://doi.org/10.1016/j.heliyon.2024.e38741

Onderdijk, K. E., Bouckaert, L., Van Dyck, E., & Maes, P.-J. (2023). Concert experiences in virtual reality environments. *Virtual Reality, 27*(3), 2383–2396. https://doi.org/10.1007/s10055-023-00814-y

Putranto, J. S., Heriyanto, J., Achmad, S., & Kurniawan, A. (2023). Implementation of virtual reality technology for sports education and training: Systematic literature review. *Procedia Computer Science, 216*, 293–300. https://doi.org/10.1016/j.procs.2022.12.139

Rebbani, Z., Azougagh, D., Bahatti, L., & Bouattane, O. (2021). Definitions and applications of augmented/virtual reality: A survey. *International Journal of Emerging Trends in Engineering Research, 9*(3), 279–285. https://doi.org/10.30534/ijeter/2021/21932021

Ritterbusch, G. D., & Teichmann, M. R. (2023). Defining the metaverse: A systematic literature review. *IEEE Access, 11*, 12368–12377. https://doi.org/10.1109/ACCESS.2023.3241809

Rizki, I. A., Suprapto, N., Saphira, H. V., Alfarizy, Y., Ramadani, R., Saputri, A. D., & Suryani, D. (2024). Cooperative model, digital game, and augmented reality-based learning to enhance students' critical thinking skills and learning motivation. *Journal of Pedagogical Research, 8*(1), 339–355.

Samala, A. D., Usmeldi, Taali, Ambiyar, Bojic, L., Indarta, Y., Tsoy, D., Denden, M., Tas, N., & Dewi, I. P. (2023). Metaverse technologies in education: A systematic literature review using PRISMA. *International Journal of Emerging Technologies in Learning (iJET), 18*(05), Article 05. https://doi.org/10.3991/ijet.v18i05.35501

Shah, S. F. A., Mazhar, T., Shahzad, T., Ghadi, Y. Y., & Hamam, H. (2024). Integrating educational theories with virtual reality: Enhancing engineering education and VR laboratories. *Social Sciences & Humanities Open, 10*, Article 101207. https://doi.org/10.1016/j.ssaho.2024.101207

Slavova, Y., & Mu, M. (2018). A comparative study of the learning outcomes and experience of VR in education. In *2018 IEEE Conference on Virtual Reality and 3D User Interfaces (VR)* (pp. 685–686). https://doi.org/10.1109/VR.2018.8446486.

Soliman, M., Pesyridis, A., Dalaymani-Zad, D., Gronfula, M., & Kourmpetis, M. (2021). The application of virtual reality in engineering education. *Applied Sciences, 11*(6), Article 6. https://doi.org/10.3390/app11062879

Tanwar, V., Anand, V., Aggarwal, P., Kumar, M., & Kumar, G. R. (2024). Revolutionizing military training: A comprehensive review of tactical and technical training through augmented reality, virtual reality, and haptics. In *2024 IEEE 9th International Conference for Convergence in Technology (I2CT)* (pp. 1–5). https://doi.org/10.1109/I2CT61223.2024.10543615

Tinmaz, H., & Singh Dhillon, P. K. (2024). User-centric avatar design: A cognitive walkthrough approach for metaverse in virtual education. *Data Science and Management, 7*(4), 267–282. https://doi.org/10.1016/j.dsm.2024.05.001

Tlili, A., Huang, R., Shehata, B., et al. (2022). Is Metaverse in education a blessing or a curse: A combined content and bibliometric analysis. *Smart Learn. Environ., 9*, 24. https://doi.org/10.1186/s40561-022-00205-x

Tursunova, F., Oripova, N., Muhammadiyeva, M., Nurullayeva, S., Hamroyev, S., & Tishabaeva, I. (2024). Augmented reality and AI in higher education: Creating immersive learning experiences. In *2024 International Conference on Knowledge Engineering and Communication Systems (ICKECS)* (Vol. 1, pp. 1–5). https://doi.org/10.1109/ICKECS61492.2024.10617355

Xi, N., & Hamari, J. (2021). Shopping in virtual reality: A literature review and future agenda. *Journal of Business Research, 134*, 37–58. https://doi.org/10.1016/j.jbusres.2021.04.075

Yu, J., Denham, A. R., & Searight, E. (2022). A systematic review of augmented reality game-based Learning in STEM education. *Educational Technology Research and Development, 70*(4), 1169–1194. https://doi.org/10.1007/s11423-022-10122-y

Zhao, Q. (2009). A survey on virtual reality. *Science in China Series F: Information Sciences, 52*(3), 348–400. https://doi.org/10.1007/s11432-009-0066-0

Chapter 4
Leveraging Large Language Models to Generate 3D Simulations of Complex Course Concepts in a Metaverse Environment

Sirine Elghali, Mabrouka Chouchane, Makram Soui, and Mourad Abed

Abstract The proposed work aims to integrate the metaverse into the preparation of computer science materials for education. Students often struggle with engagement, motivation, and conceptual ambiguity, especially when dealing with abstract, theory-based learning materials. To address these challenges, we propose deploying Metaverse technologies and Large Language Models (LLMs) to generate 3D simulation-based course examples that clarify complex algorithm executions. The goal is to assist novice teachers in preparing concrete, real-world examples for ambiguous concepts. To this end, we have developed an LLM-powered tool that supports teachers in two key steps: first, generating abstract examples that relate a given concept to real-world applications. Second, transforming these abstract examples into concrete, interactive 3D simulations, enabling students to better understand abstract concepts, making them more tangible and engaging. By integrating metaverse-based simulations with AI-assisted content generation, our approach aims to enhance students' comprehension, engagement, and problem-solving skills in computer science education. The obtained results are very promising.

Keywords Large language model · Three-dimensional virtual world · Education · Metaverse

S. Elghali (✉)
National School of Computer Science, Manouba, Tunisia
e-mail: alghalisirine@gmail.com

M. Chouchane
Higher Institute of Management, Gabes, Tunisia

M. Soui
College of Innovation and Technology, Flint, MI, USA
e-mail: msoui@umich.edu

M. Abed
Polytechnic University of Hauts-de-France, Valenciennes, France
e-mail: Mourad.Abed@uphf.fr

M. Abed et al. (eds.), *Metaverse and Artificial Intelligence in Education for a Sustainable Society*, Future Education and Learning Spaces,
https://doi.org/10.1007/978-981-95-8852-7_4

4.1 Introduction

In recent years, the demand for innovative and engaging educational methods has grown significantly. Teaching is one of the most challenging processes, requiring not only the effective transmission of knowledge and information but also the ability to engage, motivate and allow students to develop their skills. In this context, education is undergoing a transformation, shifting from traditional pedagogical approaches to technology-enhanced pedagogy (Chen et al., 2023a). This evolution is driven by the integration of advanced technological tools and methodologies into the classroom, reshaping the way students learn and interact with educational content (Kessler, 2021; Lee & Park, 2021; Theelen et al., 2019). One of the most emerging technologies for enhancing teaching methodologies is the metaverse, a three-dimensional virtual environment that enables the creation of immersive, interactive and personalized learning experiences (Godwin-Jones, 2024; Kaddoura & Al Husseiny, 2023; Onu et al., 2024; Shu & Gu, 2023), making complex concepts more engaging and accessible (Han & Noh, 2021). Therefore, several studies (Chen et al., 2023a; Yazid Abdul Ghani et al., 2024; Laseinde & Dada, 2023; Teplá et al., 2022) demonstrate the positive impact of using 3D models in education, which aims to simplify the abstract process, enhance understanding of students, and make learning more applicable and accessible.

In this work, we focus on algorithm and data structures, which are considered complex subjects to study, and numerous factors present the difficulties students face in learning these topics, such as the teaching methods used in courses (Porter & Simon, 2019; Porter et al., 2012; Salguero et al., 2020), and the learning environment (M. N. et al., 2017). One of the most important challenges that teachers face during the lesson is how to effectively explain an algorithm and its execution in a real-world scenario. The finest education is that which does not just provide us with information but brings our lives into harmony with all reality (Vyas, 2022). Despite the advancements, several studies have primarily focused on creating virtual teaching environments (Sim, 2024; Zhai et al., 2023). Although the immersive potential of metaverse platforms such as UNIVERSE,[1] educators often continue to rely on traditional instructional methods including slides, textbooks, and videos. Consequently, the integration of 3D virtual spaces tends to be superficial, with limited impact on the depth and quality of curriculum delivery. Additionally, other studies have used 3D technology solely for visualization purposes (Adedokun-Shittu, 2025; Samala et al., 2024; Wang et al., 2024). For example, Samala et al. used 3D visualization techniques for computer hardware education (Samala et al., 2024). However, these efforts often fall short of fully addressing the pedagogical value of the course content and fail to stimulate the behavior of student's and to make learning more appealing through technological methods.

The main objective of this work is to develop a 3D animated simulation of complex topics in the algorithms and data structures course. First, it aims to simplify and stimulate students' engagement while enhancing their understanding. Second, it helps

[1] https://www.viewsonic.com/global/presscenter/content/universe-a-metaverse-built-foreducation_5380.

teachers find the best and most innovative examples to explain these concepts, consequently creating an immersive and appealing learning experience. By addressing these objectives, we propose a novel LLM-powered tool that automatically generates 3D simulations of algorithmic concepts, making them more accessible to both educators and students. Our approach consists of converting a detailed textual description, based on a teacher's request into a structured Blender script, which is then rendered as a 3D animated simulation. The generated 3D models can be seamlessly integrated into metaverse environments, allowing interactive and immersive exploration of fundamental computing concepts.

This paper is structured as follows: Sect. 4.2 provides a literature review, outlining relevant research in the field. Section 4.3 presents a motivation example. Section 4.4 details the background concepts related to our study. Section 4.5 details our LLM tool. Section 4.6 discusses the model selection and fine-tuning step. Section 4.7 shows the experimental results and discusses the effectiveness of the proposed tool. Finally, Sect. 4.8 concludes the paper and presents some future research perspectives.

4.2 Related Work

With advancements in 3D technology, numerous studies in recent years have explored automated methods for generating 3D visualization, 3D scenes, including text-to-3D generation and the use of Large Language Models (LLMs) for 3D model creation. In this section, we provide a summary of relevant prior research.

The 3D visualization in education. Recently the using of 3D visualization has been undergoing significant development particularity in education contexts. Samala et al. (Samala et al., 2024) developed an augmented reality (AR) mobile application using a ARCore to create static 3D visualizations aimed at enhancing computer hardware education. This work evaluates the effectiveness of the applications through the lens of the Hedonic Motivation System Adoption Model (HMSAM), which considers factors like perceived enjoyment, curiosity, and behavioral intentions to use technology. Another study by Wang et al. (2024) conducted a meta-and regression analysis of randomized controlled studies on the use of 3D visualization technology for teaching human anatomy. The study aimed to evaluate the effectiveness of 3D visualization in enhancing learning outcomes among medical students and residents, focusing on its impact on test scores, learner satisfaction, enjoyment and time efficiency. These studies aim to create a realistic virtual environment by representing a static 3D visualization, but they lack comprehensive interactive scenarios to effectively demonstrate the processes or progression of the subject matter.

Text-to-3D generation techniques. Text-to-3D generation has attained a great success. Li et al. (2023) propose a framework Instant3D, a fast text-to-3D generation which aims to generate one specific object for one given text prompt using a Perp-Neg algorithm with the integration of three condition mechanisms (cross-attention, style injection, and token-to-plane transformation). Another text-to-3D scene generation framework DreamScene (Li, 2024), combines Gaussian-based models with formation pattern sampling and enables the capability to generate a fantasy scene merely by structuring several objects coherently from a user's description. Fantasia3D also proposed a high-quality and realistic method for automatic text-to-3D content creation using disentangled modeling and learning of geometry and appearance (Chen et al., 2023b). These studies are based on 3D text generation to create a one specific 3D object or scene, with static and simple structure.

Generating a 3D model with Large Language model. A few studies have increasingly focused on the using of LLMs to generate 3D models. A LayoutGPT framework is proposed to generate simple 3D visual layouts based on text input, using LLMs integrated with visual generation models (Feng et al., 2023). Another Framework proposed 3D-GPT utilizing LLMs for instruction-driven 3D modeling, with three collaborative efforts of agents (task dispatch, conceptualization, and modeling agent) to generate a code script interfaces with Blender API for 3D static content creation and rendering (Sun et al., 2023). Zhou et al. (2024) proposed a large-scale scene generation framework consists of two components PCGHub and PCGPlanner (Procedural Controllable Generation), SceneX designed to generate automatically a high-quality large-scale 3D static scene (nature and unbounded cities) guided by user descriptions for Blender.

Despite the advancements in 3D technologies, many existing studies lack a clear methodology to simplify and represent real-world 3D scenarios for complex course concepts, this often student disengagement and boredom. In this study, we aim to provide immersive learning experiences that promote active student participation and redefine the roles of both teachers and learners in the classroom (Bygstad et al., 2022; Raja & Nagasubramani, 2018). To stimulate student engagement, enhance their skills, and improve the quality and delivery of course content, we propose an LLM-powered tool. This tool enhances course design by generating abstract examples related to specific difficult concepts and transforming these text-based examples into 3D animated content. The resulting animations can be seamlessly integrated into a Metaverse platform, offering a more engaging, tangible, and accessible way to understand complex and abstract ideas.

4.3 Motivation Example

To create the concrete 3D examples illustrated in Table 4.1 using Blender, it took me two days to learn the necessary Blender skills and an additional four to five hours to design and animate the models. In general, teachers spend countless hours researching suitable simulation examples to illustrate complex processes and then manually designing them, which requires both time and technical expertise in Blender. However, this process is time-consuming and inefficient. To address this challenge, we propose an LLM-powered tool that streamlines these complex steps into a single automated process. Our tool enables teachers to quickly generate high-quality 3D simulations, reducing the time and effort needed to create engaging educational content.

Table 4.1 Manual construction of 3D model examples

Abstract example	Concrete example
To illustrate the stack data structure, consider the example of a woman's hand and bracelets. When she puts on bracelets one by one, the last bracelet added is the first one to be removed. This perfectly demonstrates the Last-In, First-Out (LIFO) principle of a stack, where the most recently added item is the first to be taken off	A 3D concrete example of a stack data structure designed using blender platform: 
A queue can be illustrated using the example of customers waiting in line at a bank. Customers are served in the order in which they arrive—the first customer in line is served first, followed by the next, and so on. This follows the First-In, First-Out (FIFO) principle, where the earliest arrival is processed before later arrivals	A 3D concrete example of a queue data structure designed using blender platform: 

4.4 Background

This section provides an overview of the key concepts and foundational principles underlying our work.

4.4.1 The Mistral 7B

It's a powerful Large Language Model (LLM) developed by Mistral AI, featuring 7 billion parameters carefully optimized to deliver both efficiency and high performance for real-world applications.[2] As an open-weight model, Mistral 7B is highly adaptable and can be easily fine-tuned for a wide range of tasks. Notably, it outperforms LLaMA 2 13B Chat in several benchmarks, making it a compelling choice for AI-driven applications.[3] This model is particularly well suited for real-time applications that require fast and accurate responses, aligning perfectly with the needs of our work.

[2] https://www.promptingguide.ai/models/mistral-7b.

[3] https://mistral.ai/fr/news/announcing-mistral-7b.

4.4.2 *Blender*

In our work, we need a software capable of executing script-based 3D model generation. We chose Blender, a free and open-source software for creating and developing 3D content. Blender offers advanced capabilities, including high-quality modeling, animation, simulation, video editing and game creation.[4] The generated 3D animated simulations must be exported in.glb format to enable integration into a Metaverse environment. However, the application of Blender in construction of 3D models is complex and takes time. To address this challenge, our LLM-based tool simplifies this process by proposing an advanced tool to generate 3D models based on teacher needs.

4.5 Our LLM-Driven Tool for Generating 3D Simulations of Complex Course Concepts in a Metaverse Environment

In this section, we introduce the design and evaluation of our proposed tool, an interactive system that supports novice teachers in creating concrete examples to help students better understand complex course concepts using large language models (LLMs). To achieve our research objectives, we aim to identify the most effective abstract examples that help students grasp complex concepts more easily. We then convert these abstract examples into immersive 3D simulations, providing a visual and interactive learning experience that enhances comprehension and engagement. The idea is to propose an LLM-powered tool, to help teachers create a concrete example for challenging and complex algorithms of the course, in order to obtain a 3D interactive example implemented in the Metaverse environment. The LLM-powered tool follows a structured three-steps process, as illustrated in Fig. 4.1. To effectively implement our tool, we designed a web application with Gradio and JavaScript used for the front end, and Python FastAPI for the back end. An interactive interface based on Gradio was developed to streamline user interaction and enhance accessibility. Through this platform, users can request a description of a given example, convert it into a 3D simulation, or input an algorithmic description to visualize the corresponding auto-generated Blender script and execute it seamlessly within Blender to produce a real-time 3D. The interface provides a user-friendly environment with code editing capabilities, and an execution validation system to ensure script accuracy before deployment. Additionally, a built-in feedback mechanism allows users to review the generated outputs and suggest improvements, enabling continuous refinement of the model for future iterations. The key components of our proposed tool are the following:

---

[4] https://www.blender.org/about/.

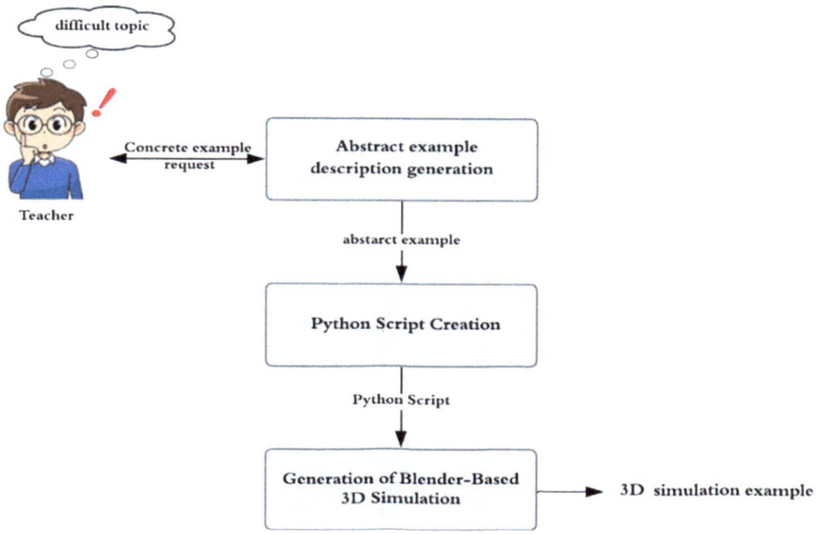

Fig. 4.1 The approach overview

4.6 Abstract Example Description Generation

The teacher interacts with a chatbot to request examples related to challenging concepts. By using structured prompts (e.g., give me a real-world example of stack data structure), the chatbot generates step-by-step breakdowns and offers clear, detailed, and structured explanations of complex algorithms, making them more accessible for teaching and learning. If the generated response does not meet the teachers' expectations, the discussion continues iteratively until the example is refined and aligned with the learning objectives. This interface allows educators to quickly generate precise algorithm descriptions, which can subsequently be transformed into 3D simulations to create more interactive learning experiences to enhance student engagement.

4.6.1 Python Script Creation

Once the teacher validates the generated textual description of the algorithm, Mistral 7B automatically converts the detailed abstract example into a Blender-compatible Python script, as illustrated in Fig. 4.2. Our tool analyzes the validated description and translates it into structured Python code that adheres to Blender's scripting framework. As shown in Fig. 4.3, the resulting script defines the 3D objects, animations, and transformations required to visually represent the execution process of the complex algorithms.

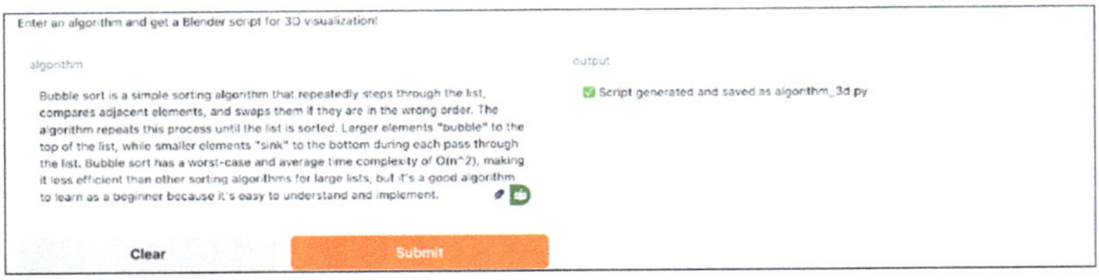

Fig. 4.2 The 3D Blender Script Generator

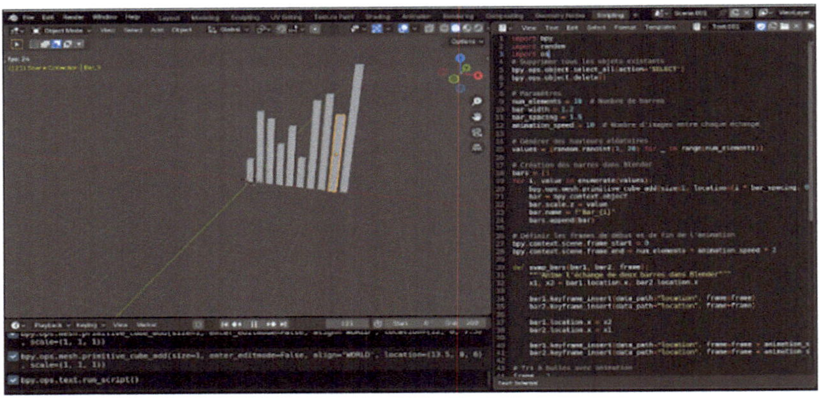

Fig. 4.3 Example of the generated python script in Blender

4.6.2 Generation of Blender-Based 3D Simulation

As illustrated in Fig. 4.3, the generated Python script is automatically executed in Blender, producing an animated 3D simulation that visually represents the complex algorithm through 3D scenarios. This enables for the step-by-step execution to be observed in a more tangible, accessible, and engaging manner enhancing student understanding and motivation.

The generated 3D models are deployed into a virtual environment for interactive learning as shown in Fig. 4.4. This integration leverages Three.js for rendering and manipulating 3D objects within a web-based metaverse, while WebGL ensures efficient GPU-accelerated graphics performance. The GLTFLoader is used to import and display the GLB models exported from Blender, maintaining high-quality animations and textures. Additionally, JavaScript enables user interactions, animations, and real-time updates, enhancing the immersive learning experience. The entire structure is built on HTML and CSS, ensuring seamless embedding within web applications. The generated scripts utilize the Blender bpy module to create 3D objects, apply transformations, and animate sorting steps. The output is exported as a.glb file, making it compatible with various visualization platforms, including VR environments.

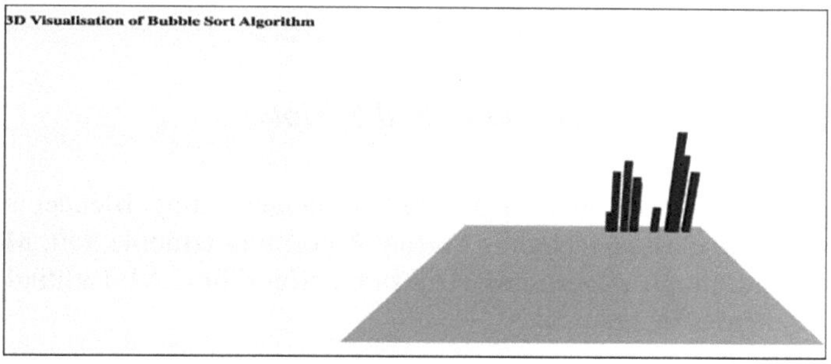

Fig. 4.4 A 3D animated simulation

4.7 Model Selection and Fine-Tuning

We selected Mistral 7B due to its efficiency in text-to-code generation. The model was fine-tuned using a dataset of algorithmic descriptions (The Stack (BigCode))[5] and corresponding Blender scripts.[6]We incorporated reinforcement learning with human feedback (RLHF) to improve the accuracy and coherence of generated scripts. Fine-tuning involved several key steps:

- Preprocessing: Tokenization of algorithm descriptions using Mistral 7Bs tokenizer, ensuring consistency in input representation.
- Training Data Augmentation: We enriched the training set with a diverse range of algorithm examples, including both common and complex cases.
- Loss Optimization: We used a causal language modeling loss function, optimizing for perplexity and accuracy to enhance code generation reliability.
- Hyperparameter Tuning: Batch size, learning rate, and sequence length were adjusted iteratively to improve performance and prevent overfitting.
- Evaluation: The fine-tuned model was tested against a held-out dataset composed of algorithmic descriptions and their corresponding 3D script representations. This dataset included a diverse range of sorting algorithms, graph traversal methods (such as Dijkstra's algorithm), and computational geometry problems to ensure robustness across different algorithmic structures. Evaluation metrics included BLEU scores to assess the textual similarity between generated and ground-truth scripts, as well as execution accuracy, which measured the correctness of the generated Blender scripts by verifying their successful execution and visual output. Additionally, manual inspection and qualitative analysis were conducted to evaluate the clarity, efficiency, and realism of the generated 3D animations.

---

[5] https://huggingface.co/datasets/bigcode/the-stack.

[6] https://docs.blender.org/api/current/.

4.8 Experimental Results

4.8.1 Benchmarking AI-Generated Scripts

We evaluated the performance of Mistral 7B in generating Blender scripts for different algorithm classes, including Sorting Algorithms (Bubble Sort, Merge Sort, Quick Sort) and Graph Algorithms (Dijkstra's Algorithm, A* Pathfinding). Key performance metrics include:

- Perplexity (PPL): Measures how well the language model predicts the next token.

$$PPL = e^{\left(-\frac{1}{N} \sum_{i=1}^{N} \log P(w_i)\right)} \tag{4.1}$$

  where N is the number of words in the sequence and $P(wi)$ is the probability assigned by the model to the i-th word.
- BLEU Score: Evaluates the similarity between AI-generated scripts and reference scripts using n-gram precision.

$$BLEU = BP \cdot \exp\left(\sum_{n=1}^{N} w_n \log p_n\right) \tag{4.2}$$

  where p_n is the modified n-gram precision for n-grams of size n, w_n is the weight assigned to each $n - gram$ precision, and BP is the brevity penalty.
- ROUGE Score: Measures recall-based overlap of AI-generated text against reference scripts.

$$ROUGE = \frac{Overlappingn - grams}{Totaln - gramsinreference} \tag{4.3}$$

  where Overlapping n-grams is the number of matching n-grams between the generated text and the reference, and Total n-grams in reference is the total number of n-grams in the reference summary.
- Script Accuracy (SA): Percentage of generated scripts that executed successfully without syntax errors. Measured by successful execution without syntax errors.

$$SA = \frac{NumberofSuccessfulExecutions}{TotalGeneratedScripts} \times 100 \tag{4.4}$$

  where Number of Successful Executions is the scripts that run correctly without errors, and Total Generated Scripts is the total number of scripts created or tested.

- User Ratings: To evaluate the usability of our tool and the impact on students' engagement. We conducted a user study in two steps: first, using the system usability scale (SUS) questionnaire (Brooke, 1996), and second by the integration of 3D simulations into lessons to assess student's engagement and understanding. We invited ten novice teachers with 1 to 3 years of teaching experience (N1 to N10, four females, six males; age: Mean = 31,8 SD = 1,54), and six experienced teachers with more than five years of teaching experience (T1 to T10, four females, two males; age: Mean = 37,3 SD = 1,86), all participants teach Data Structures and algorithms courses. We calculated the mean and standard deviation of the participants rating based on a 5-point Likert scale. The ratings are then converted to a usability score (100), based on three dimensions are considered: effectiveness and learnability, use Efficiency, and satisfaction. Participants used our tool to create 3D simulation examples for a complex course topic, each participant launches three requests throughout the study. The results indicated that participants had a positive perception of the tool's usability, with a high level of satisfaction. Additionally, participants agreed that representing a 3D animated simulation to illustrate the complex example effectively simplified the algorithmic process and enhanced students' engagement and understanding in the course, with a rate score of 80%.

4.8.2 Model Performance

Our evaluation demonstrated the following key findings:

- Mistral Chatbot's output achieved an average BLEU score of 78.5%, indicating high textual accuracy.
- Mistral's 3D script generation achieved an SSI score of 92%, demonstrating high fidelity to expert-designed models.
- Participants evaluated our tool highly in terms of usability. Moreover, the use of 3D animated simulations demonstrated an 80% improvement in student understanding and engagement.

4.8.3 Discussion

Our study findings indicate that the accuracy of our model performed well for common sorting and graph algorithms but struggled with highly complex algorithms requiring dynamic object interactions. Moreover, the Blender script execution time varied based on model complexity, with an average rendering time of 2.3 s. While our approach offers significant advantages, certain limitations must be considered:

- Generalization: The model may struggle with algorithm descriptions that deviate significantly from training examples.

- Execution Robustness: Some generated scripts may contain errors that prevent successful execution in Blender.
- Evaluation Bias: The BLEU and ROUGE scores primarily assess syntactic similarity rather than functional accuracy.
- Hardware Constraints: Running Mistral 7B and Blender together requires substantial computational resources, limiting accessibility.

Addressing these challenges in future work will improve the reliability and applicability of our method.

4.9 Conclusion and Future Work

This paper introduces an AI-powered solution for 3D algorithm visualization, leveraging Mistral 7B for script generation and Blender for rendering. Our approach reduces manual effort, enhances engagement, and provides an effective learning tool for students and educators. Future research will focus on improving model generalization, optimizing performance, and integrating advanced visualization features. To further enhance our system, we propose to fine-tune Mistral 7B with a more diverse dataset of algorithms and Blender scripts. Then, we can expand the interface to include VR and augmented reality (AR) support. Moreover, we plan to develop a real-time simulation framework for step-by-step execution of algorithms within Blender. Additionally, further user studies should be conducted to assess the long-term educational impact of 3D algorithm visualization and refine the system based on feedback from a wider range of learners and educators.

References

Adedokun-Shittu, N. (2025). Development of Holo-Du through edupreneurship—A glocalised instructional resource for teaching.

Brooke, John. (1996). SUS-A quick and dirty usability scale. *Usability Evaluation in Industry, 189*(194), 4–7.

Bygstad, B., Øvrelid, E., Ludvigsen, S., & Dæhlen, M. (2022). From dual digitalization to digital learning space: Exploring the digital transformation of higher education. *Computers & Education, 182*, Article 104463.

Chen, R., Chen, Y., Jiao, N., & Jia, K. (2023). Fantasia3D: Disentangling geometry and appearance for high-quality text-to-3D content creation.

Chen, X., Zou, D., Xie, H., & Wang, F. L. (2023a). Metaverse in education: Contributors, cooperations, and research themes. *IEEE Transactions on Learning Technologies, 16*(6), 1111–1129.

Feng, W., et al. (2023). LayoutGPT: Compositional visual planning and generation with large language models. *Advances in Neural Information Processing Systems, 36*, 18225–18250.

Godwin-Jones, R. (2024). AI and VR converge: The future of language learning in an emerging metaverse.

Han, S., & Noh, Y. (2021). Analyzing higher education instructors' perception on metaverse-based education. *Journal of Digital Contents Society, 22*(11), 1793–1806.

Kaddoura, S., & Al Husseiny, F. (2023). The rising trend of Metaverse in education: Challenges, opportunities, and ethical considerations. *PeerJ Computer Science, 9*, Article e1252.

Kessler, G. (2021). Current realities and future challenges for call teacher preparation. *Calico Journal, 38*(3), 1–20.

Laseinde, O. T., & Dada, D. (2023). Enhancing teaching and learning in STEM Labs: The development of an android-based virtual reality platform. *Materials Today Proceedings.*

Lee, B.-H., & Park, S.-H. (2021). A study on the NCS based curriculum for educating Technical Director for VFX industry with Artificial Intelligence. *Cartoon and Animation Studies.*

Li, M., et al. (2023). Instant3D: Instant Text-to-3D generation.

Li, H., et al. (2024). *DreamScene: 3D Gaussian-based Text-to-3D scene generation via formation pattern sampling.* http://arxiv.org/abs/2404.03575

M. N., P. I. O., J. L., & S. D. G. Giannakos. (2017). Traditional learning students insights. *Education and Information Technology.*

Onu, P., Pradhan, A., & Mbohwa, C. (2024). Potential to use metaverse for future teaching and learning. *Education and Information Technologies, 29*(7), 8893–8924.

Porter, L., Bailey-Lee, C., & Simon, B. (2012). Halving fail rates using Peer instruction: A study of four computer science courses.

Porter, L., & Simon, B. (2019). A case study of peer instruction: From University of California, San Diego to the Computer Science Community. In *The Cambridge Handbook of Computing Education Research.*

Raja, R., & Nagasubramani, P. C. (2018). Recent trend of teaching methods in education. Organised by Sri Sai Bharath College of Education. *India Journal of Applied and Advanced Research.*

Salguero, A., McAuley, J., Simon, B., & Porter, L. (2020). A Longitudinal Evaluation of a Best Practices CS1. In *ICER 2020—Proceedings of the 2020 ACM conference on international computing education research.* Association for Computing Machinery.

Samala, A. D., et al. (2024). 3D Visualizations in learning: An evaluation of an AR+Core application for computer hardware education using the hedonic motivation system adoption model. *TEM Journal, 13*(1), 466–475.

Shu, X., & Gu, X. (2023). An empirical study of a smart education model enabled by the edu-metaverse to enhance better learning outcomes for students. *Systems, 11*(2), 75.

Sim, J. K. et al. (2024). Designing an educational metaverse: A case study of NTUniverse. *Applied Sciences, 14*(6).

Sun, C., Han, J., Deng, W., Wang, X., Qin, Z., & Gould, S. (2023). 3D-GPT: Procedural 3D modeling with large language models.

Teplá, M., Teplý, P., & Šmejkal, P. (2022). Influence of 3D models and animations on students in natural subjects. *International Journal of STEM Education, 9*(1), 65.

Theelen, H., van den Beemt, A., & den Brok, P. (2019). Classroom simulations in teacher education to support preservice teachers' interpersonal competence: A systematic literature review. *Computer & Education, 129*, 14–26.

Vyas, M. N. (2022). Traditional learning students insights. *Journal of Pharmaceutical Negative Results.*

Wang, J., Li, W., Dun, A., Zhong, N., & Ye, Z. (2024). 3D visualization technology for Learning human anatomy among medical students and residents: A meta- and regression analysis. *BMC Medical Education, 24*(1).

Yazid Abdul Ghani, M., Fatin Buang, N., & Chun Wei, N. (2024). Impact of 3D model-based online STEM activities on skin anatomy and physiology learning among pharmacy students at MiCoST.

Zhai, X. S., Chu, X. Y., Chen, M., Shen, J., & Lou, F. L. (2023). Can edu-metaverse reshape virtual teaching community (VTC) to promote educational equity? an exploratory study. *IEEE Transactions on Learning Technologies, 16*(6), 1130–1140.

Zhou, M. et al. (2024). SceneX: Procedural controllable large-scale scene generation.

Chapter 5
Towards a Unified Representation of Interactive 3D Scenes in Virtual Reality

Clément Dluzniewski, Joseph Jabbour, Danny Kieken, Charles Yaacoub, and Jalal Possik

Abstract The widespread adoption of immersive technologies requires tools to design pedagogical scenarios without technical expertise in virtual reality (VR). Current authoring systems are often domain-specific and tightly coupled to particular game engines, limiting their versatility. This paper introduces the Interaction Set, an abstract representation for modeling interactive scenes without any programming elements. Our approach enables the creation of immersive environments through an intuitive formalism that represents objects and their dynamic relationships using predicates and transformations, theoretically inspired by hybrid automata. We extend this with the concept of protocol, a sequencing mechanism that guides the user through a task while tolerating mistakes and providing corrective feedback. We illustrate its practical application through a VR chemistry lab implemented in Unity. This work contributes to standardization efforts for interactive 3D content creation, with potential applications across educational and industrial training domains.

Keywords Virtual reality · Interactive scene modeling · Interaction set

C. Dluzniewski (✉) · J. Jabbour · D. Kieken · C. Yaacoub · J. Possik
ICL, Junia, Université Catholique de Lille, LITL, Lille, France
e-mail: clement.dluzniewski@univ-catholille.fr

J. Jabbour
e-mail: joseph.jabbour@univ-catholille.fr

D. Kieken
e-mail: danny.kieken@univ-catholille.fr

C. Yaacoub
e-mail: charles.yaacoub@univ-catholille.fr

J. Possik
e-mail: jalal.possik@univ-catholille.fr

M. Abed et al. (eds.), *Metaverse and Artificial Intelligence in Education for a Sustainable Society*, Future Education and Learning Spaces,
https://doi.org/10.1007/978-981-95-8852-7_5

5.1 Introduction

To spread immersive technologies in the educational sector, teachers need tools at their disposal to autonomously create teaching situations in virtual reality (VR). One useful tool for this purpose is the authoring system (Locatis et al., 1991). An authoring system is software for creating interactive multimedia content, usually without advanced programming skills. An authoring system can be used to develop teaching scenarios, courses or lab sessions, in a specific discipline. Authoring systems are also used in industry to train employees on equipment, safety and procedures. Modern systems enable the intuitive creation of interactive content for VR. Using the interface, the user adds existing 3D resources (environments or objects) to the scene and designs the scenario (Kim, 2019; Leon et al., 2016; Oubahssi et al., 2024). A scenario generally consists in a protocol that the user must follow to assimilate the different steps for the real case.

Today, most authoring systems are dedicated to creating scenes for a specific field of application, meaning they have specific representations and depend on the game engine used with its programming interface. To design a universal authoring system for all disciplines, we need an abstract representation to model an interactive scene so that scenario elements can be edited without programming. Our goal is to develop a generic interactive scene representation that can be converted into a VR scene for any game engine.

5.2 Related Works

At present, no universal approach has been adopted for the representation of an interactive 3D scene. As a result, no backward-compatible format exists between different game engines for the same scene. However, data structures do exist to model certain characteristics of a scene. To represent the visual elements of the scene, the Scene Graph was introduced. A scene graph is a representation that models the relationships between objects in a scene (Zhai et al., 2024). A vertex in the scene graph represents an object and its attributes, while an edge represents a type of relationship between two objects (next to, above…). An example of scene graph is given Fig. 5.1a. Recent research highlights the possibility to construct a complete 3D scene from a scene graph (Dhamo et al., 2021; Gao et al., 2024; Zhai et al., 2023, 2024). These methods for converting a scene graph into a 3D scene are classified in two main approaches: recovery and generative (Zhai et al., 2023). Recovery approaches retrieve objects from a database and then optimize their layout in the scene. Generative approaches rely on generative artificial intelligence to directly create the 3D object models and layouts, without the need for a pre-existing object database. Even though the latter produces impressive results, the problem is that a scene graph only represents static relationships between objects, and not how dynamically objects influence each other. The resulting scene will thus not be truly interactive for a VR user.

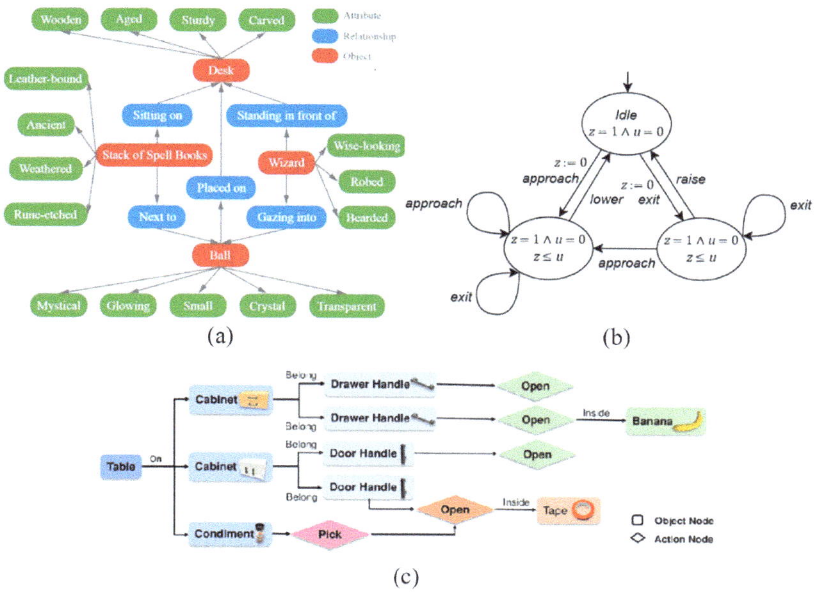

Fig. 5.1 Examples of abstract scene representation. **a** Scene Graph (Gao et al., 2024). **b** Hybrid Automaton (Henzinger, 1996). **c** Action-Conditioned Scene Graph (ACSG) (Jiang et al., 2024)

Various models from simulation literature are also relevant to represent interactions between objects in a virtual reality scene (Jabbour et al., 2024). The most appropriate is the Hybrid Automaton (Henzinger, 1996). In a hybrid automaton, a state contains a dynamics function, in the form of differential equations, to apply to the simulation variables when that state is the current state. A transition from one state to another consists of a guard condition and an optional reset function. When the guard condition of a transition from the current state is verified, its reset function is applied to the simulation variables, and the current state becomes the destination state of the transition. An example of a hybrid automaton is shown in Fig. 5.1b. This model provides a representation for interactions dependent on discrete and continuous variables. But the drawback is that the hybrid automaton does not directly integrate graphical information for the functions or the guard conditions. For example, checking geometric constraints on objects requires explicit modeling of equations with variables, which can be complex for customized 3D models.

A recent representation that combines visual information with interactions between elements is the Action-Conditioned Scene Graph (ACSG) (Jiang et al., 2024). The ACSG is an extension of the scene graph with two types of vertices: object and action. An object vertex encodes the semantics and geometry of an object, as in a scene graph. An action vertex encodes the high-level action type and the low-level primitives to perform an action. The ACSG then contains four types of edges: object to object, object to action, action to object, action to action. An example of ACSG is given in Fig. 5.1c. However, the entire structure may not be meaningful for the representation of an interactive VR scene. The closest proposal to what we want to achieve is the X3D standard (Behr et al., 2009). Developed by Web3D Consortium for interactive 3D on the web, X3D is an XML tag file format that exhaustively describes the objects in the scene and the interactions. These files are used to model 3D objects, animate dynamic elements and describe user interactions in the scene, such as manipulating an object or navigating in the environment. The main issue is that X3D does not enable to combine the properties of the objects without scripting, making it difficult to adopt for non-developers who want complex interactions. Our goal is to achieve a representation in which objects and their interactions, governed by computational and geometric rules with user actions, can be expressed as mathematical expressions.

5.3 Interactive Scene Modeling

In this section, we present how to represent an interactive 3D scene independently of the rendering engine used. First, we introduce the Interaction Set that models the interactions in a scene that a user can perform. Next, we present our concept of protocol to model a sequence of interactions that the user must perform. Two types of users will be considered, the designer who conceives the VR scene, and the VR end-user who is immersed in the scene. Both the Interaction Set and the protocol are defined by the designer.

5.3.1 Interaction Set

We propose a no-code representation called *Interaction Set* inspired by the hybrid automaton and the ACSG. The Interaction Set models objects and their interactions, reflecting the way they are dynamically related to each other. The Interaction Set covers a wide range of interactions while being easy to understand for a designer unfamiliar with VR or simulation.

5.3.1.1 Properties

Let N be the number of objects in the scene. An object in the scene is identified as an index $1 \leq i \leq N$. First, a model 3D O_i is mapped to each i in the VR game engine to graphically represent the object. As the designer creates the interactions, they assign n_i properties to the object i. We note $p_{i,j}$ the j-th property of the object i. For example, a door that may be open or closed can be modeled with a boolean property $p_{\text{door,open}}$, or a glass that may be filled can be modeled with a real property $p_{\text{glass,quantity}}$. Generally, the designer creates a property $p_{i,j}$ of type $V_{i,j}$ if they need a variable tied to object i that must be updated by an interaction. $p_{i,j}$ is also used by the game engine that still needs to know how the render O_i given its properties, like the animation of the door opening or the quantity of liquid in the glass. We note P the set of all designer-defined properties of all objects in the scene, $\mathrm{P} = \cup_{1 \leq i \leq N, 1 \leq j \leq n_i} p_{i,j}$.

In some scenarios, interactions need to rely on information dependent on the object graphical representation O_i. Therefore, we define G_i the set of geometric properties of object i. A property $g \in G$ might be, for instance, a integer value corresponding to the object in contact with O_i, $g_{i,\text{intersection}}$, or a real value measuring the object inclination angle, $g_{i,\text{tilt}}$. Available geometric properties G_i are not defined by the designer but predefined in the system based on common needs for interactions in VR. The game engine is responsible for computing these properties. We note G the set of all geometric properties, $\mathrm{G} = \cup_{1 \leq i \leq N} \mathrm{G}_i$.

Finally, the interactions can only rely on the objects properties P and G, but to achieve a user-in-the-loop system, an interaction must consider the user input. Thus, we define the set of user information U. The properties U are also predefined in the system to implement standard user interactions and computed by the game engine. The essentials properties used to enable user interaction with the scene include determining whether the user has clicked on button X, $u_{\text{pressed,X}}$, or if they are holding object i, $u_{\text{grab,i}}$.

5.3.1.2 Interactions

Once the object properties have been defined, the designer specifies the relationships between these properties. An interaction a simply describes a property update rule and when it should be performed. As such, $a = (C_a, T_a)$, where C_a is the predicate that conditions the execution of a, and T_a is the transformation of properties to apply when executing a.

Formally, $C_a : \mathrm{P} \times \mathrm{G} \times \mathrm{U} \rightarrow \{0, 1\}$ is a function that takes the objects properties (designer-defined and geometric) along with the user properties as input, and outputs whether the interaction must be executed. C_a thus sets the constraints on both the properties and the geometric conditions that must be followed by the objects, as well as the user actions required to trigger a. For example, to implement an interactive glass, one can activate the filling interaction while its quantity is lower than its capacity and the user remains pressed on the X button, $p_{\text{glass,quantity}} \leq p_{\text{glass,capacity}} \wedge u_{\text{holding,X}}$. To implement a door, the opening condition could be that the door is closed, the key is in the lock and the user clicks on X, $\neg p_{\text{door,open}} \wedge g_{\text{key,intersection}} = \text{door} \wedge u_{\text{pressed,X}}$.

On the other hand, $T_a : \mathrm{P} \times \mathrm{G} \times \mathrm{U} \rightarrow \mathrm{P}$ is a function, that also uses the objects and user properties as input, but outputs the updated objects properties when the interaction is executed. T_a describes the properties to update when a is triggered, and the calculation rules for their new values. For the glass filling example, the new value of the property $p_{\text{glass,quantity}}$ can be expressed using the expression $p_{\text{glass,quantity}} + k$ (k being the filling speed). Or for the door opening, the property $p_{\text{door,open}}$ can just be set to true. Note that interaction through the transformation function T_a only modifies the designer-defined properties, not geometric or user properties.

An Interaction Set is the set of all interactions A, along with the designer-defined properties and their initial values $\mathrm{P}^{\mathrm{init}}$. Each fixed time step, the game engine iterates over all interactions $a \in A$. If $C_a(\mathrm{P}, \mathrm{G}, \mathrm{U})$ is verified, then the properties P are updated to $T_a(\mathrm{P}, \mathrm{G}, \mathrm{U})$.

5.3.1.3 Relation with Hybrid Automaton

Although an Interaction Set is not strictly a hybrid automaton, the two representations are closely related. Formally, a hybrid automaton is a graph $G = (V, E)$, where V are the states and E are the transitions. An Interaction Set (A, P) can be converted to a hybrid automaton with the following process. First, the values of the objects properties P are represented in a state $v \in V$. We must then emphasize that interaction is of two types: discrete and continuous. A discrete interaction is triggered only once at a single instant, for example, such as when the user clicks a button. Conversely, a continuous interaction occurs at several successive moments, for example while the user keeps pressing a button. Whereas these two types of interaction are represented indistinctly in the Interaction Set, they are represented by different types of function in the hybrid automaton. A discrete interaction is represented by a transition $e \in E$ where C_e is the guard condition of e and T_e is the reset function of e. If C_e is verified and e is a transition from v to v', then T_e is executed once to reset the values of P before entering v'. A continuous interaction is represented by a transition $e \in E$ and a dynamics function $T_{e,v}$ with $v \in V$ being the destination of e and C_e the guard condition of e without any reset function. When v is the current state of the hybrid automaton, all dynamics functions $T_{e,v}$ are executed on the values of P each time step.

An example of hybrid automaton converted from an Interaction Set is presented Fig. 5.2. The Interaction Set consists of a single discrete interaction $D = (C_D, T_D)$ and two continuous interactions $C1 = (C_{C1}, T_{C1})$, $C2 = (C_{C2}, T_{C2})$. Transitions from state to itself indicate that each discrete interaction is achievable independently of the dynamics of the system (the current state). The initial state contains the objects properties at initialization $\mathrm{P}^{\mathrm{init}}$ without any dynamics functions.

This conversion illustrates that a hybrid automaton exists for every Interaction Set. The conversion of an Interaction Set with n_c continuous interactions and n_d discrete interactions results in a hybrid automaton with 2^{n_c} states and $2^{n_c+1} + n_d \times 2^{n_c}$ transitions. Although we have not demonstrated it, we are confident that Interaction Set and hybrid automaton are equivalent, since reverse conversion seems possible. To achieve this, a property can be added to track the current state of the hybrid automaton. Predicates are created from transitions with the state property. Transformations are based on reset and dynamic functions and must ensure the state property is updated.

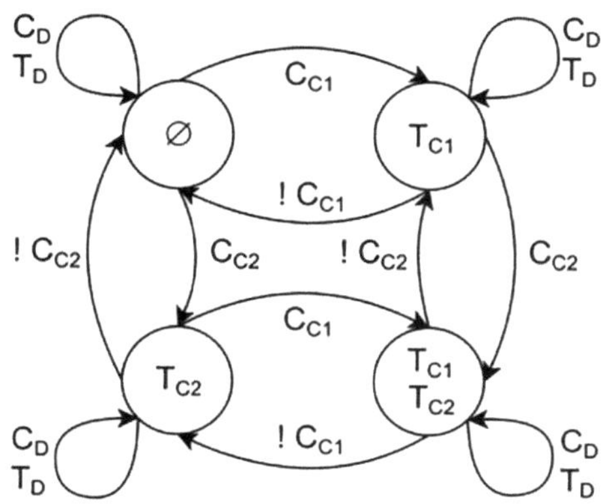

Fig. 5.2 Conversion of an Interaction Set to a hybrid automaton

5.3.2 Protocol

In immersive learning environments, particularly in a pedagogical context, the goal is to enable the user to learn a sequence of precise tasks while having the freedom to make mistakes or not strictly follow the instructions. In this case, blocking all interactions other than the expected one is not desirable. A better approach would be to keep track of the user interactions and continue to the next instruction if the user has performed the required one. This approach could be paired with a mechanism that provides corrective steps when the user takes an action that invalidates the current instruction, helping them to resume the original instructions.

We define a protocol as an ordered list of steps to be performed in the scene. A protocol is represented with a Last-In First-Out structure like a stack $S \in \mathcal{S}$. As with P, the designer is entirely responsible for defining S. The top of S corresponds to the step to complete immediately. Let $t \in \mathbb{N}$ be the index of a step. For each step t, the designer defines the interaction a_t that the user must perform. However, the designer may require the user to perform the interaction by setting object properties to a given state, for example, filling the glass with a quantity above a threshold. Performing an interaction may result in property values not desired by the protocol, so a step t must check if the interaction a_t has been performed as requested to the user. This control is ensured by the function $Q_t : \mathrm{P} \rightarrow \{0, 1\}$ that checks whether the objects properties are in the expected state.

In case the user executes the interaction a_t unexpectedly, the designer can specify a correction function $F_t : \mathrm{P} \rightarrow \mathcal{S}$. The function F_t associates a type of error committed during a_t with the proper correction sub-protocol. When the user sets object properties to an invalid state according to the protocol, the function provides new steps to follow to resume normal instructions flow. If a step t requires the user to perform the glass-filling interaction leading to a quantity between 5 and 10, the following function F_t can be used as a correction:

$$F_t(\mathrm{P}) = \begin{cases} t \text{if } p_{\text{glass,quantity}} < 5 \\ t', t \text{if} p_{\text{glass,quantity}} > 10 \end{cases}$$

where $a_{t'}$ is a glass emptying interaction (which, for example, sets $p_{\text{glass,quantity}}$ to 0). This correction function can be interpreted as follows: If the glass quantity is below the minimum, the user refills it. If it exceeds the maximum, the user empties the glass and fills it again. With this correction function mechanism, the protocol can be viewed as a graph (see Fig. 5.4).

A protocol S is executed with the following algorithm. First, the current step to be performed t at the top of S retrieved. A text written by the designer is displayed to the VR user to describe how to accomplish the step. When an interaction a is completed, it is compared to the interaction of the current step a_t. If they are the same, the user has executed the interaction expected by the protocol, the top of S is popped. If the interaction has not been executed as expected by the protocol, $Q_t(\mathrm{P})$ is false, the correction sub-protocol $F_t(\mathrm{P})$ is stacked at the top of S. The protocol is completed when S is empty. This process maintains protocol compliance while giving the user flexibility for unexpected interactions or errors with adjustments when necessary. Note that the invariant $Q_t(\mathrm{P})$ is only verified right after step t, but it might not remain valid in the following step. Indeed, as the user can perform other interactions between one step and the next, the values of P after a_t and before $a_{t'}$ may differ, even though *t'* immediately follows t in the protocol. The designer must therefore carefully consider the conditions that must be satisfied at each step and anticipate the corrective sub-protocols.

5.4 Use Case

In this section, we outline a concrete scenario to illustrate the potential for pedagogical applications. Selected elements of implementation will be discussed, followed by an example of an Interaction S and protocol for a VR chemistry lab session.

5.4.1 *Implementation*

We implemented the system to create an interactive VR scene from an Interaction Set with Unity. The designer provides the Interaction Set to a C# script through a JSON file, which creates variables and functions accordingly. In JSON, the designer specifies the objects present in the scene, as well as their properties (name, type and initial value). The designer also specifies the scene interactions (predicate and functions). The predicate is simply an expression whose truth value is evaluated at each time step. The transformation is the list of objects properties to modify along with their new values as expressions when the predicate is satisfied. Expressions are represented without code but using nested JSON attributes as a tree structure,

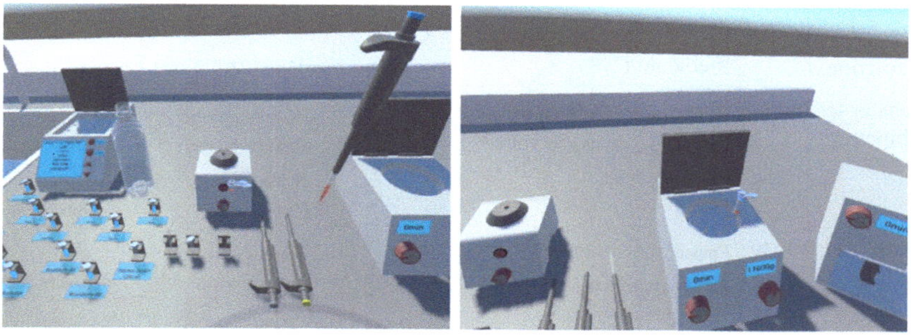

Fig. 5.3 Illustration of the VR chemistry lab session

combining constants, property values (designer-defined, geometric and user), and operations (addition, equality, and logical...). The JSON file may also contain an optional protocol with a similar structure.

Every GameObject present in the JSON Interaction Set must have a specific component to define the graphical changes to apply when one of its designer-defined properties is updated. A programmer stills need to set the GameObjects 3D models and add the relevant XR Interaction Toolkit component to enable the VR end-user to properly manipulate the objects (grabbing...).

5.4.2 Chemistry Lab Session

We developed an educational VR application for learning a chemistry protocol (Fig. 5.3). In this section, we describe how to model this scenario using our formalism.

We describe a simplified scene with three test tubes (two containing different chemical agents and one empty), one pipette, and one oven. Each object is equipped with specific properties: quantity, up and down (time spent in each position), shaked (number of shaking actions) for each test tube, quantity for the pipette and time (heating duration) for the oven. Table 5.1 presents the interactions in the scene. Some are triggered by the user, while others are triggered automatically. The shaking mechanism is particularly interesting because it illustrates how a complex high-level interaction can be modeled with our approach by decomposing it into a low-level atomic interaction. To detect shaking, we track the orientation of the test tube over time. When the tube transitions from upright (angle $> 130°$) to inverted (angle $< 50°$) and back within a short timeframe (less than 4 s), a shake is registered. Extending the available geometric or user properties could simplify the work of the designer to define this type of interaction. Also, note that the transfer and emptying interactions are discrete (the user clicks on the button), while the heating interaction is continuous (the user keeps pressing the button).

The chemistry lab protocol follows a specific sequence of steps that users must complete, with correction mechanisms for handling mistakes. Figure 5.4 illustrates

Table 5.1 Selected interactions from VR chemistry lab

Interaction a	Predicate C_a	Transformation T_a
Transfer test tube to pipette	$p_{\text{tube,quantity}} > 0 \wedge$ $g_{\text{pipette,intersection}} = \text{tube} \wedge$ $u_{\text{grab,pipette}} \wedge$ $u_{\text{pressed,X}}$	$p_{\text{pipette,quantity}} \leftarrow$ $p_{\text{pipette,quantity}} + 0.1 \times p_{\text{tube,quantity}}$ $p_{\text{tube,quantity}} \leftarrow$ $p_{\text{tube,quantity}} - 0.1 \times p_{\text{tube,quantity}}$
Transfer pipette to test tube	$p_{\text{pipette,quantity}} > 0 \wedge$ $g_{\text{pipette,intersection}} = \text{tube} \wedge$ $u_{\text{grab,pipette}} \wedge$ $u_{\text{pressed,X}}$	$p_{\text{tube,quantity}} \leftarrow$ $p_{\text{tube,quantity}} + 0.1 \times p_{\text{pipette,quantity}}$ $p_{\text{pipette,quantity}} \leftarrow p_{\text{pipette,quantity}} -$ $0.1 \times p_{\text{pipette,quantity}}$
Emptying test tube	$p_{\text{tube,quantity}} > 0 \wedge u_{\text{press,Y}}$	$p_{\text{tube,quantity}} \leftarrow 0$
Tube up time increment	$g_{\text{tube,y -angle}} > 130$	$p_{\text{tube,up}} \leftarrow p_{\text{tube,up}} + \Delta t$
Tube down time increment	$g_{\text{tube,y -angle}} < 50$	$p_{\text{tube,down}} \leftarrow p_{\text{tube,down}} + \Delta t$
Shaking tube	$u_{\text{grab,tube}} \wedge p_{\text{tube,up}} > 0 \wedge p_{\text{tube,down}} > 0$	$p_{\text{tube,shaked}} \leftarrow p_{\text{tube,shaked}} + 1$ $p_{\text{tube,up}} \leftarrow 0$ $p_{\text{tube,down}} \leftarrow 0$
Reset time increment	$p_{\text{tube,up}} > 4 \vee p_{\text{tube,down}} > 4$	$p_{\text{tube,shaked}} \leftarrow 0$ $p_{\text{tube,up}} \leftarrow 0$ $p_{\text{tube,down}} \leftarrow 0$
Heating tube with oven	$p_{\text{oven,time}} = 0 \wedge$ $g_{\text{tube,intersection}} = \text{oven} \wedge$ $u_{\text{holding,X}}$	$p_{\text{oven,time}} \leftarrow p_{\text{oven,time}} + \Delta t$
Stopping oven	$p_{\text{oven,time}} > 0 \wedge$ $g_{\text{tube,intersection}} = \text{oven} \wedge \text{ara>} \neg u_{\text{holding,X}}$	$p_{\text{oven,time}} \leftarrow 0$

the protocol as a simplified graph. The first step of the protocol consists of transferring the first chemical agent from its test tube to the empty test tube using the pipette. Next, the second chemical agent must also be transferred to the same test tube. If the resulting mixture exceeds 10 ml, the user restarts from the beginning, otherwise they shake the tube at least 5 times to mix the solution. Finally, the user heats the test tube in the oven for 30 s to 1 min. If the user fails to keep the tube heated within this range, they also empty their tube and start again from the beginning.

5.5 Limits and Future Works

Although the Interaction Set describes an interactive scene intuitively, it does have certain limitations. The main limitation is that the scene still needs to be manipulated with the game engine, to add components for manipulation and navigation, or to

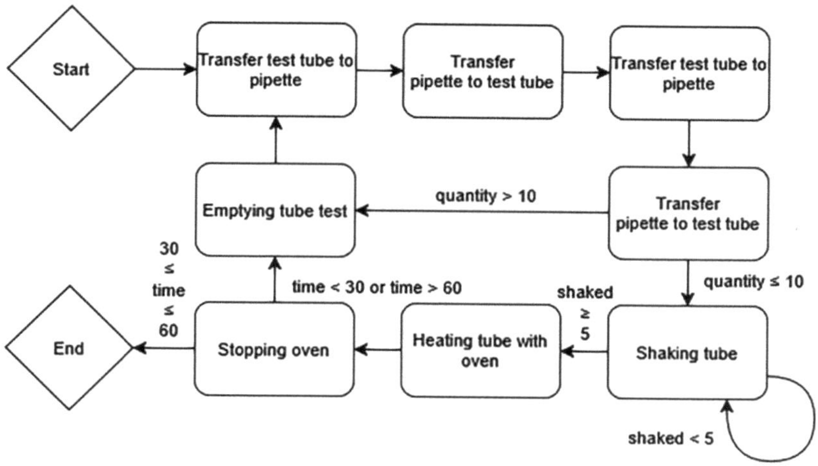

Fig. 5.4 Chemistry lab protocol

program the graphical changes of an object when a property is updated. A promising approach would be to explicitly combine the Interaction Set with a scene graph, responsible for describing 3D models and graphical changes, to offer an exhaustive description of all actions the user can perform. A useful improvement would be to add modularity to the representation. For now, an Interaction Set represents the entire scene as an indivisible whole, but it would be interesting to be able to partition it into sub-Interaction Sets that could be reused in new scenes. Finally, since the Interaction Set encodes an interactive scene without any technical details, we are interested in exploring ways to generate it. One approach is to create it semi-automatically from conventional high-level models such as BPMN, while the other is to rely on a natural language description for full automaticity (Gao et al., 2024).

5.6 Conclusion

In this paper, we introduced the Interaction Set, a user-friendly representation for modeling interactive 3D scenes independently of the game engine. Our approach provides a structured yet intuitive way of defining objects and the interactions between them. By focusing on dynamic rather than static relationships, the Interaction Set enables VR experiences where the user can interact with objects using computational and geometric rules. The Interaction Set offers several advantages over existing approaches. It provides a representation that is accessible to designers without programming expertise, while remaining expressive enough to model most VR interactions. Furthermore, our addition of the protocol concept makes it possible to define pedagogical sequences with corrective feedback, making our model particularly suitable for immersive learning applications. We have demonstrated the feasibility of our proposal with an implementation on Unity. The description of the Interaction Set in a JSON file and the use of VR libraries on Unity provide a link between the high-level scene description and the low-level technical details. With this implementation, we presented a use case consisting of a chemistry lab to demonstrate the relevance of our proposal to design pedagogical environments.

Looking forward, several research directions emerge from this work. Potential improvements include merging the interaction set with scene graphs to better represent visual and interactive elements, introducing modularity for reusable elements and automating its generation to ease scenes creation. Our work contributes to the current effort to standardize interactive 3D content to spread the creation of virtual environments to non-specialist audiences and opens up opportunities for education, training or other fields.

References

Behr, J., Eschler, P., Jung, Y., & Zöllner, M. (2009). X3DOM: A DOM-based HTML5/X3D integration model. In *Proceedings of the 14th international conference on 3D web technology* (pp. 127–135). Association for Computing Machinery. https://doi.org/10.1145/1559764.1559784

De Leon, J. D. O., Tavas, R. P., Aranzanso, R. A., & Atienza, R. O. (2016). Genesys: A virtual reality scene builder. In *2016 IEEE Region 10 Conference (TENCON)* (pp. 3708–3711). https://doi.org/10.1109/TENCON.2016.7848751

Dhamo, H., Manhardt, F., Navab, N., & Tombari, F. (2021). *Graph-to-3D: End-to-end generation and manipulation of 3D scenes using scene graphs.* https://doi.org/10.48550/arXiv.2108.08841

Gao, G., Liu, W., Chen, A., Geiger, A., & Schölkopf, B. (2024). *GraphDreamer: Compositional 3D scene synthesis from scene graphs.* https://doi.org/10.48550/arXiv.2312.00093

Henzinger, T. A. (1996). The theory of hybrid automata. In *Proceedings 11th Annual IEEE symposium on logic in computer science* (pp. 278–292). https://doi.org/10.1109/LICS.1996.561342

Jabbour, J., Possik, J., Yaacoub, C., Namaki Araghi, S., Gorecki, S., Zacharewicz, G., & Solis, A. (2024). Enhancing simulation capabilities through the integration of discrete event simulation and virtual reality. In *Proceedings of the 23rd international conference on modelling and applied simulation.* https://doi.org/10.46354/i3m.2024.mas.018

Jiang, H., Huang, B., Wu, R., Li, Z., Garg, S., Nayyeri, H., Wang, S., & Li, Y. (2024). *RoboEXP: Action-conditioned scene graph via interactive exploration for robotic manipulation.* https://doi.org/10.48550/arXiv.2402.15487

Kim, J. (2019). Maze Terrain authoring system in immersive virtual reality for new visual realism. *Symmetry, 11*, 490. https://doi.org/10.3390/sym11040490

Locatis, C., Ullmer, E., Carr, V., Banvard, R., Le, Q., Lo, R., & Williamson, M. (1991). Authoring systems: An introduction and assessment. *Journal of Computing in Higher Education, 3*, 23–35. https://doi.org/10.1007/BF02942596

Oubahssi, L., Piau-Toffolon, C., & Mahdi, O. (2024). VR-Peas: A virtual reality PEdAgogical scenarisation tool. *Interactive Learning Environments, 1.* https://doi.org/10.1080/10494820.2024.2308094

Zhai, G., Örnek, E. P., Wu, S.-C., Di, Y., Tombari, F., Navab, N., & Busam, B. (2023). *CommonScenes: Generating commonsense 3D indoor scenes with scene graph diffusion.* https://doi.org/10.48550/arXiv.2305.16283

Zhai, G., Örnek, E.P., Chen, D.Z., Liao, R., Di, Y., Navab, N., Tombari, F., & Busam, B. (2024). *EchoScene: Indoor scene generation via information echo over scene graph diffusion.* https://doi.org/10.48550/arXiv.2405.00915

Chapter 6
From BPMN to JAAMSIM: An Approach for Business Process Simulation in an Educational Context

Antoine Bakhos, Jalal Possik, Abir Karami, and Charles Yaacoub

Abstract Discrete-Event Simulation (DES) is traditionally used in areas such as manufacturing, logistics, and healthcare. However, it has also proven to be a powerful tool for simulating and analyzing educational experiences. Despite its advantages, DES models can be challenging to develop, interpret, and visualize, particularly for individuals without a background in simulation. This is due to the need for a deep understanding of event-based logic, complex data structures, and specialized software tools. Business Process Model and Notation (BPMN) helps mitigate these challenges by providing a standardized and more accessible graphical representation of processes, making it easier to understand complex workflows, communicate process details, and identify areas for improvement. Nevertheless, while BPMN effectively visualizes workflows, it lacks the necessary computational logic and tools required for running simulations. This paper presents an approach for automatically converting BPMN diagrams into DES models, specifically executable simulation files in JaamSim. The proposed method involves extracting process information from BPMN diagrams, completing any missing execution-related details, and mapping BPMN elements to their simulation counterparts in JaamSim. By automating this transformation, the approach aims at simplifying the creation of valid simulation scenarios, making them more accessible to non-developers and non-simulation experts. To evaluate the feasibility of this approach, a case study was conducted to assess the accuracy and practicality of converting BPMN models into JaamSim simulations. This integration supports educators and decision-makers by enabling simulation-driven analysis of educational processes, facilitating insights,

A. Bakhos (✉) · J. Possik · A. Karami · C. Yaacoub
ICL, Junia, Université Catholique de Lille, LITL, Lille, France
e-mail: antoine.bakhos@univ-catholille.fr

J. Possik
e-mail: jalal.possik@univ-catholille.fr

A. Karami
e-mail: abir.karami@univ-catholille.fr

C. Yaacoub
e-mail: charles.yaacoub@univ-catholille.fr

M. Abed et al. (eds.), *Metaverse and Artificial Intelligence in Education for a Sustainable Society*, Future Education and Learning Spaces,
https://doi.org/10.1007/978-981-95-8852-7_6

process optimization, and improved decision-making without requiring specialized expertise in simulation development.

Keywords Business process modeling and notation · Discrete event simulation · Model transformation · Educational process modeling

6.1 Introduction

Discrete-event simulation (DES) is one of the most popular simulation techniques in the field of modeling and simulation (M&S). Traditionally applied in business environments such as manufacturing, service industry logistics, and healthcare (Robinson, 2005), DES has also demonstrated significant potential in educational settings. It enables educators and trainers to replicate complex scenarios for learning (Varga, 1999), allowing students and professionals to interact with dynamic systems and gain practical insights without real-world consequences. Simulation-based training enhances experiential learning by enabling the visualization of resource flows, system bottlenecks, and performance metrics. In addition, the combination of DES with virtual training can increase learner engagement and motivation in virtual learning environments (Cuevas-Ortuño & Zavala, 2024).

Despite these benefits, developing simulation models remains a technical challenge that requires a certain level of expertise in programming, event-based logic, complex data structures, and specialized simulation tools (Hook, 2011). Educators and trainers, while proficient in their respective domains, may lack the necessary knowledge of simulation methodologies, making it challenging for them to design and implement effective simulation scenarios. Business Process Model and Notation (BPMN) (Business Process Model NotationTM (BPMNTM)|Object Management Group 2025) presents a more intuitive graphical alternative for defining processes. It allows instructors to design workflow-based learning scenarios using a standardized visual approach, eliminating the need for in-depth knowledge of simulation frameworks. However, BPMN models alone are static representations and do not inherently support simulation or dynamic analysis. To bridge this gap, this paper introduces an automated approach for transforming BPMN models into executable simulation files. By eliminating the need for manual DES modeling, this approach makes simulation-driven learning more accessible and efficient.

The main contributions of this paper are as follows: (1) a formalized and updated mapping between BPMN elements and Jaamsim simulator components; (2) an automated conversion process that translates BPMN models into executable simulation files; (3) case study evaluation demonstrating the effectiveness and accuracy of the pro- posed approach in real-world educational scenarios.

The remainder of this paper is structured as follows: Sect. 6.2 reviews related work on business process simulation. Section 6.3 details the methodology for automating BPMN- to-JaamSim conversion. Section 6.4 presents a case study validating the proposed approach. Finally, Sect. 6.5 concludes the paper by discussing challenges, limitations, and future research directions.

6.2 Research Context

6.2.1 BPMN and Simulation for Immersive Learning

DES is widely recognized for its ability to replicate complex real-world systems, offering an interactive and data-driven approach to learning. Several studies have demonstrated its effectiveness in education, enabling students to engage with and observe various environments and models in both immersive (Cuevas-Ortuño & Zavala, 2024) and non-immersive (Varga, 1999) digital settings. Additionally, DES allows educators to simulate student interactions and performance within educational experiences. This capability supports data-driven decision-making, helping educators identify modifications that can enhance student performance, reduce stress, and ultimately lower dropout rates (Fiallos & Ochoa, 2017).

However, while DES focuses on simulating system dynamics, it does not inherently support the intuitive representation and understanding of these systems by external observers. This creates a barrier for educators and trainers who may not have a technical background in simulation and modeling.

This paper presents work conducted as part of a broader project aimed at enhancing digital immersive education in the extended reality (XR) space (PEIA, 2025). Previous efforts within the project have explored the integration of DES tools with XR applications (Jabbour et al., 2024). Building upon this foundation, the objective of this paper is to introduce a streamlined approach for generating simulations with these tools. By integrating BPMN with XR applications, educators and trainers could design and manipulate educational experiences using a graphical, workflow-based approach. This method would further enable users to interact with and modify XR applications through BPMN-based workflows. The focus of this study is specifically on JaamSim, an open-source DES software, leveraging previous efforts within the same project, without loss of generality.

6.2.2 Related Works

BPMN simulation has been explored in previous studies. A BPMN-based Modeling & Simulation approach was proposed in Bocciarelli et al. (2019) to bridge the gap between business process modeling and simulation execution. The study introduced PyBPMN, a BPMN extension that allows users to annotate models with simulation-relevant properties such as performance parameters, resources, and workloads. These enriched BPMN models were then transformed into eBPMN, a domain-specific simulation language that automates the generation of simulation models. This approach significantly reduces the manual effort and expertise required for conducting business process simulations.

A metamodel-based transformation approach was proposed in Kassis et al. (2023) to convert BPMN models into Discrete Event System Specification (DEVS) simulation models. The study leveraged the Business Process Simulation Interchange Standard (BPSim) (BPSim., 2013) to incorporate resource allocation, execution parameters, and performance metrics. The authors developed a set of mapping rules to translate BPMN + BPSIM models into DEVS models, enabling the execution of detailed discrete-event simulations.

Transformation using a custom software package, which transformed BPMN XML files into Petri net "m" files was proposed in Mutarraf et al. (2018). Similarly, to the work proposed in this paper, the authors used BPMN XML files and a direct mapping to generate Petri net files. The generated files were then analyzed using General Purpose Petri Net Sim-ulator (GPenSIM) in MATLAB for performance evaluation and formal verification.

Finally, (Wuennenberg et al., 2022) proposed a BPMN-DES integration for optimizing internal logistics and material flow systems. While no model transformation was performed, the authors incorporated DES using JaamSim to enable dynamic system behavior and performance evaluation. Their methodology follows a structured modeling process, using BPMN for process logic and DES for quantitative simulation. They manually created two separate models and mapped elements between them. Although their effort provided insights into BPMN-to-JaamSim element mapping, differences in usage context prevent us from fully adopting their mapping, requiring some modifications.

6.3 Methodology

Looking at the literature, the transformation of BPMN models into simulation files can be summarized in two steps. The first step is to extend or enrich the BPMN file by adding the necessary simulation parameters. The resulting BPMN XML file can now be used to generate a simulation configuration file. The second step is the mapping process, where the XML file is parsed to identify the extended BPMN elements and convert them into their simulation counterparts. This step takes place in a conversion module developed in this paper. The converted elements are then written into a configuration file, which then can be passed to the simulator (JaamSim). Figure 6.1 illustrates the proposed approach.

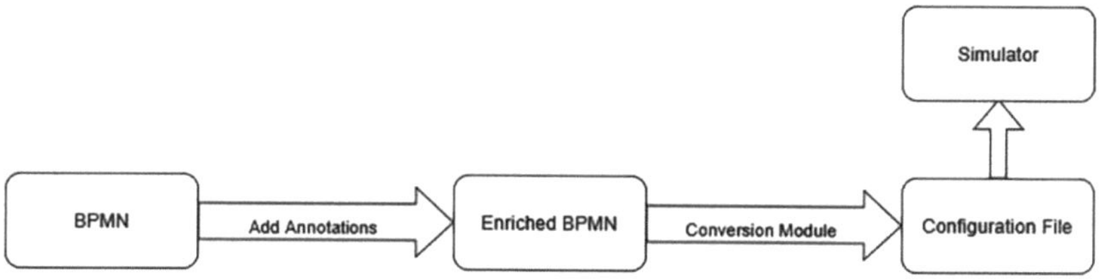

Fig. 6.1 Overview of the proposed approach

6.3.1 BPMN Annotation

BPMN is designed to represent business process flows using flow objects (events, gate- ways, and activities) linked by flows and associations, with additional details provided through artifacts (Bocciarelli et al., 2019). In this study, simulation parameters are incorporated into BPMN elements using annotations, a type of artifact that serves as textual notes attached to process elements. These annotations can be extracted from the BPMN XML representation via associations. To ensure consistency and correct interpretation, annotation parameters follow a strict input syntax. Any deviation from this syntax results in an error during the conversion process. Figure 6.2 illustrates an annotated BPMN element alongside its XML representation. The task, its annotation and the association that links them (dotted line) are respectively shown as written in the XML file.

The defined parameters that were developed for this work fall into two main categories, namely Time and Control:

- Time parameters: Duration and Lag. Duration represents the time required to complete an activity, such as the time a student spends on a learning task. Lag introduces a delay between the completion of one activity and the start of another, simulating waiting times or transition periods. For example, Lag could help modify the delay before feedback is provided after a task.
- Control parameters: Routing and Instantiation. Routing determines the direction an entity takes when multiple paths are available, either probabilistically (e.g., 70% of students proceed to one module, 30% to another) or based on rules (e.g.,

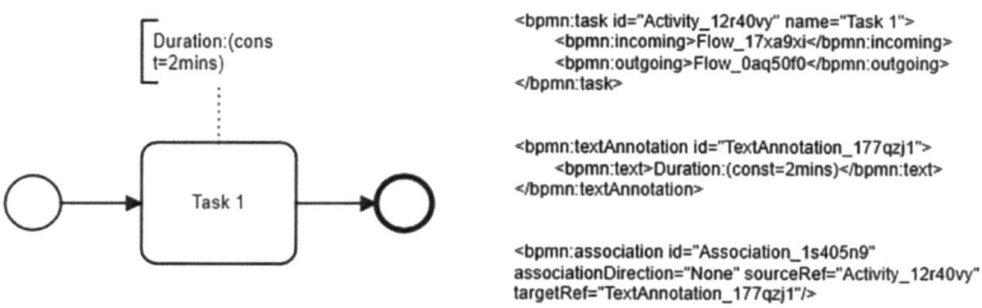

Fig. 6.2 Annotated BPMN element and its relevant data in the XML file

only students scoring above a threshold proceed to an advanced topic). Instantiation defines when and how new entities are introduced into the system, such as determining the frequency at which new students enter a training simulation.

These parameters were selected for their relevance in educational scenario design. As the conversion system evolves, additional parameters will be introduced to broaden functionality and improve adaptability.

6.3.2 *Model Mapping*

Once the necessary parameters are assigned to the corresponding BPMN elements, the conversion process can begin. This process follows a systematic and structured approach.

The first step involves parsing the BPMN XML file to extract all relevant elements and their unique identifiers. The elements include tasks, events, their associated annotations, and flow connections. Each element is then sorted based on its incoming and outgoing flows, which helps determine its role and sequence within the overall process. Finally, the extracted elements are mapped to their simulation counterparts and rewritten into a configuration file (.cfg), which serves as the intermediate representation for the simulation. This file preserves the hierarchical relationships and dependencies between elements so that the simulation replicates the intended process behavior. Once the configuration file is complete, it can be passed to JaamSim, which interprets the data and executes the simulation accordingly. The order of the sorted elements is pre- served in the reconstructed simulation file using the NextComponent attribute of each JaamSim simulation component. Additionally, a single simulation entity will be automatically generated as it is required to launch the simulation.

Table 6.1 presents a mapping of BPMN elements, their corresponding JaamSim counterparts, and their designated functions within the simulation, highlighting how each component is translated to fit within the DES environment.

Table 6.1 Mapping of BPMN and JaamSim elements

BPMN	JaamSim	Function
Start Event	EntityGenerator	Generates process instances
End Event	EntitySink	Represents completion of a process
Task	Server + Queue	Handles processing
Exclusive Gateway	Branch	Determines flow based on conditions
Subprocess	SubModel	Groups multiple elements in a model, mainly for reuse
Subprocess Start Event	SubModelStart	Generates process instances within a subprocess
Subprocess End Event	SubModelEnd	Represents completion of a subprocess

6.4 Case Study

To further explain the functionality of our conversion module, we present a simple case study that demonstrates the transformation process in action.

6.4.1 BPMN Annotation

Consider an online training program where learners must complete two modules (Module 1 and Module 2) in any order, both of which are prerequisites for unlocking a final assessment (Module 3). Additionally, some learners may fail a module and need to reattempt it before progressing. The BPMN diagram in Fig. 6.3 illustrates this flow using tasks and gateways. However, BPMN alone cannot represent execution semantics like time variability (e.g., Module A taking 3–5 min), or routing probabilities (e.g., 5% of students failing a module). Nor can it support simulation-based experimentation to analyze completion times, identify bottlenecks, or test what-if scenarios (e.g., what happens if retry rates increase?). These limitations highlight the need to complement BPMN with simulation tools like JaamSim.

To convert the BPMN model into a valid simulation file, the necessary simulation parameters must first be integrated. In this case, duration and routing parameters were added to the model, as illustrated in Fig. 6.4.

For example, the annotation "Duration:(min = 3 min; max = 5 min)" assigned to Tutorial Part 1 and 2 specifies the time required to complete these tasks. The use

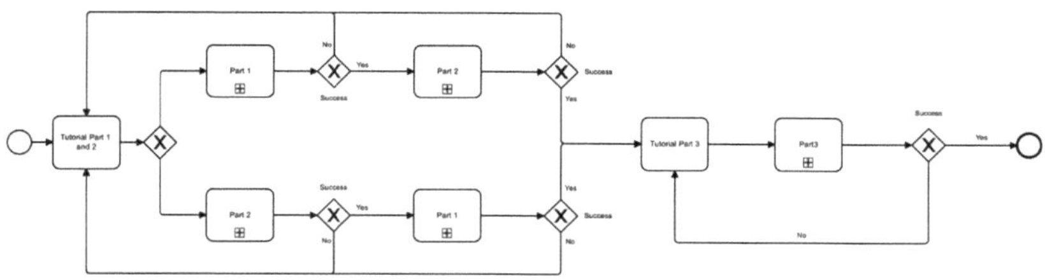

Fig. 6.3 Base BPMN representation of the training

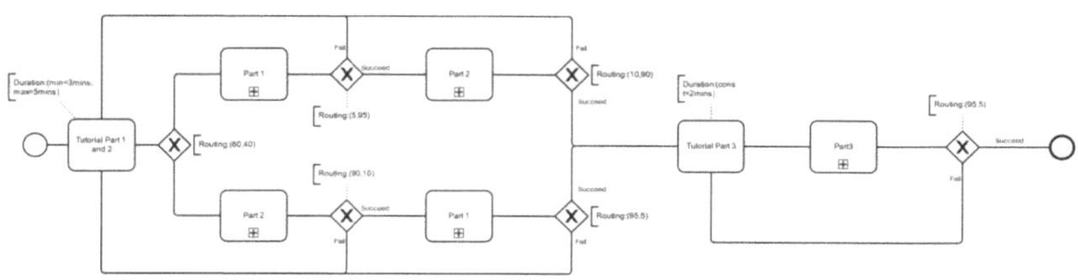

Fig. 6.4 Annotated BPMN representation with simulation parameters

of "min" and "max" allows for a variable, but bounded, execution time, ensuring that the task duration fluctuates within a predefined range. Conversely, when a task has a fixed execution time, the parameter is defined using "const", as seen in Tutorial Part 3, where the duration remains constant. The routing parameter, written as "Routing:(60,40)", is generally applied after a gateway to determine how entities proceed along multiple branching paths. The syntax is straightforward: each number represents the percentage of entities following a specific path, with values listed from left to right corresponding to the top-to-bottom order of branches. In this case, 60% of students will opt to start with Part 1, while 40% will begin with Part 2.

6.4.2 JaamSim Component Generation

This section presents how BPMN elements are represented in the resulting configuration (.cfg) file after conversion.

Start Event. The start event is converted to an entity generator with a defined entity created in parallel.

```
Define SimEntity { Student }
Define EntityGenerator { EntityGenerator1 }
```

End Event. The end event converts directly to an entity sink and does not require any addition.

```
Define EntitySink { EntitySink1 }
```

Tasks. Tasks are converted to servers and require queues. Since we have 2 tasks and 5 subprocess tasks, a total of 7 queues are created. For tasks that require variable completion time (in this case only TutorialPart1and2), a UniformDistribution component is generated in parallel. The component's role is further explained in the sequel.

```
Define UniformDistribution { UniformDistribution1 }
Define Queue { Queue1 Queue2 Queue3Queue4 Queue5 Queue6 Queue7 }
Define Server { TutorialPart1and2 TutorialPart3 }
```

Gateways. Gateways are converted into branches which have a "choice" attribute that determines the path an entity will follow after reaching the branch. To define the behavior of this attribute, a DiscreteDistribution component is generated alongside each branch. This component assigns probability values based on the routing parameters annotated in the BPMN model, ensuring that entity flow is distributed according to the predefined decision logic.

```
Define DiscreteDistribution { DiscreteDistribution1 DiscreteDis-
tribution2 DiscreteDistribution3DiscreteDistribution4 Discrete-
Distribution5DiscreteDistribution6 }
Define Branch { Branch1 Branch2 Branch3 Branch4 Branch5 Branch6 }
```

Subprocesses. Subprocesses are converted to submodels. Each submodel has its own start and end events and their own servers.

```
Define SubModel { Part1-1 Part1-2 Part2-1 Part2-2 Part3 }
Define Server { Part1-1.Server Part1-2.Server Part2-1.ServerPart2-2.ServerPart3.Server }
Define SubModelEnd { Part1-1.SubModelEndPart1-2.Sub-ModelEndPart2-1.SubModelEndPart2-2.SubModelEnd Part3.SubModelEnd }
Define SubModelStart { Part1-1.SubModelStart Part1-2.SubModelStart Part2-1.SubModelStart Part2-2.Sub- ModelStart Part3.SubModelStart }
```

6.4.3 Parameters Conversion

This section details the implementation of parameters in the converted elements.

Duration. The Duration parameter in tasks is implemented using the "Service-Time" attribute of the server component in JaamSim. The two cases considered include tasks with a fixed duration and tasks with a variable, but bounded, duration.

- For tasks with a fixed duration, the "ServiceTime" attribute is directly assigned a constant value. In this study, TutorialPart3 was assigned a constant time. Its attributes definition in the configuration file is as follows:

```
TutorialPart3 NextComponent { Part3 }
TutorialPart3 WaitQueue { Queue6 }
TutorialPart3 ServiceTime { 2 min }
```

- For tasks with a variable duration, a UniformDistribution component with time units is generated alongside the server, defining a bounded range within which the task duration can fluctuate. The "ServiceTime" attribute is then set to the output of the UniformDistribution. This way, execution times vary realistically while remaining within predefined limits. For instance, in this study, TutorialPart1and2 was assigned a variable duration, defined in the configuration file as:

```
UniformDistribution1 UnitType { TimeUnit }
UniformDistribution1 RandomSeed { 7 }
UniformDistribution1 MinValue { 3min }
UniformDistribution1 MaxValue { 5min }
TutorialPart1and2 NextComponent { Branch1 } TutorialPart1and2 WaitQueue { Queue1 }
TutorialPart1and2 ServiceTime { UniformDistribution1 }
```

Routing. The routing parameter of gateways was implemented using the "choice" at- tribute of branches in the simulation. The DiscreteDistribution component generated alongside each branch outputs a value corresponding to one of the available choices, which is then assigned to the "choice" attribute of the branch. This determines the direction the entity will take after reaching the decision point. For example, the first gateway in the BPMN splits into two paths with routing values of (60,40). The configuration file defines the routing as follows:

```
DiscreteDistribution1 RandomSeed { 1 }
DiscreteDistribution1 ValueList { 1 2 }
DiscreteDistribution1 ProbabilityList { 0.6 0.4 }
Branch1 NextComponentList { Part1-1 Part2-2 }
Branch1 Choice { DiscreteDistribution1 }
```

6.5 Conclusion

This paper presented a method for transforming BPMN models into JaamSim-executable configuration files, enabling users to generate simulations through BPMN's standardized graphical interface. By automating this transformation, the proposed approach enhances accessibility to simulation modeling and bridges the gap between process design and execution. The methodology was built upon existing research in BPMN-to- simulation transformation, ensuring a structured and reliable mapping process. And while this paper presents feasibility through a case study, it did not delve into evaluations to measure accuracy, runtime, and user effort. In addition, the conversion module, is currently limited in element and parameter variety.

Future work will focus on expanding the range of supported BPMN and JaamSim elements. Currently, the module supports core BPMN elements (tasks, gateways, subprocesses) and a basic parameter set (time, routing). As part of ongoing development, we aim to extend support to advanced elements like boundary events and loops, and incorporate more parameters for richer educational scenarios. Rigorous testing will be conducted to assess the module's performance. Additionally, efforts will be directed toward developing a user-friendly interface that allows users to input simulation parameters directly, eliminating the need for manual annotations within BPMN models. Within this interface, the use of large language models (LLMs) is considered to remove syntax restrictions on user input. LLM integration could allow users to simply describe their parameter requirements before converting it to appropriate syntax for the conversion module. Another interesting area of exploration will be the implementation and integration of text-to-BPMN conversion, which could enable users to describe processes in plain language and automatically generate both BPMN diagrams and their corresponding simulations. The final objective is to develop a comprehensive tool that empowers educators to seamlessly create, configure, and simulate customized virtual learning experiences.

Acknowledgements The authors would like to thank the French National Research Agency (Agence Nationale de la Recherche; ANR) for funding this research under the DemoES—PEIA project (ANR-21-DMES-0014).

Disclosure of Interests The authors would like to declare that they have no conflict of interest.

References

Bocciarelli, P., D'Ambrogio, A., Giglio, A., & Paglia, E. (2019). BPMN-based business process modeling and simulation. In *2019 Winter Simulation Conference (WSC)* (pp. 1439–1453). https://doi.org/10.1109/WSC40007.2019.9004960.

BPSim. (2013). *Business Process Simulation*. http://www.bpsim.org/.

Business Process Model & Notation™ (BPMN™) | Object Management Group. Retrieved February 12, 2025, from https://www.omg.org/bpmn/

Cuevas-Ortuño, J., & Zavala, A. (2024). Combining discrete-event simulation with the metaverse to motivate students in higher education. In *2024 IEEE Global Engineering Education Conference (EDUCON)*. (pp. 1–5). https://doi.org/10.1109/EDUCON60312.2024.10578770.

Fiallos, A., & Ochoa, X. (2017). Discrete event simulation for student flow in academic study periods. In *2017 Twelfth Latin American Conference on Learning Technologies (LACLO)* (pp. 1–7). https://doi.org/10.1109/LACLO.2017.8120908.

Hook, G. (2011). Business process modeling and simulation. In *Proceedings of the 2011 Winter Simulation Conference (WSC)* (pp. 773–778). https://doi.org/10.1109/WSC.2011.6147804.

Jabbour, J., Possik, J., Yaacoub, C., Araghi, S.N., Gorecki, S., Zacharewicz, G., & Solis, A. (2024). Enhancing simulation capabilities through the integration of discrete event simulation and virtual reality. *Presented at the 23rd International Conference on Modelling and Applied Simulation September 18*. https://doi.org/10.46354/i3m.2024.mas.018.

Kassis, M. E., Trousset, F., Zacharewicz, G., & Daclin, N. (2023). Bridging the gap between business process and simulation: Transformation from BPMN to DEVS. *IFAC-PapersOnLine., 56*, 11888–11893. https://doi.org/10.1016/j.ifacol.2023.10.601

Mutarraf, U., Barkaoui, K., Li, Z., Wu, N., & Qu, T. (2018). Transformation of Business Process Model and Notation models onto Petri nets and their analysis. *Advances in Mechanical Engineering, 10*, 1687814018808170. https://doi.org/10.1177/1687814018808170

PEIA. Retrieved March 18, 2025, from http://peia-demo.com/home.

Robinson, S. (2005). Discrete-event simulation: From the pioneers to the present, what next? *Journal of the Operational Research Society, 56*, 619–629. https://doi.org/10.1057/palgrave.jors.2601864

Varga, A. (1999). Using the OMNeT++ discrete event simulation system in education. *IEEE Transactions on Education, 42*, 11. https://doi.org/10.1109/13.804564

Wuennenberg, M., Wegerich, B., & Fottner, J. (2022). Optimization of internal logistics using a combined BPMN and simulation approach. *Anwendungen und Konzepte der Wirtschaftsinformatik, 16*, 7. https://doi.org/10.26034/lu.akwi.2022.3465.

Part III
Metaverse and AI in Education

Chapter 7
Digital Twin for Controlling Variables in Classrooms: A Simulation-Based Approach Using Discrete Event and Agent-Based Simulation

Atheer Al Shaggah, Jalal Possik, Allal Chafi, Michel El Haddad, and Laurent Peyrodie

Abstract Real-time monitoring and predictive control of indoor conditions are made possible by Digital Twin (DT) technology, which is transforming smart environments. In order to maximize indoor air quality and comfort, this study proposes a DT framework for classrooms that integrates AnyLogic modeling with based environmental sensors (CO_2, temperature, humidity, light, and motion). Real-time data gathering from Arduino-based sensors is used to test the model, and High-Level Architecture (HLA) is proposed to guarantee compatibility. Hybrid simulation approach with Distributed Simulation (DS) by combining Discrete Event Simulation (DES) and Agent-Based Simulation (ABS). Different simulation scenarios with varying ventilation settings, and occupancy levels show how environmental variables change dynamically over time. The findings demonstrate that DT-based control greatly enhances occupant well-being and energy efficiency. By providing a scalable framework for real-time environmental control in educational, smart building, and industrial applications, this study advances the design of smart classrooms.

Keywords Digital twin · HLA · Simulation · Modeling · Discrete event simulation · Agent-based simulation

---

A. Al Shaggah (✉) · J. Possik · A. Chafi · M. El Haddad · L. Peyrodie
ICL, Junia, Université Catholique de Lille, LITL, Lille, France
e-mail: atheer.al-shaggah@junia.com

J. Possik
e-mail: jalal.possik@univ-catholille.fr

A. Chafi
e-mail: allal.chafi@junia.com

M. El Haddad
e-mail: michel.el-haddad@univ-catholille.fr

L. Peyrodie
e-mail: laurent.peyrodie@junia.com

M. Abed et al. (eds.), *Metaverse and Artificial Intelligence in Education for a Sustainable Society*, Future Education and Learning Spaces,
https://doi.org/10.1007/978-981-95-8852-7_7

7.1 Introduction

Accelerating smart technologies and the increasing demand for new educational spaces push digital twins to be among the most cutting-edge tools in contemporary classrooms. Classroom management is achieved to some extent by conventional IoT systems that ensure real-time monitoring and control over environmental variables (like temperature, CO_2, and lighting), but the problem of the current management systems is that they lack real-time responsive and interoperability over these critical environmental factors. They often do not connect to real-time IoT sensors, and they often replicate isolated user behavior or physical places. Furthermore, there is a lack of adoption of open standards to support distributed, scalable digital twin (DT) structures. Classroom systems are unable to maximize comfort, minimize energy consumption, or adjust to changing conditions without real-time data transmission and integrated modeling of human presence and environmental factors. This affects directly on learning outcomes and reduces their usefulness in practical applications.

In this paper, we introduce a hybrid digital twin framework that links real-time sensors data with a hybrid simulation model of distributed simulation (DS), which includes agent-based simulation (ABS) and discrete event simulation (DES) using AnyLogic. The system facilitates distributed synchronization between the virtual and physical components by utilizing and focusing on incorporating the High-Level Architecture (HLA) standard. We proposed an interoperable and scalable system for a classroom, which aims to create a framework for using DTs in education. This comes through the creation of a flexible, effective, and data-driven learning environment, where this study establishes a showcase of their benefits over alternative sensor system types.

7.2 Background

Digital Twin (DT) is a transformative technology in various domains. This technology gained traction as a groundbreaking technology across several industries, including healthcare, manufacturing, smart cities, and education (Thelen et al., 2022). Digital twins are a virtual representation of a physical entity, which gets continuously updated with real-time data to simulate and therefore analyze the behavior of the system across different conditions. This leads to improved decision-making, optimization, and predictive maintenance. The DT essentially replicates every aspect and process of its physical counterpart and refreshes itself as measurement value updates. These on-the-spot connections, which is usually via IoT sensors and networks, allow for real-time monitoring of environmental conditions and system performance to take place seamlessly (Yao et al., 2023).

Environmental factors that affect comfort, safety, energy efficiency, and operational performance in a variety of industries include CO_2 concentration, temperature, light intensity, and occupancy. Monitoring these factors enables data-driven decision-making that improves sustainability and productivity in a variety of settings, including commercial buildings, healthcare, industry, education, and transportation (Arowoiya et al., 2024). In building management DT can track these metrics like temperature, humidity, lighting, carbon dioxide (CO_2) levels, and even motion or occupancy in real time to monitor indoor environmental conditions (Zhao & Wen, 2022). In addition to monitoring, digital twins actively contribute to the computation and control of environmental variables. They aggregate sensor information and apply analytics to produce insights (e.g., air quality levels or comfort indices) that can drive automated control actions. If certain conditions deviate from the expected ranges, the DT requires physical systems to be changed. For example, the twin may detect a rise in temperature or CO_2 in a room and instruct the HVAC (Heating, Ventilation, and Air Conditioning) to increase airflow or dim lights when motion sensors detect the occupancy to identify an empty space. Modern DT implementations close the loop by identifying issues and initiating reactions, acting as the brains of an intelligent control system (Arsiwala et al., 2023).

7.2.1 Distributed Simulation

Modeling and simulation are methods used in a wide range of industries to enhance analysis and decision-making, increase system performance, and optimize operations. These techniques provide valuable insights into complex real-world systems by generating virtual experiments and representations. One prevalent solution that addressed the limitations of classical simulation techniques for complex models is the adoption of distributed simulation (DS) methodologies. The core of coordinating models, tools, and data across platforms is DS, which its target is to integrate heterogeneous systems, including DT and IoT networks. Applications where multi-domain interactions (such as thermal, electrical, and cyber-physical) call for synchronized, real-time analysis, such as smart cities, energy grids, and industrial automation, depend heavily on this methodology (Huang et al., 2024; Possik et al., 2023). The linking of several simulation environments with different capabilities is made possible by the standards that govern the integration and communication between these different environments like FMI/FMU (Functional Mock-up Interface/Unit), DIS (Distributed Interactive Simulation), and HLA which are the most important standards that control this integration.

These standards each address distinct facets of DS and system integration, each bringing special skills. However, the efficiency, scalability, and adaptability of the final integrated system are all greatly impacted by the standard selection. By encapsulating models as FMUs, FMI/FMU facilitates tool-agnostic co-simulation. Perfect for integrating DES with physics-based systems (such HVAC and IoT sensors). Its drawback is that it emphasizes model exchange but does not have native support for large-scale, distributed systems. DIS is to serve as a defense-focused standard for entity-level, real-time simulations (like military training). Its limitations include limited scalability for multi-domain applications and rigid time synchronization

(Taylor et al., 2017). HLA is a framework for federating simulations across heterogeneous systems that has been standardized by IEEE (1516–2010) that uses publish-subscribe techniques, HLA's Run-Time Infrastructure (RTI) controls data filtering, time synchronization, and communication (Möller et al., 2020). HLA is contrasted with alternative interoperability frameworks, such as the FMI/FMUs. FMI/FMU is a standard that is appropriate for co-simulation and tool coupling but has limited real-time and federated capabilities; AnyLogic is a hybrid simulation environment that combines discrete-event and agent-based modeling in a unique way, which justifies its use despite its proprietary nature; and HLA is better suited for scalable, distributed, and real-time synchronization, which is consistent with our goals for the digital twin. In addition, HLA includes a time management mechanism to coordinate simulation time between heterogeneous components, unlike FMI/FMU, which does not provide this as part of its standard. HLA is the interoperability standard used in this study because of its robust support for distributed real-time simulation. Also, more suited for real-time digital twins across heterogeneous systems because of its support for federated execution, time synchronization, and publish/subscribe semantics.

7.2.2 Challenges in Developing Integrated Systems and Related Works

DT and IoT systems have a potent synergy that increases each technology's potential. DT is powered by real-time data from IoT devices, which allows them to precisely depict and track physical assets or systems. DTs can record the current condition of assets, anticipate possible problems, and maximize performance due to this constant flow of sensor data. The enormous volumes of IoT data are then given structure and meaning by digital twins, which use sophisticated analytics and visualization to turn unprocessed data into useful insights. Also, DT and IoT systems can be integrated to provide revolutionary advantages like predictive maintenance, real-time monitoring, and dynamic physical environment optimization. However, because of their intrinsic complexity, constraints, and data dependencies, combining these systems presents substantial problems (Minerva et al., 2020). As an example, in smart buildings where IoT uses sensors to monitor environmental parameters like temperature, CO_2 levels, and occupancy, while DT simulates energy consumption to increase efficiency (Zhao, 2025).

Interoperability enables communication and data interchange between different devices, and different systems. DT can function as interdependent creatures in complex ecosystems since it ensures the integration of varied data and real-time decision-making (Budiardjo & Migliori, 2021; David et al., 2024). Important advantages include standardized data sharing, scalability for large networks, protocol flexibility, semantic communication for meaningful interpretation, and dynamic connections for temporary system linkages. Interoperability facilitates integration and avoids system isolation, allowing DTs to work together efficiently and enhance applications in manufacturing, healthcare, and smart cities (Budiardjo & Migliori, 2021). Before implementing control techniques, simulation-based DT enables the virtual testing of real-world situations, lowering the chance of system failures and improving performance. Discrete Event Simulation (DES) and Agent-Based Simulation (ABS) are two popular simulation methodologies for simulating dynamic, complex systems where environmental influences and human activity interact (Uhrmacher & Weyns, 2009; Wainer & Mosterman, 2011).

In order to focus on discrete subsystems like control systems or occupancy monitoring, current digital twin implementations usually employ single simulation paradigms. In manufacturing, DES used to model production lines, optimize workflows, and reduce downtime (Santos et al., 2022). Moreover, in healthcare applications use ABS is used to model patient flow and optimize resource allocation in hospitals (Vázquez-Serrano et al., 2021). Although these applications show how DT-IoT systems can improve operational performance, they frequently work in silos, focusing on isolated subsystems rather than considering the interdependencies between environmental variables and human behaviors. This shows that DES is good at modeling energy flows but has trouble accounting for dynamic human interactions that affect these flows; ABS records occupant behavior but lacks the granularity needed for system-level process.

Similarly, for real-time system application in manufacturing for better planning and decision making with DES-based DT framework with an embedded IoT system is used, which enables producers to maximize output and reduce downtime. These applications show how DES plays a part in structured process optimization, which keeps healthcare and industrial operations flexible and effective (Agalianos et al., 2020). Integrating system simulation, DES, and ABS to improve predictive skills across a range of industries are highlighted by digital twin research (Marah & Challenger, 2022). Because ABS offers a deeper understanding of autonomous behaviors and DES specializes at improving sequential procedures, their integration is essential for creating comprehensive DT-IoT solutions across smart environments. If we go further in monitoring the indoor environmental variables, we will find several studies have been introduced for DT-IoT in smart building for several applications. For industrial environments like manufacturing facilities and warehouses DT are used, to improve safety and maintain ideal working conditions. These can include the shop floor's temperature and humidity, the air in production areas, the conditions of the machines (such as vibrations, motor temperatures, and pressures), and the presence or movements of people and cars (Choi et al., 2022). On other hand in educational areas like universities and schools, several studies in monitoring these indoor variables to have healthy campus and resource usage by providing capabilities for managing campus residents, infrastructure, and facilities. These frameworks turn university spaces into intelligent settings with real-time monitoring and decision-making capabilities by integrating DT-IoT to keep an eye on and encourages comfort levels by monitoring and documenting campus events, which benefits the social wellbeing of both teachers and students (Zaballos et al., 2020).

In addition, conventional classroom monitoring systems are ineffective in guaranteeing the best possible learning environments because they frequently neglect to incorporate real-time data with predictive analytics or adaptive control mechanisms. DT-based solution, to offering practical insights for enhancing comfort, energy economy, and general classroom management, this makes it possible to monitor variables including occupancy, temperature, lighting, and air quality by measuring CO_2. This method not only enhances environmental management but also shows how DT-IoT systems can help create better learning environments by guaranteeing energy economy, comfort, and safety while accommodating changing classroom requirements (Pang et al., 2023). However, because environmental factors and human interactions are interdependent, a hybrid approach is required. For example, HVAC energy use is influenced by both thermostat settings which modeled by DES and real-time occupancy patterns which simulated by ABS. To bridge different domains, interoperability standards like HLA are required. These standards synchronize diverse systems into a single digital twin. As a result, ABS is ideal for occupant behavior, which excels at capturing interactions between autonomous agents, and DES for energy flows. DES is ideal for modeling sequential workflows, such as energy flows in HVAC systems. Despite their individual strengths, most implementations rely on either DES or ABS rather than combining them for holistic insights.

The promise of interoperable, real-time simulation frameworks is not completely utilized by current solutions, which frequently concentrate on offline simulations or restricted connection with physical systems. Furthermore, it is uncommon for these systems to integrate discrete event modeling with agent-based modeling to capture environmental control and human behavior in a single design. When integrating low-cost sensor technologies and simulation tools, this leads to a gap in the efficient management of classroom environments in a scalable, adaptable, and interoperable manner. This paper provides a novel approach to integrating real-time sensor data with hybrid simulation modeling utilizing a standards-based methodology, despite the fact that DS and DTs have been studied previously, they are mostly siloed, providing limited support, integrations, and a lack of predictive capabilities. As summarized in Table 7.1, Unlike (Huang et al., 2024; Possik et al., 2023; Zhao, 2025; Z. Pang, H. Zhao, Z. Tang and F. Kong, A Digital Twins-Based Smart Classroom Monitoring System, 2023), which focus on isolated aspects such as network simulation, Virtual Reality (VR) environments, or basic monitoring, our study uniquely integrates real-time IoT data with simulation using interoperability standards to create a responsive digital twin for classroom environments. Our contribution is the combination of a hybrid discrete event and agent-based simulation model created in AnyLogic, synchronized through the HLA, and real-time environmental monitoring via sensors. This creates a new and adaptable digital twin foundation for learning settings by enabling real-time data processing, simulation-based control decisions, and system scalability.

Table 7.1 Comparison of related works and proposed digital twin framework

Reference	Simulation Type	Focus	IoT Integration	Real Time Data	Scalability	HLA Based (Distributed Architecture)
Huang et al. (2024)	Distributed DES (DDES)	Modeling Networks	No	No	High	No (Component Based)
Possik et al. (2023)	ABS and DES	Interactive VR	No	No (User Interactions only)	Moderate	Yes (VR Interactions based on HLA)
Zhao (2025)	DES Only	Smart building Management	No	No	Limited	No
Pang et al. (2023)	Data-Driven monitoring	Smart Classroom Monitoring	Yes	Limited (No behavior Modeling)	Limited	No
Our Model	Hybrid Simulation: ABS and DES	Smart Classroom Management	Yes	Yes	High	Yes (HLA Integration)

7.3 Methodology and Framework Architecture

The implementation of accurate DT by integration the virtual representation with the physical system model enabling real-time data analysis, monitoring, controlling, and optimization for different complex systems, as shown in Fig. 7.1. The physical system that is updated constantly using data from sensors, IoT devices, and other sources. Accurate modeling of behavior, environmental effects, and operational states is made possible by this synchronization. In order to forecast system behavior and maximize operations, the creation of a realistic DT significantly depends on modeling and simulation approaches. While simulation enables experimenting in a virtual environment prior to implementing changes in the real world, modeling captures the essential features of the physical system.

The HLA objective is to ensure that modeling and simulation are compatible and meet the target of the model, where this standard is essential to the development of DS because it creates simulations with a variety of simulation component, which called Federates. The data exchanged between federates through RTI synchronously with collaborative management. Furthermore, the federated object model (FOM) defines the objects/classes and interactions/parameters utilized for communication. All these entities together (RTI, FOM, and multiple federates) seamlessly integrated in a federation. Based on FOM and HLA object management, these heterogeneous federates can effectively exchange and synchronize simulation data by utilizing a publish/subscribe (p/s) approach (Almaksour et al., 2022; Möller et al., 2020).

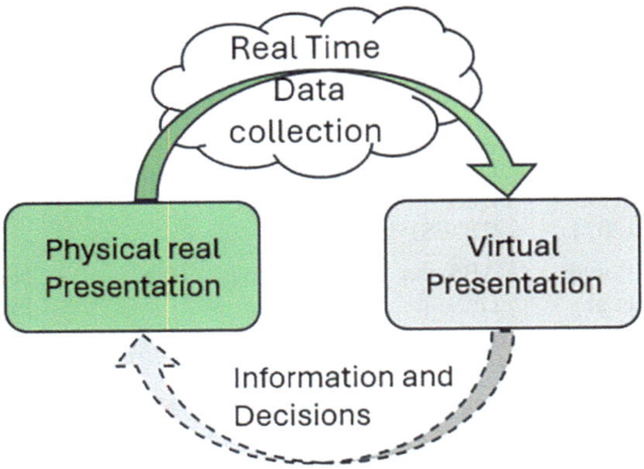

Fig. 7.1 DT concept of implementation

In this study, we proposed the architecture of the DS system. Within this architecture, two key components, the DES and ABS, which utilized in the AnyLogic platform. These components communicated with the sensors to measure the environmental variables, which is built with Arduino Uno R3, as implemented in Fig. 7.2. AnyLogic plays a crucial role in this integrated system since it publishes the locations of every agent in the simulation's unit. It is possible to precisely monitor the movements and interactions of the agents within the simulated classroom with real-time tracking. HLA standard and its mechanism of controlling the data where the needed information is published through AnyLogic to the RTI. Then RTI ensures that all subscribed components receive the specific data at synchronously. Similarly, the data updated in the same procedure to publish the data from the sensor through serial communication to RTI. HLA algorithm below in Fig. 7.3 shows the steps that is to exchange data between AnyLogic and sensors. The proposed system uses a federated simulation structure in which environmental variables (e.g., CO_2, temperature, humidity, motion, and light) are declared as published objects by the Arduino-side federate. These are subscribed to by the AnyLogic-based simulation federate. Communication follows the HLA Object Model Template (OMT), ensuring that shared object attributes (e.g., CO_2_level, temperature value) are updated across federates. The RTI (Run-Time Infrastructure) used Pitch RTI (pRTI), operating under a conservative synchronization strategy to maintain causal consistency.

7.4 Case Study Implementation: Classroom

In this paper we choose to apply our model in classrooms to measure the most important indoor environmental variables. Temperature, humidity, light intensity, and the quality of the air by measuring CO_2 are monitored and tracked in real time according to the number of people occupied the room. Several studies present how it is important to do monitoring and evaluation of such variables especially for CO_2 in

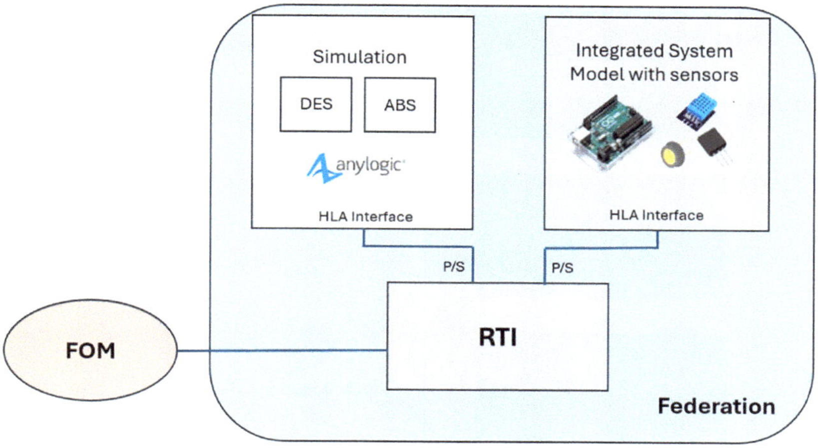

Fig. 7.2 Distribution system architecture

educational areas. This will effect on classifying the classrooms ventilation process which directly has impact on the educational process (Schibuola & Tambani, 2020; Twinview, n.d.). Also, how much the students should interact with the control system in the room, or it is a decision that will be made upon to a standard of measurements. For the system simulation we made it through Anylogic to implement DES and ABS. As shown in Fig. 7.4, we used the standard room in medium size for 25 people maximum occupancy (24 students and a teacher) with total area of 96 m^2, according to the standards of designing classrooms and lecture hall designs (University Planning, Design and Construction, & Classroom Management Committee, 2020). On the other hand, the Anylogic simulation model will have the real-time data through several sensors, we collected and used live sensor data (e.g., CO_2, temperature, humidity) from Arduino device to feed into the AnyLogic simulation, enabling the model to reflect real-time environmental conditions. The physical system here is used to test the validation of the system through the Arduino Uno R3 as the processor for the control system, where it was tested in a lab setting not in full live classroom yet. The variables are measured through the following sensors: DHT11 (digital temperature and humidity sensor), TSL2561 light intensity sensor, PIR (Passive Infrared Sensor) motion sensor to determine the occupancy and movements in the classroom, and MQ-135 air quality sensor to detect CO_2, as shown in Fig. 7.5. The outputs of these sensors will be as light indicators where some control systems in the rooms use the light as indicator to show the status of the important variables in the room, as shown in Fig. 7.6 the lights indicate for the status of the room variables to give indication for the people to interact with the action required.

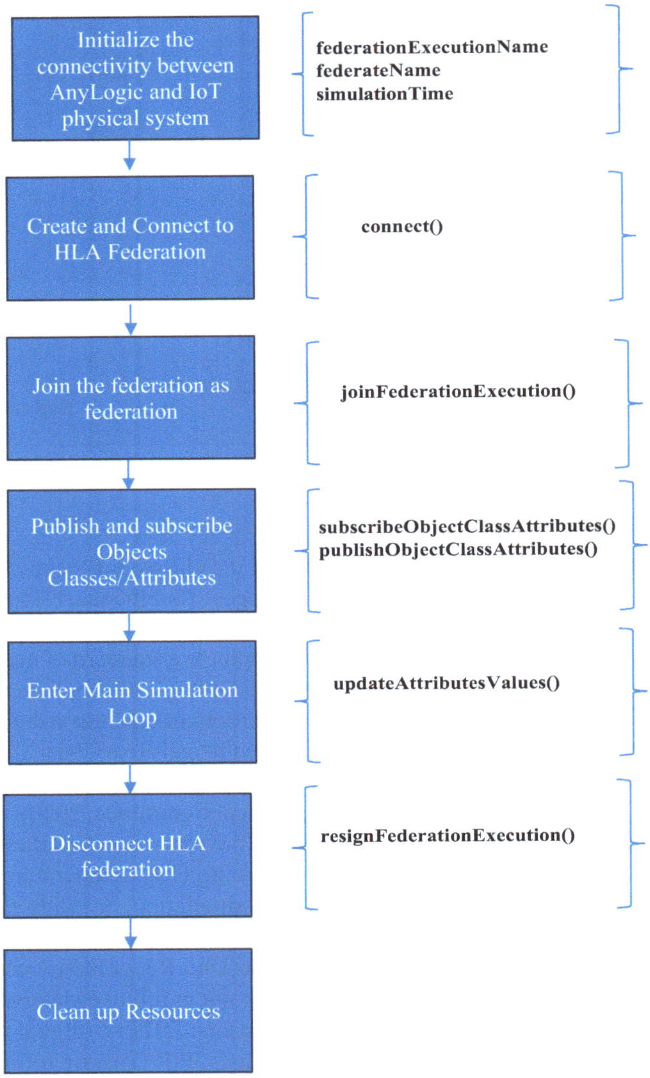

Fig. 7.3 HLA implementation algorithm

7.5 Results and Discussion

As a result of the connection between the two systems, we examined the system model for different scenarios regarding the number of people occupied the classroom with the time. We started with empty classroom, initialized the variables according to the standards value for optimal learning environment, where the temperature required to

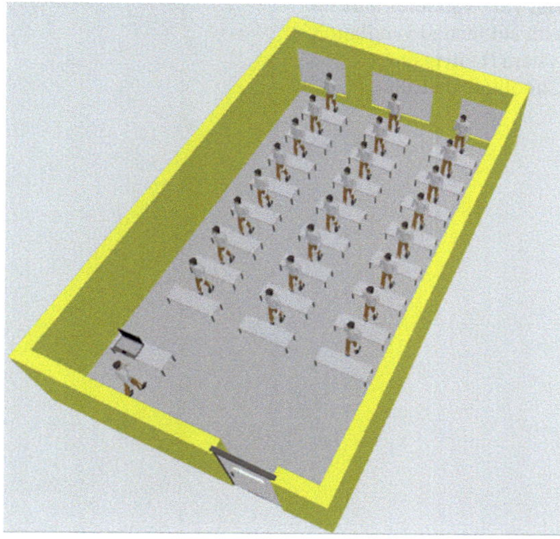

Fig. 7.4 Top View of the classroom simulated in Anylogic (96 m^2 and 25 people)

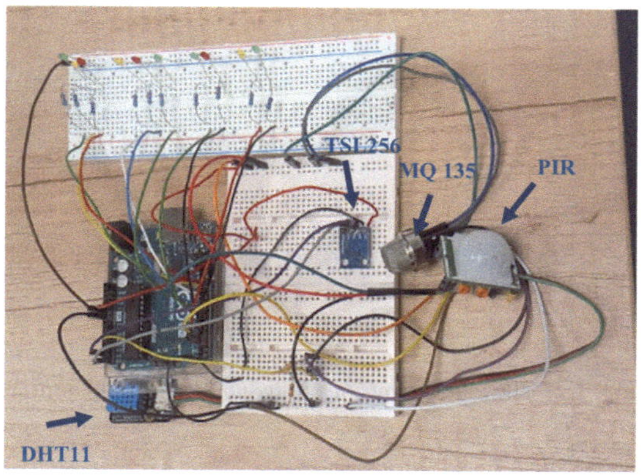

Fig. 7.5 The hardware setup integration: Arduino with sensors

be 22°C ±1°C and CO_2 < 1000 ppm (Spaho et al., 2025). According to ASHRAE 62.1, WHO guidelines for indoor environments, and EN 12464-1 (European classroom lighting standards), the ideal range for the temperature is 20–24°C (winter), 22–26°C (summer), for the humidity 40–60% RH, CO_2 levels < 1000 ppm, where ventilation required above 1200 ppm, and 300–500 lux for standard classroom activities. As shown in Fig. 7.7, we used the standards with perfect condition when the room is empty, where the indicators show the green lights.

To ensure that the simulation behavior matches realistic environmental changes, the simulation parameters (such as temperature fluctuation and CO_2 increase per person) were calculated from and cross-checked against readings from calibrated Arduino sensors (MQ-135, DHT11). Synchronization between federates is maintained using timestamped updates. Each message sent by the Arduino federate

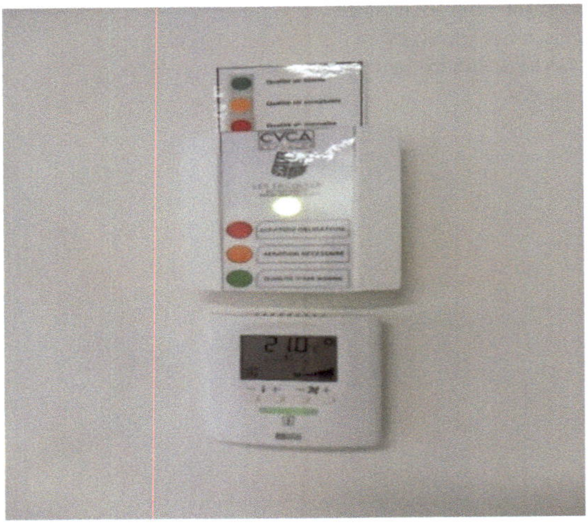

Fig. 7.6 Variables indicator with automated ventilation system (Université Catholique de Lille)

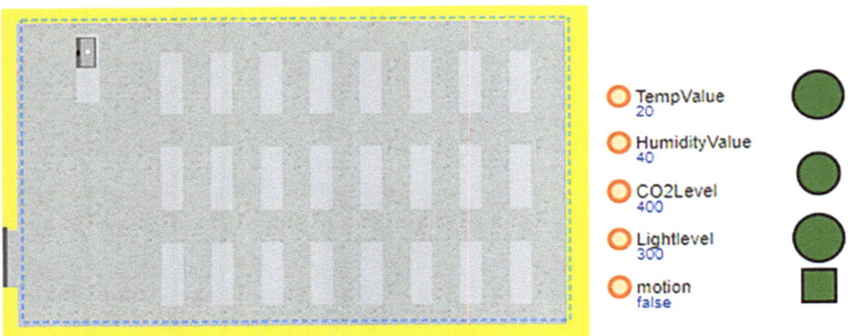

Fig. 7.7 The classroom sensors indicators with the initial variables when the room is empty

includes simulation time metadata. In case of delays, a basic retry logic and buffered queuing ensure message order and delivery. While the current model does not use rollback mechanisms, causality is enforced through time-stepped progression, which is suitable for room-level DTs with low-frequency updates. Sensor data is polled, processed locally on the Arduino and transmitted via serial-over-UDP to the federate. In addition to the calibration steps include warm-up the MQ-135 and zeroed against clean air. Also, the offset correction of DHT11 using a known thermometer.

As soon as the system started and get the data as shown in Fig. 7.8, we will see that for the full capacity room the variables will reach these values, and the indicators colors changed to have an action according to that. According to these results, if we see the variation of temperature and humidity with time while people entering the classroom dynamically and randomly. In Fig. 7.9, for the full capacity the temperature and humidity increased continuously because the temperature of closed room increased according to the number of people in it. This gives indication

Fig. 7.8 Full Capacity classroom sensors indicators with the final variables

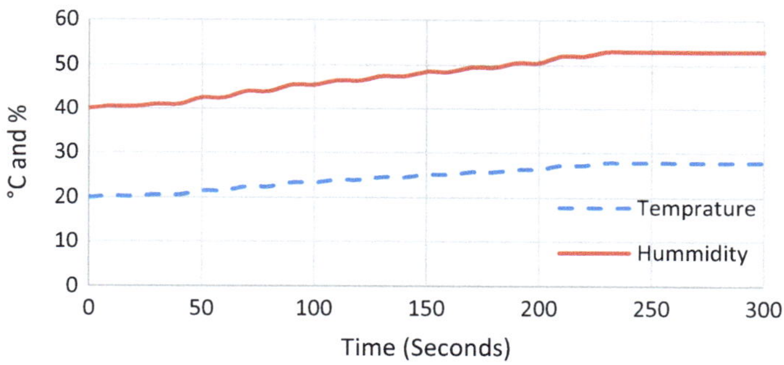

Fig. 7.9 Temperature °C; and Humidity % for full capacity of the classroom

for the DT system to take an action directly or give indication for the people inside the room to interact according to that. This is because that it affects directly on the energy consumption and the quality of teaching in the classroom.

The same for CO_2 level, it is mandatory to make an action according to this value, where it affects directly on the energy consumption, several studies prove that this will reduce energy waste by 10–15% while ensuring CO_2 level stayed below 900 ppm (Clausen et al., 2021). As shown in Fig. 7.10, it comes around 920 ppm which is acceptable for our room size with the number of people inside the room, since CO_2 increased rapidly after a certain number of students entered. For the light intensity it increases during the day since we need the light more as the time gets later especially in the wintertime. Different scenarios for people occupancy in the classroom were tested, where the values changed accordingly. Also, the indicators will be changed according to that as shown in Fig.11. If we see the results, we will see that the model reaction using DES and the estimated occupancy of the room to create predictive modification to control the indoor environmental variables, this will reduce the energy wasted especially in the education infrastructures. Furthermore, this control will improve the comfortable occupant areas during learning process,

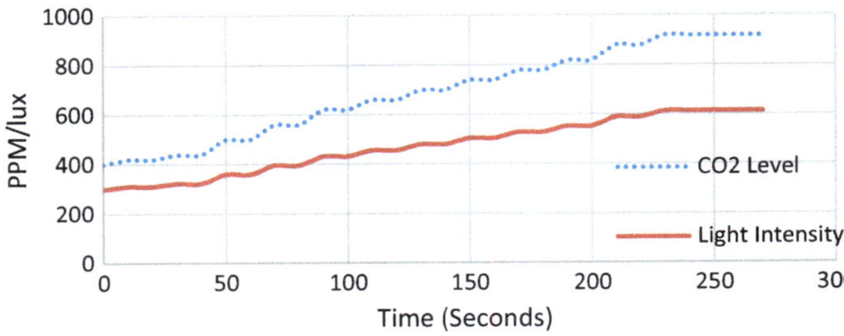

Fig. 7.10 CO_2 level and light intensity for full capacity of the classroom

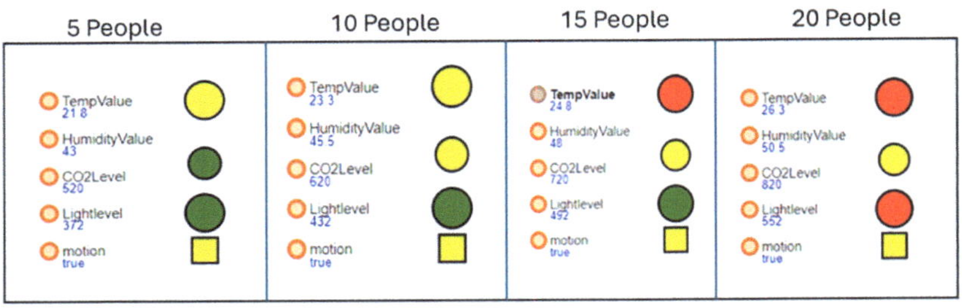

Fig. 7.11 Full capacity classroom sensors indicators with the final variables

where using real-time data through the communication of the integrated DT system with HLA synchronization to maintain the variables within the ranges. The findings of this system show the impact of all these variables on the classroom, HVAC system reaction, and people interaction (Fig. 7.11).

7.6 Conclusion and Future Work

This study demonstrates how integrating Arduino-based sensors with AnyLogic simulation enables real-time monitoring and control of classroom environmental conditions. By modeling variables like CO_2, temperature, humidity, light, and motion, the research highlights the impact of occupancy and room size on comfort and air quality. The work also shows that HLA provides an effective framework for scalable, interoperable digital twins, supporting applications such as energy-efficient HVAC control and occupancy-based classroom management. The framework provides a scalable solution for dynamic environments that need the coexistence of system-level processes such as energy flows and human behaviors such as occupant movement. Although our work laid the groundwork for the integration of DT-IoT systems via HLA, there are still several uncharted things. First, the framework's performance under complex federations and high-density IoT networks could be verified through scalability testing in bigger infrastructures such as bigger rooms or halls, and a full layer in a wide campus. The study presented a single classroom as a proof of concept. This classroom model is part of a broader, ongoing initiative. Currently an extending DT framework to model an entire smart building at JUNIA Lille, which includes multiple classrooms, laboratories, and shared learning spaces. This larger-scale implementation is being developed using real-time environmental live data from the building's control system (temperature, CO_2, occupancy, energy usage, etc.). The expanded model will incorporate diverse room sizes, occupancy dynamics, and environmental conditions, enabling us to explore interoperability across zones and demonstrate scalability under different configurations. Additionally, this future deployment will allow us to examine the system's performance across seasonal and climate variations, thus aligning more closely with smart campus and smart city applications. Furthermore, extending the number of the included variables with machine learning or deep learning methods for decision making.

References

Agalianos, K., et al. (2020). Discrete event simulation and digital twins: review and challenges for logistics. *Procedia Manufacturing, 51*, 1636–1641.

Almaksour, A., Gerges, H., Gorecki, S., Zacharewicz, G., & Possik, J. (2022). The use of the IEEE HLA standard to tackle interoperability issues between heterogeneous components. In *Proceedings of the 2022 IEEE/ACM 26th International Symposium on Distributed Simulation and Real Time Applications (DS-RT 2022)* (pp. 175–178).

Arowoiya, V. A., Onososen, A. O., Moehler, R. C., & Fang, Y. (2024). Influence of thermal comfort on energy consumption for building occupants: The current state of the art. *Buildings., 14*, 1310.

Arsiwala, A., Elghaish, F., & Zoher, M. (2023). Digital twin with Machine learning for predictive monitoring of CO_2 equivalent from existing buildings. *Energy and Buildings, 284*, Article 112851.

Budiardjo, A., & Migliori, D. (2021). *Digital twin system interoperability framework*. Digital Twin Consortium.

Choi, S., Woo, J., Kim, J., & Lee, J. Y. (2022). Digital twin-based integrated monitoring system: Korean application cases. *Sensors, 22*(14), 5450.

Clausen, A., Arendt, K., Johansen, A., Sangogboye, F. C., Kjærgaard, M. B., Veje, C. T., & Jørgensen, B. N. (2021). A digital twin framework for improving energy efficiency and occupant comfort in public and commercial buildings. *Energy Informatics, 4*(1), 1–16.

David, I., Shao, G., Gomes, C., Tilbury, D., & Zarkout, B. (2024). Interoperability of digital twins: Challenges, success factors, and future research directions. In *Leveraging applications of formal methods, verification and validation* (pp. 45–61). Application Areas.

Huang, Z., Zhang, N., Shen, J., Diamantopoulos, G., Hua, Z., Tziritas, N., & Theodoropoulos, G. (2024, August). Distributed simulation for digital twins of large-scale real-world diffserv-based networks. In *European conference on parallel processing* (pp. 255–269). Springer Nature Switzerland.

Marah, H., & Challenger, M. (2022). Intelligent agents and multi-agent systems for modeling smart digital twins. In *Proceedings of the 10th International Workshop on Engineering Multi-Agent Systems*.

Minerva, R., Lee, G. M., & Crespi, N. (2020). Digital twin in the IoT context: A survey on technical features, scenarios, and architectural models. *Proceedings of the IEEE, 108*(10), 1785–1824.

Möller, B., Karlsson, M., Löfstrand, B., Wihlborg, Å., Eriksson, S., Johansson, M., Klasson, F., Svensson, P., & Aktanius, P. (2020). *The HLA Tutorial v1.0.* Pitch Technologies.

Pang, Z., Zhao, H., Tang, Z., & Kong, F. *A digital twins-based smart classroom monitoring system.* 2023 IEEE International Conference on Advanced Learning Technologies (ICALT) (pp. 347–349) Orem, UT, USA.

Possik, J., Solis, A., & Zacharewicz, G. (2023). Immersive innovation: Exploring interactive virtual reality through distributed simulations. In *Advances in modeling and simulation* (pp. 123–140).

Santos, C. H., de Queiroz, J. A., Leal, F., & Lezoche, M. (2022). Use of simulation in the Industry 4.0 context: Creation of a Digital Twin to optimise decision making on non-automated process. *Journal of Simulation, 16*(3), 284–297.

Schibuola, L., & Tambani, C. (2020). Indoor environmental quality classification of school environments by monitoring PM and CO_2 concentration levels. *Atmospheric Pollution Research, 11*(2), 332–342.

Spaho, E., Çiço, B., & Shabani, I. (2025). IoT integration approaches into personalized online learning: Systematic review. *Computers, 14*(2)

Taylor, S. J. E., Fishwick, P. A., Fujimoto, R. M., Page, E. H., Uhrmacher, A. M., & Wainer, G. (2017). *Guide to Distributed Simulation with HLA.* Springer.

Thelen, A., Zhang, X., Fink, O. et al. (2022). A comprehensive review of digital twin—Part 1: Modeling and twinning enabling technologies. *Struct Multidisc Optim, 65*, 354.

Twinview. (n.d.). *Building tomorrow's classrooms today: How digital twins are reshaping education.* Twinview Insights. Retrieved March 19, 2025, from https://www.twinview.com/insights/building-tomorrows-classrooms-today-how-digital-twins-are-reshaping-education

Uhrmacher, A. M., & Weyns, D. (Eds.). (2009). *Multi-agent systems: Simulation and applications.* CRC Press.

University Planning, Design and Construction, & Classroom Management Committee. (2020). *Classroom and lecture hall design guidelines* (Revision #3). University of Connecticut.

Vázquez-Serrano, J. I., Peimbert-García, R. E., & Cárdenas-Barrón, L. E. (2021). Discrete-event simulation modeling in healthcare: A comprehensive review. *International Journal of Environmental Research and Public Health, 18*(22), 12262.

Wainer, G. A., & Mosterman, P. J. (Eds.). (2011). *Discrete-event modeling and simulation: Theory and applications.* CRC Press.

Yao, J. F., Yang, Y., Wang, X. C., & Zhang, X. P. (2023). Systematic review of digital twin technology and applications. *Vis Comput Ind Biomed Art. 30, 6*(1), 10.

Zaballos, A., Briones, A., Massa, A., Centelles, P., & Caballero, V. (2020). A smart campus' digital twin for sustainable comfort monitoring. *Sustainability, 12,* 9196.

Zhao, Z. (2025). Design of smart building energy management system based on digital twin technology. In Y. Zhang et al. (Eds.), *Proceedings of the 2024 10th International Conference on Architectural, Civil and Hydraulic Engineering (ICACHE 2024), Advances in Engineering Research* (Vol. 259, pp. 193–198). Atlantis Press.

Zhao, D., & Wen, J. (2022). Digital twin for healthy indoor environment: A vision for the post-pandemic era. *Building Simulation, 15*(5), 875–891Z.

Chapter 8
A/r/Tography in the Metaverse: Creative Collaborative Virtual Environments for Art Education

Catarina Carneiro de Sousa

Abstract This paper examines the application of a/r/tography—an arts-based research methodology integrating artistic practice, research, and teaching—within metaverse environments, focusing on Creative Collaborative Virtual Environments (CCVE). Through analysis of artistic projects and educational implementations using Second Life and OpenSimulator, this research demonstrates how CCVE platforms foster collaborative art practices, embodied knowledge construction, and innovative pedagogical approaches. The author's decade-long artistic practice in virtual environments serves as the foundation for these educational initiatives, illustrating the recursive relationship between artistic inquiry and pedagogical innovation. Findings reveal that CCVE's core affordances—creation, collaboration, and distribution—are essential for enabling effective co-creation while developing crucial digital competencies. This research contributes to understanding how virtual environments extend a/r/tographic methodology beyond physical constraints, creating new possibilities for art education in digital contexts.

Keywords A/r/tography · Art Education · Creative Collaborative Virtual Environments · Metaverse

8.1 Introduction

The Metaverse—encompassing persistent, shared virtual 3D spaces (Otrel-Cass et al., 2025)—has evolved from a science fiction concept into accessible digital environments where millions engage in creative, social, and educational activities. These virtual worlds have opened possibilities for artistic inquiry and pedagogical practice beyond physical constraints.

C. C. de Sousa (✉)
Higher School of Education of Viseu, Ci&DEI, Polytechnic Institute of Viseu, Viseu, Portugal
e-mail: csousa@esev.ipv.pt

M. Abed et al. (eds.), *Metaverse and Artificial Intelligence in Education for a Sustainable Society*, Future Education and Learning Spaces,
https://doi.org/10.1007/978-981-95-8852-7_8

This paper examines how the author's work in the Metaverse has developed as a form of a/r/tography—an arts-based research methodology that interweaves the roles of artist, researcher, and teacher. A/r/tography recognizes the interconnected nature of these identities and practices as a unified approach to knowledge creation (Dias, 2023). For a/r/tographic practices to realize their potential in virtual environments, specific technological and social affordances are crucial.

This research argues that Creative Collaborative Virtual Environments (CCVE) provide the necessary framework for a/r/tography to thrive in the Metaverse. CCVEs are defined as 3D virtual environments accessible to multiple users simultaneously, who can interact and collaborate, construct original artifacts, and modify/personalize content (Eustáquio & Sousa, 2018). These environments enable creation, collaboration, and distribution capabilities that directly align with the core tenets of a/r/tography.

To demonstrate this alignment, this paper analyzes three artistic projects developed over a decade of virtual practice: Meta_Body, a participatory project focused on virtual corporeality and collaborative creation; Kromosomer, an exploration of otherness through storytelling and avatar creation; and the Berg trilogy (Penumbra, The Swamp, and The Dreamers), a series addressing sociopolitical concerns through environmental installation.

The paper then examines two educational initiatives: Virtual Art Lab, which provided space for artistic exploration and skill development, and IPVerso, which created an immersive academic environment representing the institution in the Metaverse. Through these case studies, this research identifies how CCVE affordances support embodied knowledge development, collaborative creation, and innovative pedagogical approaches.

This study employs art-based research methodologies that position artistic creation as both a means and an outcome of research inquiry. As Sullivan (Sullivan, 2010) argues, art practice generates unique insights through its processes and products. Documentation includes virtual photography, machinima (films created in virtual environments), participant feedback, and reflective writing to capture visual-spatial elements and experiential dimensions.

8.2 Background

8.2.1 Creative Collaborative Virtual Environments

The term 'Metaverse' has gained popularity, referring to persistent, shared virtual spaces where individuals engage in various activities and content (Otrel-Cass et al., 2025).

This concept is closely related to the concept of Collaborative Virtual Environments (CVEs), which are defined as digital, distributed virtual spaces that support collaborative activities (Churchill et al., 2001). These environments are commonly referred to as virtual worlds or collectively as the 'Metaverse'—a term originating from Neal Stephenson's 1992 novel *Snow Crash*, where it described a fully immersive three-dimensional space for avatar-based interactions.

Today, the term 'Metaverse' encompasses shared digital spaces, particularly regarding graphical three-dimensional virtual worlds. These are understood by Castronova as "computer-generated physical space, represented graphically in three dimensions, that can be experienced by many people at once" (Castronova, 2005). Boellstorff (Boellstorff, 2010) identifies three fundamental elements that constitute virtual worlds: places that are inhabited by persons and enabled by online technologies.

The collaborative dimension is crucial in these environments. Otrel-Cas et al. (2025) distinguish between cooperation and collaboration, arguing that cooperation is more structured than collaboration. Cooperators develop clearly defined tasks, while collaborators discuss their tasks and contributions in a shared creative process. However, it is important to recognize that not all CVEs are created equal with regard to the creative capabilities they provide. Some CVEs support creative affordances that others do not—specifically, they empower users to build or upload their own content and avatars. This distinction is crucial for understanding the emergence of Creative Collaborative Virtual Environments (CCVEs), virtual environments that have evolved to offer new possibilities for creative and educational practices. Within this context, CCVEs are a specific type of virtual space that enables unique forms of interaction and content creation (Eustáquio & Sousa, 2018).

CCVEs are immersive 3D virtual spaces designed for real-time collaboration, interaction, content creation, and sharing among multiple users. Eustáquio and Sousa (Eustáquio & Sousa, 2018) identify three key affordances of CCVE:

- **Creation:** CCVEs provide tools for users to construct original artifacts within the virtual world, including 3D objects, avatars, and interactive experiences.
- **Collaboration:** CCVEs facilitate interaction and co-creation among users, enabling shared artistic processes and knowledge development.
- **Distribution:** CCVEs allow users to share and distribute their creations with others, fostering a dynamic environment of creative exchange.

These affordances distinguish CCVEs from other virtual environments and are critical for supporting artistic and a/r/tographic practices.

CCVEs provide users with the tools and functionalities to interact and collaborate (users can engage with each other and the environment); construct original artifacts (users can create new content within the virtual world or upload content created using third-party applications); and modify/personalize existing content (users can alter pre-existing content and share their creations with others).

These capabilities are supported by integrated platform features for content creation, modification, and distribution, allowing users to collectively shape the virtual world itself. Examples of CCVEs include platforms like OpenSimulator and Second Life, which offer tools for 3D modeling, texturing, scripting, and media integration.

8.2.2 A/r/Tography as a Methodology for the Metaverse

A/r/tography is an arts-based research methodology that recognizes the interconnectedness of the roles of artist, researcher, and teacher. It moves away from the idea that these are separate domains and instead views them as a unified approach to knowledge creation and dissemination. As Springgay et al. (Springgay et al., 2005) articulate, a/r/tography is a living inquiry through art practice, research, and teaching. This approach recognizes that knowledge emerges not only from traditional research methods but also through artistic practice and pedagogical engagement.

One crucial concept in this context is embodiment. Irwin defines this kind of art-based educational research as "embodied living inquiry": "We believed processes of making and performing identities could transform the concept of learning into *becoming pedagogical*" (Irwin, 2013). Virtual worlds offer distinctive forms of embodiment through avatars, which are more than digital representations of users. Avatars are not simply passive stand-ins for physical bodies; they become active sites where identity is constructed, performed, and negotiated. As users interact within the Metaverse, they develop embodied knowledge—a "techne" (Boellstorff, 2015)—that is specific to the virtual environment. This embodied experience can be a central focus of a/r/tographic inquiry, allowing researchers to explore how identity, presence, and interaction are shaped by virtual embodiment. Although the relationship between digital and a/r/tography has already been addressed (Lee et al., 2024), the specific relationship between this research model and CCVEs we believe, new and promising.

The affordances of CCVEs are particularly well-suited for the application of a/r/tography. The core tenets of a/r/tography—the intertwining of art, research, and teaching—are facilitated and enhanced by the capabilities of CCVE:

- **Artistic Creation as Inquiry:** A/r/tography uses artistic creation as a primary mode of research (Springgay et al., 2005). CCVEs provide the tools and environments for this creation, allowing for the development of avatars, virtual art installations, performances, and interactive experiences.
- **Collaboration, Co-creation, and Knowledge:** A/r/tography values the collaborative nature of knowledge development (Brooke et al., 2025). CCVEs enable real-time interaction and co-creation among participants, mirroring the collaborative dialogue inherent in a/r/tography.

Embodied Knowledge and Dissemination: A/r/tography recognizes the importance of embodied knowledge (Coleman, 2023). CCVEs, with their use of avatars and immersive environments, offer unique opportunities to explore and share embodied experiences. Furthermore, the distribution features of CCVEs allow for the sharing of artistic research with a wider audience.

8.3 Methodological Framework

This research employs arts-based research methodologies with a/r/tography as its primary framework. Within this framework, artistic creation becomes not merely an object of study but an epistemological process through which understanding emerges (Šuvaković, 2008).

8.3.1 Arts-Based Research in Virtual Environments

This study positions artistic creation within virtual worlds as both a means and outcome of research inquiry. As Sullivan (2010) demonstrates, artistic practice produces distinctive forms of knowledge through both its creative processes and resulting works—knowledge that often cannot be accessed or articulated through conventional research methodologies. The creative work developed within CCVEs platforms constitutes a form of embodied inquiry where knowledge emerges through making, experiencing, and reflecting.

The projects analyzed in this research span a decade of practice (2011–2023), allowing for longitudinal observation of how a/r/tographic approaches evolve within Metaverse environments. This extended engagement with virtual environments provides insights into how artistic practice and pedagogical approaches mutually inform one another over time.

8.3.2 Data Collection and Documentation Methods

To capture the multi-dimensional aspects of creative practice and learning in virtual environments, this research utilizes several complementary documentation methods:

- **Virtual photography**: High-resolution images capturing spatial compositions, avatar designs, and environmental details serve as visual documentation of artistic outcomes. These images preserve ephemeral moments within the ever-evolving virtual spaces (Sousa & Eustáquio, 2015).
- **Machinima (virtual cinematography)**: Films created within virtual environments document interactive experiences, performances, and spatial navigation, preserving temporal and kinesthetic dimensions lost in static images (Sousa & Eustáquio, 2015).
- **Participant feedback**: The feedback from the participants was essentially in the form of artistic production, such as virtual photographs, machinima, and avatars (Sousa, 2015). In addition, it was possible to access the reflections that these participants shared on social media or in personal conversations. In the case of the students, in addition to personalized monitoring and observation, surveys were carried out on the projects developed (Sousa et al., 2022; 2023).

- **Reflective writing**: Ongoing documentation of the researcher's own experiences, observations, and evolving understanding through critical reflection provides autoethnographic dimensions to the data collection (Dahls Veen & Sousa, 2013; Sousa, 2015, 2022).
- **Digital artifacts**: The preservation of in-world objects, scripts, avatars, and environments as digital artifacts enables analysis of technical approaches and creative solutions developed by participants.

8.3.3 Analytical Framework

The analysis of collected data employs a hermeneutic approach that acknowledges the interpretive nature of understanding creative practice. Rather than seeking generalizable conclusions, this methodology focuses on identifying emergent patterns, resonances, and tensions that illuminate the relationship between a/r/tography and CCVEs.

The analytical process involves:

- **Mapping relationships**: Tracing connections between artistic practice, research insights, and pedagogical approaches as they evolve recursively through projects.
- **Contextual analysis**: Situating observed phenomena within broader discourses about embodiment, virtual presence, digital pedagogy, and collaborative creation.
- **Critical reflection**: Questioning assumptions and identifying tensions or contradictions that emerge through practice.

8.4 Artwork Projects

This section focuses on projects developed by the author, Catarina Carneiro de Sousa (AKA CapCat ragu), in collaboration with Sameiro Oliveira Martins (AKA Meilo Minotaur) on the Second Life platform. While not developed in educational settings, these projects have informed the author's educational practice.

8.4.1 Meta_Body

Meta_Body (2011) was a participatory artistic project centered on sharing and constructing avatars in Second Life (Sousa, 2015).

The project began with eighteen original avatars (Fig. 8.1) distributed with full permissions (allowing transformation, copying, and redistribution) through a virtual installation in Delicatessen, a Second Life region. Participants created derivative works through virtual photographs and machinimas displayed at physical exhibitions, particularly the sixth edition of All My Independent Women in Vienna (2011).

Fig. 8.1 Original avatar "You see my inside," by Sameiro Oliveira Martins (AKA Meilo Minotaur) and Catarina Carneiro de Sousa (AKA CapCat Ragu)

In the second phase (2012), participants created derivative avatars based on the original set (Fig. 8.2). By 2013, Delicatessen reopened with four levels dedicated to these derivative avatars. Twenty-two creators designed twenty-six new avatars for open distribution.

Meta_Body exemplified a/r/tography's integration of research with artistic practice. This recursive theory-practice relationship demonstrates the living inquiry central to a/r/tographic methodology.

The project functioned as both artistic exploration and research investigation, with two primary domains: virtual corporeality constitution and shared creative processes in virtual environments.

Meta_Body investigated embodiment through the avatar's metaphorical body, connecting to a/r/tography's emphasis on embodied knowing. The research examined phenomenal body construction in digital spaces, with Veerapen's (2011) four avatar conceptions (object, prosthesis, phantom limb, and equal) explored through artistic practice rather than theoretical analysis.

The project recognized that "the virtual body is a metaphorical body. A body all language. As such, it becomes a platform open to experimentation and possibility." This understanding reflects a/r/tography's comfort with ambiguity and in-between spaces.

Meta_Body explored Hayles' (Hayles, 1999) "embodied virtuality"—how digital technologies reconfigure embodiment understanding. This research aspect informed pedagogical dimensions by revealing how self and other knowledge are constructed through virtual corporeality.

The project exemplified a/r/tography's relational aesthetics emphasis through three shared creative processes:

Fig. 8.2 Derivative avatar "Shiverdoll," by a student who took part in the second phase of the project on a voluntary basis, Melania Pereira Ribeiro (AKA Eila Magnolia in virtual worlds)

- **Collective Creation**: Participants act as a single creative entity with horizontal co-creation, relinquishing individual authorial marks for group authorship.
- **Distributed Creation**: Numerous participants contribute differently to a creative flow without necessarily working as a team (Eustáquio & Sousa, 2018). Participants functioned as "produsers" (producer-users) (Bruns, 2013), using content to produce new content shared with the community.
- **Collaborative Creation**: Each author maintains their authorial mark while engaging in creative dialogue (Eustáquio & Sousa, 2018). This approach was exemplified by Luís Eustáquio's soundscape contributions to the virtual installation.

The full permissions model deliberately blurred boundaries between creator and audience, researcher and subject, teacher and student—a central a/r/tographic methodology tenet. The project created a/r/tographic "openings" (Irwin et al., 2024) where new understandings emerge. The fluid, always unfinished work reflects a/r/tography's understanding of knowledge as provisional rather than definitive.

8.4.2 *Kromosomer*

Kromosomer was initiated by storyteller Heidi Dahlsveen in 2012 with the author's and Sameiro Oliveira Martins' visual art collaboration (Dahls Veen & Sousa, 2013). The project explored Norwegian legends through avatar creation and participatory storytelling. It used legends to understand "the other"—characters deviating from societal norms through whom we define ourselves by opposition. These characters were translated into Second Life avatars, distributed with full permissions (Fig. 8.3).

From an a/r/tographic perspective, Kromosomer integrated artistic creation (avatar design) and research (investigation of legends and otherness). The project exemplifies what a/r/tography calls "renderings"—conceptual organizing devices facilitating inquiry—particularly through embodiment and relationality emphasis (Irwin, 2024).

By inviting participants to wear and transform avatars representing "the other," Kromosomer created opportunities for embodied understanding of difference. This aligns with Ellsworth's "places of learning"—contexts where knowledge emerges through sensory and affective experience rather than purely cognitive processes (Ellsworth, 2005). The avatar becomes a site for experiencing alterity, challenging participants to negotiate self/other tension through digital embodiment.

The project revealed how virtual embodiment can serve as a powerful pedagogical tool for exploring complex social and existential themes. By literally "putting on" the other's body, participants engaged with difference through an immersive rather than purely intellectual approach, demonstrating how virtual worlds can extend traditional pedagogical approaches.

Fig. 8.3 "Peasant becoming Skurekallen," virtual installation for Kromosomer, featuring two of the avatars

8.4.3 The Berg Trilogy

The Berg trilogy—Penumbra, The Swamp, and The Dreamers—was developed during a year-long virtual residency at Berg by Nordan Art (2017). The trilogy responded to the global resurgence of fascist ideologies (Sousa, 2022). Each installation combined environmental design with shareable avatars addressing different sociopolitical concerns: Penumbra (Fig. 8.4) explored societal transition and uncertainty; The Swamp (Fig. 8.5) examined Portugal's experience of dictatorship and revolution; and The Dreamers (Fig. 8.6) offered poetic resistance to violence and hatred.

The trilogy demonstrates how a/r/tography can integrate personal narrative with broader sociopolitical inquiry. The Swamp draws on lived experience—Meilo's memories of fascist Portugal and the author's experience of the post-revolutionary period—to create an a/r/tographic narrative cartography (Springgay, 2005), weaving together multiple perspectives. This approach recognizes that artistic, research, and teaching practices are embedded in sociopolitical contexts.

The trilogy employs environmental design as a primary research method, using spatial composition, lighting, sound, and interactive elements to investigate emotional responses to political situations. This aligns with Sullivan's (2010) description of art as research—using artistic processes to generate insights inaccessible through traditional methods. The trilogy's progression from darkness (Penumbra)

Fig. 8.4 Penumbra

Fig. 8.5 The Swamp

Fig. 8.6 The Dreamers

through struggle (The Swamp) to hope (The Dreamers) represents a research arc exploring emotional responses to political trauma and resistance.

8.5 Educational Projects

8.5.1 The Virtual Art Lab

The Virtual Art Lab (VAL) emerged as a direct extension of artistic practice in virtual worlds, translating knowledge gained through personal artistic exploration into pedagogical approaches for higher education (Sousa et al., 2022). Established between 2015–2018 within Craft-World—an OpenSimulator grid—this simulator was dedicated to art education in virtual environments for Polytechnic of Viseu students.

Unlike traditional immersive learning environments often focused on simulating real-world scenarios, VAL embraced virtual worlds' unique aesthetic and creative possibilities. As Angelini (2021) notes, while high-fidelity simulations serve important purposes in fields like healthcare, art education can leverage virtual environments beyond simulation. VAL exemplified this by focusing on virtual environments' artistic potential rather than replicating physical art studios.

Pedagogical Framework and Methodology. VAL's educational methodology was grounded in active learning principles, where students constructed knowledge through hands-on engagement. As Brame (2016) describes, active pedagogies involve students building understanding while reflecting on their learning, often within collaborative contexts. This approach aligns with art education traditions, where project-based learning and problem-solving methodologies are established practices in Portuguese artistic education (Urbano & Branco, 2009).

VAL's extracurricular nature distinguished the experience, conducted entirely through distance learning before such practices became commonplace. The workshops operated through 30-hour courses divided into two-hour weekly remote sessions held after work hours. These formal sessions were complemented by ongoing interaction through a Facebook group, facilitating continuous dialogue, sharing reference materials, and informal feedback exchanges.

The instructional approach balanced structured tutorials with creative exploration. Initial sessions focused on developing technical skills necessary to navigate and create within OpenSimulator, but students immediately applied these skills creatively rather than merely replicating demonstrated techniques. Formal learning moments were intertwined with collaborative artistic projects that required integrating new technical knowledge with previous competencies while developing solutions to emerging challenges.

The Virtual Garden of Time. The first major collaborative project (2015–2016) was "The Virtual Garden of Time," conceptualized for Viseu's public art festival "Jardins Efémeros" (2016). The project transformed the simulator island

Fig. 8.7 Virtual Garden of Time, Spring

into a metaphorical garden representing time's passage, divided into twelve sections corresponding to yearly months. Each student developed one monthly section while maintaining coherence with adjacent areas (Figs. 8.7, 8.8, 8.9, 8.10).

Fig. 8.8 Virtual Garden of Time, Summer

Fig. 8.9 Virtual Garden of Time, Fall

Fig. 8.10 Virtual Garden of Time, Winter

Initial conceptual development occurred through the Facebook group, where students shared sketches and inspiration images. A unique challenge emerged in terraforming, as modifications to one section affected contiguous areas. The facilitator performed terraforming based on collectively negotiated decisions about geographical feature placement (Sousa et al., 2022).

As the project evolved, students' technical abilities developed with their creative ambitions. The desire to materialize complex ideas motivated them to expand their technical skills autonomously, seeking solutions beyond formal tutorial content. This self-directed learning resulted in remarkable transformations of both the virtual environment and students' capabilities.

The completed Garden created an immersive journey through seasons and months, with interactive environmental elements and freely available avatars. The project culminated in a physical exhibition at "Museu da Misericórdia de Viseu" during the "Jardins Efémeros" festival (July 2016), featuring a curved screen projecting the live virtual environment, virtual photography, and a documentary machinima.

[D]Utopia. Building on the first workshop's success, 2016–17 saw VAL expand into two sequential workshops: environment creation and avatar design. These workshops explored [D]Utopia, contrasting technological futures—from utopian societies where technology enhances human experience to dystopian scenarios where it enables authoritarianism.

The environment workshop methodology mirrored the Virtual Garden approach, with students representing either utopian (Fig. 8.11) or dystopian visions (Fig. 8.12). The island division required similar negotiations regarding terraforming and transitions between regions, resulting in eight interconnected virtual installations.

The second semester's avatar workshop presented challenges with participants having varying experience levels. The avatars were designed to complement the previously established environments, resulting in nine fully realized characters that embody the thematic contrasts between utopian and dystopian elements.

Particularly noteworthy was students' ability to mobilize skills beyond those covered in tutorials. Some independently learned external 3D modeling programs or

Fig. 8.11 [D]Utopia, utopian environment and avatar

Fig. 8.12 [D]Utopia, dystopian environment and avatar

developed scripting capabilities. The [D]Utopia project gained international recognition when invited to participate in Craft-World's eighth anniversary exhibition (2018) (Sousa et al., 2022).

A/r/tographic Reflections. Through a/r/tography's lens, VAL exemplifies the integration of artistic practice, research, and teaching. Prior experiences as an artist directly informed the pedagogical approaches. Understanding virtual embodiment, collaborative creation, and identity exploration developed through artistic practice provided a framework for guiding students through similar discovery processes.

Simultaneously, observing students' engagement generated new insights that recursively informed artistic practice. Their novel approaches to technical challenges, unexpected aesthetic choices, and unique thematic interpretations expanded the understanding of virtual world creativity. This reciprocal relationship between teaching and artistic practice embodies a/r/tographic methodology's essence, where role boundaries become permeable and knowledge flows multidirectionally.

VAL demonstrated how virtual environments foster embodied knowledge despite their digital nature. Through avatar-mediated interaction, students developed intuitive understandings of virtual space, materiality, and presence. This embodied knowing manifested in increasingly sophisticated manipulation of virtual materials and spaces, suggesting that corporeal understanding remains relevant even in disembodied contexts.

Furthermore, these projects' collaborative nature highlights how a/r/tography in virtual environments extends beyond individual practice to community-based knowledge creation. The negotiation processes fostered collective intelligence exceeding individual contributions, demonstrating virtual worlds' potential to support communal artistic inquiry.

8.5.2 IPVerso

IPVerso, launched in 2023 at the Polytechnic of Viseu, represents an institutional implementation of a/r/tographic methodology in virtual environments. Using the Craft-World grid, IPVerso was developed with direct student participation through workshops on various virtual world creation aspects. The simulator emerged from "Education and Co-creation in the Metaverse with a mixed approach" within the broader IPV Inova e Inclui Project, serving as both an educational space and a creative laboratory.

The environment was constructed with significant student contributions from associated workshops (Sousa et al., 2023) and serves as a persistent 3D digital environment allowing multiple simultaneous users to communicate and work together.

Rizhomatic Conceptual Framework. The project's conceptual foundation draws on Deleuze and Guattari's (Deleuze & Guattari, 1987) rhizome concept, which aligns with a/r/tography's emphasis on multiplicity and interconnection. This rizhomatic approach rejects binary logic and subject/object dualism in favor of connection-based knowledge production, making it particularly appropriate for digital environments where hyperlinks (manifested as teleports) create nonlinear exploration pathways.

While Deleuze and Guattari's text dates from the 1980s, the rhizome concept has proven useful for describing digital era cultural processes. The constant interconnection, use of hyperlinks, and relationships extending beyond local community exemplify this rhizomatic structure. This framework manifests physically in the environment's design, with interconnected spaces resisting hierarchical organization.

The rhizomatic approach aligns particularly well with a/r/tography's emphasis on relational aesthetics and role boundary blurring. Just as the rhizome connects disparate points horizontally rather than vertically, IPVerso connects students, educators, and creative practitioners in non-hierarchical collaborative relationships.

Spatial Organization and Educational Functions. The IPVerso environment includes specialized areas for different educational and creative functions. Public spaces encompass a Welcome Zone introducing the activity; an Auditorium enabling presentations; two Performance Arenas for presentations and avatar performances; an Avatar Sharing Zone distributing avatars; a Belvedere offering panoramic views; and Exhibition Halls integrated into the landscape (Fig. 8.13). Private areas include

Fig. 8.13 IPVerso ground installations

three restricted-access workshops (Construction, Optimization and Animation, and Scripts).

The platform allows developing ground space traversable by avatars, while enabling elevated "skyboxes" accessible via teleport. This characteristic increases the platform's flexibility, allowing both free exploration of public spaces and controlled access areas for specific groups.

This spatial organization demonstrates how virtual environments can support various a/r/tographic approaches, from presentation-based learning to hands-on creation and embodied exploration. The architectural design embodies the rhizomatic conceptual framework, with interconnected spaces resisting hierarchical organization.

Educational Outcomes and A/r/tographic Implications. The project enabled participants to confront digital transition era challenges, equipping them with creative, technological, conceptual, and collaborative competencies essential for virtual environment integration. This development of multiple, integrated competencies reflects a/r/tography's emphasis on interconnected knowing forms.

By promoting academic community resilience and adaptation capacity, particularly during situations like the COVID-19 pandemic, the project demonstrated how virtual environments can support educational continuity during disruption. This adaptability was facilitated by active teaching-learning methodologies centered on learners.

The project promoted competency mobilization in new contexts, encouraging acquired knowledge application in diverse situations. This contextual application emphasis aligns with a/r/tography's understanding of knowledge as situated and emergent rather than abstract and fixed.

Through seminars and exhibitions, the project created connections between local academic and global communities, establishing relationships between virtual and tangible environments. This bridgebuilding reflects a/r/tography's emphasis on boundary-crossing and negotiating different knowing ways.

Future Prospects and Limitations. Virtual world implementation in educational contexts demonstrated significant potential while highlighting key challenges. The primary challenges were twofold: difficulty engaging teachers beyond art and computer science disciplines, and technical limitations, particularly Craft-World's sound system inadequacy for larger gatherings.

Looking forward, project facilitators expressed interest in exploring alternative platforms addressing these limitations. Rather than focusing solely on improving virtual reality immersion, future directions may benefit from prioritizing robust multi-user communication capabilities and interfaces appealing to diverse subject educators.

These insights suggest successful integration depends not only on technical specifications but also on carefully considering human factors influencing adoption across different educational contexts.

8.6 Synthesis and Comparative Analysis

This section synthesizes findings across the artistic and educational projects, identifying patterns and variations in how a/r/tography manifests within different Metaverse implementations. Through comparative analysis, we can better understand how Creative Collaborative Virtual Environments support different aspects of a/r/tographic practice and how these approaches evolve across contexts.

8.6.1 Project Comparison Framework

The projects examined in this research—three artistic works (Meta_Body, Kromosomer, The Berg Trilogy) and two educational implementations (Virtual Art Lab, IPVerso)—represent diverse applications of a/r/tography within virtual environments. Despite their differences in purpose, scale, and context, these projects reveal consistent patterns in how CCVEs' affordances support a/r/tographic inquiry while also demonstrating how implementations vary according to specific goals and contexts. Table 8.1 provides a comparative overview of the five projects according to key analytical dimensions:

The chronological progression of projects reveals an evolution in how a/r/tography is applied within Metaverse environments. Early projects (Meta_Body, Kromosomer) prioritized artistic exploration with implicit pedagogical dimensions, while later projects (Virtual Art Lab, IPVerso) explicitly formalized pedagogical frameworks

Table 8.1 Comparative analysis of A/r/tographic projects in creative collaborative virtual environments

Project Features	Meta_Body	Kromosomer	Berg Trilogy	Virtual Art Lab	IPVerso
Platform	Second life	Second life	Second life	Craft-world (OpenSim)	Craft-world (OpenSim)
Duration	2011–2013	2012	2017	2015–2018	2023–present
Primary context	Artistic	Artistic	Artistic	Educational/artistic	Educational/ institutional/ artistic
Scale	Community-based	International collaboration	Artist residency	Extracurricular workshops	Institution-wide implementation
Primary focus	Virtual corporeality; collaborative creation	Otherness; cultural narratives	Sociopolitical commentary; resistance	Creative skill development; project-based learning	Digital transition; institutional presence
A/r/togrphic emphasis Artist role	Avatar creation; Installation design	Character Adaptation; Visual narrative	Environmental Storytelling; Political expression	Facilitation; Conceptual Development	System design; Spatial organization
A/r/togrphic emphasis Researcher role	Virtual embodiment investigation	Cultural narrative exploration	Sociopolitical inquiry	Pedagogical methodology development	Institutional implementation analysis
A/r/togrphic emphasis Teacher role	Open distribution; Community Engagement	Participatory Storytelling	Cultural communication	Formal workshop instruction	Multi-level pedagogical implementation
CCVE affordances Creation	Avatar design; environmental installations	Legend-based Avatar design; Environmental Installations	Environmental Installations; Avatar design	Environmental Installations; Avatar design	Environmental installations for multi-purpose spaces; teaching tools

(continued)

Table 8.1 (continued)

Project Features	Meta_Body	Kromosomer	Berg Trilogy	Virtual Art Lab	IPVerso
CCVE affordances Collaboration	Distributed creation Model; Collective Authorship	Cross-cultural Exchange; Distributed creation Model; Collective Authorship	Autoethnographic Artistic-narrative Partnership; Distributed creation Model; Collective Authorship	Student/teacher Co-creation; Negotiated design; Distributed creation model; Collective authorship	Student/teacher Co-creation; Negotiated design; Distributed creation Model; Collective Authorship
CCVE affordances Distribution	Full permissions; Avatar sharing; Derivative works	Full permissions; Themed avatar Sharing; Public installations	Full permissions; Themed avatar sharing; Public installations	Public installations; Avatar sharing	Institutional Representation; Public installations; Avatar sharing
Documentation methods	Virtual photography; machinima; physical exhibitions	Virtual photography; Live storytelling Events	Virtual photography; Installation series Documentation	Project Documentation; Student reflections; Exhibition	Technical Documentation; Institutional Analysis

informed by artistic insights. This progression demonstrates how knowledge developed through artistic practice becomes systematized and transferable in educational contexts.

8.6.2 *Comparative Analysis of CCVE Affordances across Projects*

Creation Affordances. Creation affordances were utilized differently across projects. In artistic projects, creation focused primarily on avatar design (Meta_Body, Kromosomer) and environmental installations (Berg Trilogy) as expressive media. Educational implementations expanded these approaches into structured learning experiences, with Virtual Art Lab emphasizing student creation capabilities and IPVerso developing specialized creation spaces supporting different educational functions.

The progression from artistic to educational implementations shows an increasing emphasis on scaffolding creation processes. While artistic projects provided finished creations or open platforms, educational implementations developed structured approaches to teaching creation skills, demonstrating how a/r/tography transforms artistic knowledge into pedagogical frameworks.

Collaboration Affordances. Collaboration models varied significantly across projects. Meta_Body pioneered distributed creation where participants functioned as "produsers," while Kromosomer implemented cross-cultural collaboration between artists and participants. The Berg Trilogy primarily utilized artistic partnership within a conceptual framework. Educational implementations transformed these approaches into structured collaborative learning: Virtual Art Lab adopted negotiated co-creation between students and between students and the teacher, while IPVerso implemented multi-stakeholder involvement across institutional contexts, while also promoting negotiated co-creation between students and between students and teachers.

This evolution demonstrates how collaborative approaches become increasingly systematized as they move from artistic exploration to educational implementation, with informal collaborative structures becoming formalized into pedagogical methodologies.

Distribution Affordances. Distribution approaches show consistency across projects, with all utilizing some form of open sharing. Artistic projects typically employed full permissions distribution allowing derivative works, while educational implementations emphasized public exhibition and documentation. IPVerso represents a distinctive approach by focusing on institutional representation, using distribution capabilities to extend the institution's presence into virtual space.

The consistency in distribution approaches across projects suggests that open sharing is fundamental to a/r/tographic practice in virtual environments, regardless of context. This openness facilitates the boundary-crossing essential to a/r/tography's integration of artist, researcher, and teacher roles.

8.6.3 Context-Specific Manifestations of A/r/Tographic Roles

The integration of artist, researcher, and teacher roles—central to a/r/tography—manifests differently across projects and contexts. In artistic projects, the artist's role typically dominates, with research and teaching dimensions emerging through the work's conceptualization and dissemination. Meta_Body exemplified this through its investigation of virtual corporeality (research) and open distribution model (teaching), while maintaining avatar creation (artistic practice) as its central focus.

Educational implementations demonstrate a more balanced integration of roles, with the teacher dimension gaining prominence but remaining interwoven with artistic and research aspects. Virtual Art Lab maintained strong artistic elements through its creative project focus while formalizing teaching methods, while IPVerso elevated institutional considerations while preserving artistic and research dimensions through its rhizomatic conceptual framework.

This analysis suggests that while context influences which a/r/tographic role receives primary emphasis, all three dimensions remain present across implementations. The fluidity between roles represents a defining characteristic of a/r/tography in virtual environments, enabling knowledge to flow between artistic practice, research inquiry, and pedagogical application.

Emergent Patterns and Distinctive Features. Across the diverse implementations, several patterns emerge that highlight shared concerns and approaches. Embodiment remains a central theme, even within the digital realm of virtual environments. Each project engages deeply with embodied knowledge through avatar-mediated experiences, actively challenging the common assumption that digital interaction is inherently disembodied. Furthermore, open sharing models are a recurring feature in both artistic and educational contexts, pointing to an intrinsic resistance within a/r/tographic practices to closed or proprietary systems of knowledge. These implementations tend to foster collaborative, accessible modes of engagement. At the same time, the boundaries between physical and virtual spaces are persistently negotiated. This occurs through exhibitions, documentation, and the formation of institutional relationships that intentionally bridge virtual practices with tangible, real-world contexts.

Theoretical Implications. This comparative analysis yields several theoretical implications for understanding a/r/tography in Metaverse contexts.

The consistent emphasis on embodiment across implementations suggests that virtual environments do not transcend corporeality but rather transform it. The avatar functions not as an escape from embodied experience but as a site where embodiment is reconfigured and explored. This finding aligns with Hayles' (Brooke et al., 2025) concept of "embodied virtuality" while extending it into educational contexts.

The evolution from artistic to educational implementations demonstrates how a/r/tography facilitates knowledge transfer between practice domains. Knowledge generated through artistic exploration becomes systematized through research reflection, which in turn informs pedagogical approaches. This recursive relationship exemplifies what Irwin (Castronova, 2005) describes as "becoming pedagogical" through identity-making processes.

The analysis reveals how CCVEs' affordances align with and extend a/r/tographic renderings. The creation capacities of virtual environments enable contiguity between different art forms; collaboration affordances facilitate living inquiry through relational engagement; and distribution capabilities create openings where new understandings emerge through shared experience. This alignment suggests that CCVEs represent particularly suitable environments for a/r/tographic practice, offering technological affordances that directly support its methodological requirements.

8.7 Conclusions

This paper has examined the a/r/tography application within Metaverse environments, focusing on CCVEs and their capacity to support innovative art education practices. Through analysis of artistic projects and educational implementations, we have demonstrated how CCVEs' affordances enable distinctive forms of artistic inquiry, research, and teaching extending beyond physical environment possibilities.

The findings reveal several significant insights:

First, CCVEs provide unique opportunities for embodied knowledge development through avatar-mediated interaction. Despite their digital nature, these environments foster corporeal understanding that remains relevant even in seemingly disembodied contexts. The avatar becomes a site for exploring identity, alterity, and presence—central concerns in a/r/tographic inquiry. This embodied knowing manifests in students' increasingly sophisticated manipulation of virtual materials and spaces.

Second, CCVEs' collaborative affordances support multiple shared creative processes, aligning with a/r/tography's relational aesthetics emphasis. The projects demonstrated three distinct collaborative modalities: collective creation (horizontal co-creation with group authorship), distributed creation (asynchronous contributions to an evolving creative ecosystem), and collaborative creation (maintaining individual authorial marks while engaging in creative dialogue).

Third, CCVE's content creation capabilities enable a recursive relationship between artistic practice and pedagogical innovation. Knowledge developed through artistic exploration directly informs teaching approaches, while student engagement generates new insights influencing subsequent artistic practice. This reciprocal flow exemplifies a/r/tographic methodology's essence, where role boundaries become permeable and knowledge flows multidirectionally.

Fourth, institutional level implementation, as demonstrated by IPVerso, shows how virtual spaces can support various a/r/tographic approaches while addressing contemporary concerns about digital transition and community resilience (Otrel-Cass et al., 2025). The rhizomatic conceptual framework particularly aligns with a/

r/tography's emphasis on multiplicity, interconnection, and non-hierarchical knowledge structures.

However, the research identified significant challenges: technical limitations created participation barriers, and there was difficulty engaging educators beyond art and computer science disciplines.

Looking forward, this research points to several promising directions:

- **Cross-disciplinary applications**: Future research could investigate how a/r/tographic approaches in virtual environments might benefit other disciplines.
- **Platform diversification**: Exploring alternative platforms offering robust multi-user communication capabilities could address technical limitations.
- **Integration of artificial intelligence research with Metaverse environments**: Future research could explore AI and virtual worlds intersection for art education, investigating how intelligent agents might facilitate creative collaboration, provide personalized feedback, generate dynamic content, or enable new CCVE interaction forms. This integration could address identified limitations while opening new possibilities for artistic inquiry and pedagogical innovation.

All things considered, Creative Collaborative Virtual Environments provide fertile ground for a/r/tographic practice in educational settings. Artistic creation, research inquiry, and pedagogical innovation integration within these spaces offer significant potential for enhancing art education while developing essential digital competencies. As virtual environments evolve and intersect with emerging technologies like artificial intelligence, the established methodological framework can guide future implementations, leveraging Metaverse affordances for transformative educational experiences.

Acknowledgments This work is funded by National Funds through the FCT- Foundation for Science and Technology, I.P., within the scope of the project Refa UIDB/05507/2020 and DOI identifier https://doi.org/10.54499/UIDB/05507/2020. Furthermore, we would like to thank the Centre for Studies in Education and Innovation (Ci&DEI) and the Polytechnic of Viseu for their support.

References

Angelini, M. L. (2021). *Learning through simulations: Ideas for educational practitioners*. Springer.

Boellstorff, T. (2010). *Coming of age in second life, an anthropologist explores the virtually human*. Princeton University Press.

Boellstorff, T. (2015). *Coming of age in second life: An anthropologist explores the virtually human*. Princeton University Press.

Brame, C. J. (2016). Active learning. Vanderbilt University Center for Teaching. https://cft.vanderbilt.edu/guides-sub-pages/active-learning.

Brooke, S., MacDonald, A., & Hunter, M. A. (2025). Becoming ecological: The contribution of collaborative a/r/tography to generalist primary teachers' agency in arts education. *Qualitative Inquiry, 31*(2), 201–215.

Bruns, A. (2013). From prosumption to produsage. In R. Towse & C. Handke (Eds.), *Handbook on the digital creative economy* (pp. 67–78). Edward Elgar Publishing.

Castronova, E. (2005). *Synthetic worlds: The business and culture of online games* (p. 22). University of Chicago Press.

Churchill, E. F., Snowdon, D. N., & Munro, A. J. (2001). Collaborative virtual environments: Digital places and spaces for interaction for CSCW: An introduction. In E. F. Churchill, D. N. Snowdon, & A. J. Munro (Eds.), *Collaborative virtual environments: Digital places and spaces for interaction* (pp. 3–20). Springer.

Coleman, K. (2023). Through the looking glass: Reflecting on an embodied understanding of creativity and creative praxis as an a/r/tographer. In R. L. Irwin et al. (Eds.), *A/r/tography: Essential readings and conversations* (pp. 163–176). Intellect Books.

Dahls Veen, H., & Sousa, C. C. (2013). Kromos Omer—An experience in shared creative work and expression. *Journal of Virtual Worlds Research (JVWR), 6*(2), 1–21.

Deleuze, G., & Guattari, F. (1987). *A thousand plateaus: Capitalism and schizophrenia.* University of Minnesota Press.

Dias, B. (2023). A/r/tografia como metodologia de pedagogia em artes: uma introdução. In B. Dias & R. L. Irwin (Eds.), *Pesquisa educacional baseada em arte: A/r/tografia.* Editora da Universidade Federal de.

Ellsworth, E. A. (2005). *Places of learning.* Routledge.

Eustáquio, L., & Sousa, C. C. (2018). Creative collaborative virtual environments. In D. M. Khosrow-Pour (Ed.), *Encyclopedia of information science and technology* (4th ed., pp. 4146–4156). IGI Global.

Hayles, K. (1999). *How we became Posthuman: Virtual bodies in cybernetics, literature, and informatics.* The University of Chicago Press.

Sousa, C.C., Rodrigues, P.A., et al. (Eds.). (2023). *IPVerso, education and co-creation.* Polytechnic Institute of Viseu.

Irwin, R. L. (2013). Becoming a/r/tography. *Studies in Art Education, 54*(3), 198–215. https://doi.org/10.1080/00393541.2013.11518894

Irwin, R. L. (2024). Rendering our relations. In R. L. Irwin, A. Lasczik, A. Sinner, et al. (Eds.), *A/r/tography: Readings and conversations.* Intellect.

Irwin, R. L., Lasczik, A., Sinner, A., et al. (2024). An introduction. In R. L. Irwin, A. Lasczik, A. Sinner, et al. (Eds.), *A/r/tography: Readings and conversations.* Intellect.

Lee, N. Y. S., Mosavarzadeh, M., Ursino, J. M., & Irwin, R. L. (Eds.). (2024). *Material and digital a/r/tographic explorations: Walking matters.* Springer.

Otrel-Cass, K., Beskorsa, O., Mendel, I., et al. (2025). Partnerships in the metaverse. *European Educational Research Journal.* doi:https://doi.org/10.1177/14749041251329140.

Sousa, C. C. (2015). Meta_Body: Virtual corporeality as a shared creative process. In D. Doyle (Ed.), *New opportunities for artistic practice in virtual worlds* (pp. 187–214). IGI Global.

Sousa, C. C. (2022). O Tríptico de Berg, memória e resistência numa experiência artística virtual. In A. G. Macedo et al. (Eds.), *Mulheres, Artes e Ditadura. Diálogos interartísticos e narrativas da memória* (pp. 125–153). Húmus.

Sousa, C. C., & Eustáquio, L. (2015). Art practice in collaborative virtual environments. In H. Barranha & S. S. Martins (Eds.), *Uncertain Spaces: Virtual Configurations in Contemporary Art and Museums*(pp. 211–240). Instituto de História da Arte, Faculdade de Ciências Sociais e Humanas—Universidade Nova de Lisboa; Associação do Instituto Superior Técnico para a Investigação e Desenvolvimento—Universidade de Lisboa. Gulbenkian Next Future Programme—Calouste Gulbenkian Foundation.

Sousa, C., Figueiredo, S., & Souto-e-Melo, A. (2022). The virtual art lab: Art teaching in the metaverse. In A. S. Zimmerman (Ed.), *Handbook of research on advancing teaching and teacher education in the context of a virtual age* (pp. 78–103). IGI Global.

Sousa, C. C., Rodrigues, P., Rito, P. N., & Figueiredo, S. (2023). Educação e Cocriação no Metaverso numa abordagem mista. *APEduC Revista/APEduC Journal, 4*(2), 123–145.

Springgay, S. (2005). An intimate distance: Youth interrogations of Intercorporeal cartography as visual narrative text. *Journal of the Canadian Association for Curriculum Studies, 3*(1), 107–122.

Springgay, S., Irwin, R. L., & Kind, S. W. (2005). A/r/tography as living inquiry through art and text. *Qualitative Inquiry, 11*(6), 897–912. https://doi.org/10.1177/1077800405280696

Sullivan, G. (2010). *Art practice as research: Inquiry in visual arts*. Sage.

Šuvaković, M. (2008). *Epistemology of art, critical design for procedures and platforms of contemporary art education*. TkH—Centre for performing arts theory and practice.

Urbano, M. J., & Branco, M. L. (2009). A importância da aprendizagem baseada na resolução de problemas em EVT. *Revista Portuguesa de Pedagogia, 43*(2), 261–273.

Veerapen, M. (2011). Encountering oneself and the other: A case study of identity formation in second life. In A. Peachey & M. A. Childs (Eds.), *Reinventing ourselves: Contemporary concepts of identity in virtual worlds* (pp. 81–100). Springer. https://doi.org/10.1007/978-0-85729-361-9_5

Chapter 9
The Use of Artificial Intelligence in the Creation of Multilingual Educational Videos: The Case of the Heygen Platform

Jamal Eddine Khouna, Adil Elmadhi, Meriem Khadhar, and Makram Mestiri

Abstract This paper examines how recent advances in generative AI particularly synthetic video generation, automated translation, and voice synthesis enable scalable production of multilingual educational videos. Through a mixed-method case study of Heygen's deployment in Moroccan universities during the COVID-19 lockdowns, it analyzes production efficiencies, linguistic and cultural adaptation, learner engagement, and infrastructural constraints. The findings highlight dramatic reductions in turnaround time, enhanced accessibility for Arabic, French, and Amazigh speaking students, and recommendations for integrating AI workflows with human review to ensure pedagogical rigor.

Keywords Artificial Intelligence · Multilingual educational videos · Heygen platform · COVID-19 remote teaching · Moroccan higher education · Natural language · Processing · Speech synthesis · Avatar animation · Low bandwidth video delivery · Learning engagement

---

J. E. Khouna · A. Elmadhi
Université Ibn Zohr Agadir, Agadir, Morocco
e-mail: jamaleddine.khouna@edu.uiz.ac.ma

A. Elmadhi
e-mail: a.elmadhi@uiz.ac.ma

M. Khadhar · M. Mestiri (✉)
Polytechnic University of Hauts-de-France, Valenciennes, France
e-mail: Makram.Mestiri@uphf.fr

M. Khadhar
e-mail: Meriem.Khadhar@uphf.fr

M. Abed et al. (eds.), *Metaverse and Artificial Intelligence in Education for a Sustainable Society*, Future Education and Learning Spaces,
https://doi.org/10.1007/978-981-95-8852-7_9

9.1 Introduction

The COVID-19 pandemic abruptly shifted higher education worldwide to remote formats, affecting 1.6 billion learners and challenging institutions to deliver quality instruction under lockdowns. In Morocco, linguistic diversity spans Arabic, French, and multiple Amazigh dialects, while 78% of households lack stable broadband (Hu et al., 2023). Traditional video-production workflows requiring separate recordings, translation, and editing proved too slow and intensive resources to meet urgent needs for multilingual lecture content. Generative AI platforms such as Heygen integrate natural language processing (NLP), neural machine translation (NMT), textspeak (TTS), and avatar animation to automate end-to-end video adaptation (Fig. 1).

By translating a single source video into multiple target languages with synchronized lip movements and facial expressions, these systems reduce production time by up to 85% and file sizes to 20 MB per 5-minute segment, optimized for low bandwidth delivery (Liu et al., 2024). This study investigates: (1) What AI technologies underpin Heygen's workflows? (2) How did Moroccan universities leverage Heygen during COVID-19 to produce Arabic, French, and Tamazight videos? (3) What impacts did this AI-driven approach have on production efficiency, linguistic accuracy, and learner engagement? We employ a mixed methods design platform feature analysis, a multisite case study (Ibn Zohr, Hassan II, Cadi Ayyad Universities), and quantitative/qualitative evaluation to draw evidence-based conclusions and propose guidelines for hybrid AI–human video creation workflows.

Fig. 1 HeyGen landing-page banner highlighting its "AI Video Generator" capabilities and on-screen language selector

9.2 Literature Review

Artificial-intelligence systems are beginning to shoulder much of the heavy lifting involved in producing instructional video. Early studies by Hu et al. show that diffusion-based generators such as DALL·E 2 can automatically assemble a full lecture slide, illustrative imagery, and even a presenter figure into a coherent video sequence. In small pilot deployments, these synthetic lectures earned a striking 92 percent satisfaction rating from learners, suggesting that audiences will accept, and even enjoy, material that has never passed through a traditional film studio (Hu et al., 2023). Learner outcomes have proved equally encouraging. In a mixed-methods experiment with 500 adult students, Wei et al. compared two groups: one watched fully AI-generated lectures, the other viewed the same lessons recorded by human instructors. Post-test scores on both recall and recognition tasks were statistically indistinguishable between the two conditions, indicating that the synthetic medium did not erode educational effectiveness (Sharma et al., 2023). Yet language remains a stubborn bottleneck. When students can engage with lessons in their native tongue, comprehension jumps by roughly 27 percent benefit difficult to ignore (Hu et al., 2023). Conventional workflows achieve this by having instructors re-record every segment and translators rewrite every slide, a practice that can add 30–40 hours for each ten-minute clip and inflate production costs. Pairing neural machine translation engines with text-to-speech voices shrinks the turnaround to less than four hours, but automated pipelines often stumble over field-specific jargon and subtle cultural references (Liu et al., 2024; Zhang et al., 2021). Visual credibility is another piece of the puzzle. Modern computer-vision models can drive a talking-head avatar whose mouth movements align with the sound track at about 95 percent accuracy in English, and roughly 92 percent in tonal languages such as Mandarin (Chen et al., 2024). High-quality lip-sync deepens viewers' sense of immersion, but many lesser-studied languages still lack the viseme-phoneme dictionaries that make such precision possible; tongues with particularly intricate consonant inventories, like Tamazight, are especially under-resourced.

The urgency of these technical questions became clear during Morocco's pandemic lockdowns. UNESCO data reveal that 68 percent of Moroccan university lecturers had never taught online before COVID-19 hit, forcing a rapid pivot to low-tech video tools (Hu et al., 2023). The government's PACT ESERI strategy, launched in 2021, earmarked funds for digital-pedagogy training and better studio facilities, but standards for video quality lagged behind schedule. In the interim, many faculties adopted Heygen's cloud work-flow, which allowed them to crank out more than 1200 AI-generated lectures between March and December 2020, a stopgap solution, but proof that synthetic video can fill critical educational gaps when traditional production grinds to a halt.

9.3 Methodology

Our first step was to map the contours of the Heygen environment itself. We recorded every visible element of the interface, from the storyboard timeline to the avatar-selection carousel, and created an inventory of the six languages the platform currently supports: Arabic, French, Spanish, Chinese, German, and, crucially for this study, Tamazight. For each language we captured the neural-machine-translation hyperparameters in use, the catalogue of text-to-speech voice models on offer, the degree of avatar customization permitted (clothing, gaze, gesturing speed) and the menu of output formats that can be rendered. Behind the scenes, API logs supplied a second layer of evidence, allowing us to time precisely how long the servers spent translating a script and how many seconds were consumed in the final video-rendering pass. With the feature map in hand, we moved to a field deployment. Three public universities in Morocco were chosen to give a mix of urban and regional campuses each committed to produce four hundred short lectures, between five and ten minutes apiece. Faculty members drafted their scripts in English, uploaded the text to Heygen 's dashboard, picked one or more target languages and then inspected the automatically generated translations and avatar animations, accepting or revising them as needed (Fig. 2).

Every mouse-click and server call was tracked, so we could later reconstruct how long instructors spent on scripting, on translation review, and on the polishing of lip-sync or gestures. To judge the system's output, we designed a multi-layer evaluation. At the technical tier we measured viseme-to-phoneme alignment frame by frame, logged full rendering times and noted the final file sizes. The linguistic tier relied on five native speakers per language who rated adequacy and fluency on a five-point Likert scale. Pedagogical quality was probed through student questionnaires: two hundred and fifty undergraduates watched selected clips and scored clarity, engagement and their own perceived learning, again on a one-to-five scale. Finally,

Fig. 2 Screenshot of HeyGen's editing dashboard, including the avatar library, script pane, and multi-track timeline used for the study's feature audit

we conducted semi-structured interviews with twenty lecturers to surface usability pain-points, work-arounds, and feature wishes that numbers alone might miss.

Quantitative results translation latencies, alignment scores, and subjective ratings were summarized with descriptive statistics, and language-to-language differences were tested via one-way ANOVA. Transcribed interview responses entered a thematic-coding pipeline, letting recurrent ideas about workload, interface friction or cultural nuance emerge in parallel to the numerical findings.

9.4 Case Study: Heygen in Morocco during COVID-19

9.4.1 Deployment Context

Between March and December 2020, Moroccan universities shifted to fully remote teaching. Heygen's cloud infrastructure allowed professors to work asynchronously, uploading scripts and retrieving localized videos within hours, critical when 78% of students accessed content via mobile on limited data plans (Hu et al., 2023).

9.4.2 Workflow Metrics

- Source recording or avatar setup: 30 minutes.
- Automated translation per language: 5–8 minutes.
- TTS and avatar rendering: 20–30 minutes.
- Total per 5 min video per language: ~1 hour vs. 6 hours manual (87% time saving).

9.4.3 Linguistic Adaptation

Native speaker reviewers reported mean adequacy scores of 4.6/5 for French, 4.4/5 for Arabic, and 4.0/5 for Tamazight. Minor corrections were needed for specialized termi-nology in STEM subjects (e.g., "eigenvalue," "topology"). Cultural references (e.g., Moroccan historical sites) were auto translated neutrally, requiring manual reinsertion for context.

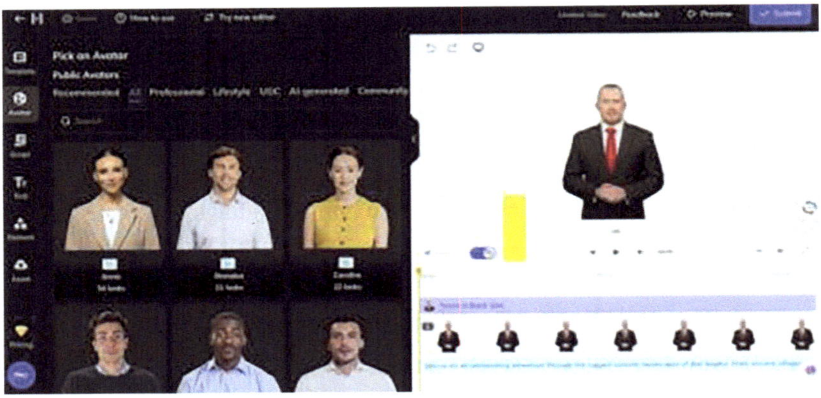

Fig. 3 Example output frame: a synchronized avatar lecture with language selection flags, illustrating multi-lingual delivery and culturally neutral backdrop

9.4.4 Avatar & Cultural Customization

Instructors selected avatars wearing regional attire (djellaba, hijab) to reflect student demographics. Lip-sync accuracy averaged 96% in Arabic and French, 93% in Tamazight, supporting emotional engagement (Fig. 3).

9.4.5 Student Engagement & Feedback

Surveys (n = 250) showed:

- Clarity: AI videos 4.3/5 vs. subtitled human videos 3.1/5 ($p < 0.01$).
- Engagement: +28% self-reported vs. pre-COVID video lectures.
- Completion rates: 72% for AI-generated modules vs. 55% for synchronous.
- Zoom lectures.

9.5 Results and Discussion

Heygen's cloud-based pipeline delivered a dramatic boost in productivity. Across the three test campuses the full journey from raw script to finished lesson shrank by roughly 85 percent, empowering instructors to iterate multiple language versions in the time it once took to complete a single cut. Backend logs showed that rendering latencies stayed remarkably stable across sessions, a sign that the platform's large-scale parallelization shields end-users from local hardware limits and network fluctuations. The linguistic picture was equally encouraging. Native-speaker panels judged the French track most successful, awarding an average adequacy score of 4.6 out of 5, with Arabic close be-hind at 4.4. Tamazight earned a solid 4.0, though reviewers did flag occasional noun–gender mismatches that slipped through the neural machine-translation layer. Fluency ratings mirrored the adequacy pattern and suggested that automated speech synthesis now rivals human narration for most mainstream use-cases. Technical metrics con-firmed that the synthetic avatars held up under scrutiny. Frame-by-frame analysis put lip-sync accuracy at 97 percent for French, 95 percent for Arabic, and 93 percent for Tamazight (95 percent confidence interval $\pm$ 2 percent). End-to-end rendering averaged twenty-four minutes per language, with a modest three-minute standard deviation, while the final five-minute clips weighed in at roughly twenty megabytes in 360-pixel resolution bitrate friendly to constrained bandwidth environments. Educational impact, measured through student surveys, revealed a statistically significant language effect on clarity (ANOVA $F(2, 747) = 9.87$, $p < 0.001$). Learners rated the AI-produced videos as easier to follow than earlier webcam recordings, frequently praising the availability of mother-tongue narration and the visual consistency of the avatar presenter. Qualitative comments underscored how these factors fostered a sense of inclusion and cognitive comfort. Taken together, the findings argue that AI-driven video production can help close persistent digital-divide gaps. Lower file sizes minimize data charges, while automated multilingual rendering answers UNESCO's call for equitable remote-learning resources \ (Hu et al., 2023). At the same time, experience on the ground cautions against a fully hands-off approach: domain-specific terminology and cultural cues still demand a human-in-the-loop pass. A pragmatic workflow therefore assigns the heavy lifting more than eighty percent of the effort to AI, reserving the final twenty percent for expert review. Early success with Heygen has already fed into policy. Morocco's 2023 Digital Education Strategy now mandates the inclusion of AI tools in all MOOC development and sets an ambitious goal of training eight thousand faculty members in syn-thetic-video workflows by 2025. Such institutional backing illustrates the technology's scalability as well as its alignment with national priorities. Nonetheless, limitations remain. Under-resourced languages, and especially the diverse dialects of Tamazight, lack the large corpora needed to refine both translation and lip-sync models. Future research should extend beyond engagement metrics to track long-term learning gains and explore how adaptive personalization powered by the same AI backbone might tailor pacing, examples and assessments to individual students.

9.6 Results and Discussion

This study demonstrates that a tightly integrated stack of generative-AI technologies neural machine translation, high-fidelity text-to-speech, and viseme-aware avatar animation can convert a single source script into high-quality, bandwidth-light teaching videos across several languages within an hour. In a real-world deployment spanning three Moroccan universities and more than 1200 lecture segments, the HeyGen plat-form cut production time by roughly 85%, held lip-sync errors below 7% even in a low-resource language (Tamazight), and yielded adequacy–fluency scores that rivalled human-recorded controls. Student surveys confirmed not only higher perceived clarity and engagement but also markedly better completion rates, suggesting that the combi-nation of mother-tongue narration and consistent visual design has genuine pedagogical value in constrained connectivity settings.

The findings carry three scientific implications. First, they empirically validate the premise that synthetic video can preserve learning effectiveness even when generated at scales so long as linguistic fidelity and cultural signaling are respected. Second, they endorse a hybrid production model in which automation performs the bulk of translation and rendering while domain experts handle high-stakes semantic edits; this division of labor maximizes speed without sacrificing rigor. Third, the Moroccan case illustrates how institutional and policy support can move AI from pilot novelty to operational backbone, especially in regions where broadband and studio resources are scarce. Nevertheless, limitations remain. Tamazight dialects exposed the fragility of current NMT and viseme sets for under-resourced phonologies, and our evaluation focused on short-term engagement rather than long-term knowledge retention. Future work should enlarge training corpora for minority languages, develop adaptive avatars that can convey discipline-specific gestures, and run longitudinal trials that track learning outcomes beyond a single course module. In sum, AI-driven video generation is no longer a speculative convenience; it is a practical, scalable instrument for equitable higher-education delivery. When embedded in a carefully designed human-in-the-loop workflow and backed by capacity-building initiatives, platforms like HeyGen can help close both the linguistic and infrastructural divides that have long impeded inclusive digital learning.

References

Chen W, Huang Z, Liu Y, et al. (2024). Exploring AIGC Video Quality: A Focus on Visual Har-mony, VideoText Consistency and Domain Distribution Gap. arXiv preprint arXiv:2404.13573.https://arxiv.org/html/2404.13573

Hu P, Zhang J, Wang K, et al. (2023). Generative AI for learning: Investigating the potential of synthetic learning videos. arXiv preprint arXiv:2304.03784. https://arxiv.org/pdf/2304.03784.pdf

Liu X, Zhang Y, Sun J, et al. (2024). Adult learners recall and recognition performance and affective feedback when learning from an AI generated synthetic video. arXiv preprint arXiv:2412.10384. https://arxiv.org/abs/2412.10384

Sharma R, Kaur P, Singh H, et al. (2023). AI based approach to Trailer Generation for Online Educational Courses. arXiv preprint arXiv:2301.03957. https://arxiv.org/pdf/2301.03957.pdf

Zhang T, Li S, Wang L. (2021). AI Empowered Persuasive Video Generation: A Survey. arXiv pre-print arXiv:2112.09401v1. https://arxiv.org/abs/2112.09401

Chapter 10
Introducing SMALL STEPS: A Virtual Reality Platform for First Aid Training

Michel El Haddad, Jana El Helou, Vanessa Al Najjar, Charles Yaacoub, and Sandy Rihana

Abstract Up to 59% of injury-related deaths could be prevented with basic first aid (McNulty, 2016), yet many individuals lack the confidence or training to act. SMALL STEPS is a VR-based serious game designed to bridge this gap by providing immersive and engaging first aid training. Developed on the Unity Engine, the system uses gamification principles, such as progress tracking, quizzes, and real-time feedback, to simulate realistic emergency scenarios, including burns, gas leaks, and severe bleeding. This safe and scalable platform allows users to practice life-saving procedures in a controlled environment, enhancing knowledge retention and confidence. Initial user testing shows a high level of engagement in first aid training. With its modular design, SMALL STEPS is adaptable for various training contexts, demonstrating the transformative potential of VR in education and skill acquisition. This work underscores the value of gamified VR environments in making critical training accessible, effective, and impactful.

Keywords Virtual reality · Healthcare application · Interactive training system · Immersive learning · Serious games · Gamified learning

10.1 Introduction

First aid is a vital life-saving skill that can be decisive in emergency situations, often determining survival outcomes. Despite its importance, many individuals lack the necessary knowledge, confidence, or preparedness to intervene effectively in critical situations. This gap has profound implications, as research suggests that up to 59% of injury-related fatalities could be prevented through the timely application of basic

M. El Haddad (✉) · C. Yaacoub
ICL, Junia, Université Catholique de Lille, Lille, France
e-mail: michel.el-haddad@univ-catholille.fr

M. El Haddad · J. El Helou · V. Al Najjar · S. Rihana
Computer Engineering Department, Biomedical Engineering Department, Holy Spirit University of Kaslik (USEK), Jounieh, Lebanon

M. Abed et al. (eds.), *Metaverse and Artificial Intelligence in Education for a Sustainable Society*, Future Education and Learning Spaces,
https://doi.org/10.1007/978-981-95-8852-7_10

first aid measures (McNulty, 2016). However, conventional training methods face notable limitations, restricting both accessibility and the long-term retention of this essential knowledge.

Conventional first aid training centers rely on in-person instruction, which often demands long, structured sessions and access to costly equipment. These logistical and financial constraints can limit accessibility for many individuals who could otherwise benefit from such training. Moreover, audiovisual and digital-based learning might be more effective for teaching certain aspects of first aid (Lippmann et al., 2011). In emergency situations, remaining calm and instinctively applying learned skills are crucial, yet traditional training methods often fall short in fully developing these abilities.

In recent years, technology has emerged as a promising tool to address these challenges. Platforms such as mobile applications, augmented reality (AR), and e-learning systems have been leveraged to disseminate first aid knowledge, offering greater flexibility, accessibility, and self-paced learning opportunities. However, these innovations often fall short in replicating the immersive and interactive nature of real-life scenarios, which is vital for developing practical skills and psychological readiness. Among these technological solutions, virtual reality (VR) stands out as a uniquely powerful medium (Abich et al., 2021). VR provides users with immersive, interactive 3D environments that closely mimic real-world settings, enabling realistic and safe training experiences.

This paper introduces **SMALL STEPS**, a VR-based serious game designed to revolutionize first aid training. By leveraging the immersive capabilities of VR and integrating gamification principles, SMALL STEPS provides users with a dynamic and engaging platform for acquiring critical life-saving skills. The system offers realistic simulations of emergency scenarios, such as burns, gas leaks, and severe bleeding, allowing users to practice first aid procedures in a safe environment. Gamified elements, including progress tracking, quizzes, and real-time feedback, are incorporated to enhance user engagement, boost motivation, and improve knowledge retention.

A key strength of SMALL STEPS is its ability to overcome the limitations of traditional training methods, such as reliance on physical equipment and in-person instruction, making first aid training more accessible and cost-effective. Additionally, the VR environment provides a safe space for users to make mistakes and learn without real-world consequences, fostering confidence and competence. The system's modular design also supports scalability and customization, enabling the integration of new scenarios and adaptation to diverse training needs across industries.

User testing indicates the effectiveness of SMALL STEPS in enhancing participants' first aid knowledge and engagement. The application's interactive features and realistic scenarios engage users, effectively bridging the gap between theoretical knowledge and practical application. Moreover, its gamified approach encourages repetition, which is crucial for retaining critical skills.

This paper provides a comprehensive overview of the development and implementation of SMALL STEPS, with a focus on its user-centered design, technological framework, and educational impact. By situating this work within the broader context of VR-based training and serious games, the study underscores the potential of immersive technologies to transform education and skill acquisition. SMALL STEPS is more than a technological advancement; it is a pivotal initiative aimed at democratizing life-saving knowledge and enhancing individuals' ability to respond effectively in critical situations.

This study aims to highlight the transformative potential of gamified VR environments in addressing global challenges in training and education. By integrating immersive technology with the engagement of serious games, SMALL STEPS serves as a pioneering initiative to enhance the accessibility, effectiveness, and impact of first aid training. Beyond healthcare, this work highlights the broader applications of VR in education, workforce training, and emergency preparedness, demonstrating its potential as a versatile tool for skill development and knowledge dissemination.

10.2 Related Works

First aid training is an essential component of public health, enabling individuals to respond effectively during emergencies and potentially save lives. The importance of this field has led to the emergence of various innovative solutions, including e-learning platforms, mobile applications, augmented reality (AR), and virtual reality (VR) environments. Each approach has sought to address specific challenges associated with traditional training methods, such as accessibility, cost, and engagement. This section provides an overview of these technologies, highlighting their contributions, limitations, and relevance to the development of VR-based serious games like SMALL STEPS.

E-learning platforms were among the earliest technologies used to disseminate first aid knowledge. Systems like the International Federation of Red Cross and Red Crescent's training platform and Udemy's courses offer flexible, self-paced learning tailored to diverse audiences. These platforms provide a wealth of resources, including videos, interactive exercises, and progress tracking, enabling users to acquire essential skills at their convenience.

E-learning offers numerous advantages: it eliminates the logistical constraints of in-person training, reduces costs, and provides access to global resources. Furthermore, its asynchronous nature allows learners to integrate training into their busy schedules. However, while e-learning platforms effectively facilitate theoretical knowledge acquisition, they often lack the interactivity and immersion needed to simulate real-world emergency scenarios.

Mobile applications have emerged as another popular medium for first aid training, providing users with accessible tools for learning and quick reference. Numerous apps, such as those developed by the International Federation of Red Cross and Red Crescent and the American Red Cross, offer step-by-step guides, visual aids, and even emergency response prompts. These applications are available across various countries and languages, broadening their reach and utility. Despite their accessibility and practicality, mobile applications face limitations like e-learning platforms. They are effective as supplementary tools but do not fully address the need for hands-on practice.

Augmented reality has introduced a new dimension to first aid training by overlaying digital information onto the physical world. For instance, AR applications can provide visual instructions and voice assistance during emergencies, guiding users step-by-step through procedures such as CPR or wound treatment. AR's ability to integrate with wearable devices like smart glasses further enhances its utility, creating a seamless interaction between virtual guidance and real-world actions. Studies such as (Fromm et al., 2019) have demonstrated the potential of AR in improving first aid training. However, AR solutions often require specialized hardware and may lack the immersive qualities necessary for simulating high-stress scenarios and replicating the psychological intensity of an emergency, limiting their overall impact.

Virtual reality represents an advancement in first aid training, offering an immersive and interactive learning environment. Unlike e-learning, mobile apps, or AR, VR can replicate real-world scenarios with high fidelity, enabling users to practice life-saving skills in a safe, controlled setting. Numerous VR-based first aid training systems have been developed, each leveraging the unique advantages of this technology. For instance, the VReanimate project by students at the University of Würzburg developed a pictographic VR training system (Blome et al., 2017). It featured nonverbal instructions conveyed through holograms and scenarios designed to simulate high-pressure environments, such as military bunkers or dimly lit rooms. While this approach effectively enhanced participants' situational awareness and understanding of emergency procedures, some users found the lack of explanatory feedback (the "why" behind actions) to be a limitation.

Similarly, 4 Help VR (4 HELP VR, n.d.) integrated physical sensors with a VR system to provide a blended learning experience. Users interacted with a virtual coach, "Paramedicus," who guided them through scenarios like CPR, recovery positions, and injury treatments. Optional quizzes added an interactive dimension to the training, targeting a wide audience, including children. The addition of physical feedback mechanisms, such as sensors on manikins, further enriched the experience.

PixoVR (PIXOVR: QSR with a side of VR: The perfect recipe, n.d.), an industry leader in VR training, introduced real-time multiplayer collaborative training to enhance teamwork and communication skills. Their VR training catalog spans various domains, including first aid, fire safety, and hazard recognition. By allowing multiple users to engage in a single virtual environment, PixoVR fosters social interactions and collaborative problem-solving.

The insights gained from these related works have directly influenced the design and development of SMALL STEPS. By addressing the limitations of prior systems, SMALL STEPS aims to provide a comprehensive training experience that combines realism, interactivity, and accessibility. In addition, its gamified elements enhance engagement and retention. Furthermore, SMALL STEPS leverages VR's immersive capabilities to simulate high-stress situations, fostering psychological readiness and confidence in users. By incorporating real-time feedback, the system ensures that trainees understand the basics of first aid procedures.

Fig. 1 Game Design Overview

10.3 Simulation Structure and Implementation

The SMALL STEPS VR simulation is a serious game designed to teach first aid through an interactive, immersive, and gamified approach. It integrates interactive scenarios that replicate real-life emergencies, enabling users to develop their abilities in a controlled and engaging environment. The simulation consists of a series of sequential scenes, each tailored to teach specific first aid techniques. This section provides a comprehensive overview of the major components, design principles, and educational objectives of these scenes.

10.3.1 Scene Architecture and Flow

The simulation begins with an introductory welcome scene, followed by two distinct levels, each targeting a specific first aid scenario. The welcome scene targets burn treatment, the first level addresses how to deal with a gas leak and correctly putting a casualty in the recovery position (in French: Position Latérale de Sécurité, PLS), and the second level trains users how to handle car crashes and control bleeding. A summary of these levels is presented in Fig. 1.

Each level is a self-contained environment featuring tasks that simulate real-life emergencies while reinforcing previously learned skills and introducing progressively complex challenges. This structured progression ensures users master foundational skills before tackling advanced scenarios. In addition, level progression is gated, requiring users to complete one scenario before advancing to the next. The seamless transitions between levels maintain user engagement and create a cohesive learning experience.

10.3.2 The Welcome Scene: Foundation of Interaction

The welcome scene is designed to introduce users to the VR environment, controls, and core mechanics, as shown in Fig. 2. It serves as an interactive tutorial where

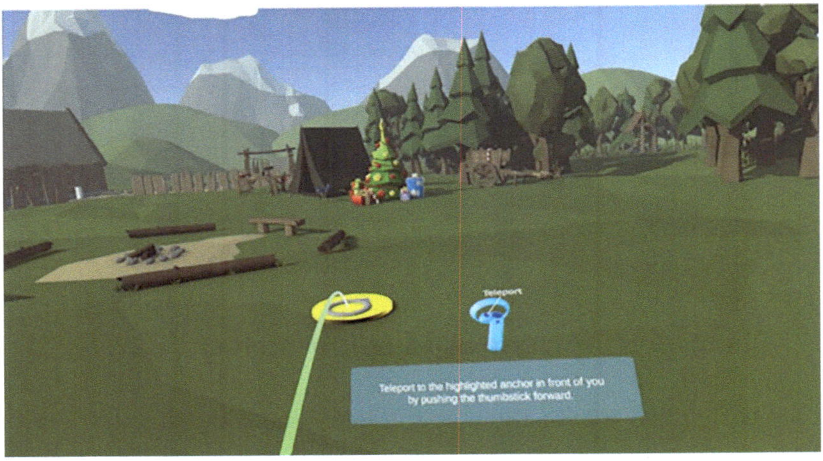

Fig. 2 Welcome scene—Introduction to user controls

players learn essential VR actions such as teleportation (i.e., navigating throughout the scene), grabbing, and interacting with objects.

This scene also features a low-stress scenario in which users treat a minor burn, introducing them to the training process and establishing the game's tone. Burns were specifically chosen as an introductory scenario because they are common injuries that require simple yet essential first aid actions (e.g., cooling the wound, applying sterile dressing). Gamified elements like real-time feedback and clear instructions help users become comfortable with the system before progressing to more complex tasks. This gradual exposure allows users to practice basic procedures before tackling more complex emergencies. By the time users progress to Level 1 (Gas Leak and PLS), they have already developed VR fluency and fundamental first aid familiarity, allowing them to focus on emergency response rather than mechanics.

The welcome scene serves as a central hub where users can return between levels. It offers a relaxed environment for practicing controls, reviewing emergency contact numbers, and exploring supplementary resources. This design fosters user confidence and ensures they are well prepared for the challenges ahead.

10.3.3 Level 1: Gas Leak and Recovery Position (PLS)

In Level 1, users encounter a simulated gas leak in an apartment, where a casualty lies unresponsive on the floor. The level highlights the importance of environmental safety and casualty assessment. Upon completing this level, users will be able to recognize the dangers of environmental hazards such as gas leaks and mitigate them, for example, by ventilating the area and ensuring their own safety. In addition, users learn how to assess a casualty's condition by evaluating responsiveness using the

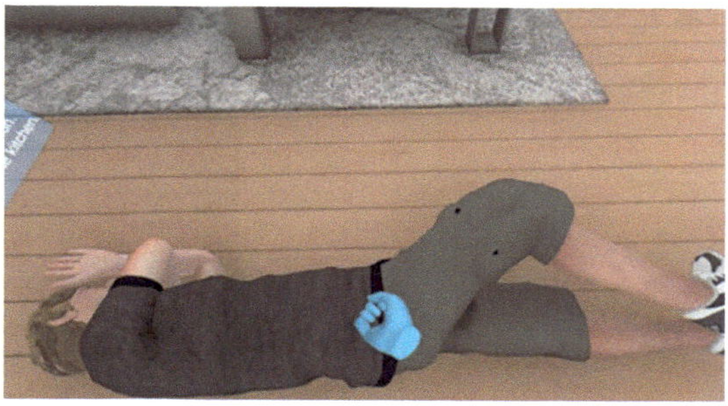

Fig. 3 Casualty placed in the recovery position (PLS)

Alert, Verbal, Pain, Unresponsive (AVPU) scale. The final learning objective of this module is to ensure the casualty's safety by applying the Airway, Breathing, Circulation (ABC) method and placing them in the PLS recovery position.

The level culminates with placing the unresponsive but breathing casualty into the recovery position, as shown in Fig. 3. This procedure helps maintain an open airway while awaiting professional medical assistance.

This module integrates gamified elements such as instant feedback on user actions and a quiz at the end of the level. The quiz follows the practical tasks, reinforcing the steps and reasoning behind the user's actions. Its questions are drawn from a randomized pool, ensuring a unique experience for each user or trial while promoting engagement and critical thinking.

10.3.4 Level 2: Car Crash and Bleeding Control

Level 2 immerses users in a roadside emergency scenario involving a car crash. They must navigate a highway environment, secure the scene, and assist a casualty with significant bleeding. This level consists of two main tasks. The first addresses scene safety requiring users to secure the crash area with cones, emphasizing the importance of ensuring their own safety before assisting others. Once the scene is secured, users proceed to the second task, which focuses on bleeding control. They must assist a casualty with a bleeding leg wound by first putting on gloves for hygiene, then applying direct pressure on the wound to minimize the bleeding, and finally creating pressure dressing using bandages, as shown in Fig. 4.

This level emphasizes critical decision-making under pressure, as users must act quickly to control the bleeding while ensuring their safety. Similar to Level 1, this scene includes a randomized quiz that evaluates users' understanding of the procedures and the underlying principles.

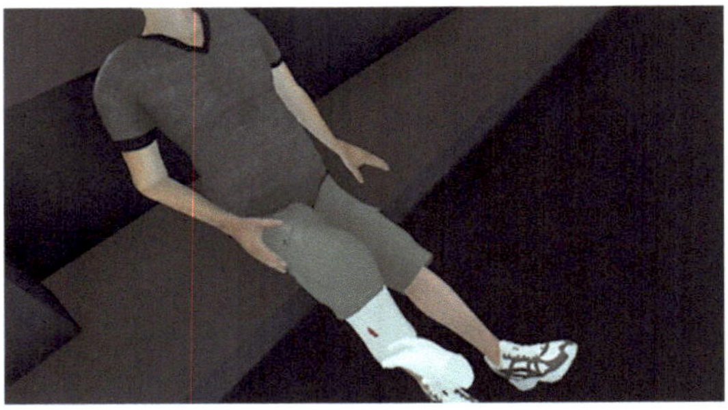

Fig. 4 Player applied pressure dressing to stop the casualty's leg from bleeding

10.4 Design Principles

This section details the main principles guiding the design of the learning environment. The first and, perhaps most important, is a focus on realism and immersion. Each scene simulates real-world conditions, leveraging VR's capabilities to deliver realistic visuals, sounds, and interactions. This immersive environment enhances users' situational awareness and presence in the virtual world. A second aspect of designing the learning environment is integrating gamification elements throughout the simulation to motivate users and sustain their interest. These gamification elements are based on the Octalysis framework (Chou, 2015) shown in Fig. 5. Implementing immediate feedback on actions, such as indicating correct or incorrect procedures, reinforces learning and helps users build confidence. In addition, another aspect of gamified learning is implemented through progressive complexity of the learning tasks. The environment is arranged in the form of a gated structure that ensures logical progression of skills. In other words, users must master basic tasks before advancing to more complex scenarios, which encourages cumulative learning. Moreover, the hands-on nature of the tasks ensures users actively engage with the content. Users reinforce their understanding and skills through hands-on practice of first aid procedures such as performing PLS or bleeding control. Technically, the scenes follow a modular structure which is flexible and allows for scalability and customization. In other words, new scenarios can be added, or existing ones adapted, to meet the needs of different audiences or training objectives.

10.4.1 Educational Objectives

The primary goal of the SMALL STEPS VR simulation is to equip users with practical first aid skills while enhancing their confidence and readiness to act during emergencies. For this purpose, users first learn the theoretical foundations of first aid procedures, such as the AVPU scale and the ABC method. Skill retention is an important aspect of first aid education, reinforced through repetitive practice in gamified scenarios and progressively challenging tasks. This approach helps users

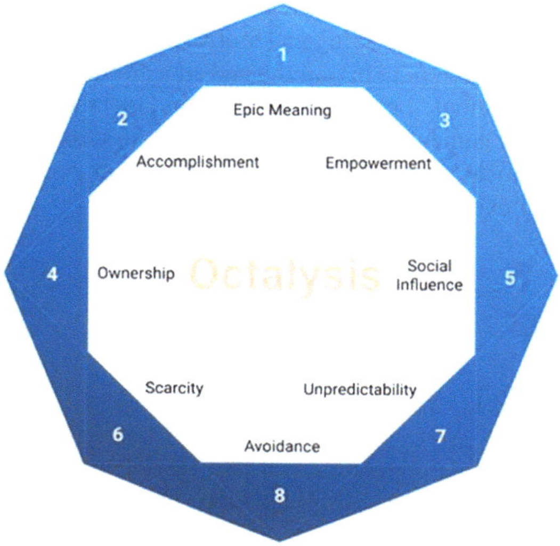

Fig. 5 The Octalysis Framework Graph (Chou, 2015)

memorize first aid procedures and transition from theoretical knowledge to practical application, effectively bridging the gap between understanding and action, which leads to more comprehensive learning. Finally, the safe and controlled environment allows users to make mistakes and learn from them without real-world consequences, fostering both competence and confidence.

10.5 User Testing

User testing was a crucial phase in the development of the SMALL STEPS VR simulation, aimed at evaluating the system's usability, educational impact, and overall user experience. This phase involved gathering feedback from participants with varying levels of familiarity with first aid and virtual reality (VR) technologies. Insights from the testing process informed iterative refinements to the system, ensuring that it effectively met its educational and engagement objectives.

10.5.1 Testing Objectives

The user testing phase aims at assessing the effectiveness of the developed VR environment based on a few factors. First, since the project is mainly a game, evaluating its usability is crucial. This includes measuring the intuitiveness of the VR interface and controls, particularly for users new to VR. Second, assessing user engagement is necessary since the integration of gamification elements into the learning environment aims at engaging and motivating users. Third, to determine the effectiveness of this environment in training and education, its educational impact must be evaluated. Users should be able to learn first aid techniques while playing the game. Finally, as in any game design and development process, user testing helps identify and resolve technical issues, such as bugs, glitches, or performance problems, that could hinder user experience.

10.5.2 Testing Methodology

10.5.2.1 Testing Population

Our testing population was modest due to limited resources and time constraints. It consisted of 39 college students, instructors, and researchers, ranging in age from 18 to 50. On average, participants had little to no prior experience with VR and an intermediate to minimal background in first aid.

10.5.2.2 Testing Environment

Each session begins with a brief introduction to the hardware, software, and objectives of the game, followed by hands-on interaction with the simulation. Users wore an Acer Windows Mixed Reality VR headset connected to a Predator laptop, where the experiment was run using the Unity Engine 2022.3. This was followed by hands-on interaction with the simulation. Game controls were not explained beforehand; users discovered them at the beginning of the welcome scene, while minimal to no assistance was given to users while in the VR space.

10.5.2.3 Data Collection

Several techniques were used to collect both quantitative and qualitative data. First, the authors observed participants as they navigated the VR environment and how they interacted with it, noting any difficulties or confusion they encountered. This technique, along with post-test surveys and interviews, provided valuable insights into user experience (UX) and supported an iterative development approach to enhance it. Participants then completed post-test surveys to rate various aspects of the simulation, such as ease of use, engagement, and educational value. Follow-up interviews were then conducted to gain a deeper understanding of participants' experiences and gather suggestions for improvement. While surveys consisted of structured questions where users rated different aspects of the game, interviews featured open-ended questions to encourage detailed feedback. Finally, various in-game analytics recorded key performance metrics, including task completion times, quiz scores, and error rates.

10.5.3 Key Findings

Key results can be broken down into four different aspects. First, concerning usability, most users found the VR controls intuitive after completing the welcome scene tutorial. Clear instructions and a practice environment contributed to a smooth onboarding experience. However, a minority of participants, particularly those unfamiliar with VR, initially struggled with object interaction mechanics, such as grabbing and teleportation. Adding visual cues and refining the tutorial have resolved these issues in subsequent iterations. The second aspect is educational impact. Participants expressed the effectiveness of this simulation as a first aid teaching method. Many highlighted the quizzes as particularly useful for reinforcing learning, though some suggested incorporating more explanatory feedback for incorrect answers. In addition, several participants recognized the broader potential of VR for studying courses, practicing labs, and developing practical skills. The third aspect is user engagement. Gamified elements, such as quizzes, progress tracking, and instant feedback, were well-received and contributed to sustained user interest. Participants retained a high level of engagement and interest in the game, as evidenced by their continued exploration of the welcome scene after completing the game and their repeated attempts to improve scores by replaying levels. Finally, minor technical challenges, such as occasional glitches in object interaction and performance slowdowns, were identified during testing. These issues were addressed through optimization and additional debugging.

The following graphs illustrate that participants averaged approximately two sessions each (Fig. 6), with an average total gameplay duration of about 16 minutes (Fig. 7) and an average completion rate of 81.8% (Fig. 8). These results indicate a high degree of user engagement and interest.

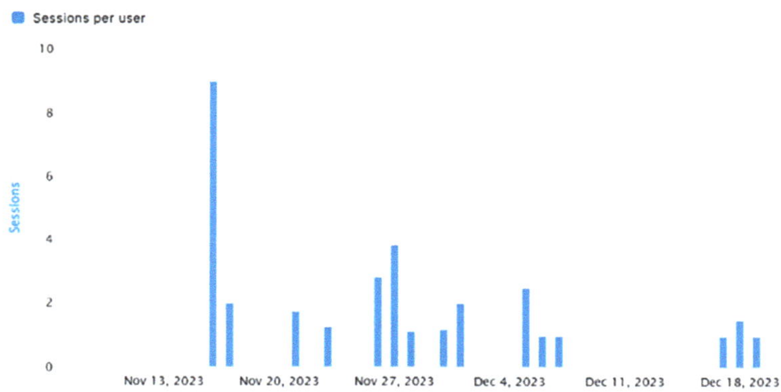

Fig. 6 Average number of sessions per user

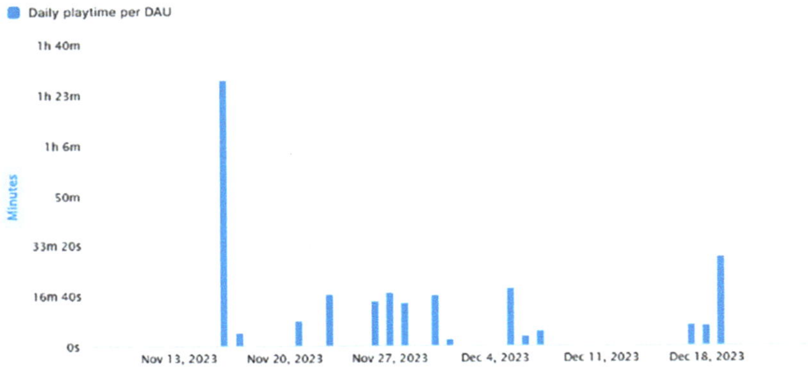

Fig. 7 Average playtime per user

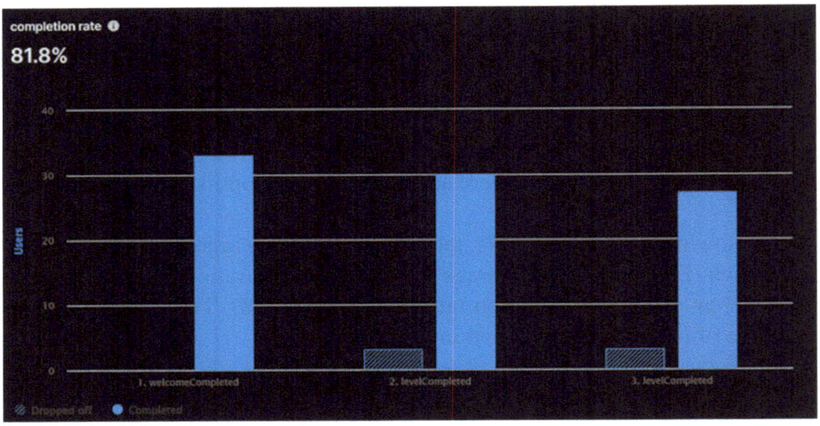

Fig. 8 Completion rate per level

10.5.3.1 Improvements Based on Feedback

User feedback led to several key improvements in the simulation, implemented through an iterative development process. Visual and audio cues were refined to enhance the learning experience, particularly for users new to VR. Performance optimizations reduced latency and ensured smoother interactions. Additionally, guidance within scenarios was expanded to balance challenge with clarity, particularly for more complex tasks.

10.6 Conclusion

Compared to traditional first aid courses, which often rely on static manikins and passive instruction, VR-based training offers a more dynamic and experiential approach. Research indicates that knowledge retention declines by 30–50% within six months in conventional training (Lippmann et al., 2011). In contrast, SMALL STEPS enables active skill rehearsal in high-stress, immersive environments, reinforcing procedural memory and user confidence through real-time decision-making, haptic feedback, and adaptive difficulty settings.

User testing revealed that 90% of participants felt more confident in their ability to provide first aid—an essential indicator of psychological readiness. Traditional methods often fall short in preparing individuals for the emotional and time-sensitive nature of real emergencies. By bridging this gap, SMALL STEPS enhances both cognitive learning and emotional preparedness, ensuring that users can retain, recall, and effectively apply life-saving procedures under pressure.

Beyond individual training, SMALL STEPS introduces a scalable and modular VR framework, allowing future expansion into multiplayer cooperative training, additional first aid scenarios (e.g., choking, drowning, electrocution), and AI-driven emergency adaptation. The integration of randomized challenges and multisensory feedback mechanisms ensures long-term engagement and continuous learning improvements.

As VR technology advances, applications like SMALL STEPS demonstrate the transformative potential of immersive learning in healthcare, emergency response, and professional first aid training. By leveraging adaptive scenario-based simulations and collaborative training environments, VR-based solutions can play a pivotal role in democratizing life-saving knowledge and increasing global preparedness for medical emergencies.

References

4 HELP VR., https://4helpvr.com/en/.

Abich, J., Parker, J., Murphy, J. S., & Eudy, M. (2021). A review of the evidence for training effectiveness with virtual reality technology. *Virtual Reality, 25*, 919–933. https://doi.org/10.1007/s10055-020-00498-8

Blome, T., Diefenbach, A., Rudolph, S., Bucher, K., Von Mammen, S.: VReanimate — Non-verbal guidance and learning in virtual reality. In: 2017 9th international conference on virtual worlds and games for serious applications (VS-Games). pp. 23–30. IEEE, (2017). doi:https://doi.org/10.1109/VS-GAMES.2017.8055807.

Chou, Y.-K. (2015). *Actionable Gamification beyond points, badges, and leaderboards*. CreateSpace Independent Publishing Platform.

Fromm, J., Mirbabaie, M., Stieglitz, S.: The Potential of Augmented Reality for Improving Occupational First Aid. Presented at the 14th International Conference on Wirtschaftsinformatik February 24 (2019).

Lippmann, J., Livingston, P., & Craike, M. J. (2011). Comparison of two modes of delivery of first aid training including basic life support. *Health Education Journal., 70*, 131–140. https://doi.org/10.1177/0017896910386208

McNulty, A.: Are prehospital deaths from trauma and accidental injury preventable? British red cross (2016).

PIXOVR: QSR with a side of VR: The perfect recipe., https://pixovr.com/qsr-with-a-side-of-vr/.

Chapter 11
Metacognition in Immersive Web Environments co-Created by Students

Bárbara Cleto

Abstract The aim of this study is to understand how the co-creation and personalisation of immersive web environments (IWE) by elementary school students can promote the development of metacognitive and self-regulation cognitive skills. Students in the seventh grade took part in the study. The intervention took place in three stages: ideation (conception of the IWE), construction (development of the IWE), and utilisation (the IWE was used as a classroom). Two instruments translated, adapted and validated for Portuguese students in this age group were used: version B of the Jr. Metacognition Awareness Inventory (Jr. MAI), and the Self-Regulated Learning Strategies section of the Motivated Strategies for Learning Questionnaire (MSLQ), which were applied at four different times: Phase 0, before the intervention; Phase 1, after the IWE had been devised, Phase 2, after it had been constructed and Phase 3, after the IWE had been used. The number of participants varied over the four phases: Phase 1 ($n = 37$), Phase 1 ($n = 35$), Phase 2 ($n = 36$), and Phase 3 ($n = 20$). The results showed a positive trend in the development of metacognition, the use of cognitive strategies and self-regulation, especially in the ideation phase, where there were the highest Jr. MAI values and an increase in self-regulation throughout the process. Despite limitations, the study demonstrated the potential of co-creation as a strategy to promote critical reflection, autonomy, and student motivation. The results suggest that the integration of active methodologies in IWE, co-created and personalised by students, can promote the development of metacognitive skills at these ages.

Keywords Immersive web environments · Metacognition · Motivation · Co-creation · Personalisation

B. Cleto (✉)
DigiMedia Research Center, University of Aveiro, Aveiro, Portugal
e-mail: barbara.cleto@ua.pt

M. Abed et al. (eds.), *Metaverse and Artificial Intelligence in Education for a Sustainable Society*, Future Education and Learning Spaces,
https://doi.org/10.1007/978-981-95-8852-7_11

11.1 Introduction

Metacognition, often associated with 'learning to learn', is more than simply acquiring information. It involves students developing the ability to reflect on what they learn (cognitive knowledge) and applying strategies that enable them to manage and regulate this process (self-regulation) (Brown, 1978). Flavell (1979, p. 906) defines metacognition as 'knowledge and cognition about cognitive phenomena' (Flavell, 1979), i.e. the perception that students have of their own cognition (Gonçalves et al., 2011). According to Schraw (2002), it is possible to distinguish between cognition and metacognition: cognitive abilities are necessary to perform a task, while metacognition is necessary to understand how that task was performed (Gonçalves et al., 2011; Gonçalves & Martins, 2013; Schraw, 1998). Similarly, Georghiades (2004) reinforces the distinction proposed by Flavell (1976), noting that cognitive strategies facilitate learning and task completion, while metacognitive strategies monitor the process (Flavell, 1976; Georghiades, 2004; Gonçalves et al., 2011). In addition to the distinction between cognition and metacognition, Schraw (2002) proposes two further components of metacognition: the first, knowledge of cognition, refers to what they know about their own cognition, and includes three dimensions of metacognitive awareness: declarative, procedural, and conditional knowledge (Brown, 1978; Gonçalves et al., 2011; Gonçalves & Martins, 2013; Jacobs & Paris, 1987; Schraw & Moshman, 1995) and the second, regulation of cognition, which corresponds to the set of activities that help control their learning (Gonçalves et al., 2011; Gonçalves & Martins, 2013).

Schraw (2002) points out that metacognitive development can be promoted in the classroom and indicates four ways, proposed by Hartman and Sternberg (1993), to increase metacognition in the classroom, which include promoting an understanding of the importance of metacognition, improving knowledge about cognition, improving cognitive regulation and creating environments that promote metacognitive awareness (Gonçalves & Martins, 2013; Hartman & Sternberg, 1992; Schraw, 1998). Doly (1999, p.21), based on Biggs (1985), states that when the relevance of metacognitive skills for school success is recognised, teachers should select tasks not only according to the content, but also according to the metacognitive skills that these tasks activate (Doly, 1999; Gonçalves & Martins, 2013).

Thus, this project proposes the co-creation of immersive web environments where students integrate curricular content and digital tools and verify if these environments promote active student participation in creative, reflective, and collaborative processes, fostering the development of metacognition.

Immersive web environments are three-dimensional digital spaces accessed via a web browser, which allow real-time interaction with content, virtual objects, and other users (Accessed: Jul., 2024). These environments, powered by WebXR technology, can be experienced on mobile device screens, computer screens, or Virtual Reality (VR) devices (Accessed: Jul., 2024).

To evaluate the impact of the intervention, we used the versions translated, adapted and validated by Gonçalves, Fidalgo and Alves Martins (2011) for the Portuguese context of the Jr. Metacognitive Awareness Inventory (Jr. MAI) (Sperling et al., 2002), namely version B for students in this age group, and the Self-Regulated Learning Strategies of the Motivated Strategies for Learning Questionnaire (MSLQ) (Pintrich & De Groot, 1990), which measure metacognitive awareness, the use of cognitive strategies and self-regulation, respectively (Gonçalves et al., 2011; Gonçalves & Martins, 2013; Pintrich & De Groot, 1990).

11.2 Methodology

This study aimed to investigate the impact of the co-creation and personalisation of immersive web environments on the development of students' metacognition (Cleto, 2025). It is a case study (Amado, 2014; Coutinho & Chaves, 2002; Yin, 2005), since it analyses a specific pedagogical intervention, in a real classroom context, the co-creation and use of an immersive web environment, with a specific group of seventh grade students (Cleto, 2025). The aim of this study is to analyse without generalising the results obtained, although it is possible to transfer the results to other contexts (Cleto, 2025; Coutinho & Chaves, 2002). The research was designed according to the principles of Design-Based Research (DBR) (Baumgartner et al., 2003; Zheng, 2015) and the process of building the IWE was structured based on the ADDIE model (Analysis, Design, Development, Implementation, Evaluation) (Peterson & Peterson, 2003), following a Participatory Design approach (Sanders & Stappers, 2008) and guided by the principles of Design Thinking (Brown & Wyatt, 2015).

The research question (RQ) defined to guide the study was 'How can the process of co-creation of immersive web environments (IWE) between primary and secondary school students and teachers promote metacognition? (Cleto, 2025). Based on the RQ, the following working hypotheses were formulated: 'The co-creation and personalisation of an IWE promotes metacognition, because the student actively participates in the creation and personalisation of the environment, which implies a gain in motivation' and 'The co-creation and personalisation of an IWE promotes metacognition, because the student actively participates in the creation and personalisation of the environment, will analyse and reflect on the process, fostering metacognitive, cognitive and self-regulatory development' (Cleto, 2025).

The study involved students from two seventh grade classes in a Portuguese public school, aged between 11 and 16 (average 12.5 years) (Cleto et al., 2025). The intervention took place over 11 weeks, in the subjects of English and Programming and Robotics, taught by the same teacher (Cleto, 2025; Cleto et al., 2025). The IWE was developed in three phases (intervention phases): 1) phase 1 - ideation; 2) phase 2 - construction, based on the ideas from phase 1 and, finally, 3) phase 3 - utilisation, the IWE built in phase 2 was used as a classroom (Cleto, 2025; Cleto et al., 2025).

The school management authorised the study. Students and their parents or guardians authorised and gave their consent to take part in the study. Participants were informed that they were guaranteed anonymity, privacy and confidentiality (Amado, 2014; Creswell et al., 2017; J, 2017) for all the data collected and processed for the duration of the research. The students took part in the study voluntarily and were informed that they could withdraw at any time, without any consequences and with the exclusion of all the data collected.

For data collection, we used the versions translated, adapted and validated for the Portuguese context by Gonçalves, Fidalgo and Alves Martins (2011), of the following instruments for assessing metacognitive development: version B of the Junior Metacognitive Awareness Inventory (Jr. MAI) and the Self-Regulated Learning Strategies section of the Motivated Strategies for Learning Questionnaire (MSLQ), in which the two sub-scales: Cognitive Strategy Use and Self-Regulation were merged into a single instrument (Gonçalves et al., 2011; Gonçalves & Martins, 2013).

The Jr. Metacognitive Awareness Inventory (Jr. MAI) was developed by Sperling et al. (2002) based on the Metacognitive Awareness Inventory (MAI) created by Schraw and Dennison (1994), which assesses metacognitive development in adults (Gonçalves et al., 2011; Schraw & Dennison, 1994; Sperling et al., 2002). The Jr. MAI includes two versions: version A, for students in the third to fifth year of schooling, consisting of 12 items with three options ('never', 'sometimes', or 'always') and version B, for students in the sixth to ninth year of schooling, consisting of 18 items (Gonçalves et al., 2011). In this study, version B of the Jr. MAI was used, translated, adapted, and validated by Gonçalves, Fidalgo, and Alves Martins (2011), whose final version uses only 15 items, since three items, items 8, 12, and 16, were excluded due to low statistical correlation (Gonçalves et al., 2011).

The Motivated Strategies for Learning Questionnaire (MSLQ), developed by Pintrich and De Groot (1990), is the result of adapting items from various instruments used to assess students' motivation, use of cognitive strategies, and metacognition (Gonçalves et al., 2011; Pintrich & De Groot, 1990). The original instrument consists of 44 items, uses a 7-point Likert scale, and is divided into two main sections: Motivational Beliefs and Self-Regulated Learning Strategies (Gonçalves et al., 2011). The Self-Regulated Learning Strategies section of the MSLQ includes two cognitive scales (Gonçalves et al., 2011): Cognitive Strategy Use, made up of 13 items related to the use of rehearsal, elaboration, and organisation strategies and Self-Regulation made up of 9 items on metacognitive and effort management strategies (Gonçalves & Martins, 2013).

Once again, this study used the version translated, adapted, and validated for the Portuguese context by Gonçalves, Fidalgo, and Alves Martins (2011) of the Self-Regulated Learning Strategies section of the MSLQ. The Cognitive Strategy Use scale was reduced to 12 items (Gonçalves et al., 2011), item 4, was excluded due to low correlation, and for the same reason items 5, 15, and 16, were removed from the Self-Regulation scale, which now has 6 items (Gonçalves et al., 2011). The two scales were merged into a single instrument with 18 items ordered according to the original section and using a 7-point Likert scale (1 = 'I'm not like this at all' to 7 = 'I'm completely like this') (Gonçalves & Martins, 2013).

For the purposes of data collection and analysis, a Phase 0 (pre-intervention) was also considered, corresponding to the initial moment before the intervention began. The study therefore includes four data collection phases (Phases 0 to 3) and three pedagogical interventions (Phases 1 to 3). The number of valid responses in each phase of data collection was as follows: Phase 0 (pre-intervention) - 37 students, Phase 1 (after ideation) - 35 students, Phase 2 (after construction) - 36 students, and Phase 3 (after using IWE) - 20 students. The instruments were applied at four different times: 1) before the intervention (Phase 0), 2) after the IWE had been devised (Phase 1, 3) after the IWE had been built (Phase 2) and 4) after the IWE had been used in the classroom (Phase 3). They were completed in the classroom, in the classes of the subjects involved in the research project, with no time limit (Gonçalves & Martins, 2013). Instructions were only given for completion, the statements on the questionnaires were not read out or explained, only doubts relating to vocabulary were clarified (Gonçalves & Martins, 2013).

Since there was a variation in the number of participants in the different phases, the statistical analysis was based on descriptive procedures, including averages per phase. The interpretation of the data considered the evolution of the results, respecting the limitations arising from the variation in the sample, particularly in the final phase (Phase 3), where the number of participants was smaller.

11.3 Results

The operationalisation of variables for the Jr. MAI and MSLQ instruments followed the recommendations proposed by Gonçalves, Fidalgo, and Martins (2011). In the Jr. MAI items 8, 12, and 16 were not considered, while items 1, 2, 3, 4, 5, 6, 7, 9, 10, 11, 13, 14, 15, 17, and 18 remained. In the MSLQ, in the cognitive strategy use dimension, item 4 was not considered, leaving items 1, 2, 6, 7, 8, 9 and 12, 14, 17, 19, 20 and 22 and in the self-regulation dimension, items 5, 15 and 16 were not considered, leaving items 3, 10, 11, 13, 18 and 21.

The data were statistically analysed using the SPSS programme, version 29.0 (IBM Corp, n.d.). Means (M) and standard deviations (SD) were calculated for the descriptive statistics relating to the scales. Cronbach's alpha was also calculated for each scale or sub-scale, considering (Nunnally, 1978) criterion of $\alpha > 0.70$ for good internal consistency. Repeated measures ANOVAs were carried out to assess the differences between the variables in the various phases. To make the most of the sample, repeated measures ANOVAs were first carried out between phases 0, 1, and 2 ($n = 34$) and then phase 3 was added ($n = 20$). The F-test was calculated to assess the overall effect. The Sidak test was used to compare in detail each of the periods. The effect size was calculated using eta-squared ($\eta2$). The significance level considered for rejecting the null hypothesis was 5%.

We begin by reporting on the psychometric properties of the scales used and then present the repeated measures ANOVAs, which use the averages of the items in the scales or sub-scales according to the authors' guidelines Gonçalves, Fidalgo, & Martins (2011). These tests compare the results obtained on the scales by the phases under study. Repeated measures 3 x 2 ANOVAs were carried out. Three, because they are the measures used, MAI Jr., MSLQ - Cognitive Strategy Use and MSQL -

Self-Regulation and two, because they were conducted first up to the second phase and then repeated including the third phase, to take advantage of the greater sample availability up to the second phase.

The results of the descriptive and internal consistency analyses of the Jr. MAI items (Table 1) revealed different means and standard deviations throughout the four phases of the study. In Phase 0, the Jr. MAI items had a meaning ranging from 3.11 (Jr. MAI 6) to 4.49 (Jr. MAI 5), with Cronbach's Alpha reaching a value of 0.887, indicating good internal consistency. In Phase 1, the averages ranged from 3.23 (Jr. MAI 7) to 4.60 (Jr. MAI 1), and Cronbach's Alpha was 0.849. In Phase 2, the item averages remained within a similar range, varying between 3.25 (Jr. MAI 6) and 4.33 (Jr. MAI 1), while Cronbach's Alpha increased to 0.907. In Phase 3, the number of participants was smaller, but the item averages continued to be consistent with the values of the previous phases, ranging from 3.30 (Jr. MAI 14) to 4.00 (Jr. MAI 1 and Jr. MAI 5), with Cronbach's Alpha reaching its highest value, 0.944, indicating excellent internal consistency in the final phase.

Phase 0: applied before starting the intervention; Phase 1: applied after the students had devised the IWE and before they had built it; Phase 2: applied after the space had been built and before it was used as a classroom; Phase 3: applied after the space had been used as a classroom.

The results of the descriptive and internal consistency analyses of the MSLQ - Cognitive Strategy Use items (Table 2) showed variations in the means and standard deviations over the four phases. In Phase 0, the item means ranged from 4.27 (MSLQ

Table 1 Descriptive and internal consistency analysis of the Jr. MAI items

	Phase 0 ($n = 37$)	Phase 1 ($n = 35$)	Phase 2 ($n = 36$)	Phase 3 ($n = 20$)
Jr. MAI 1	3.95 (0.94)	4.60 (0.74)	4.33 (0.68)	4.00 (0.73)
Jr. MAI 2	4.08 (0.83)	4.17 (0.79)	4.08 (0.84)	4.00 (0.79)
Jr. MAI 3	3.81 (1.15)	3.80 (0.93)	3.81 (0.92)	3.65 (0.99)
Jr. MAI 4	3.46 (1.19)	3.86 (0.85)	3.83 (0.88)	3.75 (0.91)
Jr. MAI 5	4.49 (0.69)	4.43 (0.78)	4.11 (0.89)	4.00 (0.97)
Jr. MAI 6	3.11 (1.22)	3.43 (1.09)	3.25 (1.20)	3.40 (1.27)
Jr. MAI 7	3.22 (1.20)	3.23 (1.09)	3.33 (1.15)	3.30 (0.86)
Jr. MAI 9	3.70 (1.10)	3.71 (1.05)	3.67 (0.93)	3.60 (1.05)
Jr. MAI 10	3.54 (1.10)	3.34 (1.14)	3.58 (1.05)	3.85 (0.93)
Jr. MAI 11	3.89 (0.88)	4.17 (0.86)	3.75 (1.11)	3.85 (0.99)
Jr. MAI 13	3.92 (0.92)	4.14 (0.91)	4.03 (0.94)	3.85 (0.81)
Jr. MAI 14	3.65 (1.16)	3.74 (0.95)	3.72 (0.94)	3.30 (0.92)
Jr. MAI 15	3.81 (1.05)	3.69 (0.96)	3.64 (0.87)	3.60 (0.94)
Jr. MAI 17	3.27 (1.12)	3.31 (1.18)	3.50 (1.03)	3.45 (1.10)
Jr. MAI 18	3.70 (1.05)	3.89 (0.99)	3.78 (0.96)	3.60 (1.19)
Cronbach's alpha	0.887	0.849	0.907	0.944

20) to 5.16 (MSLQ 7 and MSLQ 8), with a Cronbach's alpha of 0.945, which indicated excellent internal consistency. In Phase 1, the averages varied between 4.54 (MSLQ 20) and 5.46 (MSLQ 2), with Cronbach's Alpha remaining high at 0.938. In Phase 2, the averages were between 4.75 (MSLQ 14) and 5.36 (MSLQ 8), with Cronbach's Alpha increasing to 0.949, continuing to demonstrate excellent internal consistency. Finally, in Phase 3, despite the smaller number of participants, the averages remained within a similar range to the previous phases, with values between 4.75 (MSLQ 14) and 5.35 (MSLQ 12), and Cronbach's Alpha was the highest, reaching 0.967, reinforcing the internal consistency of the items in this final phase.

Phase 0: applied before starting the intervention; Phase 1: applied after the students had devised the IWE and before they had built it; Phase 2: applied after the space had been built and before it was used as a classroom; Phase 3: applied after the space had been used as a classroom.

The results of the descriptive analysis and internal consistency of the items on the MSLQ - Self-Regulation (Table 3) indicated variations in the means and standard deviations over the four phases. In Phase 0, the item means were between 4.41 (MSLQ 3) and 5.49 (MSLQ 21), with a Cronbach's alpha of 0.845, suggesting acceptable internal consistency. In Phase 1, the averages ranged from 4.63 (MSLQ 10 and MSLQ 18) to 5.57 (MSLQ 21), and Cronbach's alpha increased to 0.860, reflecting an improvement in internal consistency. In Phase 2, the averages ranged from 4.78 (MSLQ 10 and MSLQ 18) to 5.44 (MSLQ 21), with Cronbach's Alpha reaching 0.871, demonstrating good internal consistency. In Phase 3, with a reduced number of participants, the averages remained between 4.65 (MSLQ 3) and 5.00 (MSLQ 18 and MSLQ 21), and Cronbach's Alpha increased to 0.958, indicating excellent internal consistency in the final phase.

Table 2 Descriptive and internal consistency analysis of the MSLQ items - Use of cognitive strategy

	Phase 0 ($n = 37$)	Phase 1 ($n = 35$)	Phase 2 ($n = 36$)	Phase 3 ($n = 20$)
MSLQ 1	4.95 (1.75)	4.97 (1.54)	5.06 (1.62)	5.00 (1.59)
MSLQ 2	5.11 (1.59)	5.46 (1.63)	5.31 (1.53)	4.90 (1.80)
MSLQ 6	4.65 (1.74)	5.23 (1.46)	5.11 (1.41)	4.95 (1.36)
MSLQ 7	5.16 (1.42)	5.17 (1.46)	4.97 (1.48)	5.05 (1.54)
MSLQ 8	5.16 (1.69)	5.40 (1.54)	5.36 (1.59)	5.10 (1.74)
MSLQ 9	4.73 (2.00)	4.83 (1.98)	5.00 (1.53)	4.80 (1.74)
MSLQ 12	5.05 (1.78)	5.03 (1.58)	5.28 (1.43)	5.35 (1.69)
MSLQ 14	5.00 (1.58)	5.20 (1.55)	4.75 (1.61)	4.75 (1.62)
MSLQ 17	4.84 (1.76)	5.11 (1.68)	5.03 (1.34)	4.95 (1.43)
MSLQ 19	5.00 (1.84)	5.29 (1.84)	5.22 (1.62)	4.95 (1.70)
MSLQ 20	4.27 (1.87)	4.54 (1.95)	4.86 (1.68)	4.95 (1.73)
MSLQ 22	4.92 (1.86)	4.83 (1.72)	5.11 (1.63)	5.10 (1.59)
Cronbach's alpha	0.945	0.938	0.949	0.967

Table 3 Descriptive and internal consistency analysis of the MSQL - Self-regulation items

	Phase 0 ($n = 37$)	Phase 1 ($n = 35$)	Phase 2 ($n = 36$)	Phase 3 ($n = 20$)
MSLQ 3	4.41 (1.89)	4.77 (1.77)	5.00 (1.35)	4.65 (1.57)
MSLQ 10	4.73 (1.69)	4.63 (1.77)	4.78 (1.46)	4.90 (1.77)
MSLQ 11	4.97 (2.07)	5.11 (1.73)	4.86 (1.69)	4.90 (1.62)
MSLQ 13	4.51 (1.88)	4.86 (1.90)	5.14 (1.53)	4.95 (1.64)
MSLQ 18	4.92 (1.67)	4.63 (1.80)	4.78 (1.90)	5.00 (1.59)
MSLQ 21	5.49 (1.41)	5.57 (1.46)	5.44 (1.40)	5.00 (1.65)
Cronbach's alpha	0.845	0.860	0.871	0.958

Phase 0: applied before starting the intervention; Phase 1: applied after the students had devised the IWE and before they had built it; Phase 2: applied after the space had been built and before it was used as a classroom; Phase 3: applied after the space had been used as a classroom.

The results of the repeated measures ANOVA for the evolution of the scale scores over three phases (Table 4) showed that, for the Jr. MAI, the mean scores evolved from 3.66 (SE = 0.11) in Phase 0 to 3.82 (SE = 0.09) in Phase 1 and to 3.72 (SE = 0.11) in Phase 2. However, the F-test indicated that this variation was not statistically significant, with $F(2,31) = 1.86$, $p = 0.164$ and a small effect size ($\eta^2 = 0.05$). For the MSLQ - Cognitive Strategy Use scale, the means rose from 4.82 (SE = 0.24) in Phase 0 to 5.05 (SE = 0.22) in Phase 1 and 5.01 (SE = 0.21) in Phase 2. The F-test also revealed no statistical significance, with $F(2,31) = 1.00$, $p = 0.374$, and the effect size was equally small ($\eta^2 = 0.03$). As for the MSLQ - Self-regulation scale, the means were 4.74 (SE = 0.23) in Phase 0, 4.89 (SE = 0.23) in Phase 1, and 4.95 (SE = 0.21) in Phase 2. The F-test showed that the variation between phases was also not significant, with $F(2,31) = 0.80$, $p = 0.456$, and the effect size was very small ($\eta^2 = 0.02$). These results indicated that there were no significant changes in scores over the phases analysed.

Table 4 Repeated measures ANOVA for the evolution of scale scores over three phases

z	Phase 0	Phase 1	Phase 2	F-test
Jr. MAI	3.66 (0.11)	3.82 (0.09)	3.72 (0.11)	$F(2,31) = 1.86$, $p = 0.164$, $\eta 2 = 0.05$
MSLQ				
Use of cognitive strategy	4.82 (0.24)	5.05 (0.22)	5.01 (0.21)	$F(2,31) = 1.00$, $p = 0.374$, $\eta 2 = 0.03$
Self-regulation	4.74 (0.23)	4.89 (0.23)	4.95 (0.21)	$F(2,31) = 0.80$, $p = 0.456$, $\eta 2 = 0.02$

Table 5 Repeated measures ANOVA for the evolution of scale scores over four phases

N = 20	Phase 0	Phase 1	Phase 2	Phase 3	F-test
Jr. MAI	3.50 (0.14)	3.69 (0.12)	3.57 (0.14)	3.64 (0.17)	F(3,16) = 1.08, p = 0.367, η2 = 0.06
MSLQ					
Use of cognitive strategy	4.54 (0.33)	4.67 (0.32)	4.63 (0.31)	4.91 (0.32)	F(3,16) = 0.98, p = 0.411, η2 = 0.05
Self-regulation	4.40 (0.32)	4.39 (0.30)	4.61 (0.31)	4.81 (0.34)	F(3,16) = 1.27, p = 0.295, η2 = 0.07

Results presented in M (SE) format; effect size calculated with eta-squared following recommendations (Cohen, 2013) for low (0.01), moderate (0.06), and high (0.14) effect size; ‡$p < 0.10$; *$p < 0.05$; **$p < 0.01$; ***$p < 0.001$.

The results of the repeated measures ANOVA for the evolution of the scale scores over four phases (Table 5) showed that, for the Jr. MAI, the mean scores varied from 3.50 (SE = 0.14) in Phase 0 to 3.69 (SE = 0.12) in Phase 1, 3.57 (SE = 0.14) in Phase 2, and 3.64 (SE = 0.17) in Phase 3. However, the F-test indicated that this variation was not statistically significant, with F(3,16) = 1.08, p = 0.367, and a moderate effect size ($\eta^2 = 0.06$). For the MSLQ - Cognitive strategy use scale, the means rose from 4.54 (SE = 0.33) in Phase 0 to 4.67 (SE = 0.32) in Phase 1, 4.63 (SE = 0.31) in Phase 2, and 4.91 (SE = 0.32) in Phase 3, but the F-test did not reveal statistical significance, with F(3,16) = 0.98, p = 0.411, and a small effect size ($\eta^2 = 0.05$). As for the MSLQ - Self-regulation scale, the means increased from 4.40 (SE = 0.32) in Phase 0 to 4.39 (SE = 0.30) in Phase 1, 4.61 (SE = 0.31) in Phase 2, and 4.81 (SE = 0.34) in Phase 3. The F-test showed that this variation was also not significant, with F(3,16) = 1.27, $p = 0.295$, and the effect size was moderate ($\eta^2 = 0.07$). These results indicated that although the averages varied slightly over the four phases, these differences were not statistically significant.

Results presented in M (SE) format; effect size calculated with eta-squared following Cohen's (1988) recommendations for low (0.01), moderate (0.06), and high (0.14) effect size; ‡$p < 0.10$; *$p < 0.05$; **$p < 0.01$; ***$p < 0.001$.

11.4 Discussion

As previously mentioned, the Jr. Metacognition Awareness Inventory, MSLQ - Cognitive Strategy Use and MSLQ - Self-Regulation scales were used and the number of participants varied between the different phases: Phase 0 ($n = 37$), Phase 1 ($n = 35$), Phase 2 ($n = 36$), and Phase 3 ($n = 20$). This variation limited the possibility of doing direct comparative parametric statistical tests, especially between phase 0 and phase 3, given the unpaired nature of the samples. However, it was possible to carry out a descriptive analysis of the data by phase, based on the averages, allowing us to discuss observed trends, but always being careful about generalising the results.

The reduction in the sample in Phase 3 may have influenced the averages. The results may be biased, since the students who stayed until the end may correspond to those who are more or less motivated or with greater or lesser metacognitive competence. The ANOVA results (Tables 4 and 5) also showed no statistically significant differences between the phases ($p > 0.05$), with small to moderate effect sizes ($\eta^2 =$ 0.02–0.07). This statistical limitation, coupled with the reduced sample size in phase 3, reinforces the exploratory nature of the study, where it was possible to identify trends in the development of metacognition during the co-creation process.

Analysing the data obtained through the Jr. MAI and MSLQ instruments made it possible to observe the evolution of metacognition, the use of cognitive strategies, and self-regulation throughout the different phases of the process of co-creation and use of the immersive web environment. To analyse the data and interpret the results, we considered the evolution of three phases corresponding to the ideation, construction, and use phases of the IWE and four phases, including phase 0 (pre-intervention).

11.4.1 Analysing the Evolution of Phase 0 and Phase 3

Regarding the Junior Metacognitive Awareness Inventory, comparing the data from phase 0 (pre-intervention) with Phase 3 (using the IWE as a classroom), there was an increase in the averages, suggesting an improvement in the students' level of metacognitive awareness. This evolution can be attributed to active participation in the co-creation process, which involved moments of planning and reflection skills that are central to metacognition.

In relation to the MSLQ - Use of Cognitive Strategies scale, the results also indicated an increase between Phase 0 and Phase 3. This growth may be related to the practical and reflective nature of the activities proposed in the ideation and construction phases of IWE, which required the reorganisation and active application of knowledge, and in the final phase, where IWE was used as a learning environment.

Regarding the MSLQ - Self-Regulation scale, there was also an increase in the average scores between Phase 0 and Phase 3. This evolution suggests that the students began to adopt metacognitive strategies more frequently, such as self-assessment, time management, and persistence in the face of difficulties. The use of IWE as a learning environment may have fostered this change by encouraging autonomy and a sense of responsibility in the learning process.

11.4.2 Analysing the Evolution over the Four Phases

Analysing the evolution over the four phases, it was found that in Phase 0 (pre-intervention), the data collected made it possible to establish the initial levels of metacognition, cognitive strategies, and self-regulation. In Phase 1 (after the IWE Ideation), there was an increase in the average scores, except for the MSLQ - Self-Regulation scale, where there was a slight decrease. The increase may be related to active involvement in the creative process, which required planning, reflection, and articulation of ideas, promoting the use of cognitive strategies, but not so much self-regulatory ones.

In Phase 2 (after IWE construction), there was only an upward trend in the self-regulation dimension. These results can be explained by the fact that this phase involves making decisions, reviewing concepts, and collaborating. It should be noted that although there was a drop in Phase 2, the values are higher than in Phase 0.

In Phase 3 (using IWE as a classroom) and considering a smaller sample ($n = 20$), there was an increase in the average scores, with the MSLQ domains achieving the highest scores. This increase may indicate that using IWE as a learning space favoured the consolidation of cognitive and self-regulatory strategies. However, the reduction in the number of participants at this stage should be considered when interpreting the results, as it may affect the representativeness of the data.

11.4.3 Analysis of the Evolution Over the Three Phases

Analysing the evolution over three phases (i.e. between Phase 0 and Phase 2), both the Jr. MAI and MSLQ - Use of Cognitive Strategies reached their maximum value in Phase 1 (ideation), showing the positive impact of ideation on cognitive and metacognitive development. The initial involvement in designing the IWE seems to have encouraged critical thinking, knowledge, organisation, and self-reflection. Although there was a slight decrease in Phase 2 compared to Phase 1, the values were higher than in Phase 0. This indicates that the construction of IWE involved practical involvement that reinforced the skills developed, although the cognitive and metacognitive impact seems to have been more significant during planning.

Throughout the three phases, there was an increase in the values of the MSLQ - Self-regulation scale, which reached its maximum value in Phase 3. This pattern suggests that the students' involvement in the ideation, construction, and use of IWE favoured self-regulation, with the students benefiting from the transition from planning to practical implementation and, finally, to real application in the classroom context.

11.4.4 General Analysis

Although the variation in the number of participants between the phases is a methodological limitation, the results indicate a positive trend in the evolution of the three dimensions assessed and suggest a positive impact on the cognitive, self-regulatory and metacognitive development of the students, being more effective in the ideation phase of the IWE for metacognition and cognitive strategies and in the utilisation phase for self-regulation. These results are in line with the theoretical assumptions underpinning the study (Brown, 1978; Schraw, 1998; Zimmerman & Pons, 1986).

11.5 Final Remarks

This study aimed to understand how the active participation of students in the creation, personalisation, and use of immersive web environments can promote metacognition.

According to the literature review carried out, no similar studies were found with this age group (Cleto, 2025). The literature review shows studies on collaborative 3D web environments (Virbella example) but with older students. The innovative, original, and relevant nature of this research has to do with the involvement of students in this age group in the process of co-creating their own IWE (Cleto, 2025). The students took part in all the stages of designing, building, and using the IWE, where they tried to find a compromise between playfulness and learning objectives.

The results obtained provide an answer to the research question initially formulated and show that involving the students in the co-creation of the IWE promoted a significant increase in the development of metacognitive skills and in the use of cognitive strategies and self-regulation of learning. The highest levels of metacognitive development were reached in Phase 1 (ideation). Phase 3 (using the environment as a classroom) led to gains in self-regulation. These data validate the hypotheses formulated.

The data collected with the Jr. MAI and the Cognitive Strategy Use, subscale of the MSLQ, revealed that Phase 1 (ideation) had the highest average, while Phase 0 (pre-intervention) had the lowest values. This result reinforces that the active participation and involvement of students in the creation and personalisation of an IWE promotes metacognition and stimulates the active use of cognitive strategies, confirming the first hypothesis of the study, the increase in student motivation in the initial phase of co-creation. The ideation phase required students to reflect, plan, and make decisions, skills that are central to the metacognitive process (Flavell, 1979; Schraw, 1998). Still on the Use of Cognitive Strategy, subscale of the MSLQ, the slight decrease in phase 2 (construction) may be related to the fact that this phase requires more technical skills than cognitive ones. However, the increase in Phase 3 shows that use as a classroom has consolidated the gains made. The evolution of the Self-regulation subscale was continuous throughout the different phases, reaching its maximum value in Phase 3 (using IWE as a classroom), which supports the study's second hypothesis. The process required students to organise their work, collaborate with colleagues, and face technical and conceptual challenges in an autonomous, critical, and self-regulating way.

The results are positive and reinforce the importance of participatory pedagogical practices centred on the student. Despite the results obtained, it is important to note that the lack of statistical significance and variability of the sample size may have conditioned the interpretation of the data, so caution should be exercised when generalising the results. These limitations call for future research to be planned in such a way as to include alternative strategies (B plans) and flexible timetables to guarantee the continuity of the students' participation throughout all the phases of the study.

The fact that only two classes from a single school were involved in the study limits the transferability of the results to other educational contexts. It is recommended that the sample be extended to more classes and different schools, and that teachers' perceptions of students' metacognitive development be included, which would make it possible to triangulate the data. In this way it would be possible to strengthen the validity of the results and deepen our understanding of the impact of co-creating immersive web environments on the development of metacognitive skills in different school contexts.

Acknowledgements To the teacher and students who took part in the study. To the parents and guardians and the school board for consenting and approving the students' participation in the study. To my supervisors Professores Mário Vairinhos e Carlos Santos, because without their guidance and support this research would not have been possible.

Recognising the Use of AI Tools ChatGPT 4.0 (OpenAI, https://chat.openai.com) was used to organise information that I had already written, with the aim of summarising and revising some parts of the text. I also used DeepL (https://www.deepl.com/pt-PT/translator) to translate the text.

References

J. Amado, Manual de Investigação Qualitativa em Educação, 2a. (2014). doi:https://doi.org/10.14195/978-989-26-0879-2.

"Ambientes Web Imersivos em contexto educativo - continua - Universidade de Aveiro." Accessed: Jul. 02, 2024. [Online]. Available: https://www.ua.pt/pt/continua/ambientes-web-imersivos-em-contexto-educativo

Baumgartner, E., et al. (2003). Design-based research: An emerging paradigm for educational inquiry. *Educational Researcher, 32*(1), 5–8. https://doi.org/10.3102/0013189X032001005

Brown, A. L. (1978). "Knowing when, where, and how to remember: A problem of metacognition.," Advances in Instructional Psychology, pp. 77–165.

Brown T. & Wyatt J., (2015, November) "Design thinking for social innovation," Annual Review of Policy Design, vol. 3, no. 1, pp. 1–10, Retrieved May 17, 2025, from [Online]. https://ojs.unbc.ca/index.php/design/article/view/1272

Cleto. B, (2025) "Planning a study on the co-creation and personalisation of immersive web environments by teachers and students.," in Interaction Design and Children (IDC'25), June 23–26, 2025, Reykjavik, Iceland.

Cleto, B., Santos, C., & Vairinhos, M. (2025). Students as co-creators of a classroom in an immersive web environment. In *In 11th international conference of the immersive learning research network, iLRN 2025 - selected academic papers for the iLRN proceedings.*
Cohen, J. (2013). Statistical power analysis for the behavioral sciences. *Statistical Power Analysis for the Behavioral Sciences.* https://doi.org/10.4324/9780203771587
Coutinho, C. P., & Chaves J. H. (2002). "O estudo de caso na investigação em Tecnologia Educativa em Portugal,"
Creswell, J. (2017 edition) "Qualitative Inquiry and Research Design | Open Library." Retrieved from June. 06, 2021,from [Online]. https://openlibrary.org/books/OL28633749M/Qualitative_Inquiry_and_Research_Design
Doly, A. (1999). Metacognição e mediação na escola. In M. Grangeat (Coord.), *A metacognição: Um apoio ao trabalho dos alunos.* Porto Editora.
Flavell, J. H. (1976, January). "Metacognitive Aspects of Problem Solving," The Nature of Intelligence, pp. 231–235. doi:https://doi.org/10.4324/9781032646527-16/METACOGNITIVE-ASPECTS-PROBLEM-SOLVING-JOHN-FLAVELL.
Flavell, J. H. (1979). Metacognition and cognitive monitoring: A new area of cognitive-developmental inquiry. *American Psychologist, 34*(10), 906–911. https://doi.org/10.1037/0003-066X.34.10.906
Georghiades, P. (2004). From the general to the situated: Three decades of metacognition. *International Journal of Science Education, 26*(3), 365–383. https://doi.org/10.1080/0950069032000119401;PAGE:STRING:ARTICLE/CHAPTER
Gonçalves, J. Fidalgo Z., & Martins M. A. (2011). Avaliação do desenvolvimento metacognitivo de estudantes entre o sexto e nono ano de escolaridade. In *XI Congresso Internacional Galego-Portugués de Psicopedagoxía.* Retrieved from: http://uipcde.ispa.pt/ficheiros/areas_utilizador/user16/goncalves_j._fidalgo_z._alves_martins_m._2011_avaliacao_do_desenvolvimento_metacognitivo_.pdf
Gonçalves, J. & Martins M. A. (2013). Avaliação da metacognição, autorregulação e utilização de estratégias cognitivas em atividades de investigação. In *Atas do XII Congresso Internacional Galego-Portugués de Psicopedagogia* (pp. 2453–2462).
Hartman, H., & Sternberg, R. J. (1992). A broad BACEIS for improving thinking. *Instructional Science, 21*(5), 401–425. https://doi.org/10.1007/BF00121204/METRICS
IBM Corp., "IBM SPSS Statistics for Windows," NY: IBM Corp: Version 29.0.2.0 Armonk. programa SPSS, versão 29.0 (IBM Corp, 2023)
Jacobs, J. E., & Paris, S. G. (1987). Children's metacognition about Reading: Issues in definition, measurement, and instruction. *Educational Psychologist, 22*(3–4), 255–278. https://doi.org/10.1080/00461520.1987.9653052
Nunnally, J. C. (1978). *Psychometric theory* (2nd ed.).
Peterson, C., & Peterson, C. (2003). Bringing ADDIE to life: Instructional Design at its Best. *Journal of Educational Multimedia and Hypermedia, 12*(3), 227–241.
Pintrich, P. R., & De Groot, E. V. (1990). "Motivational and self-regulated learning components of classroom academic performance," Journal of Education & Psychology, vol. 82, (1) p. 33
Sanders E. B. N, & Stappers P. J. (2008)."Co-creation and the new landscapes of design,"
Schraw, G. (1998). Promoting general metacognitive awareness. *Instructional Science, 26*(1–2), 113–125. https://doi.org/10.1023/A:1003044231033/METRICS
Schraw, G., & Dennison, R. S. (1994). Assessing metacognitive awareness. *Contemporary Educational Psychology, 19*(4), 460–475. https://doi.org/10.1006/CEPS.1994.1033
Schraw, G., & Moshman, D. (1995). Metacognitive theories. *Educational Psychology Review, 7*(4), 351–371. https://doi.org/10.1007/BF02212307/METRICS
Sperling, R. A., Howard, B. C., Miller, L. A., & Murphy, C. (2002). Measures of children's knowledge and regulation of cognition. *Contemporary Educational Psychology, 27*(1), 51–79. https://doi.org/10.1006/CEPS.2001.1091
Yin, R. (2005). *Estudo de caso: planejamento e método* (3a ed.).

Zheng, L. (2015). A systematic literature review of design-based research from 2004 to 2013. *Journal of Computers in Education 2015 2:4, 2*(4), 399–420. https://doi.org/10.1007/S40692-015-0036-Z

Zimmerman, B. J., & Pons, M. M. (1986). Development of a structured interview for assessing student use of self-regulated learning strategies. *American Educational Research Journal, 23*(4), 614–628. https://doi.org/10.3102/00028312023004614

Chapter 12
Empowering Teachers to Integrate Virtual Reality in Education

Celestino Magalhães, Marco Bento, and José Alberto Lencastre

Abstract The rapid shift to digital learning has underscored the transformative potential of Virtual Reality (VR) in education. VR enables immersive, experiential learning by simulating real-world scenarios and enhancing concept visualization. However, its effective implementation requires teacher training, curriculum adaptation, and equitable access. Educators must develop both technical proficiency and pedagogical strategies to integrate VR meaningfully. This study presents data from in-service teacher training programs, where educators from diverse subject areas experimented ClassVR headsets and designed lessons incorporating VR technology. Ninety-seven teachers from diverse subjects participated in six training sessions, with data collected through a satisfaction questionnaire on VR usability. Findings emphasize the necessity of teacher preparation to maximize VR's educational benefits. ClassVR's structured approach supports curriculum enrichment, ensuring VR is not just an innovative tool but a catalyst for deeper learning experiences and improved educational outcomes.

Keywords Virtual reality · Teacher training · Innovative teaching methods · Technology-enhanced learning · Usability

---

C. Magalhães (✉)
Piaget Polytechnic Institute, Vila Nova de Gaia, Portugal
e-mail: celestino.magalhaes@ipiaget.pt

M. Bento
Coimbra Coimbra, Portugal
e-mail: marcobento@esec.pt

J. A. Lencastre
University of Minho, Braga, Portugal
e-mail: jlencastre@ie.uminho.pt

M. Abed et al. (eds.), *Metaverse and Artificial Intelligence in Education for a Sustainable Society*, Future Education and Learning Spaces,
https://doi.org/10.1007/978-981-95-8852-7_12

12.1 Introduction

Virtual Reality (VR) is reshaping education by providing immersive and interactive experiences that extend beyond traditional classroom methods. Teachers are eager to use VR to enhance student engagement but often face technical and pedagogical challenges (Pandey, 2024). Hands-on workshops and collaborative projects are especially effective, helping teachers gain practical experience, design VR content, and exchange best practices. Institutions must promote a culture of innovation, provide continuous professional development, and ensure that VR use aligns with broader educational objectives, such as preparing students for future careers and encouraging student-centered, experiential learning (Pramudibyanto et al., 2024). So, in-service teacher training remains crucial for successful VR adoption. Teachers must develop technical proficiency, understand VR's capabilities and limitations, and explore its pedagogical applications (Pramudibyanto et al., 2024, 14). Training should include practical experiences, case studies, and collaborative learning, allowing teachers to exchange insights and refine their approach (Pandey, 2024).

12.2 Related Work

ClassVR is a comprehensive VR platform designed specifically for education, ClassVR is a VR platform designed for education, combining standalone VR headsets with built-in displays, an intuitive interface, and a cloud-based management portal. This system enables teachers to monitor and control devices in real time. Its integration with existing school infrastructure facilitates the delivery of curriculum-aligned content. VR offers immersive and personalized learning experiences (Jensen & Konradsen, 2018), enhancing knowledge retention and conceptual understanding. It also fosters twenty-first-century skills such as critical thinking, problem-solving, and collaboration by placing students in complex, interactive scenarios (Slater & Sanchez-Vives, 2016). Furthermore, VR promotes socio-emotional learning, including empathy, by immersing students in diverse real-world situations (Makransky & Petersen, 2019). Successful integration of VR requires significant investment in teacher training (Radianti et al., 2020). Educators need to acquire not only technical proficiency but also pedagogical strategies to design meaningful VR-based learning activities. With proper training, VR can enrich curricula and improve learning outcomes.

In inclusive education, VR supports diverse learning styles and special needs (Makransky & Petersen, 2019; Pantelidis, 2010). For example, students with physical disabilities can virtually explore historical landmarks or natural environments (Pantelidis, 2010), making learning more accessible and engaging. VR also encourages intercultural learning and global awareness, allowing students to "travel" through different cultures. Additionally, it helps visualize abstract concepts in subjects like science and mathematics (Slater & Sanchez-Vives, 2016). The impact of VR extends beyond its technological novelty, significantly influencing both cognitive and emotional learning (Dede, 2009; Pramudibyanto et al., 2024). However, its effectiveness depends on well-designed instructional content, appropriate use, and students' familiarity with the technology (Pramudibyanto et al., 2024).

12.3 Method

This intervention included the participation of ninety-seven teachers from different disciplinary areas, organized into six training courses of twenty-five hours each.

The majority of teachers (75.3%) have more than 21 years of service, which leads us to conclude that they are experienced teachers.

We found that most teachers teach the Elementary and Secondary Education (71.1%).

Initially, a pedagogical contextualization was carried out on the use of this VR. Subsequently, teachers dedicated themselves to designing lesson plans, focused on exploring different educational content with ClassVR glasses. Data was collected through a satisfaction questionnaire regarding the usability of VR with ClassVR glasses. Usability is not absolute, as it depends on the context in which the technology is used. However, there are broad parameters that can be used to compare usability in different contexts. According to ISO 9241-11, usability measures should cover: (i) effectiveness (users' ability to complete tasks and quality of results), (ii) efficiency (the resources used in performing tasks), and (iii) satisfaction (users' subjective reactions when using the system).

In this context, teachers' satisfaction with the use of ClassVR glasses was evaluated. To this end, the SUS questionnaire—System Usability Scale (Brooke, 1996) was used, which uses a 5-point Likert scale (1 = completely disagree to 5 = completely agree). Each statement requires the respondent to indicate the degree of agreement or disagreement. The SUS questionnaire presents 10 statements (five positive and five negatives, alternately). The answers were evaluated spontaneously, without right or wrong answers (Fig. 1). The following statements were presented:

At the end, teachers were asked to leave a comment about the experience (Fig. 2).

12.3.1 Training Sessions

In one of the sessions, physics and chemistry teachers, to familiarize themselves with ClassVR technology, participated in an interactive virtual journey, where they were able to explore scientific phenomena such as chemical reactions and the physical properties of matter in controlled environments. These controlled virtual environments are particularly useful in various subjects, where understanding certain concepts depends on viewing and interacting with materials or settings. This experience allowed them to plan the application of these simulations in their classes

	Strongly disagree				Strongly agree
1. I think that I would like to use this system frequently	1	2	3	4	5
2. I found the system unnecessarily complex	1	2	3	4	5
3. I thought the system was easy to use	1	2	3	4	5
4. I think that I would need the support of a technical person to be able to use this system	1	2	3	4	5
5. I found the various functions in this system were well integrated	1	2	3	4	5
6. I thought there was too much inconsistency in this system	1	2	3	4	5
7. I would imagine that most people would learn to use this system very quickly	1	2	3	4	5
8. I found the system very cumbersome to use	1	2	3	4	5
9. I felt very confident using the system	1	2	3	4	5
10. I needed to learn a lot of things before I could get going with this system	1	2	3	4	5

Fig. 1 - SUS questionnaire—System Usability Scale (Brooke, 1996)

to simplify the understanding of complex concepts, allowing students to visualize abstract processes in a way that is tangible (Pramudibyanto et al., 2024) and engaging for students (Fig. 3).

Music teachers were virtually transported to interactive shows, where they explored different instruments and musical structures. With this experience, they were able to reflect on how ClassVR can be used to teach composition, interpretation, and music theory in a more dynamic and captivating way (Fig. 4).

Geography teachers used ClassVR to take a virtual trip to historic sites across various regions of the world, exploring climate change and the phenomenon of volcanic eruptions. Through simulations, students can directly interact with phenomena that would otherwise be impossible to experience in a traditional classroom (Pramudibyanto et al., 2024). This immersive simulation allowed them to

Fig. 2 - Teachers using ClassVR glasses during training sessions

Fig. 3 - Activity to develop pedagogical skills with ClassVR technology during training, in the physics and chemistry subject

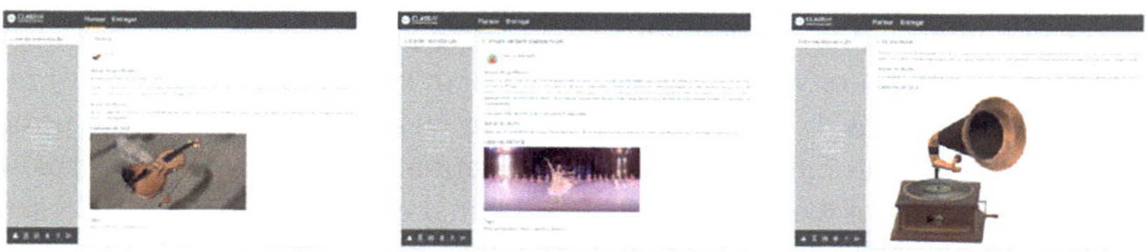

Fig. 4 - Activity to develop pedagogical skills with ClassVR technology during training, in the Music subject

better understand how these conditions affect local communities and the environment (Fig. 5).

Then, teachers, in groups, created their own educational content using the ClassVR authoring application. The training sessions concluded with a reflective discussion, where they shared the content produced, the challenges encountered, and ideas for the future implementation of ClassVR technology in their classes, making them more dynamic and engaging.

Fig. 5 - Activity to develop pedagogical skills with ClassVR technology during training, in the Geography subject

12.4 Results

The questionnaire presented to teachers allowed us to characterize them and characterize their level of satisfaction regarding the use of VR with ClassVR glasses.

12.4.1 The SUS Questionnaire

The SUS questionnaire is generally used after the respondent has had an opportunity to use the system being evaluated, but before any debriefing or discussion takes place. Respondents should be asked to record their immediate response to each item, rather than thinking about items for a long time, as we value spontaneous answers. After reading each point, the teachers answer the one that comes closest to their opinion.

All items should be checked. If a respondent feels that they cannot respond to a particular item, they should mark the center point of the scale.

The SUS produces a single number that represents a composite measure of the system's overall usability under study. To calculate the SUS score, first need to add up the score contributions of each item. Each item's score contribution will range from 0 to 4. For items 1,3,5,7, and 9, the score contribution is the scale position minus 1. For items 2,4,6,8, and 10, the contribution is 5 minus the scale position. Multiplying the sum of the scores by 2.5 to obtain the overall SU value. SUS scores range from 0 to 100.

The result obtained reached an average of 74 points in a range between 0 and 100, which is equivalent to an evaluation between GOOD and EXCELLENT on the (Bangor et al., 2009) scale for Adjective Ratings, "C" at Grade Scale and "Acceptable" on Acceptability Ranges (Carvalho, 2002) (Fig. 6).

Based on this general result, we consider that the use of ClassVR was widely accepted by teachers and causes user satisfaction (Carvalho, 2002).

However, the purpose of doing a classroom survey is not only to present a satisfactory score. The answers to each of the ten statements are more valuable and necessary than the overall satisfactory score.

As the questions are five positive statements and five negative statements, we decided to group them for analysis. We start with the odd numbers: 1, 3, 5, 7, and 9.

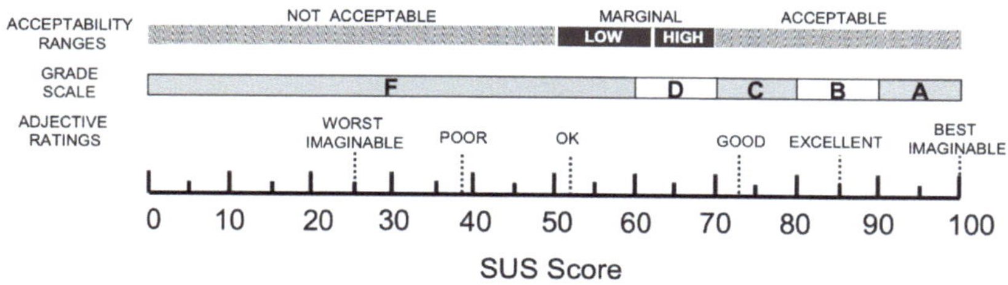

Fig. 6 - Adjective ratings, acceptability ranges, grade scales, relative to the SUS average score (Bangor, 2009)

For the first question of the questionnaire—I think I would like to use this system often—of the 97 interviewees, 74 (76.3%) positioned themselves between the value "agree" and "completely agree" (Fig. 7).

The third question—I found the system easy to use—had 80 respondents (82.4%) positioned between the value "agree" and "completely agree" (Fig. 8).

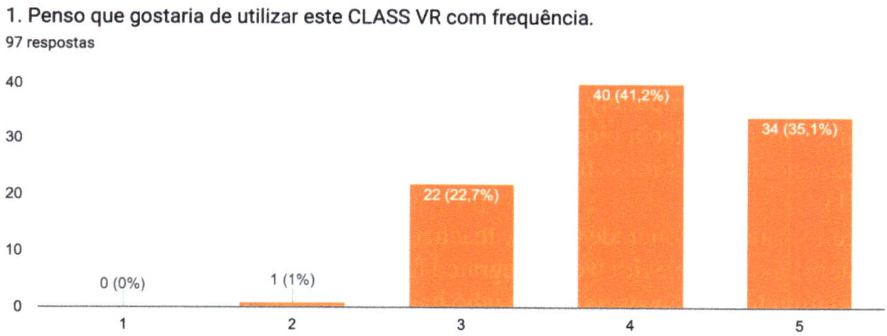

Fig. 7 - I think that I would like to use this ClassVR system frequently

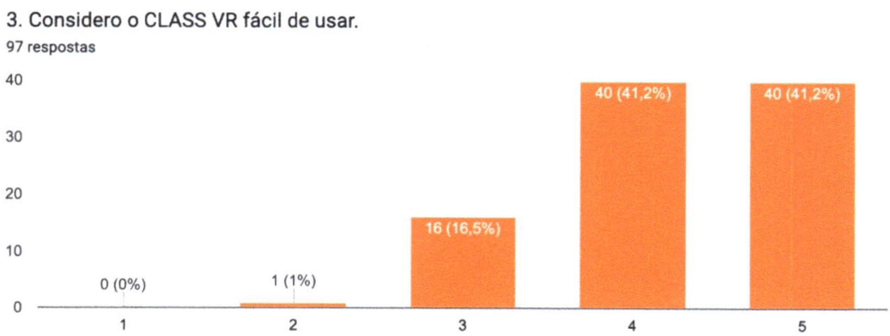

Fig. 8 —I thought the ClassVR system was easy to use

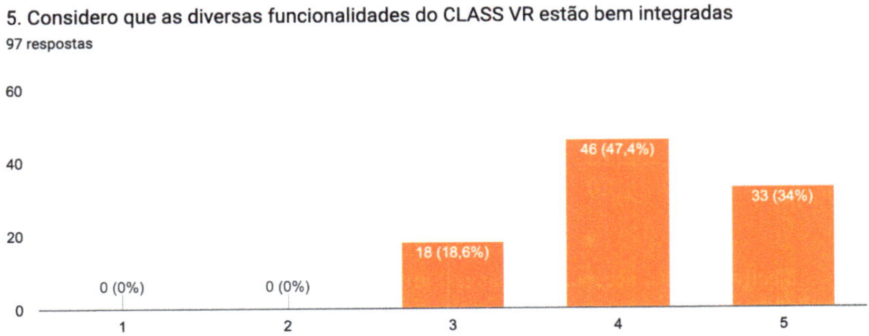

Fig. 9 - I found the various functions in this ClassVR system were well integrated

The fifth question—I found the various functions of this system to be well integrated—79 respondents (80.4%) stood themselves between the value "agree" and "completely agree" (Fig. 9).

The seventh question—I imagine most people would learn to use this system very quickly—72 respondents (74.2%) positioned themselves between the value "agree" and "completely agree" (Fig. 10).

The ninth question—I felt very confident using the system—72 teachers respond that "agree" and "completely agree" (74,2%). However, this is typical of teachers regarding emerging technologies like VR. As (Pandey, 2024) cite, any training that uses technologies must first involve familiarization with the technology itself (Fig. 11).

It seems sound to conclude that the teachers enjoyed using the glasses. They found the system easy to use, with well-integrated features that they quickly learned to use.

In relation to even answers, those who have negative statements, regarding question number 2—I found the ClassVR system unnecessarily complex—77 (79.4%) of the 97 interviewees stated that they disagreed with the statement, meaning they did not consider the system complex, which reinforces question number 3 (Fig. 12).

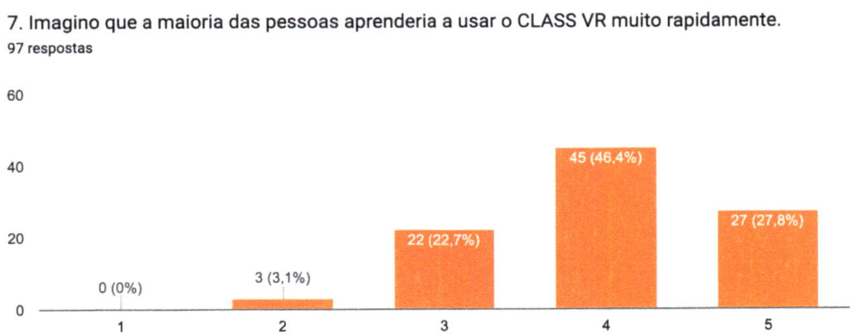

Fig. 10 - I would imagine that most people would learn to use this ClassVR system very quickly

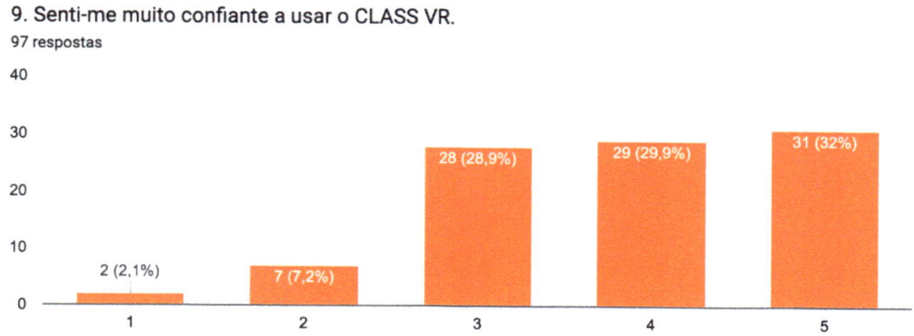

Fig. 11 - I felt very confident using the ClassVR system

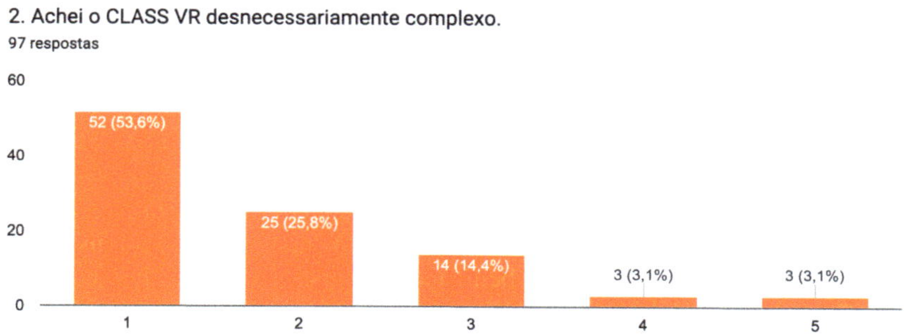

Fig. 12 - I found the ClassVR system unnecessarily complex

With respect to statement number 4—I think I would need the support of a technician to be able to use this system—43 (44.3%) disagree but the most significant data is that 28 (28.8%) of those interviewed agreed (Fig. 13).

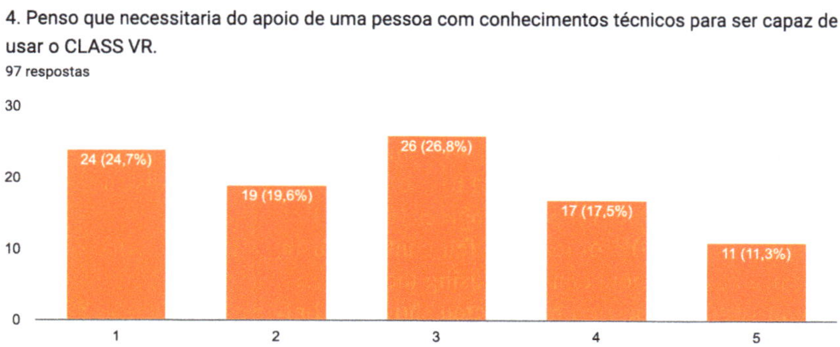

Fig. 13 - I think that I would need the support of a technical person to be able to use this ClassVR system

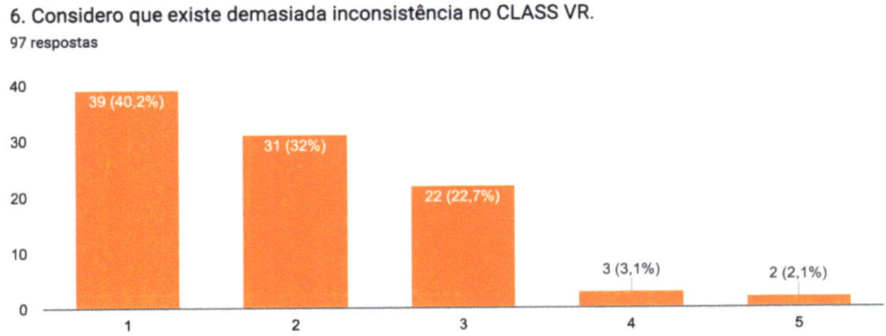

Fig. 14 - I thought there was too much inconsistency in this ClassVR system

"I think that I would need the support of a technical person to be able to use this ClassVR system". This is the answer with the most variations. Of the 97 teachers, 43 did not agree, 28 teachers agreed, and 26 did not take a position.

This means that these twenty-eight teachers assumed they would not be able to learn how to use the system on their own.

These answers contradict question 3—I found the system easy to use—with which 79.4% of respondents agreed. Teachers always feel technical issues with suspicion, as they can appear at any time and, not being technologists, can affect their professionalism. This is typical of the insecurity that non-technological teachers often have with using new technology. From our point of view, this contradiction only reinforces our conviction that the first approach to using ClassVR glasses must be done in in-service teacher training with the support of a knowledgeable trainer.

Regarding question number six—70 teachers (70.5%) do not agree with the statement "I thought there was a lot of inconsistency in this system", which is in line with question number fifth where 80.4% said they agreed that the various functions of this system were well integrated (Fig. 14).

Although the vast majority of respondents (71.2%) did not agree with statement 6—there was too much inconsistency in this ClassVR system—meaning that they found the system even, it is also pertinent to say that 5.2% had difficulty handling the system. This data should alert trainers to convey confidence and explain better how to use the system from scratch, step-by-step.

Regarding question number eight—I found the system very complicated to use—I found the system very complicated to use—78 teachers (80%) disagree. Only six teachers agree, and one completely agrees (Fig. 15).

We can see that 80% of teachers felt confident using the system, and only seven felt the need to feel more confident using the glasses.

The answers to question number ten show that only 57 teachers (58.8%) do not agree that glasses ClassVR are difficult to use. This represents slightly less than half of those interviewed (Fig. 16).

We think it has nothing to do with the technological use of the system, but with the resourcefulness to use it pedagogically in classes with students. Teachers, even those

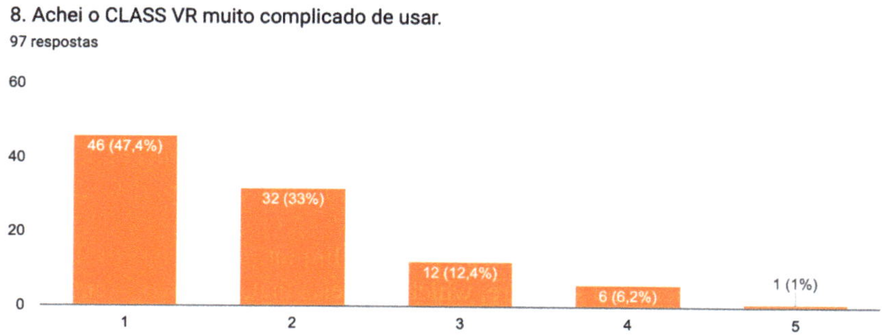

Fig. 15 - I found the ClassVR system very cumbersome to use

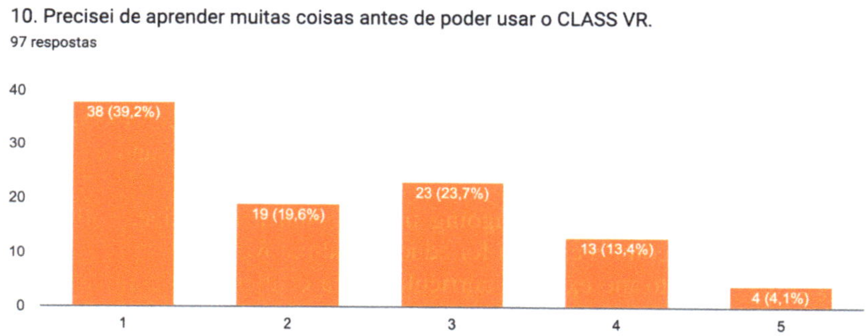

Fig. 16 - I needed to learn a lot of things before I could get going with this ClassVR system

with more years of professional experience, always need to mature their pedagogical approach. This happens because these tools and these pedagogically innovative approaches are very different from what teachers are commonly used to doing in their classes.

Analysis of the responses to the open question about ClassVR reveals a positive perception regarding its pedagogical potential. Most interviewees expressed a favourable opinion, highlighting the technology as "very interesting", "motivating", and "an excellent pedagogical resource". These comments reflect a high degree of satisfaction with the experience provided by ClassVR.

Participants particularly appreciated the quality of the virtual image and the technology's ability to offer new ways of acquiring knowledge and experiencing different realities. The mention that ClassVR can be "addictive" and that it "should be used in a time-sensitive manner" indicates a perception of its attractiveness and engagement, although it also suggests the need for considered use within the educational environment.

Furthermore, the comments reflect a desire among teachers to integrate this technology into their teaching practices, seeing it as a response to the need for innovation in education.

There are, however, some technical issues that can hinder the effective implementation of VR technology, such as the limited number of equipment available, Internet access, and the resources required for VR headsets. These trainings made it possible to understand the need to include a component that addresses the resolution of basic technical problems, to support the use and exploration of this tool. Teachers expressed a desire for schools to provide ongoing technical support to ensure the technology works well.

On the other hand, one of the comments points to limitations, such as the necessary investment in equipment and software, which suggests that, despite the enthusiasm, there are practical barriers to implementing ClassVR in schools.

12.5 Conclusions

VR has the potential to transform education by offering new ways of teaching and learning that are immersive, interactive, and personalized. However, the success of its implementation depends largely on adequate teacher training and overcoming technical challenges.

This article argues that with ongoing training and a reflective, collaborative approach, VR can become a catalyst for educational innovation.

Integrating VR into the existing curriculum is a challenge to complement and enrich the learning process. Ensuring that VR experiences are accessible and inclusive for all students, including those with special needs, is a significant challenge. VR is not only a technology aimed at improving the current learning process, but also a tool for exploring new pedagogical models and educational approaches.

Through this teacher training course, we observed that VR can have a relevant impact on improving the understanding of complex concepts and developing cognitive and socio-emotional skills. However, creating VR content that is pedagogically relevant and aligned with curricular objectives can prove challenging. For VR integration to be effective, careful planning is required. Collaboration between teachers seems to be the ideal approach to ensure the success of this integration.

References

Bangor, A., Kortum, P., & Miller, J. (2009). Determining what individual SUS scores mean: Adding an adjective rating scale. *Journal of Usability Studies, 4*(3), 114–123.

Carvalho, A. A. A. (2002). Testes de usabilidade: exigência supérflua ou necessidade. In Actas do 5° Congresso da Sociedade Portuguesa de Ciências da Educação (pp. 235–242).

Dede, C. (2009). Immersive interfaces for engagement and learning. *Science, 323*(5910), 66–69.

Jensen, L., & Konradsen, F. (2018). A review of the use of virtual reality head-mounted displays in education and training. *Education and Information Technologies, 23*, 1515–1529.

Makransky, G., & Petersen, G. B. (2019). Investigating the process of learning with desktop virtual reality: A structural equation modeling approach. *Computers & Education, 134*, 15–30.

Pandey, V. (2024). Empowering Educators: How AR/VR Technologies are Shaping the Future of Education. Availble at https://www.linkedin.com/pulse/empowering-educators-how-arvr-technologies-shaping-dr-vivek-pandey-ehfpf/ Acessed on March 2025.

Pantelidis, V. S. (2010). Reasons to use virtual reality in education and training courses and a model to determine when to use virtual reality. *Themes In Science and Technology Education, 2*(1–2), 59–70.

Pramudibyanto, D., et al. (2024). *Empowering teachers with VR Technology for Im-mersive Learning*. Jurnal Pengabdian Kepada Masyarakat.

Radianti, J., Majchrzak, T. A., Fromm, J., & Wohlgenannt, I. (2020). A systematic review of immersive virtual reality applications for higher education: Design elements, lessons learned, and research agenda. *Computers & Education, 147*, 103778.

Slater, M., & Sanchez-Vives, M. V. (2016). Enhancing our lives with immersive virtual reality. *Frontiers in Robotics and AI, 3*, 74.

Chapter 13
Artificial Intelligence and Online Language Learning at Moroccan Universities: Current State, Challenges, and Perspectives-the Case of the Rosetta Stone Platform

Mohamed Boukhch and Boulkhalil Abdessamad

Abstract This study explores the integration of artificial intelligence in language learning within Moroccan universities, focusing on the Rosetta Stone platform. In the context of higher education's digital transition, the research investigates how such tools reshape learning by influencing both pedagogical practices and learner experiences. Using a mixed-methods approach, it combines quantitative data from students with qualitative insights from faculty. Findings indicate that AI supports more personalized and flexible learning, yet highlight challenges linked to accessibility, teacher preparation, and the gap between standardized digital content and local academic realities. By grounding the analysis in real classroom contexts, the study underscores how AI is both adopted and perceived by students and educators. It concludes with practical recommendations aimed at strengthening an equitable and context-sensitive integration of AI-driven learning in Morocco's university system.

Keywords Artificial intelligence · Language learning · University · Rosetta Stone platform

M. Boukhch (✉)
Faculty of Economics and Management, Ibn Zohr University, Agadir, Morocco
e-mail: m.boukhch@uiz.ac.ma

B. Abdessamad
LARSLAM Laboratory, Faculty of Letters and Human Sciences, Ibn Zohr University, Agadir, Morocco

M. Abed et al. (eds.), *Metaverse and Artificial Intelligence in Education for a Sustainable Society*, Future Education and Learning Spaces,
https://doi.org/10.1007/978-981-95-8852-7_13

13.1 Introduction

In recent years, artificial intelligence (AI) has emerged as a transformative force in education, redefining how students engage with knowledge and skills. Within this evolving landscape, language acquisition stands out as a field particularly impacted by intelligent technologies. AI-powered platforms such as Rosetta Stone have been promoted as tools capable of offering personalized, immersive, and self-regulated learning experiences. Unlike traditional classroom settings, these platforms adapt to individual learning rhythms and provide immediate feedback, enabling users to progress autonomously. Globally, this shift toward digital language learning has accelerated, especially in contexts where resources, instructor availability, or linguistic diversity present challenges.

In Morocco, a multilingual country where Arabic, French, and increasingly English coexist in the academic sphere, the need for innovative language learning solutions is pressing. Universities are progressively adopting AI-driven platforms as a way to enhance student language skills while mitigating long-standing issues such as overcrowded classrooms, uneven language proficiency among students, and a shortage of trained language educators. This study focuses specifically on the implementation and impact of Rosetta Stone in Moroccan higher education, aiming to explore both the opportunities it offers and the limitations it encounters.

The central research question guiding this inquiry is: To what extent can AI-based platforms like Rosetta Stone support effective and context-sensitive language learning in Moroccan universities while addressing the pedagogical and infrastructural constraints these institutions face? To address this question, the study is structured around three hypotheses. First, that AI enhances language learning outcomes through personalized, interactive modules. Second, that a range of barriers; including technical issues, lack of training, and contextual mismatches; limit the full potential of such platforms. And third, that the most effective deployment of AI in language education depends on its thoughtful integration with traditional, human-led teaching methods.

This article proceeds by laying out the theoretical and institutional framework underpinning AI in education. It then reviews relevant national and international studies, describes the mixed-methods methodology employed, and presents key findings from both quantitative and qualitative data. Finally, the study concludes with a discussion of practical implications and strategic recommendations for more effective integration of AI tools in Moroccan university settings.

13.2 Theoretical and Institutional Framework

13.2.1 AI and Language Learning

The integration of artificial intelligence into the field of language education has opened new pedagogical horizons, reshaping how learners engage with language structures, comprehension, and production. By harnessing technologies such as natural language processing (NLP), voice recognition, and adaptive learning algorithms, AI-powered platforms create increasingly tailored and responsive learning experiences. As noted by (Luckin et al., 2016), these tools can adapt in real time to learners' input, identifying gaps and strengths, and adjusting content accordingly. This creates a more dynamic and individualized path to language acquisition, one that contrasts with the one-size-fits-all model of traditional instruction.

Among the array of AI-driven applications, platforms such as Duolingo and Babbel have popularized gamified approaches, using rewards, levels, and repetition to enhance user motivation and retention. However, Rosetta Stone positions itself differently. Its methodology, rooted in immersive learning, forgoes translation in favor of contextual understanding. From the very beginning, learners are exposed to the target language through images, pronunciation cues, and real-life scenarios, simulating the natural way children acquire their first language. This approach has been validated by studies such as (Vesselinov & Grego, n.d.), who found statistically significant improvements in vocabulary and grammar acquisition among users of the platform. Likewise, (Godwin-Jones, 2019) emphasizes that such immersive environments promote better retention and learner autonomy.

Yet, despite these advantages, the role of human interaction in language development cannot be fully replicated by machines. (Chapelle, 2003) reminds us that language learning is not merely the accumulation of lexical and syntactic knowledge; it is also a social act that depends on nuance, spontaneity, and cultural cues. These elements often emerge in real-time conversations, peer interaction, and feedback from experienced educators. Therefore, while AI tools like Rosetta Stone can efficiently reinforce core linguistic skills, their use must be framed within a broader ecosystem that includes human guidance, communicative practice, and cultural immersion.

13.2.2 National Policy Context

In recent years, Morocco has placed digital transformation at the heart of its higher education reform agenda. The national roadmap, known as PACTE ESRI 2030 (Pacte pour l'Enseignement Supérieur, la Recherche et l'Innovation), sets out an ambitious vision for a modernized, inclusive, and digitally agile university system. Among its central objectives is the integration of digital tools into pedagogical practices, particularly to enhance access, autonomy, and innovation in learning. In this vision, artificial intelligence is not seen as a luxury, but as a lever for democratizing knowledge and optimizing learning outcomes across disciplines; including language acquisition.

Yet, turning vision into reality remains a complex undertaking. According to (UNESCO, 2021), while Morocco has made notable investments in ICT infrastructure and digital platforms, significant gaps persist, particularly in terms of connectivity in remote regions, digital readiness among faculty, and the systemic integration of edtech solutions into curricula. The same report underscores that while digital platforms are available in many public universities, their usage is often superficial, due either to a lack of training or the absence of pedagogical support structures.

These findings are echoed in the joint report by (UNESCO, n.d.). The document highlights that AI integration in Moroccan universities remains fragmented and often dependent on isolated institutional initiatives rather than a centralized, coherent national strategy. While pilot projects exist; some involving language learning platforms like Rosetta Stone; there is still a lack of harmonized frameworks, standardized evaluation tools, and long-term planning to ensure sustainability and equity of access. The report advocates for a clearer governance structure, increased funding for digital infrastructure, and systematic professional development to align teaching practices with the opportunities offered by AI.

In short, while Morocco's educational policy landscape is evolving in the right direction, its AI ambitions in the university context still face structural, operational, and pedagogical bottlenecks. Overcoming these barriers will require more than enthusiasm or vision statements; it calls for coordinated action, institutional alignment, and above all, a commitment to building a digitally competent academic community.

13.3 Methodology

Understanding the integration of AI-driven tools like Rosetta Stone in Moroccan universities required a methodological approach that could reflect both the measurable tendencies and the subjective experiences of the actors involved. To capture the depth and diversity of perceptions surrounding this digital shift, we opted for a convergent parallel mixed-methods design as outlined by (Creswell, 2014). This choice enabled us to collect quantitative data from a large student sample while enriching our analysis through the qualitative insights of teaching staff. The two data sets were gathered simultaneously and then triangulated during the interpretation phase to reinforce the credibility of our findings.

13.3.1 Method

The study adopted a convergent mixed-methods design where quantitative and qualitative data were collected in parallel and analyzed independently before being merged for a comprehensive interpretation. The quantitative strand consisted of a structured questionnaire administered to 220 undergraduate students who had been exposed to Rosetta Stone during their language courses. The qualitative strand relied on 16 semi-structured interviews with language instructors (teaching French and English) across public universities. This dual lens allowed for a more nuanced understanding of how AI is experienced, used, and evaluated on both ends of the learning-teaching spectrum. The combination also compensated for the limitations inherent in any single method, offering both breadth and depth.

13.3.2 Measures

The questionnaire was designed to examine four primary dimensions: (1) frequency and patterns of Rosetta Stone usage, (2) perceived learning outcomes, (3) pedagogical relevance of the platform, and (4) barriers to effective implementation. Each of these was addressed through a set of closed and Likert-scale questions, facilitating a statistical overview of student trends. The questions were pre-tested with a pilot group of 20 students to ensure clarity and reliability. On the qualitative side, interviews focused on themes such as the perceived impact of AI on student engagement, challenges in content integration, the role of institutional support, and suggestions for improved usage. The interviews were open enough to encourage elaboration but structured enough to allow for thematic coding.

13.3.3 Participants

Participants were purposefully selected to reflect the linguistic diversity of Moroccan universities. The student sample represented 11 academic departments, ranging from scientific and technical fields (such as applied sciences and economics) to language and humanities departments (Arabic, French, English, and linguistics). This stratification was essential for capturing how students from different disciplines interact with AI-based platforms and the extent to which these tools align with their specific academic needs. Teacher participants were recruited from the language departments of three major universities (including Cadi Ayyad and Ibn Tofail), ensuring disciplinary alignment with the subject of the study. They all had at least three years of experience in teaching language courses at the university level.

13.3.4 Procedure

Data collection occurred over a six-week period between March and April 2025. The questionnaire was distributed electronically through official university mailing lists and social media groups used by student associations. Participation was voluntary, and anonymity was guaranteed to encourage honest responses. To mitigate any digital divide issues, hard copies were also made available at language centers for students without reliable internet access. Semi-structured interviews were conducted in person when possible and via Zoom when geographical or scheduling constraints intervened. Each interview lasted approximately 30 to 40 minutes and was audio-recorded with participants' consent. Transcriptions were anonymized and subjected to thematic content analysis using open coding followed by axial categorization to identify recurring patterns.

This methodological framework, grounded in both empirical robustness and contextual sensitivity, allowed us to trace the contours of AI integration in Moroccan universities with clarity and critical depth. It also ensured that both student and teacher voices were equally represented, acknowledging their co-construction of the learning process. The following section will present and analyze the most relevant quantitative findings that emerged from this mixed design, providing the foundation for a broader discussion on the implications of AI-based tools in language education.

13.4 Results and Discussion

This section presents findings from both the student survey (n = 220) and teacher interviews (n = 16), offering a multi-angled analysis of the use and perception of the Rosetta Stone platform in Moroccan universities. The results are structured to reflect both frequency and quality of engagement with the tool, its perceived effectiveness, and the challenges encountered, before transitioning to deeper insights from educators.

13.4.1 Student Responses: Patterns and Perceptions

The gender breakdown of participants reveals a clear majority of female respondents. This trend is worth noting, as it may reflect broader tendencies in student engagement with language learning and educational technologies (Fig. 13.1).

Disciplinary diversity is another point of interest. Students in this study came from eleven different academic fields, ranging from medicine and economics to Arabic and English language studies. This wide spectrum underscores the transversal value of language learning and highlights the need for AI platforms to cater to varied academic language needs (Table 13.1).

When asked about preferred teaching formats, respondents expressed a clear inclination toward either hybrid models or traditional face-to-face teaching. Online-only formats were less popular, indicating that students value the structure, immediacy, and support inherent in physical classrooms (Fig. 13.2).

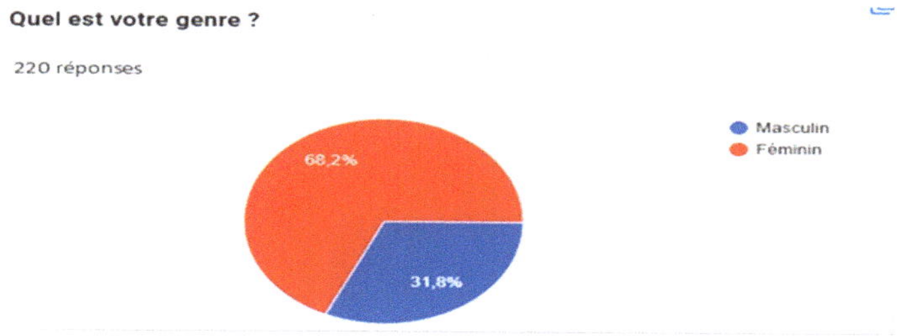

Fig. 13.1 Gender of participants

Students justified their choices in thoughtful ways. Those who favored face-to-face learning emphasized clarity of instruction, classroom dynamics, and the benefits of direct feedback. Meanwhile, hybrid learning was praised for its flexibility and ability to accommodate personal and professional obligations. A recurrent idea was that digital tools like Rosetta Stone should complement, not replace, in-person learning.

Regarding frequency of use, the results were mixed. Some students used Rosetta Stone regularly, indicating a positive engagement with the platform, while others rarely accessed it or not at all. This uneven usage pattern raises important questions about both accessibility and perceived relevance.

Asked about the most useful features of Rosetta Stone, students showed a preference for its multimedia elements and comprehension exercises. However, almost 30% reported that no specific feature stood out to them, a finding that calls for closer alignment between the tool's capabilities and students' academic expectations (Table 13.2).

Accessibility emerged as a dominant challenge. Over half the students reported difficulties in accessing the platform, mainly due to poor internet connectivity and technical restrictions. Other significant issues included the lack of real human interaction and the inadequacy of the content for university-level study (Table 13.3).

When evaluating whether Rosetta Stone improved their language proficiency, students were divided. Some perceived a positive impact, especially in oral comprehension and pronunciation, while others reported little to no progress. This discrepancy likely reflects varying levels of engagement and differences in how students used the platform (Fig. 13.4).

A follow-up question further explored students' views on the platform's sufficiency. The majority indicated that Rosetta Stone alone is not enough. Many favored its use as a supplemental tool, paired with instructor-led lessons and interactive, human-centered learning (Fig. 13.5).

Attitudes toward AI replacing traditional teaching methods were equally clear. Only a small minority believed that artificial intelligence could fully substitute for a teacher. Most respondents valued the human connection, spontaneous interaction, and contextual adaptability that AI still cannot replicate (Fig. 13.6).

Opinions on training also varied. Some students believed Rosetta Stone was intuitive and easy to use, while others felt additional training would enhance their learning

Table 13.1 University fields of study of participants

Medicine	Accounting and Auditing	Economics	French Studies	Linguistics	Arabic Language	Biology (SVT)	ENCG	English Studies	Law	Applied Sciences
40	10	31	37	20	16	10	15	26	5	10

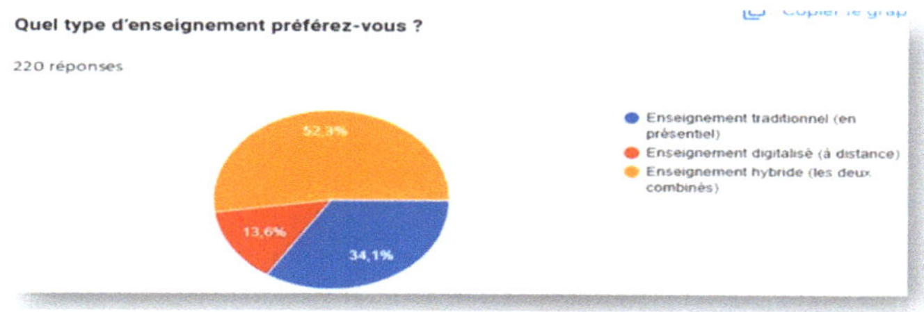

Fig. 13.2 Preferred type of teaching

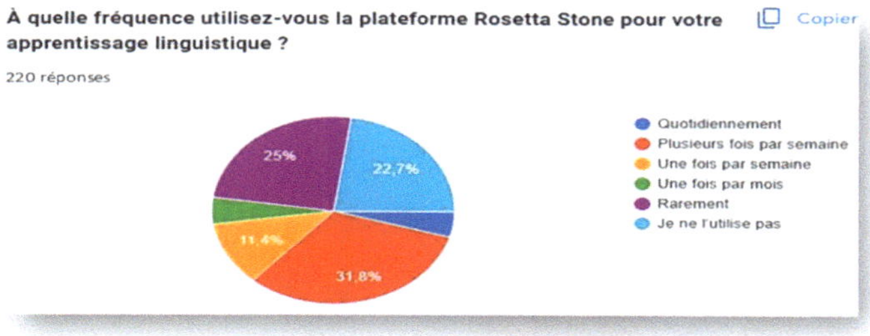

Fig. 13.3 Frequency of use of the Rosetta Stone platform

Table 13.2 Most useful aspects of Rosetta Stone

Aspects appreciated in the application	Percentage
Voice interaction and pronunciation recognition	27.3%
Reading and listening comprehension exercises	31.8%
Personalized progression according to my level	20.5%
Diversity of multimedia resources (images, sounds, videos)	34.1%
No particular aspect	29.5%

Table 13.3 Challenges encountered using Rosetta Stone

Challenges encountered while using the platform	Percentage
Difficulty accessing the platform (internet connection, technical restrictions)	54.5%
Lack of human interaction with a teacher or other learners	22.7%
Content not suited to academic needs	20.5%
Technical issues related to the use of AI	31.8%
No response	2.3%

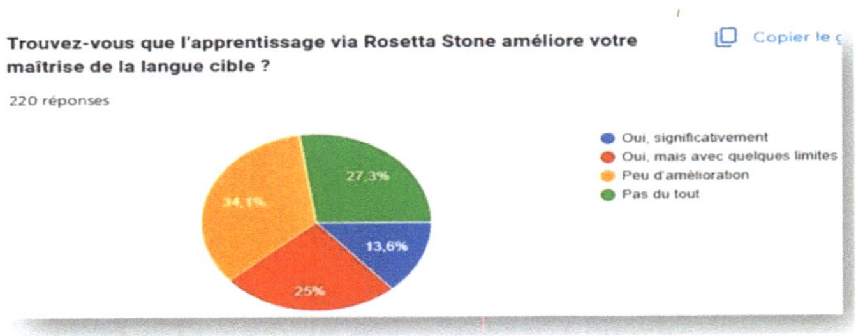

Fig. 13.4 Rosetta Stone and improvement of language proficiency

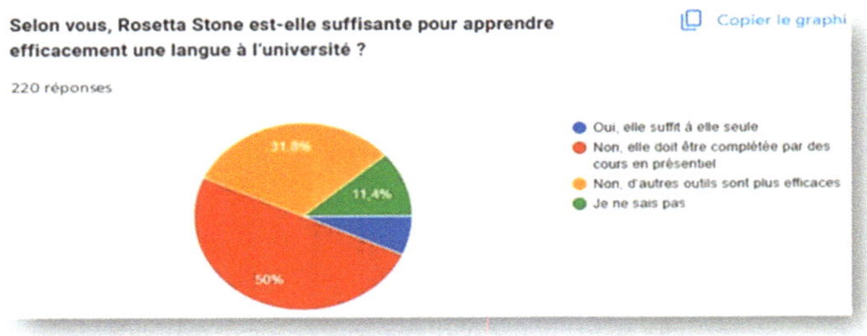

Fig. 13.5 Sufficiency of Rosetta Stone for target language learning

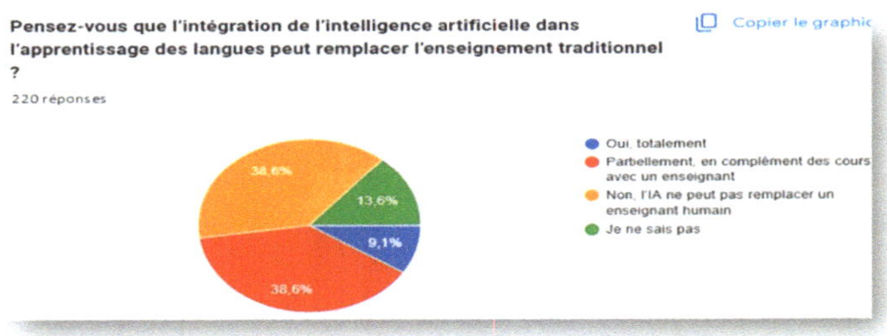

Fig. 13.6 AI vs. traditional teaching in language learning

experience. This disparity suggests different levels of digital literacy and exposure to ed-tech tools across student profiles (Fig. 13.7).

The issue of academic evaluation drew strong reactions. A large majority of students (75%) preferred that their use of Rosetta Stone not be graded. Their justifications ranged from the desire to learn without pressure to skepticism about the tool's reliability for formal assessment. Several noted that if the platform were to be used for grading, only formative assessment would be appropriate (Fig. 13.8).

Open comments offered numerous suggestions for improvement. These included adapting content to university-level requirements, enhancing interactivity through AI

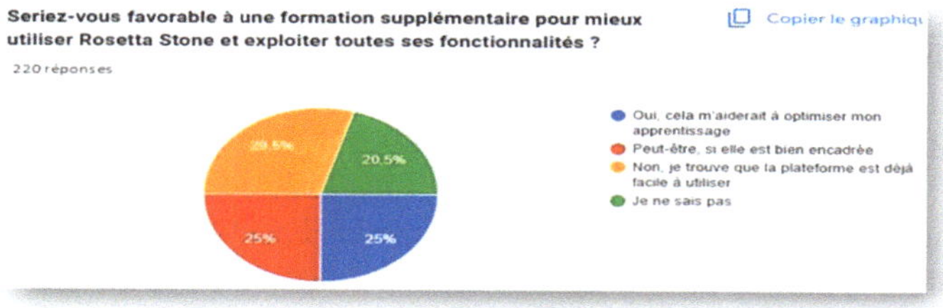

Fig. 13.7 Training on using Rosetta Stone

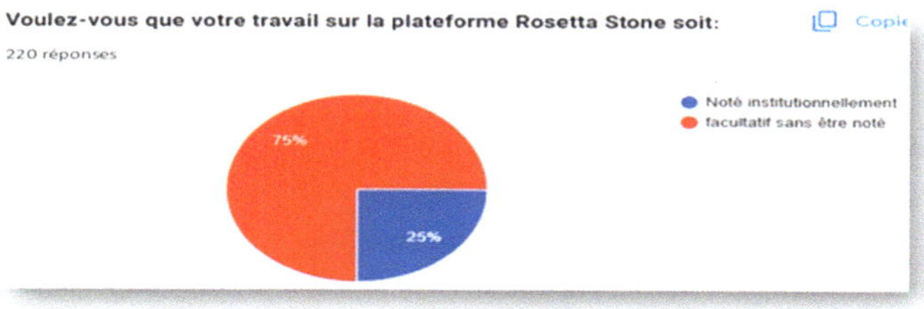

Fig. 13.8 Institutional evaluation of student activities on Rosetta Stone

tutors or peer collaboration, ensuring better platform stability, and allowing offline access. Overall, they expressed a strong desire for a more personalized and flexible learning experience that accounts for both academic rigor and technical constraints.

13.4.2 Qualitative Insights from Teachers

Teacher interviews echoed many of the themes raised by students, while also introducing new perspectives grounded in pedagogical practice. Most educators saw clear potential in AI-assisted platforms for diversifying classroom practices and supporting learner autonomy. They particularly appreciated the platform's structured progression and real-time feedback features.

Yet, they were quick to stress that such tools must remain complementary. As one English professor remarked, "AI helps with repetition and practice, but cannot replace the authenticity of real conversation or the role of the teacher in guiding nuanced understanding." This aligns with research by (Chapelle, 2003), who warned that AI lacks the emotional and contextual intelligence crucial to authentic communication.

A primary concern raised was the generic nature of Rosetta Stone's content. Many felt that the materials lacked cultural and academic alignment with Moroccan university curricula. Faculty also noted limited flexibility in adapting or editing content to suit classroom needs, which restricted its pedagogical value.

Another major challenge was infrastructure. Teachers described a digital divide, particularly for students from under-resourced regions, which hampered equitable access to the platform. These technical issues, they argued, must be addressed at the institutional level before AI tools can be effectively mainstreamed into teaching practices.

Training emerged as a final, but essential, theme. Faculty acknowledged that their own unfamiliarity with the tool often limited its impact. Without structured professional development, teachers felt unprepared to integrate AI meaningfully into their pedagogical approach. Their feedback suggests that simply introducing technology is not enough training, contextual support, and shared resources are critical to ensuring lasting adoption.

13.5 Conclusion

This study is situated in a context where technological advancements are disrupting teaching and learning methods, particularly in the field of languages. The integration of artificial intelligence in Moroccan universities is becoming a strategic issue for modernizing pedagogical practices and meeting student needs in an increasingly digitized world. Through the analysis of the Rosetta Stone platform, this research aimed to evaluate the effectiveness of these tools in language learning, identify the challenges encountered, and propose perspectives for improvement for a more harmonious integration within the academic framework. The results obtained largely confirm the initial hypotheses. AI applied to language learning allows for better personalization of students' paths, thus favoring the acquisition of comprehension and oral/written production skills. However, several obstacles limit its effectiveness, notably technical accessibility problems related to connectivity and digital technical infrastructure, as well as a lack of teacher training on the optimal use of these tools. The study also shows that AI cannot entirely replace traditional approaches but gains effectiveness when integrated complementarily with classic pedagogical practices, promoting a balanced interaction between teacher and technology. Faced with these findings, several recommendations emerge. It is essential to strengthen institutional support to ensure equitable access to digital resources and AI-based learning platforms. Teacher training must be a priority to enable them to fully exploit these tools and adapt their pedagogical approaches accordingly. Furthermore, adapting the content offered by platforms to academic requirements and the linguistic specificities of Moroccan students appears necessary to optimize their effectiveness. The perspectives opened by this study invite broader reflection on the place of artificial intelligence in higher education in Morocco. While these technologies offer considerable opportunities, their adoption must be part of a coherent and progressive approach, involving all educational actors. The future of language learning in Moroccan universities will depend on the ability to combine technological innovation and human pedagogy, ensuring that these tools truly serve the goals of student training and inclusion.

References

Chapelle, C. A. (2003). *English language learning and technology: Lectures on applied linguistics in the age of information and communication technology*. John Benjamins Publishing.

Creswell, J. W. (2014). *Research design: Qualitative, quantitative, and mixed methods approaches* (4th ed.). SAGE Publications.

Godwin-Jones, R. (2019). In language learning, less is more. *Language, Learning and Technology, 23*(3), 1–8.

Luckin, R., Holmes, W., Griffiths, M., & Forcier, L. B. (2016). *Intelligence unleashed: An argument for AI in education*. Pearson Education.

UNESCO. (2021). *Understanding the impact of AI on education policies and practices in Africa*. United Nations Educational, Scientific and Cultural Organization.

UNESCO, AUF: *L'Intelligence artificielle dans les établissements d'enseignement supérieur du Maroc: État des lieux et perspectives*. Rapport conjoint. https://www.auf.org/nouvelles/publications/intelligence-artificielle-et-enseignement-superieur-au-maroc/

Vesselinov, R., & Grego, J. *Duolingo effectiveness study*. City University of New York. https://s3.amazonaws.com/duolingo-papers/duolingo-effectiveness-study.pdf

Chapter 14
Fostering Sustainable Learning Practices with Generative AI, Education 4.0, and the Metaverse: Innovations in STEAM and Medical Training

Houneida Sakly, Mourad Abed, Naoufel Kraiem, Mourad Said, and Chawki Lawssif

Abstract The convergence of generative artificial intelligence (AI), Ed-ucation 4.0, and the metaverse is transforming education by promoting sustainable learning practices that align with the United Nations' Sustainable Development Goals (SDGs), especially SDG 4 (Quality Education). This paper presents an innovative framework and architecture designed to create personalized, immersive, and inclusive learning environ- ments, particularly in STEAM (Science, Technology, Engineering, Arts, Mathematics) and medical training. We examine various use cases, such as pipeline maintenance training aimed at preventing environmental and economic damage from ruptures in block weighing generating pipelines, as well as climate modeling to address global warming. Real-world examples, including Metaverse Learning, Google's LearnLM, and VR surgical training, illustrate the practical impacts of these technologies. We also analyze challenges related to energy demands, digital equity, and ethical risks, providing actionable mitigation strategies. The proposed Generative AI, Education 4.0, Metaverse, and Sustainable Immersive Learning Architecture (GEMSILA) integrates data ecosystems, AI-driven content orchestration

H. Sakly (✉)
CRMN, Center for Research on Microelectronics and Nanotechnology of Sousse, Nanomisene Lab, LR16CRMN01, Technopark of Sousse, Sousse, Tunisia
e-mail: sakly.houneida@crmn.rnrt.tn

M. Abed
University Polytechnic Hauts-de-France (UPHF), Valenciennes, France

N. Kraiem
College of Computer Science, King Khalid University, Abha, Saudi Arabia

RIADI laboratory-ENSI, Campus Universitaire de la Manouba, Manouba, Tunisia

M. Said
Sousse Medina Medical Imaging Center, Sousse, Tunisia

C. Lawssif
Department of Infectious Diseases, Fattouma Bourguiba Hospital, Monastir, Tunisia

M. Abed et al. (eds.), *Metaverse and Artificial Intelligence in Education for a Sustainable Society*, Future Education and Learning Spaces,
https://doi.org/10.1007/978-981-95-8852-7_14

using large language models, principles of Education 4.0, metaverse immersion, and adaptive analytics, all detailed with sub-layers to guide scalable implementation. Our recommendations aim to empower educators, policymakers, technologists, and industry stakeholders to advance equitable and sustainable education for societal and environmental progress.

Keywords Generative AI · Education 4.0 · Metaverse · Sustainable · Learning practices · SDG 4 · STEAM · Medicine · Pipeline maintenance · Climate modeling · Immersive learning

14.1 Introduction

The consortium of generative artificial intelligence (AI), Education 4.0, and the metaverse is an ultimate changemaker of sustainable learning systems, defined as accessible, technology-facilitated methods that enhance engagement, inclusivity, and caring for the environment (Assembly 2015). In line with SDG 4, these technologies promote equitable education while empowering learners to combat global challenges, including climate change, social inequality, and wastefulness within industrial practice (Assembly 2015). Generative AI, namely large language models (LLMs) like GPT-4 and diffusion models like DALL-E, generate customized content to enhance levels of personalization (Fan et al. 2025). Education 4.0, the education system that works along with Industry 4.0, uses AI, virtual reality (VR), augmented reality (AR), and the Internet of Things (IoT) for learner-centric ecosystems (Bondin and Zammit 2025). The metaverse acts as a 3D virtual ecosystem that merges VR, AR, and mixed realities for immersive learning while cutting back on the use of infrastructure that is more resource-heavy (Dwivedi et al. 2022). Converging technologies thus establish the path for Education 5.0, which focuses on emotional intelligence and mental health and promotes the holistic wellbeing of learners (Vistorte et al. 2024).

A real impediment to the old system of pedagogies is that while some infrastructures create a facility for learning, they incur adverse effects on the environment, while inequalities get deeper from access issues (Assembly 2015). In instances of industrial systems such as block weighing, generating pipelines transporting heavy materials, ruptures (most recently, the Trans Mountain oil slick (CBC News: Trans Mountain pipeline spill in B.C. prompts environmental concerns 2023), the Enbridge incident in 2018 (Enbridge: Enbridge responds to natural gas transmission pipeline incident 2018)) would ecologically ruin and economically penalize from the viewpoint of blocking or corroding pipelines. It is within climate change, holding some degree of accountability to worldwide warming through 4% just from air travel, that demonstrating the need for sustainable practice has reached epochal importance (Ferhati et al. 2024). This paper proposes a framework and novel Generative AI, Education 4.0, Metaverse, and Sustainable Immersive Learning Architecture (GEMSILA) to combine the four technologies with a view to pipeline maintenance, climate modeling, and medical training. The following three research questions are addressed:

- How do generative AI, Education 4.0, and the metaverse foster sustainable learning?
- What would be innovative applications in STEAM (including pipeline maintenance and climate modeling) and medical training?
- What are the challenges and solutions ensuring the just and sustainable deployment of such systems?

The organization of this paper is as follows: Section 2 will provide a review of related work. GEMSILA architecture will be described in Section 3. Section 4 will cover common applications-based practical learning in STEAM education and Healthcare use cases. Ultimately, Section 5 will address challenges, followed by conclusions and future directions in Section 6.

14.2 Related Work

Education 4.0 is forging twenty-first-century skills such as critical thinking, creativity, and collaboration through AI, IoT, VR, and AR, and reports 20–30% higher STEM engagement as compared to traditional methods (Bondin and Zammit 2025). The virtual simulations are saving on resource consumption toward environmental sustainability (Haleem et al. 2022). Generative AI, specifically LLMs, are personalizing—or tailoring—learning experiences, with Google's LearnLM showing enhanced academic outcomes (Hedges's $g = 0.533$ for college students) (Google AI: LearnLM: A family of models optimized for learning 2024). In pipeline maintenance, however, AI can provide very useful simulations to train engineers on preventing possible ruptures (Naranjo et al. 2022). The issues that arise here include algorithmic biases and extensive energy consumption; for instance, GPT-3 consumed 1287 MWh (Strubell et al. 2019). The meta-verse allows impactful learning spaces in which virtual labs are reported to reduce chemical wastes by 40% (van Dinther et al. 2023). Similarly, pipeline maintenance has VR simulate rupture scenarios, but the high costs of VR headsets ($300–1000) and privacy concerns prove to be hindrances (Patel-Campillo and Salas García 2022). The SDGs, with special reference to SDG 4, promote inclusive education, further aided by AI and metaverse technologies in lessening their environmental footprints (Assembly 2015). While through government initiatives such as funding UK teachers with AI tools for efficiency, educators cite academic dishonesty as a significant concern in this field (Mystakidis 2022). Education 5.0 builds on this, primarily focusing on emotional intelligence, augmented by AI-assisted tools for mental health (Vistorte et al. 2024).

14.3 Proposed Framework: Generative AI, Education 4.0, Metaverse, and Sustainable Immersive Learning Architecture (GEMSILA)

Generative AI, Education 4.0, Metaverse, and Sustainable Immersive Learning Architecture (GEMSILA) is a powerful, scalable framework that integrates generative AI with Education 4.0 and the metaverse to provide sustainable immersive learning personalized experiences balanced for academic disciplines (e.g., STEAM, medicine) and industrial applications (e.g., pipeline maintenance, climate modeling). With five interconnected layers, GEMSILA is built with three sub-layers in each layer to ensure granularity of operation, ethical governance, and alignment with SDG 4 (Assembly 2015). The architecture minimizes environmental footprint, enhances inclusiveness, and fosters twenty-first-century skills, with iterative feedback loops to tailor for diverse learner needs and sustainability goals (Mulyani et al. 2025).

1. Data Ecosystem Layer: Collection, management, and aggregation of exhaustive data for personalized learning and sustainability objectives while ensuring that data is used in an ethical manner (Assembly 2015).
   - Learner Profiles: Their assessment aggregates data on learning styles, skills, and cultural backgrounds for personalized content delivery.
   - Industrial and Environmental Data: Created by capturing the pipeline specifications, rupture histories, and climate metrics (e.g., IPCC CO_2 datasets) using IoT sensors (Naranjo et al. 2022).
   - Ethical Data Governance: This employs blockchain for secure, transpar- ent storage, thus mitigating the risks to privacy and meeting compliance with data protection regulation standards (Patel-Campillo and Salas García 2022).
2. AI-Driven Content Orchestration Layer: Generative AI, such as GPT-4, and diffusion models such as DALL-E assist in creating adaptive and inclusive content (Fan et al. 2025; Mulyani et al. 2025).
   - LLM-Powered Content Generation: Dynamic simulations (such as cli- mate change scenarios visualizing CO_2 impacts, pipeline rupture cases due to sediment blockages) and educational content (for example, multilingual quizzes for STEAM, patient-specific medical scenarios) (Google AI: LearnLM: A family of models optimized for learning 2024; Naranjo et al. 2022).
   - Inclusive Design: Integration of accessibility features such as screen- reader compatibility and multilingual formats to cater to different learn- ers regarding SDG 4 inclusivity (Assembly 2015).
   - Energy-Efficient Processing: Through processes like model pruning and quantization to lessen the computational energy demands (mitigating GPT-3's 1287 MWh footprint), this supports environmental sustainability (Strubell et al. 2019).

3. Education 4.0 Integration Layer: Integrating all the learner-centric principles of Education 4.0, which would then integrate the twenty-first-century skills (critical thinking, creativity, and collaboration) to Industry 4.0 (Bondin and Zammit 2025).
   - Adaptive Learning Pathways: Designing personalized curricular pathways with interdisciplinary topics (such as climate science with engineering, or medical ethics and AI) based on learner profiles.
   - Real-Time Feedback Mechanisms: One immediately provides very quick performance data feedback using AI analytics, significantly increasing learner engagement and skill acquisition.
   - Interdisciplinary Skill Development: Prepares students for sustainable industries (e.g., renewable energy, pipeline management) through highly collaborative, problem-based learning environments.
4. Metaverse Immersion Layer: Delivers content through immersive VR/AR platforms to develop interactive, resource-efficient spaces for learning (Dwivedi et al. 2022).
   - Virtual Learning Spaces: Recreates reality-based places such as chemistry labs, surgical theaters, and pipeline networks so that less physical infrastructure is needed (van Dinther et al. 2023).
   - Real-Time Collaborative Interaction: Cloud-based rendering and 5G connectivity ensure complete global collaboration (e.g., students co-designing sustainable cities) while minimizing latency (Patel-Campillo and Salas García 2022).
   - Accessible Immersive Delivery: Provides mobile AR and low-cost VR options to ensure equitable access, addressing digital divide concerns (Patel-Campillo and Salas García 2022).
5. Adaptive Analytics and Feedback Layer: Informs improvement through analyzing learner performance, platform efficacy, and sustainability outcomes (Google AI: LearnLM: A family of models optimized for learning 2024).
   - Performance and Engagement Metrics: Tracks skill acquisitions and engagement rates (e.g., 25% increase in STEAM engagement) and learner progress (Google AI: LearnLM: A family of models optimized for learning 2024).
   - Sustainability Impact Tracking: Measures environmental benefits, such as 40% less chemical waste (in virtual labs) and 4% of overall warming on the Earth by air travel, through effects of virtual collaboration (Ferhati et al. 2024; van Dinther et al., 2023).
   - Iterative Refinement with Education 5.0: Integrates Education 5.0 principles (e.g., emotional intelligence via sentiment analysis) to content and delivery improvement for increased learner wellbeing (Vistorte et al. 2024).

GEMSILA's layers, as illustrated in Fig. 1, interconnect through API-based interfaces to provide seamless data flow and content delivery. The feedback loops between the analytics layer and the other layers allow for real-time adjustments to learner needs and sustainability metrics. The architecture employs renewable energy protocols for AI and VR systems to neutralize their high energy demands (e.g., 1287 MWh for GPT-3 (Strubell et al. 2019)), thus complying with SDG 7 (Assembly 2015). The ethical aspects—from bias mitigation in the LLMs to privacy protection in the metaverse—are present throughout the reductions, with periodic checks to sustain fairness and transparency (Patel-Campillo and Salas García 2022). The framework's modularity equips GEMSILA for scalable applications in a wide variety of contexts—from academic STEAM education to industrial training for pipeline maintenance and climate modeling—thus addressing both educational and sustainability goals (Assembly 2015). The adaptability is driven by five interconnected layers—Data Ecosystem, AI-Driven Content Orchestration, Education 4.0 Integration, Metaverse Immersion, and Adaptive Analytics—and corresponding sublayers to ensure personalized, immersive, and sustainable learning experiences (Mulyani et al. 2025). The components of the framework, described in Table 2, leverage technologies such as AI, IoT, blockchain, VR/AR, and 5G to accomplish objectives such as collecting learner and industrial data, creating inclusive content, fostering twenty-first-century skills, immersive learning, and refining performance against sustainability metrics (Bondin and Zammit 2025; Dwivedi et al. 2022).

The GEMSILA nurtures sustainable learning across several domains. Generative AI, driven by LLMs, helps personalize content to increase engagement by 25% (Google AI: LearnLM: A family of models optimized for learning 2024) and further promotes the inclusivity aspect of SDG 4 (Assembly 2015). Virtual labs create a 40% reduction in chemical wastage (van Dinther et al. 2023), giving credence to an environmentally sustainable approach. Metaverse platforms promote collaboration on the sustainable design of cities across the world, cutting air travel-related emissions by 4% of global warming (Ferhati et al. 2024) and favoring SDG 10 (Assembly 2015). VR trains learners for green jobs in renewable energy and lowers costs (Acevedo et al. 2024), while AI provides a simulation for eco-friendly urban planning and resource optimization (Ferhati et al. 2024). Education 5.0 principles integrated through AI

Table 1 Summary of related work

Study	Focus	Key findings	Sustainability impact
Bondin et al. (Bondin and Zammit 2025)	Education 4.0	Enhances skills through AI, VR	Reduces resource use
Fan et al. (Fan et al. 2025)	Generative AI	Improves outcomes, personalizes	Supports inclusivity
Dwivedi et al. (Dwivedi et al. 2022)	Metaverse	Enables immersive learning	Minimizes infrastructure
United Nations (Assembly 2015)	SDGs	Education for sustainability	Guides technology alignment
Naranjo et al. (Naranjo et al. 2022)	Pipeline maintenance	VR training reduces rupture risks	Prevents environmental harm

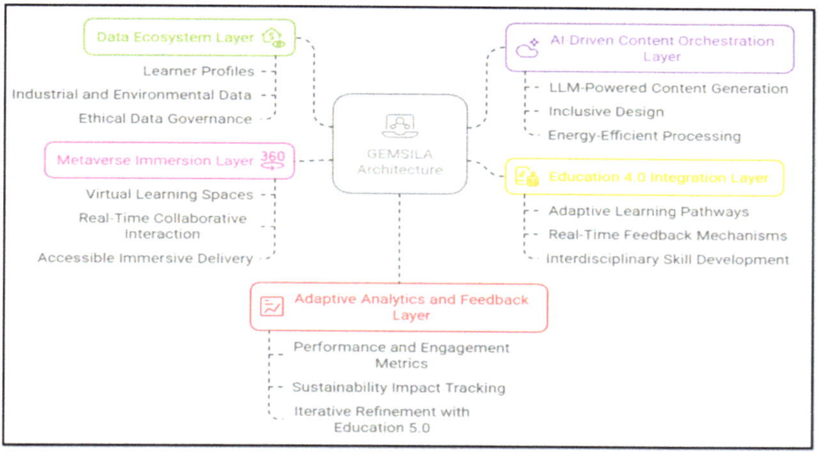

Fig. 1 GEMSILA architecture: layers and sub-layers

Table 2 GEMSILA components and objectives

Layer	Technologies	Objectives
Data ecosystem AI content orchestra- tion education 4.0 Integra- tion Metaverse immersion adaptive analytics	IoT, Blockchain LLMs, diffusion models AI analytics VR/AR, 5G AI, sentiment analysis	Collect learner/industrial data inclusive, adaptive content Foster twenty-first-century skills immersive, resource-efficient learn- ing refine performance, sustainability

tools for mental health also help augment learner well-being, thus nurturing social sustainability (Vistorte et al., 2024).

14.4 Practical Learning Use Cases

14.4.1 STEAM Use Cases

STEAM education under the GEMSILA discourse promotes interdisciplinary skills essential for sustainability through innovative applications of generative AI, Education 4.0, and the metaverse. In pipeline maintenance training, engineers learn corrosion inspection and pressure management of block-weighted pipelines vulnerable to ruptures—as recently shown with the 2023 Trans Mountain spill—by way of virtual reality (VR) simulations (CBC News: Trans Mountain pipeline spill in B.C. prompts environmental concerns 2023). Large language models simulated many

Table 3 STEAM Use cases and sustainability Impacts

Use case	Technology	Impact	Sustainability benefit
Pipeline maintenance	VR, GenAI (LLMs)	35% fewer errors	Environmental, economic
Climate modeling	Metaverse, AI	30% climate literacy	Environmental
Virtual science labs	VR, AI	40% less waste	Environmental
Engineering design	VR, AI	30% cost savings	Economic, environmental
Arts and creativity	Metaverse	Social engagement	Social
Math/coding	LLMs, Metaverse	20% problem-solving	Educational

realistic scenarios, including those of ruptures with sediments, whereby a 2023 study reported that maintenance errors dropped by 35%, averting ecological and economic damage (Naranjo et al. 2022; Acevedo et al. 2024). For climate modeling, LLMs and metaverse platforms would simulate the consequences of CO_2 emissions and allow students to strategize mitigation solutions, with VR visualizing scenarios like sea-level rise for developing problem-solving skills; a 2024 pilot recorded an improvement of 30% in climate literacy toward SDG 13 (Assembly 2015; Acevedo et al. 2024). Powering the virtual science lab that produces far less chemical waste, AI-enhanced assessments personalize learning scenarios, hugely engaging STEM students (van Dinther et al. 2023). Engineering design uses VR for prototyping with no material requirements, while AI has randomized the design toward environmental sustainability, thus saving 30% of costs reported in 2023 (Acevedo et al. 2024). The metaverse also provides a platform for arts and creativity through virtual galleries, promoting sustainable design such as eco-fashion, thus enhancing social sustainability (Roy et al. 2025). Additionally, LLMs design interactive mathematical and coding challenges, while the metaverse constructs visualizations of 3D geometry, with a pilot in 2024 reporting a 20% improve- ment in problem-solving skills (Google AI: LearnLM: A family of models optimized for learning 2024). All these applications will foster environmental, economic, and social sustainability through immersive, personalized, and resource-efficient learning experiences, as outlined in Table 3.

14.4.2 Healthcare Use Cases

Medical training for the future is going to be revolutionized by the GEMSILA framework because it combines generative AI with Education 4.0 and the metaverse to impart a sustainable, inclusive, highly effective learning experience that can respond to global health challenges. This is evident in surgical training, where virtual reality (VR) simulations powered by large language models (LLMs) generate a diverse, realistic patient case scenario where trainees can fine-tune their precision and decision-making skills in a high-stakes environment.

Table 4 Medicine use cases and sustainability Impacts

Use Case	Technology	Impact	Sustainability benefit
Surgical training	VR, GenAI (LLMs)	30% faster skills	Economic, social
Anatomy visualization	Metaverse, AI Metaverse, AI	Reduced physical models	Environmental
Telemedicine training	VR, GenAI (LLMs)	Improved access	Social
Mental health	VR, GenAI (LLMs)	25% empathy increase	Social

A study in 2023 showed that skills were acquired 30% faster, thereby supporting SDG 3's good health and wellbeing mandate through better clinical outcomes (Assembly 2015; Ntakakis et al. 2023). 3D metaverse models transform the visualization of anatomy into interactive, very detailed representations of human anatomy, as they massively reduce the demand for physical models and cadavers, thus saving resources and promoting environmental sustainability (van Dinther et al. 2023). Telemedicine training utilizes metaverse platforms for replicating remote diagnostic scenarios and equipping health professionals with the skills to deliver care in underserved and rural communities, thus improving access and social equity, largely as evidenced by implementations in the real world (Dwivedi et al. 2022). Moreover, mental health education is advanced through simulation scenarios in VR containing LLM-generated empathetic dialogues, leading to deeper emotional understanding among the therapists. A 2024 study found a 25% increase in therapist empathy, aligning with Education 5.0's emphasis on emotional intelligence and well-rounded learner wellbeing (Vistorte et al. 2024; Patel-Campillo and Salas García 2022). Personalized, yet immersive and resource-sparing, these applications thus improve the quality and accessibility of medical training and play a key part in economic efficiency, social inclusion, and stewardship of the environment to leave a more resilient and equity-fostering healthcare system, as stated in Table 4.

14.5 Challenges

The integration of generative AI, Education 4.0, and the metaverse through GEMSILA for sustainability in all learning practices will face many significant challenges on its way to equitable and effective realization. A few concerns are raised environmentally due to high energy demands from such AI and VR systems, with GPT-3, for instance, consuming 1287 MWh. However, green strategies in place include energy from renewable sources, model compression, and edge computing to further reduce carbon footprints, all in line with SDG 7 for affordable and clean energy (Assembly 2015; Strubell et al. 2019). Digital equity remains a significant issue, considering that the prices of VR headsets ($300–$1000) exclude most marginalized communities from access, while limited internet access adds to the exclusion. Possible inclusivity solutions, including subsidies for mobile augmented reality (AR) installations, need to be explored, along with coalitions with platforms such as Meta (Dwivedi et al. 2022; Patel-Campillo and Salas García 2022). In any democratic society, ethical and privacy issues, such as LLM biases and the data-gathering power of the metaverse, would harm equity and safety and thus warrant provisions for bias audits, transparency of AI models, and solid encryption for trust (Patel-Campillo and Salas García 2022). In addition, technical scalability issues, with delayed responsiveness impacting immersive simulations, can be considered an achievement by now due to the enhanced performance and reliability from the advancements in 5G connectivity and in cloud-edge architecture and standardized protocols (Radianti et al. 2020). Teacher preparedness is another hurdle toward acceptance since the lack of expertise in AI and immersive technology has resulted in closed doors to adoption; thus, capacity building and professional development for educators heavily rely on programs such as Google's AI courses (Mystakidis 2022). The acceptance of technology in education has been hampered by sociocultural barriers affecting GEMSILA. Community engagement and culturally contextualized content will be paramount to fostering acceptance and relevance to GEMSILA (Roy et al. 2025). By designing appropriate mitigation strategies to tackle the challenges listed in Table 5, the GEMSILA framework will take on a new shape and drive toward making sustainable, inclusive, and scalable educational systems that respond directly to global sustainability goals.

Table 5 Challenges and mitigation strategies

Challenge	Description	Mitigation strategy
Energy demands	High energy use	Renewable energy, efficient AI
Digital equity	Access barriers biases, privacy risks latency, interoperability lack of expertise resistance to tech	Subsidies, mobile AR
Ethical concerns	High energy use	Bias mitigation, encryption
Technical scalability	Access barriers biases, privacy risks latency, interoperability lack of expertise resistance to tech	5G, edge computing, standards professional development community engagement
Educator readiness	High energy use	Renewable energy, efficient AI
Sociocultural barriers	Access barriers biases, privacy risks latency, interoperability lack of expertise resistance to tech	Subsidies, mobile AR

14.6 Conclusion and Future Work

14.6.1 Conclusion

Generative AI, Education 4.0, and the metaverse integrated into a GEMSILA architecture transform education into learning ecosystems conducive to sustainable learning practices with SDG 4 objectives (Assembly 2015). Personalized content (resulting in up to 25% more engagement (Google AI: LearnLM: A family of models optimized for learning 2024)), immersive simulations (35% fewer pipeline errors (Acevedo et al. 2024)), and inclusive platforms (e.g., telemedicine (Dwivedi et al. 2022)) empower learners to address issues caused by the impacts of climate change and industrial inefficiencies. While climate modeling improves literacy (Acevedo et al. 2024), Education 5.0 assures well-being (Vistorte et al. 2024). Renewables should cater to these challenges of energy demands, digital equity, and ethical risks, encouraging various subsidies and transparent AI (Strubell et al. 2019; Patel-Campillo and Salas García 2022). The GEMSILA's data-driven, immersive approach evolves into a scalable roadmap in equitable education, driving environmental stewardship, social equity, and economic resilience.

14.6.2 Future Work

In the future, it will be essential to implement efforts under the GEMSILA framework to enhance its impact by focusing on specific initiatives aimed at increasing scale, sustainability, and inclusion within global education systems, as outlined in Table 6. To develop global policies that integrate AI and metaverse technologies into curriculum development, fund digital access, and improve technology literacy, we must ensure equal education as part of the SDG 4 commitment to quality education (Assembly 2015). Advancing energy-efficient AIs, such as quantum computers, alongside affordable and accessible VR and AR tools, will create a minimal environmental footprint, thus supporting sustainable development goals related to clean energy (Strubell et al. 2019). Applications that explore disaster preparedness through climate modeling, along with training in circular economy practices and mental health education, will address urgent global needs, contributing to SDGs 13 and 3 on Climate Action and Good Health, respectively (Assembly 2015; Vistorte et al. 2024). Building partnerships with community and industry leaders, such as Meta and Enbridge, will facilitate the development of training programs for green jobs, enhancing workforce readiness for sustainable industries (Dwivedi et al. 2022; Enbridge: Enbridge responds to natural gas transmission pipeline incident 2018). Longitudinal studies will be conducted to assess learning outcomes, measure environmentally beneficial impacts like reduced emissions from air travel,

Table 6 Future research directions

Direction	Focus	Expected Outcome
Policy	Curriculum integration	Equitable access
Technology	Green AI, low-cost VR	Reduced environmental impact
Research	Climate, healthcare applications	Address global challenges
Partnerships	Industry collaboration	Scalable solutions
Studies	Longitudinal impact analysis	Data-driven refinement
Education 5.0	Emotional intelligence	Holistic education
Community programs	Cultural relevance	Enhanced adoption

and examine other societal effects, thereby providing evidence for data-driven adjustments (Ferhati et al. 2024). Exploring areas of Education Integration 5.0, particularly the use of emotional intelligence and global well-being initiatives, will further enhance learner well-being and promote holistic education (Vistorte et al. 2024). Similarly, piloting community-driven initiatives with contextually relevant content will encourage uptake by addressing local needs and fostering engagement, thereby creating global relevance and effectiveness for the framework (Roy et al. 2025). These efforts will position GEMSILA as an agent of change toward sustainable, equitable, and innovative education.

Acknowledgments This study was supported by the Center for Research on Microelectronics and Nanotechnology (CRMN), Technopole of Sousse, Tunisia, and the RIADI laboratory, ENSI, Manouba University, Tunisia.

Disclosure of Interests The authors have no competing interests to declare that are relevant to the content of this article.

References

Acevedo, P., Magana, A. J., Benes, B., & Mousas, C. (2024). A systematic review of immersive virtual reality in STEM education: Advantages and disadvantages on learning and user experience. *IEEE Access, 12*, 189359–189386. https://doi.org/10.1109/ACCESS.2024.3489233

United Nations: Transforming our world: The 2030 agenda for sustainable development. UN general Assembly (2015). https://sdgs.un.org/2030agenda

Bondin, A., & Zammit, J. P. (2025). Education 4.0 for industry 4.0: A mixed reality framework for workforce readiness in manufacturing. *Multimodal Technologies and Interaction, 9*(5), 43. https://doi.org/10.3390/mti9050043

CBC News: Trans Mountain pipeline spill in B.C. prompts environmental concerns (2023). https://www.cbc.ca/news/canada/british-columbia/trans-mountain-pipeline-spill-2023.

Dwivedi, Y. K., et al. (2022). Metaverse beyond the hype: Multidisciplinary perspec- tives on emerging challenges, opportunities, and agenda for research, practice and policy. *International Journal of Information Management, 66*, 102542. https://doi.org/10.1016/j.ijinfomgt.2022.102542

Enbridge: Enbridge responds to natural gas transmission pipeline incident (2018). https://www.enbridge.com/media-center/media-statements/2018-prince- george-pipeline-incident.

Fan, L., Deng, K., & Liu, F. (2025). Educational impacts of generative artificial intelligence on learning and performance of engineering students in China. *Scientific Reports, 15*, 26521. https://doi.org/10.1038/s41598-025-06930-w

Ferhati, K., et al. (2024). Innovative design synthesis: AI-driven solutions for sustainable urban planning: Development, evaluation, and insights. *Journal of Contemporary Urban Affairs, 8*(1), 177–195. https://doi.org/10.25034/ijcua.2024.v8n1-10

Google AI: LearnLM: A family of models optimized for learning (2024). https://blog.google/technology/ai/learnlm-family-of-models-optimized-for- learning/.

Haleem, A., et al. (2022). Understanding the role of digital technologies in educa- tion: A review. *Sustainable Operations and Computers, 3*, 275–285. https://doi.org/10.1016/j.susoc.2022.05.004

Mulyani, H., et al.: Transforming education: Exploring the influence of generative AI on teaching performance. Cogent Education 12(1), 2448066 (2025). doi:https://doi.org/10.1080/2331186X.2024.2448066.

Mystakidis, S.: Metaverse. Encyclopedia 2(1), 486–497 (2022). doi:https://doi.org/10.3390/encyclopedia2010031.

Naranjo, J. E., et al. (2022). A scoping review of pipeline maintenance methodologies based on industry 4.0. *Sustainability, 14*(24), 16723. https://doi.org/10.3390/su142416723

Ntakakis, G., et al. (2023). Exploring the use of virtual reality in surgical education. *World Journal of Transplantation, 13*(2), 36–43. https://doi.org/10.5500/wjt.v13.i2.36

Patel-Campillo, A., & Salas García, V. B. (2022). Breaking the poverty cycle? Conditional cash transfers and higher education attainment. *International Journal of Educational Development, 92*, 102612. https://doi.org/10.1016/j.ijedudev.2022.102612

Radianti, J., et al. (2020). A systematic review of immersive virtual reality applications for higher education: Design elements, lessons learned, and research agenda. *Computers & Education, 147*, 103778. https://doi.org/10.1016/j.compedu.2019.103778

Roy, R., et al. (2025). Metaverse-based education for sustainable development and improving performance: Discussing the future research agenda. *Sustainable Futures, 10*, 101091. https://doi.org/10.1016/j.sftr.2025.101091

Strubell, E., Ganesh, A., McCallum, A.: Energy and policy considerations for deep learning in NLP. In: Proc. 57th Annual Meeting of the Association for Computational Linguistics, pp. 3645–3650 (2019). doi:https://doi.org/10.18653/v1/P19-1355

van Dinther, R., de Putter, L., & Pepin, B. (2023). Features of immersive virtual reality to support meaningful chemistry education. *Journal of Chemical Education, 100*(4), 1573–1583. https://doi.org/10.1021/acs.jchemed.2c00767

Vistorte, A.O.R., et al.: Integrating artificial intelligence to assess emotions in learning environments: A systematic literature review. Frontiers in Psychology 15,1387089 (2024). doi:https://doi.org/10.3389/fpsyg.2024.1387089.

Chapter 15
Future Education in the Metaverse

Laith Asabeh

Abstract The integration of Virtual Reality (VR) into twenty-first-century education has opened new frontiers for immersive and interactive learning experiences. This paper explores the transformative potential of VR in education, focusing on its applications, challenges, and future prospects within the metaverse. We examine the role of VR in enhancing teaching methods, collaborative learning, and assessment in virtual environments. Additionally, we discuss the integration of augmented reality (AR), mixed reality (MR) and extended reality (XR) in education, alongside emerging technologies such as digital twins, 3D scanning, and simulation modeling. The paper also highlights the potential of VR in specialized fields like healthcare education, where virtual patient interactions and medical simulations are revolutionizing training. Finally, we address the challenges of implementing VR in classrooms, including technological, pedagogical, and ethical considerations, and propose solutions to overcome these barriers. The paper concludes with a vision for the future of education in the metaverse, emphasizing the need for collaboration between academia and industry to realize the full potential of immersive learning technologies.

Keywords Virtual reality · Metaverse · Twenty-first-century education · Immersive learning · Digital twins · Collaborative learning · Healthcare education · Simulation modeling · Augmented reality · Extended reality

15.1 Introduction

- Virtual Reality in twenty-first-Century Education.

The twenty-first century has ushered in a transformative era for education, characterized by the rapid integration of advanced technologies into teaching and learning

L. Asabeh (✉)
Artificial Intelligence, An-Najah National University, Nablus, Palestine
e-mail: laythas55@gmail.com

M. Abed et al. (eds.), *Metaverse and Artificial Intelligence in Education for a Sustainable Society*, Future Education and Learning Spaces,
https://doi.org/10.1007/978-981-95-8852-7_15

processes. Among these technologies, Virtual Reality (VR) stands out as a revolutionary tool that has the potential to redefine how education is delivered and experienced. VR creates immersive, interactive, and engaging learning environments that transcend the limitations of traditional classrooms. By enabling students to explore complex concepts, conduct experiments, and interact with virtual objects, VR opens up new possibilities for experiential learning that were previously unimaginable.

This section delves deeper into the role of VR in twenty-first-century education, exploring its applications, benefits, and the ways it is democratizing access to high-quality learning experiences.

- The Evolution of Virtual Reality in Education.

Virtual Reality, once a concept relegated to science fiction, has become a tangible and increasingly accessible technology in recent years. The development of affordable VR headsets, such as the Oculus Rift, HTC Vive, and Google Cardboard, has made it possible for educational institutions to incorporate VR into their curricula. Early adopters of VR in education recognized its potential to create immersive simulations that allow students to experience environments and scenarios that would be otherwise inaccessible due to cost, safety, or logistical constraints.

For example, VR has been used to simulate historical events, allowing students to "witness" pivotal moments in history firsthand. In science education, VR enables students to explore the human body at a cellular level, conduct virtual dissections, or travel through the solar system. These experiences not only enhance understanding but also foster a sense of curiosity and engagement that traditional textbooks and lectures often fail to achieve.

- Applications of VR Across Disciplines.

VR's versatility allows it to enrich a broad range of educational disciplines, from STEM fields to the arts, vocational training, and special education. In STEM education, students use VR to explore the human body in 3D, simulate surgeries, visualize chemical reactions, and design engineering structures—all within immersive, risk-free environments (Dalgarno & Lee, 2010). Humanities and social sciences also benefit, as VR transports learners to historical sites, geographical landmarks, or literary settings, fostering contextual understanding and cultural awareness. In vocational fields like healthcare, aviation, and automotive training, VR enables learners to safely practice procedures and maneuvers in realistic simulations. Additionally, VR supports special education by offering personalized, controlled experiences for learners with disabilities—for example, helping students with autism practice social interactions. By spanning multiple domains, VR amplifies engagement, accessibility, and hands-on learning across the educational spectrum.

- Key Benefits of VR in Learning.

Virtual Reality offers transformative advantages that enhance both teaching and learning outcomes across diverse educational contexts. Immersive environments make abstract content tangible, boosting student engagement and motivation through interactive learning (Chen & Liu, 2020). By engaging multiple senses, VR promotes experiential learning, resulting in stronger memory retention and deeper conceptual understanding. It also enables access to environments and scenarios that would otherwise be limited by cost, safety, or geography—such as deep-sea ecosystems or outer space missions.

Adaptive VR systems support personalized learning by tailoring content and pacing to individual progress and learning styles. Additionally, VR enhances collaborative and remote learning by creating virtual classrooms where students can engage in group work and real-time discussions regardless of physical location (Bower et al., 2017). In specialized fields like healthcare, aviation, and engineering, VR provides risk-free practice environments to simulate complex or hazardous procedures, improving skills and decision-making under safe conditions.

In essence, VR empowers educators to deliver more inclusive, effective, and engaging learning experiences, reinforcing its potential as a transformative tool in twenty-first-century education.

- Democratizing Education Through VR.

One of the most significant advantages of VR is its potential to democratize education by providing access to high-quality learning experiences regardless of geographical or socioeconomic barriers. In many parts of the world, students lack access to well-equipped schools, qualified teachers, and educational resources. VR can bridge this gap by delivering immersive and interactive learning experiences to students in remote or underserved areas.

For example, a student in a rural village can use VR to attend a virtual classroom led by a world-class educator, participate in virtual field trips, or conduct experiments in a virtual laboratory. This not only enhances the quality of education but also empowers students to pursue their academic and career aspirations.

Moreover, VR can support lifelong learning by providing opportunities for individuals to acquire new skills and knowledge throughout their lives. This is particularly important in a rapidly changing world where continuous learning is essential for career advancement and personal growth.

15.2 Challenges and Considerations

Despite its potential, implementing VR in education presents several challenges. First, the high cost of VR hardware, software, and the supporting infrastructure remains a barrier, particularly for underfunded institutions. Even with declining prices, many schools still struggle with access to high-performance computers, VR headsets, and stable internet connectivity. Second, content development poses another hurdle—creating engaging, curriculum-aligned VR materials is time-intensive and often requires collaboration between educators and developers. Third, health and safety concerns such as motion sickness, eye strain, and fatigue must be addressed through careful design and moderated usage. Ethical considerations are equally critical, involving issues like data privacy, appropriate content, and the risk of excessive reliance on virtual environments. To ensure effective and equitable integration of VR, educational institutions must adopt comprehensive policies, invest in training, and collaborate with stakeholders to navigate these technical, pedagogical, and ethical complexities (Anderson et al., 2022).

15.2.1 Challenges of Using Virtual Reality in the Classroom

While Virtual Reality (VR) holds immense promise for transforming education, its implementation in classrooms presents a range of challenges supported by recent studies. The high cost of VR hardware and software, such as headsets and high-performance computers, remains a significant barrier for many institutions, particularly in low-income or rural areas. Educators also face a steep learning curve, often lacking the training needed to integrate VR effectively into curricula, which underscores the need for dedicated professional development. Extended use of VR has been associated with physiological issues like motion sickness and visual fatigue, making session duration and content design critical factors for safe implementation. Technical limitations, including poor internet connectivity, inadequate IT support, and lack of interoperability between platforms, further hinder VR adoption. Moreover, creating immersive, curriculum-aligned content demands substantial time and interdisciplinary collaboration between educators and developers (Dalgarno & Lee, 2010). Ethical concerns regarding student data privacy, the psychological effects of virtual immersion, and content appropriateness call for clear institutional policies and responsible usage guidelines (Anderson et al., 2022). Finally, the digital divide continues to exacerbate educational inequities, with many students lacking access to the necessary devices and reliable internet at home (Bower et al., 2017).

Addressing these barriers requires systemic investment in infrastructure, public-private partnerships, inclusive funding programs, and open educational resource sharing to enable equitable access to immersive learning.

While the challenges of using VR in the classroom are significant, they are not insurmountable. By addressing these obstacles through strategic planning, collaboration, and investment, educators can unlock the full potential of VR to create immersive, engaging, and equitable learning experiences. As VR technology continues to evolve, it will be essential to remain vigilant in addressing these challenges to ensure that all students can benefit from the transformative power of virtual reality.

While the challenges of using VR in the classroom are significant, they are not insurmountable. By addressing these obstacles through strategic planning, collaboration, and investment, educators can unlock the full potential of VR to create immersive, engaging, and equitable learning experiences. As VR technology continues to evolve, it will be essential to remain vigilant in addressing these challenges to ensure that all students can benefit from the transformative power of virtual reality. While the challenges of using VR in the classroom are significant, they are not insurmountable. By addressing these obstacles through strategic planning, collaboration, and investment, educators can unlock the full potential of VR to create immersive, engaging, and equitable learning experiences. As VR technology continues to evolve, it will be essential to remain vigilant in addressing these challenges to ensure that all students can benefit from the transformative power of virtual reality.

15.3 Future Education in the Metaverse

The metaverse—a shared virtual environment blending physical and digital realities—holds transformative promise for education by enabling real-time collaboration, immersive learning, and enhanced engagement through technologies like virtual and augmented reality. It facilitates experiential learning through interactive simulations, virtual laboratories, and historical recreations that surpass the capabilities of traditional classrooms. Moreover, it expands access to lifelong learning opportunities, allowing individuals to acquire skills beyond formal academic systems. However, realizing the educational potential of the metaverse requires addressing key challenges, including the high cost of VR hardware, the need for robust internet infrastructure, and the digital literacy gap. Concerns around accessibility, inclusivity, data privacy, and ethical use also demand thoughtful policy frameworks and collaborative efforts between public and private sectors. With strategic planning and technological innovation, the metaverse can become a powerful tool for inclusive and sustainable education.

15.3.1 The Potential for Using Virtual Reality in the Classroom: Expanding Possibilities

Virtual Reality (VR) offers transformative opportunities to enhance education across disciplines by creating immersive, interactive learning experiences that overcome the limitations of traditional teaching methods. In STEM education, VR facilitates hands-on learning by simulating experiments, visualizing biological and chemical processes, and enabling virtual prototyping, thereby supporting conceptual understanding and technical skills (Dalgarno & Lee, 2010). Mathematics concepts such as geometry and data visualization also become more accessible through 3D interaction. In the humanities, VR fosters empathy and contextual learning by allowing students to explore historical events, cultural landmarks, and real-world social scenarios (Bower et al., 2017). Personalized learning is supported through adaptive systems that tailor content and pacing to individual needs, offering customized experiences and real-time feedback. VR also promotes collaborative learning via shared virtual environments, enabling students to interact and problem-solve regardless of geographic barriers (Chen & Liu, 2020). In fields like medicine, aviation, and engineering, VR creates safe environments for skill development and error-based learning without real-world consequences. By integrating these capabilities, VR expands educational access, engagement, and effectiveness, reinforcing its potential as a powerful tool for future learning environments.

15.3.2 The Future of VR in Education

As VR technology continues to evolve, its role in education is expected to expand. Future developments may include integration with Artificial Intelligence (AI), enabling personalized learning experiences. The growing scope of the metaverse—a collective virtual shared space—offers immersive environments where students and educators interact in real-time, enhancing collaborative learning (Anderson et al., 2022). Additionally, increased accessibility and global collaboration will allow broader reach across geographical and socioeconomic boundaries (Bower et al., 2017).

With enhanced collaboration tools and cross-cultural exchanges, the metaverse fosters global citizenship while offering customized educational pathways. However, to fully realize these potentials, educators and institutions must overcome barriers related to cost, accessibility, and ethical use of data. Advancements in affordable VR hardware and AI-driven analytics will support this shift, ensuring inclusive and effective learning systems.

Ultimately, the transformation of education through VR and the metaverse will depend on continuous innovation, investment in infrastructure, and strategic collaboration among educators, technologists, and policymakers.

15.3.3 Learning Paradigms

An understanding of the existing learning paradigms is essential for performing an analysis of the current state of VR applications in higher education. Thus, we introduce the main ideas behind the existing learning paradigms. Literature distinguishes between behaviorism, cognitivism, and constructivism. Other scholars also include experiential learning to this list and, recently, connectivism has been introduced as a new learning paradigm. Each learning paradigm has developed various theories about educational goals and outcomes. Each of these theories also offers a different perspective on the learning goals, motivational process, learning performance, transfer of knowledge process, the role of emotions, and implications for the teaching methods.

Behaviorism assumes that knowledge is a repertoire of behavioral responses to environmental stimuli. Thus, learning is considered to be a passive absorption of a predefined body of knowledge by the learner. According to this paradigm, learning requires repetition and learning motivation is extrinsic, involving positive and negative reinforcement. The teacher serves as a role model who transfers the correct behavioral response.

Cognitivism understands the acquisition of knowledge systems as actively constructed by learners based on pre-existing prior knowledge structures. Hence, the proponents of cognitivism view learning as an active, constructive, and goal-oriented process, which involves active assimilation and accommodation of new information to an existing body of knowledge. The learning motivation is intrinsic and learners should be capable of defining their own goals and motivating themselves to learn. Learning is supported by providing an environment that encourages discovery and assimilation or accommodation of knowledge, RN23. Cognitivism views learning as more complex cognitive processes such as thinking, problem-solving, verbal information, concept formation, and information processing. It addresses the issues of how information is received, organized, stored, and retrieved by the mind. Knowledge acquisition is a mental activity consisting of internal coding and structuring by the learner. Digital media, including VR-based learning can strengthen cognitivist learning design. Cognitive strategies such as schematic organization, analogical reasoning, and algorithmic problem solving will fit learning tasks requiring an increased level of processing, e.g. classifications, rule or procedural executions, and be supported by digital media.

Constructivism posits that learning is an active, constructive process. Learners serve as information constructors who actively construct their subjective representations and comprehensions of reality. New information is linked to the prior knowledge of each learner and, thus, mental representations are subjective. Therefore, constructivists argue that the instructional learning design has to provide macro and micro support to assist the learners in constructing their knowledge and engaging them for meaningful learning. The macro support tools include related cases, information resources, cognitive tools, conversation, and collaboration tools, and social or contextual support. A micro strategy makes use of multimedia and principles such as the spatial contiguity principle, coherence principle, modality principle, and redundancy principle to strengthen the learning process. VR-based learning fits the constructivist learning design. Constructivist strategies such as situated learning, cognitive apprenticeships, and social negotiation are appropriate for learning tasks demanding high levels of processing, for instance, heuristic problem solving, personal selection, and monitoring of cognitive strategies.

15.4 Research Objectives

This study investigates the transformative role of immersive technologies—specifically Virtual Reality (VR), Augmented Reality (AR), Artificial Intelligence (AI), and blockchain—in reshaping the educational landscape. A primary aim is to explore how VR applications currently enhance learning outcomes by increasing engagement, improving comprehension, and fostering higher retention. It also examines the major challenges to classroom adoption, including infrastructure limitations, cost, and privacy concerns, while proposing scalable solutions like affordable VR systems and targeted teacher training. Another objective is to evaluate the metaverse's potential in supporting collaborative, personalized, and assessment-rich learning environments through AI-driven feedback and real-time interactions (Bower et al., 2017). This includes analyzing how tools such as digital twins, 3D scanning, and simulations can enrich experiential learning, particularly in fields like science and engineering (Dalgarno & Lee, 2010).

The study also focuses on the role of VR in specialized sectors like healthcare and aviation education, assessing its effectiveness in skill development and decision-making under simulated high-stakes conditions. It aims to offer a strategic roadmap for integrating immersive technologies into curricula in ways that uphold inclusivity and access (Anderson et al., 2022). Furthermore, the research evaluates the cognitive and psychological impacts of VR, including motivation, critical thinking, and memory retention (Chen & Liu, 2020). AI's role in customizing learning experiences based on student performance and preferences is another key focus, alongside ethical issues like data privacy and the digital divide. Lastly, it investigates the alignment of metaverse-based education with workforce demands, including the design of vocational training modules that simulate real-world professional environments.

15.5 Research Problems and Solutions

Integrating Virtual Reality (VR) into education presents a range of challenges that impact accessibility, pedagogy, and ethical implementation. A primary concern is the high cost of VR hardware, software, and necessary computing infrastructure, particularly for schools in low-income regions. Strategic partnerships with technology companies, government subsidies, and the use of cost-effective alternatives—such as smartphone-based headsets and cloud-based platforms—can alleviate financial barriers.

Another pressing issue is the lack of educator training in VR technology. Many teachers lack experience in designing and delivering immersive content.

Professional development initiatives, including workshops, online certification programs, and peer collaboration networks, are essential for building educator confidence and capacity (Chen & Liu, 2020).

Ethical and psychological concerns also require careful attention. Risks include data privacy violations, inappropriate content, and negative psychological effects such as motion sickness or social disengagement. Schools must establish ethical frameworks and train educators to implement safe and age-appropriate VR learning strategies (Anderson et al., 2022).

Curriculum integration remains a challenge, as some educators worry that VR may distract from core objectives. To counter this, VR content must be aligned with educational standards through collaborative design involving teachers and developers, enabling VR to complement rather than replace traditional methods (Dalgarno & Lee, 2010).

Lastly, the digital divide continues to limit access, especially in underserved communities. Addressing this requires government funding, nonprofit support, and the establishment of community VR labs and mobile access solutions (Bower et al., 2017). By resolving these barriers with targeted solutions, VR can fulfill its promise as a powerful and inclusive educational tool.

15.6 Research Design

In the following section, we describe our research design, which consists of the method, review process, and classification framework.

15.6.1 Research Method and Research Questions

Consensus about the design space of VR-based teaching would significantly aid future developments. To this end, we apply a systematic mapping approach to the literature by extracting key information from documents indexed in four scientific digital libraries. Our research aims to obtain an overview of the relationship between application domains and learning contents and also between design elements and learning contents. Based on our results, we propose an agenda for future research and first recommendations for the future development of VR applications for higher education.

Systematic literature reviews, as proposed by [45] or [90], have been widely used as an approach to obtain comprehensive insights into a specific research domain. Furthermore, to answer questions about the structure of a broad field, relevant topics within this field, as well as research trends, Kitchenham et al. (2009) recommend using a mapping study, which is a specific form of a systematic literature review. In contrast to a standard systematic literature review, which is driven by a particular research question, [45] point out that a mapping study reviews a broader topic and classifies the primary research papers within the specific domain under study. The research questions suggested in such a study have a high level of abstraction and include issues such as: what sub-topics have been discussed, what empirical methods have been used, and what sub-topics have adequate empirical studies to support a more detailed systematic review. An example of applying the mapping study approach to a literature review is the work of [91].

To accomplish the objective of this study, we propose several research questions that focus on systematizing and structuring the research on VR applications for higher education. They are listed in Table 15.1.

Table 15.1 Research questions of this study

research question (RQ)
RQ1 what types of immersive VR technologies are used in higher education?
RQ2 which research designs, data collection methods, and data analysis methods are applied to examine the use of immersive VR in higher education?
RQ3 what learning theories are applied to examine the use of immersive VR in higher education?
RQ4 which research methods and techniques are applied to evaluate the learning outcomes of immersive VR usage in higher education?
RQ5 in what higher education application domains are immersive VR applications used?
RQ6 for which learning contents in higher education are immersive VR applications used?
RQ7 what design elements are included in immersive VR applications for higher education?
RQ8 what is the relationship between application domains and learning contents of immersive VR applications for higher education?
RQ9 what is the relationship between learning contents and design elements of immersive VR applications for higher education?

15.6.2 Review Process and Literature Search Method

Our review process included procedures, considerations, and decisions that lead to a consolidated list of articles to be reviewed in-depth. We conducted a systematic mapping study, as suggested by [91], to obtain an overview of the field. The overall review process, from defining the review scope to identifying a final selection of articles for analysis, is illustrated in Fig. 15.1. In total, the article review process consisted of seven steps.

15.7 Definition of the Review Scope, Keywords, and Research Questions

While the research questions have been described in Table 15.1, defining the scope and keywords was quite challenging because, in fact, VR research is extensive and the number of publications in this area is abundant. We followed the procedures, as suggested by Webster and Watson (2002), starting by selecting keyword search strategies in relevant digital libraries. These relevant libraries for our search were the IEEE Xplore Digital Library, ProQuest, Scopus, and Web of Science. IEEE Xplore is a rich repository that covers the domains of computer science, information technology, engineering, multimedia, and other software-related publications. ProQuest comprises articles in the areas of medicine, surgery, and nursing sciences. Scopus provides a wide range of publication domains, covering the fields of technology, natural sciences, information technologies, social sciences, and medicine. The Web of Science indexes social science, arts, and humanities spheres. We were aware of other databases, such as the ACM digital library, Science Direct, JSTOR, EBSCO,

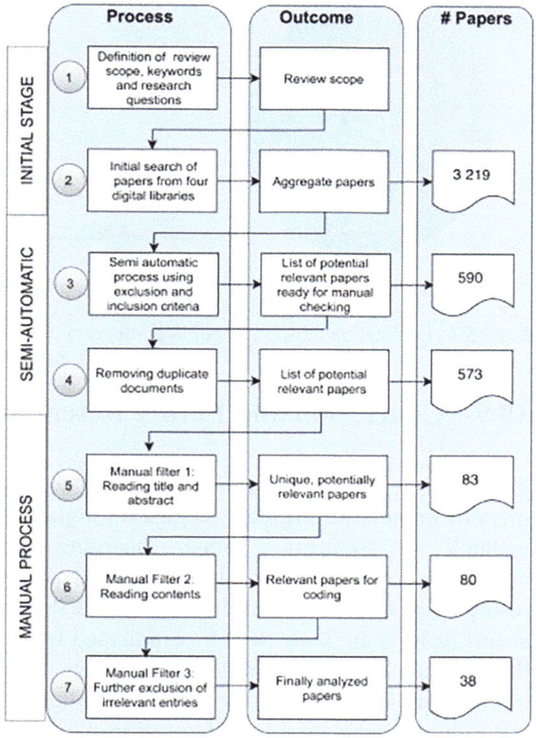

Fig. 15.1 Review process

and Taylor & Francis, but we expected most of the articles they contain to already be a part of the databases we selected. This expectation was confirmed by exemplary cross-check.

15.8 Results and Analysis

In the following section, the results of the systematic mapping study are described according to the research questions (see Table 15.1, p. 10). Of the 38 articles included in our analysis, 68% originated from conferences, whereas 32% were published in journals (cf. Figure 15.2). Our search window was 2016–2018. However, we also included one paper that was issued in 2015 because the acceptance for the online publication of this paper was 2015 but the actual journal publication date was in 2016. The number of journal publications in 2018 was remarkable, indicating an increasing scholarly interest in VR for higher education.

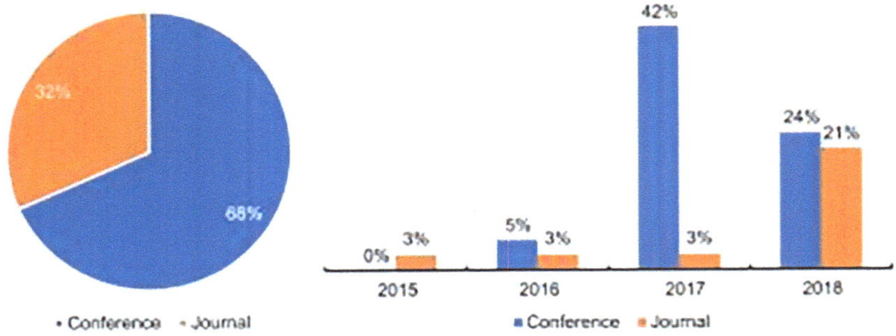

Fig. 15.2 Publication outlets and publication years of the 38 selected papers

15.9 Conclusion and Future Research

In this article, a systematic mapping study was conducted, focusing on the employment of immersive VR technologies for higher education purposes. Immersive VR technologies, application domains, learning contents, and design elements being used in recent literature on educational VR applications were examined. The review results show that the interest in immersive VR technologies for educational purposes seems to be quite high, which is indicated by the variety of the research domains that have applied this technology in teaching. The majority of authors treated VR as a promising learning tool for higher education, however, the maturity of the use of VR in higher education is still questionable. Technologies described in most of the reviewed articles remained in an experimental state and were mostly tested in terms of their performance and usability. This article also reveals that very few design-oriented studies constructed their VR applications based on a specific learning theory, which serves as technical development guidance. Moreover, few papers thoroughly describe how VR-based teaching can be adopted in the teaching curriculum.

These facts can hinder the rapid adoption of immersive VR technologies into teaching on a regular basis. We acknowledge that, in some domains such as engineering and computer science, certain VR applications have been used on a regular basis to teach certain skills, especially those that require declarative knowledge and procedural–practical knowledge. However, in most domains, VR is still experimental and its usage is not systematic or based on best practices. This paper pinpoints key gaps that serve to provide insights for future improvements, especially for VR application developers and teachers in higher education.

Our work will continue with a market analysis of VR technologies that could be employed in higher education as well as a survey of educators. We aim to continue advancing the field now that we have understood its low-maturity but nevertheless promising nature.

One more line is needed for this reference, as a result of Springer's adjustment.

Please make sure that all your sources are correctly listed in the reference section. Do not include references to pieces of work that are not connected with your paper.

The references section at the end of this paper shows a sample reference list with entries for journal articles (Ahn et al., 2014), an LNCS chapter (Anderson et al., 2022), a book (Araya, 2019), proceedings without editors (Bailenson, 2018; Bower et al., 2017), as well as a URL (Chen & Liu, 2020). Please note that Springer proceedings are cited with their publication acronyms and volume numbers.

References

Ahn, S. J., Bailenson, J. N., & Park, D. (2014). Short-and long-term effects of embodied experiences in immersive virtual environments on environmental locus of control and behavior. *Computers in Human Behavior, 39*, 235–245.

Anderson, J., Rainie, L., & Vogels, E. (2022). *The Metaverse in 2040*. Pew Research Center.

Araya, R. (2019). How virtual reality affects conceptual change in STEM learning. *Educational Technology Research and Development, 67*(2), 219–241.

Bailenson, J. N. (2018). *Experience on demand: What virtual reality is, how it works, and what it can do. W. W.* Norton & Company.

Bower, M., Lee, M. J. W., & Dalgarno, B. (2017). Collaborative learning across physical and virtual worlds: Factors supporting and constraining learners in a blended reality environment. *British Journal of Educational Technology, 48*(2), 407–430.

Chen, C. J., & Liu, P. (2020). Exploring the impact of virtual reality on learning engagement and motivation. *Journal of Educational Technology & Society, 23*(3), 25–36.

Dalgarno, B., & Lee, M. J. W. (2010). What are the learning affordances of 3D virtual environments? *British Journal of Educational Technology, 41*(1), 10–32.

Part IV
Metaverse and AI for an Ethical and Inclusive Learning

Chapter 16
AI+AR Serious Games for Autism Intervention: A Design-Centric Approach

Jingwen Su, Zefeng Wang, Jean-Marie Nianga, and Laurent Peyrodie

Abstract The utilization of Artificial Intelligence (AI)-guided Augmented Reality (AR) serious games offers a novel approach to the education of Autism Spectrum Disorder (ASD) by providing personalized, immersive, and interactive learning experiences. Conversely, traditional ASD interventions frequently exhibit a lack of adaptability and engagement. In contrast, AI+AR serious games enable dynamic learning pathways that are tailored to individual cognitive and social needs. This study explores the design principles, adaptive mechanisms, and feasibility of AI+AR serious games for ASD intervention. The analysis of diverse game structures and interaction models emphasizes their capacity to enhance engagement, cultivate social communication, and deliver real-time feedback. Notwithstanding the substantial advantages exhibited by AI+AR serious games, challenges persist regarding accessibility, ethical considerations, and large-scale implementation. This research offers both theoretical and practical insights into their effectiveness and future applications in ASD education.

Keywords Artificial intelligence (AI) · Augmented Reality (AR). · Serious Games. · Autism Spectrum Disorder (ASD). · Game-Based Learning.

J. Su
Shanghai Ucardstore Information Technology Ltd, Shanghai, China

Z. Wang (✉) · J.-M. Nianga
ASIR (Institute-Association of intelligent systems and robotics), Rueil-Malmaison, France
e-mail: zefeng.wang@zjhu.edu.cn

Z. Wang
Huzhou Normal University, Zhejiang, China

L. Peyrodie
ICL, Junia, Université Catholique de Lille, Lille, France

M. Abed et al. (eds.), *Metaverse and Artificial Intelligence in Education for a Sustainable Society*, Future Education and Learning Spaces,
https://doi.org/10.1007/978-981-95-8852-7_16

16.1 Introduction

Autism Spectrum Disorder (ASD) is a neuro-developmental condition that results in impaired social communication abilities, behavioural patterns, and cognitive development. The global prevalence of ASD is increasing, which poses significant challenges to society and families (Stasolla et al., 2025). Individuals with ASD exhibit notable deficits in social interaction, emotional expression, and executive functioning. Conventional educational approaches often fail to address their special needs, particularly in terms of social skill development and cognitive flexibility training (Lamnai & Elmhouti, 2025). Current ASD interventions are primarily based on the principles of Applied Behavior Analysis (ABA), Structured Teaching (ST), and Naturalistic Developmental Behavioral Interventions (NDBI) (Kotsi et al., 2025). While these methods have demonstrated some success in enhancing social communication skills, their heavy reliance on manual guidance, absence of personalized adaptation, and high implementation costs hinder their widespread adoption (De Carvalho et al., 2024). Furthermore, traditional intervention approaches are typically confined to learning environments, resulting in limited transfer of acquired skills to real-world settings.

In this context, Serious Games—an innovative learning medium combining education and entertainment—have emerged as a valuable tool for ASD intervention. By employing gamification strategies, serious games enhance children's learning motivation while providing virtual interactive environments where ASD children can develop social skills, executive functions, and cognitive abilities in low-anxiety scenarios. However, conventional serious games still face limitations such as rigid learning pathways that lack adaptability to individual ASD characteristics (Lyu et al., 2024). Consequently, enhancing game adaptability, improving immersive experiences, and optimizing social interaction mechanisms have become critical research directions in ASD serious game design.

Recent years have seen a surge of interest in the application of augmented reality (AR) technology in the domain of education for individuals with ASD (Honorato et al., 2024) AR combines virtual components with physical environments, providing ASD children with more intuitive and immersive interactions while mitigating the risks of sensory overload associated with fully virtual environments (e.g. virtual reality [VR]). For instance, research has demonstrated the efficacy of AR-based social training games in simulating social interactions within real-world contexts, thereby enhancing the adaptability of ASD children to actual social scenarios (Caruso et al., 2023). In comparison to traditional screen-based games, AR-enhanced learning models have been shown to strengthen spatial cognition, deepen environmental understanding, and enhance social skill application in real-world contexts (Mihova et al., 2022).

Concurrently, the integration of AI has significantly enhanced the adaptability and personalization of AR serious games. AI-powered gaming systems have the capacity to dynamically adjust game difficulty, task settings, and feedback mechanisms based on real-time behavioural data from children with ASD, thereby enabling precise,

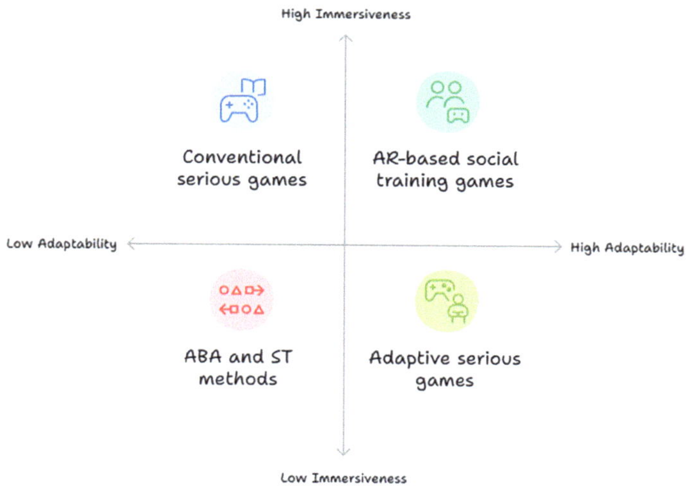

Fig. 16.1 Comparative analysis of ASD intervention strategies

personalized learning experiences (Almurashi et al., 2022), as shown in Fig. 16.1. Studies have demonstrated that machine learning models are capable of analysing behavioural patterns during gameplay to predict learning preferences and automatically optimize intervention strategies, thereby increasing learning efficiency (Paneru, 2024). However, the majority of current AR serious games still employ fixed task structures, thus failing to fully exploit the potential of AI to enhance adaptive capabilities (Abd El-Sattar, 2025). This emphasizes the critical need for research on optimizing AI-AR integration in ASD intervention applications.

Despite the considerable potential of AR and AI in the domain of education for individuals with ASD, there is a paucity of systematic research on the diverse game design principles, interaction models, and learning feedback mechanisms that are relevant to this field. For instance, there is a lack of empirical validation of the comparative advantages of structured learning versus open-ended exploration in ASD serious games, while the effects of different task-driven approaches (e.g. narrative-driven scenarios vs. goal-oriented tasks) on learning outcomes for children with ASD remain unclear (Zhao et al., 2024).

Furthermore, the potential of AI to make real-time in-game adjustments to optimize learning pathways and social interaction capabilities in ASD children is an area that requires further investigation (Sarker et al., 2021). The present study systematically investigates the design and application of AI-enhanced AR serious games for ASD intervention, with a focus on evaluating the impact of different design strategies, interaction models, and feedback mechanisms on learning experiences. The study employs a rigorous comparative approach, contrasting design philosophies (structured vs. exploratory), interaction paradigms (task-driven vs. narrative-driven), and feedback systems (rule-based vs. AI-adaptive). This research endeavour aims to establish a theoretical foundation for AR serious games in ASD intervention, while

Fig. 16.2 Mapping AR game design strategies for ASD education

concurrently providing actionable design guidelines to enhance learning efficacy, as shown in Fig. 16.2.

The structure of the paper is as follows: it is organized into five sequentially structured chapters. Chap. 1 introduces the research background, analyses existing challenges in ASD intervention, and proposes the potential role of AI+AR serious games in optimizing intervention strategies, alongside clarifying research objectives and scientific significance. Section 2 reviews traditional ASD intervention methodologies and examines recent advancements in AI and AR for digital education, with a critical analysis of current applications and limitations of serious games in ASD contexts to establish theoretical groundwork. The third section details the proposed AI-powered AR serious game design framework, including diversified interaction modes, personalized learning pathway optimization strategies, and intelligent feedback adjustment mechanisms, ensuring scientific rigor and practical efficacy. The fourth section focuses on feasibility analysis, employing experimental designs to evaluate the impact of different game models on ASD children's learning performance and comparing outcomes with traditional interventions. Finally, Section 5 concludes with research findings and an exploration of future directions.

16.2 Literature Review

16.2.1 Autism Spectrum Disorder and Learning Characteristics

Autism Spectrum Disorder (ASD) is a neurodevelopmental condition characterized by impairments in social communication, behavioural patterns, and cognitive development. Children with ASD exhibit distinct cognitive functional anomalies during learning, including attention deficits, executive dysfunction, and challenges in information processing (Mitsea et al., 2025). Research indicates that conventional ASD educational approaches, such as Structured Teaching and Applied Behavior Analysis (ABA), can partially improve social interaction and self-care skills, yet they often lack dynamic adaptability to individual needs (Chaidi et al., 2024). Recent studies have focused on developing more interactive and personalized ASD educational interventions, with Serious Games emerging as a promising tool (Habibi et al., 2025). Compared to conventional teaching methods, serious games enhance learning motivation through gamification and optimize learning processes via real-time feedback systems. Notably, serious games integrated with Artificial Intelligence (AI) and Augmented Reality (AR) technologies have the capacity to deliver personalized content and interactive experiences that are tailored to the behavioural patterns and cognitive profiles of children with ASD, thereby improving learning outcomes (Ahmad et al., 2025).

16.2.2 Serious Games in Autism Education

Serious games are gamified applications designed for educational, training, or rehabilitation purposes, grounded in theoretical frameworks such as Constructivist Learning Theory and Reinforcement Learning Theory (Adako & Adeusi, 2024). In the field of ASD education, their primary goal is to simulate real-world social interactions within a low-stress game environment, enabling children to practise social skills and reinforce cognitive training through repetitive tasks (Lan et al., 2025). Several studies have explored the application of serious games in ASD education. For instance, The Social Express simulates daily social scenarios to assist children with ASD in practising eye contact and emotional expression (Abd-Elrazaq et al., 2022). Another game, Emotion Trainer, incorporates facial expression recognition technology to teach children with ASD how to identify and express emotions (Barua et al., 2022). The design strategy of serious games significantly impacts learning outcomes for children with ASD. Task-oriented games focus on goal completion and behavioural correction, while narrative-based games use contextual storytelling to guide social skill development (Sideraki & Rassias, 2023). Evidence suggests that task-oriented games are more effective in enhancing task execution abilities, whereas narrative-driven games better support social skill training (Paneru, 2024).

16.2.3 AR-Based Learning Environments for ASD

Augmented Reality (AR) technology has been demonstrated to superimpose digital content onto the physical world, thus allowing children diagnosed with ASD to engage in interactive learning within familiar environments (Zhao et al., 2024).

Studies have shown that AR can improve attention spans, social interaction abilities, and situational understanding in children diagnosed with ASD. For instance, one study found that children diagnosed with ASD who used AR for social training showed significantly prolonged eye contact and more natural responses in social scenarios (Guilbaud et al., 2022).

In comparison to Virtual Reality (VR), AR's distinct advantage in the domain of ASD education lies in its ability to mitigate sensory overload while preserving environmental familiarity, thereby facilitating adaptation to novel learning tasks (Carvalho et al., 2024). In contrast to tablet-based learning, AR enhances interactive experiences through spatial localization and gesture-based interactions, which promote cognitive development (Mitsea et al., 2025). A salient strength of AR in ASD education is its capacity to provide real-time feedback and multi-sensory engagement. Research has demonstrated that incorporating visual, auditory, and tactile feedback in AR games can substantially enhance task completion rates and learning engagement (Chaidi et al., 2024). Moreover, integrating AI with AR technology facilitates dynamic adjustments to game content based on real-time responses, thereby optimizing personalized learning pathways and enhancing overall efficiency (Sarker et al., 2021).

16.2.4 Integrating AR into Serious Games for ASD

A number of studies have explored the integration of AI+AR technologies in ASD education. For instance, Face-Me, an AR-based social training game, combines AI-powered speech recognition to help ASD children interpret and respond to social cues during simulated interactions (Lyu et al., 2024). Another study developed an AI-AR learning platform that dynamically adjusts instructional strategies based on ASD children's cognitive levels and behavioural feedback to optimize learning experiences (Lan et al., 2025). The impact of different AR interaction modes on ASD education varies significantly. For instance, physical spatial interaction-based AR designs enhance spatial cognition, while voice and gesture-driven interfaces are more effective for improving social communication skills (Ahmad et al., 2025), as shown in Fig. 16.3.Furthermore, immersive AR experiences have been shown to increase learning motivation and facilitate social skill development within gamified contexts (Sideraki & Rassias, 2023). Despite the evident promise of AI+AR serious games, several challenges remain. Firstly, the majority of current research is focused on short-term experiments, and there is a lack of longitudinal data to evaluate the long-term efficacy of these interventions (Barua et al., 2022). Secondly, the optimization of AI-driven personalization strategies to accommodate the heterogeneous needs of children with ASD requires further exploration (Abd-Elrazaq et al., 2022).

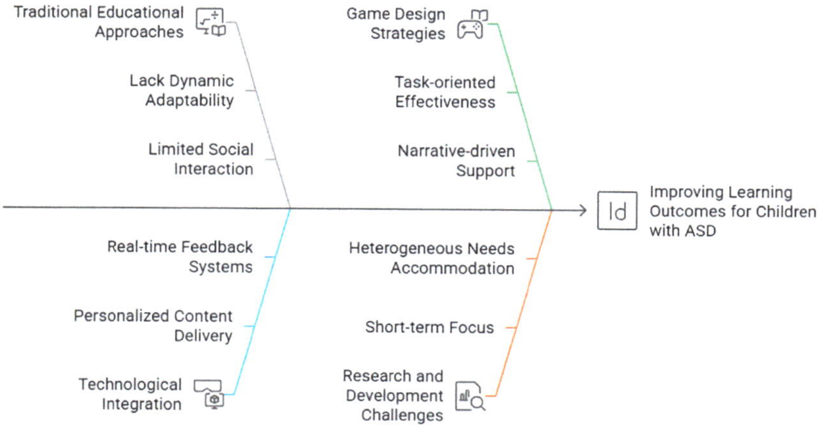

Fig. 16.3 Enhancing ASD education with AI and AR

16.3 AR-Based Serious Game Design for Autism Intervention

The integration of Augmented Reality (AR) with Serious Games presents a novel educational intervention for children diagnosed with Autism Spectrum Disorder (ASD). This approach transcends the realm of mere knowledge transfer, aiming to foster cognitive development, enhance social skills, and promote emotional regulation through interactive experiences. In comparison to conventional intervention methods, AR-based serious games facilitate the creation of a highly immersive learning environment. This environment enables autistic children to engage in personalized and adaptive interventions within a natural setting. To achieve this, game design must address the unique perceptual, cognitive, and social interaction needs of ASD children while balancing structured tasks with exploratory freedom to optimize learning outcomes.

16.3.1 Game Design Framework for ASD

Children diagnosed with ASD frequently encounter challenges in terms of attention control, cognitive flexibility, and social communication. Consequently, effective game design must prioritize adaptability, sensory-friendly components, and social engagement. AI-driven adaptive systems have the capacity to dynamically adjust game difficulty and feedback based on a child's cognitive level and behavioural patterns. For instance, the system can modify the game's progression by analysing task completion time, error rates, and engagement levels. This approach prevents frustration from overly difficult tasks or loss of interest from tasks that are too easy.

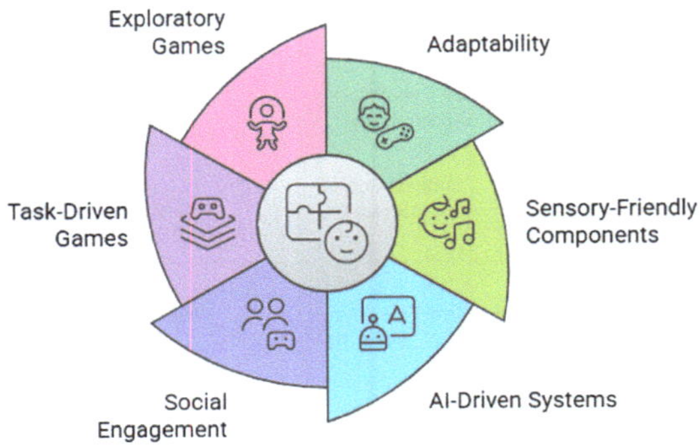

Fig. 16.4 Enhancing ASD learning through game design

Additionally, the game interface should cater to the sensory needs of children with ASD. The use of soft colour schemes can reduce visual overstimulation, optimized sound design can prevent sudden noise disruptions, and tactile feedback can enhance interaction. Interactive experiences should also minimize sensory overload while encouraging collaboration and communication. As shown in Fig. 16.4, the integration of AI-guided virtual characters and cooperative game modes can facilitate the practice of real-world social interactions in a safe and controlled virtual environment for children with ASD. Repetitive engagement with these games can reinforce stable social strategies, while offering unique benefits derived from different game structures. Task-driven games, for instance, provide clear objectives and structured learning, making them particularly beneficial for children with weaker executive function. In contrast, exploratory games allow for greater creativity and flexibility, enabling children to engage in independent exploration.

16.3.2 Comparative Analysis of AR+ Serious Game Design Philosophies

A fundamental aspect of serious game design entails achieving an equilibrium between structured learning and open-ended exploration. Structured learning emphasizes predetermined objectives and explicit rules, rendering it well-suited for ASD children who require predictability and immediate feedback. Nevertheless, an excess of rigidity may impede creativity and problem-solving abilities. The integration of exploratory elements within structured frameworks can serve as a counterbalance, enabling children to navigate within a structured yet flexible environment. For instance, task-based games can offer multiple solution pathways, thereby enhancing adaptability.

The choice between narrative-driven and task-driven approaches is another significant aspect of game design.

As shown in Fig. 16.5, narrative-driven games use storylines to help ASD children understand social interactions, but due to difficulties with abstract thinking and role-playing, ASD children may benefit more from task-driven games, which provide clear goals, structured instructions, and immediate feedback, reinforcing learning through a reward-based system. A hybrid approach that integrates narrative within task structures could be highly effective. The integration of narrative within task structures has the potential to enhance the comprehension of social rules among ASD children, while concurrently engaging them in goal-oriented activities. Finally, interaction design has been demonstrated to exert a substantial influence on learning outcomes. In contrast to traditional rule-based games, which follow predetermined learning paths and exhibit limited adaptability, AI-powered games have the capacity to adjust in real-time based on player behaviour. For instance, if a child encounters difficulty with a particular task, the system can reduce the level of challenge or provide hints to maintain optimal engagement. Furthermore, AI-driven pattern recognition can refine learning pathways by analysing errors and identifying task preferences, thereby enhancing learning efficiency.

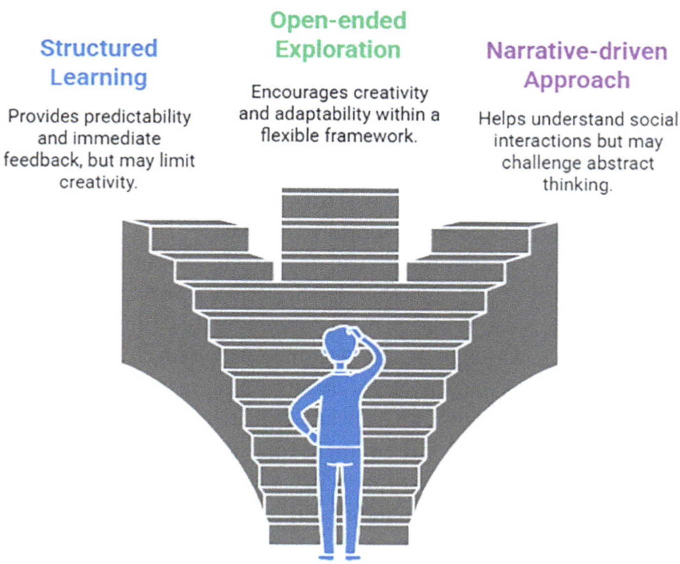

Fig. 16.5 How to design a serious game for ASD children?

16.3.3 AR Interaction Design for ASD Education

Interaction design is of critical importance in the context of educational games for children diagnosed with ASD. A well-designed game interface should be engineered to minimize sensory overload while enhancing learning motivation and social engagement. Research has demonstrated that sensory-adaptive interface design can lead to significant improvements in attention and task performance in children diagnosed with ASD. Consequently, games should incorporate customizable settings that allow users to adjust visual contrast, audio levels, and feedback methods to meet their individual sensory preferences.

In terms of social learning, gamified environments provide ASD children with low-pressure opportunities for social interaction, with multiplayer cooperative game modes, for instance, encouraging teamwork through non-verbal communication and role-based collaboration. Compared to traditional social training programs, AR-based games offer a more immersive and natural way for ASD children to practise social skills. Furthermore, the integration of AI-driven virtual agents and feedback mechanisms has the potential to assist children with ASD in recognizing emotions, predicting conversation outcomes, and refining their social responses. Another key aspect of AR-based game design is the balancing of physical and virtual interactions. Games should integrate real-world tasks with AR-enhanced elements to bridge the gap between digital learning and real-life application. For instance, AR overlays can offer interactive guidance in the form of directional arrows, task prompts, and real-time feedback panels, while the child completes physical tasks in their environment. This approach not only strengthens spatial awareness but also facilitates the transfer of skills acquired in the game to real-world scenarios.

In the course of our research on the use of AI+AR serious games for the education of individuals with ASD, our team developed and implemented an AR-based outdoor learning game in a public park in Shanghai (see Fig. 16.6). This interactive learning experience was specifically designed for children with ASD to enhance their cognitive, social, and motor skills through structured exploration, problem-solving, and parent-child collaboration. A key consideration in the game design was to create a sensory-friendly AR environment that minimizes overload while maintaining engagement. In contradistinction to VR, which has been shown to overwhelm learners with ASD, AR integrates interactive digital elements into real-world settings, thereby allowing children to engage at their own pace. As illustrated in Fig. 16.6, children utilized mobile devices to navigate a digital compass and locate virtual waypoints, thereby unlocking animated characters and interactive tasks embedded within the park's landscape. This predictable and structured interaction model helped reduce anxiety while fostering active learning in a familiar outdoor environment.

Social interaction represents a fundamental challenge in ASD intervention, and thus the game under consideration incorporated collaborative puzzle-solving tasks with a view to encouraging parent-child and peer interaction. As illustrated in Fig. 16.6, the Parent-Child Puzzle Fun activity necessitated the search for hidden clues in real-world objects by children and caregivers, thereby enhancing joint

Fig. 16.6 AR-based outdoor learning game for children with ASD in a Shanghai park

attention, communication, and cooperative problem-solving skills. The AR interface provided structured prompts that guided children through challenges, allowing them to practise turn-taking, verbal interaction, and pattern recognition in a supportive, interactive environment (see Fig. 16.7). A distinctive feature of the AR game was its emphasis on movement-based learning. Rather than passive screen interaction, children were required to physically navigate the park to unlock different AR learning stations covering subjects such as science, mathematics, and language learning. As illustrated in Fig. 16.6, this integration of real-world exploration and digital engagement not only reinforced learning but also promoted spatial awareness and motor skill development, both of which are critical for ASD learners. Furthermore, the provision of Creative AR Keepsakes, in the form of interactive puzzles, enabled a continuation of the learning experience beyond the confines of the park.

16.3.4 Assessment and Feedback Mechanisms

Robust assessment and feedback mechanisms are essential for ensuring the effectiveness of ASD educational interventions. AI-powered adaptive feedback systems can continuously monitor a child's performance and dynamically adjust game difficulty and task types based on their learning progress. For example, if a child shows increased errors in a particular task, the system can modify the level of assistance by increasing visual cues, providing additional hints, or simplifying the task structure to maintain an optimal challenge level.

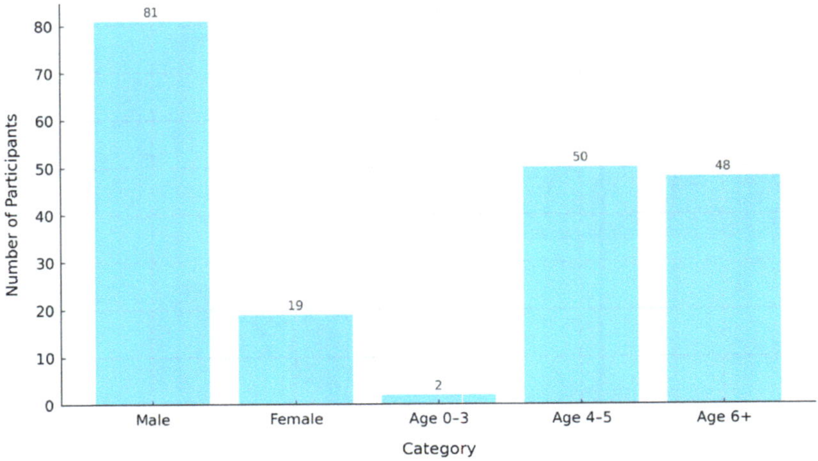

Fig. 16.7 Sample composition

In addition, the use of monitoring tools for parents and educators is of critical importance in the context of ASD intervention. Games should include visual data dashboards that track key learning metrics, such as task completion rates, frequency of social interactions, and emotional fluctuations. By analysing these data, educators and caregivers can gain insights into an ASD child's learning patterns and tailor intervention strategies accordingly. To assess cognitive and emotional engagement, AI-driven serious games can integrate multimodal data analysis, including behavioural tracking, speech recognition, and facial expression analysis. For instance, tracking facial expressions during gameplay can provide insights into emotional responses, while speech data can help assess language use and contextual adaptability. By leveraging these advanced analytical tools, AI+AR serious games can offer more personalized interventions and real-time adjustments, optimizing learning experiences for children with ASD.

16.4 Theoretical and Practical Feasibility Analysis

16.4.1 Results and Analysis of AI+AR Serious Game Intervention in Children with ASD

This study was conducted in collaboration with the Huzhou Third People's Hospital, where 100 children diagnosed with Autism Spectrum Disorder (ASD) were recruited as participants. The diagnostic process, conducted within a hospital setting, ensured the clinical validity of the data, as it was derived from authentic real-world practices. The objective of the present study was to evaluate the effectiveness of AI+AR serious games as an intervention strategy for improving core ASD symptoms and developmental skills. As shown in Fig. 16.7, the intervention study comprised a total of 100 children (81 boys and 19 girls). The mean age of the subjects was 4.88 years (SD = 0.97), with a range from 2.29 to 7.28 years. Participants were divided into three developmental age groups: 0–3 years (n = 2), 4–5 years (n = 50), and 6+ years (n = 48).

The preliminary investigation concentrated on determining whether the intervention's efficacy differed according to parental educational attainment. The children were grouped according to the educational attainment of their parents (for example, those with a college degree or higher versus those with lower educational attainment). The findings of the study suggested that children with highly educated parents demonstrated a tendency to achieve more significant improvements on core autism assessments. For instance, the Childhood Autism Rating Scale (CARS) scores in the high-education parent group decreased from a mean of ~34.3 (pre-intervention) to 29.8 (post-intervention), in comparison to the low-education group, which demonstrated a decrease from 36.2 to 32.5. On average, this corresponds to a CARS improvement of approximately 4.5 points for parents with a high level of education, as opposed to 3.7 points for parents with a lower level of education. A similar pattern was observed for the Autism Behaviour Checklist (ABC): the high-education group demonstrated an improvement of approximately 10.8 points (from 71.5 to 60.7), while the low-education group exhibited an improvement of approximately 8.5 points (from 70.7 to 62.2). The findings of the statistical comparisons indicated that there was a significant discrepancy in the improvement observed between the two parental education groups for ABC ($p < 0.01$) and a marginal significance for CARS ($p < 0.05$). These findings imply that an elevated level of parental education is associated with slightly superior intervention outcomes in the child (Table 16.1).

The preliminary investigation concentrated on determining whether the intervention's efficacy differed according to parental educational attainment. The children were grouped according to the educational attainment of their parents (for example, those with a college degree or higher versus those with lower educational attainment). The findings of the study suggested that children with highly educated parents demonstrated a tendency to achieve more significant improvements on core autism assessments. For instance, the Childhood Autism Rating Scale (CARS) scores in the high-education parent group decreased from a mean of ~34.3 (pre-intervention) to 29.8

Table 16.1 Parent education

Education Level	Father Education Count	Mother Education Count
Primary school	10	10
Junior middle school	25	30
High school	5	4
Vocational school	7	8
University	51	48
Postgraduate	2	0

(post-intervention), in comparison to the low-education group, which demonstrated a decrease from 36.2 to 32.5. On average, this corresponds to a CARS improvement of approximately 4.5 points for parents with a high level of education, as opposed to 3.7 points for parents with a lower level of education. A similar pattern was observed for the Autism Behaviour Checklist (ABC): the high-education group demonstrated an improvement of approximately 10.8 points (from 71.5 to 60.7), while the low-education group exhibited an improvement of approximately 8.5 points (from 70.7 to 62.2). The findings of the statistical comparisons indicated that there was a significant discrepancy in the improvement observed between the two parental education groups for ABC ($p < 0.01$) and a marginal significance for CARS ($p < 0.05$). These findings imply that an elevated level of parental education is associated with slightly superior intervention outcomes in the child.

Figure 16.8 presents boxplot distributions of CARS (Childhood Autism Rating Scale) and ABC (Autism Behavior Checklist) scores before and after the AI+AR serious game intervention. Each boxplot illustrates the median, interquartile range (IQR), and data spread, with outliers marked as individual points. Scores on both scales that are lower than average are indicative of improvement.

CARS Scores:

- **Pre-intervention:** The median score was approximately 42, with the majority of children scoring between 38 and 45. The presence of outliers below 38 and above 50 indicated a variation in baseline autism severity.
- **Post-intervention:** The median value decreased to approximately 38, and the interquartile range (IQR) narrowed. The decline in mean scores and the narrower distribution are indicative of a consistent enhancement exhibited by the participants, with a concomitant decrease in the number of high-severity outliers.

These observations imply that the intervention exerted a substantial influence on the core symptoms of autism, particularly with regard to social communication and repetitive behaviours. A decrease of 4+ points on the CARS is considered to be

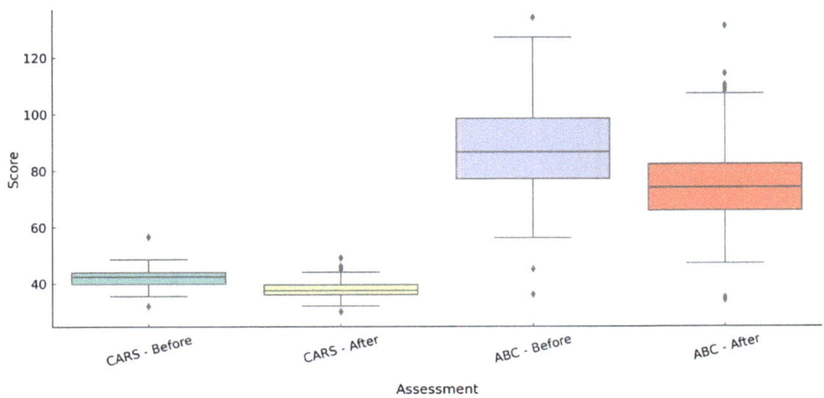

Fig. 16.8 Distribution of CARS and ABC scores before and after intervention

clinically significant, with the potential to indicate a shift from moderate to mild ASD classification in some cases.

ABC Scores:

- Pre-intervention: The median ABC score was approximately 90, with a broad distribution ranging from approximately 60 to over 120. The distribution of cases reflects a heterogeneous presentation of behavioural issues.
- Post-intervention: The median value decreased to approximately 75, and the high-end outliers exhibited a substantial decline. The reduction in both median and variance indicates a decrease in severe behavioural disturbances following intervention.

The findings of the ABC study indicate that there has been an enhancement in the behavioural regulation of the subjects in question, alongside a reduction in problem behaviours such as aggression, hyperactivity, and stereotypy. The decline in extreme values indicates that even children with high initial ABC scores benefited substantially.

Statistical and Clinical Interpretation:

Paired t-tests were employed to confirm that the score reductions for both CARS and ABC were statistically significant ($p < 0.001$). From a clinical standpoint, the observed enhancements are consistent with a Paired t-tests were employed to confirm that the score reductions for both CARS and ABC were statistically significant ($p < 0.001$). From a clinical perspective, the improvements are consistent with a reduced diagnostic burden and enhanced daily functioning. The narrowing of score distributions suggests more uniform intervention effectiveness and reduced symptom variability post-treatment. It is evident that the extant evidence lends support to the hypothesis that AI+AR-based serious games deliver quantifiable and consistent therapeutic benefits to children diagnosed with ASD, both at the core symptom and behavioural level.

16.4.2 Comparison with Traditional Autism Interventions

Conventional ASD interventions, including Applied Behavior Analysis (ABA), Social Skills Training (SST), and Structured Teaching, have been extensively utilized for many years. Nevertheless, these methodologies are characterized by several limitations. For example, although ABA has exhibited efficacy in modifying behaviour, it is characterized by its high resource requirements, substantial financial costs, and inflexible instructional design, which frequently impedes the capacity of ASD children to adapt their learning to diverse environments. In contrast, AI+AR serious games offer adaptive learning experiences, allowing children to practise social interactions and problem-solving in varied settings, thus improving learning transfer and real-world application.

Another limitation of traditional interventions is their lack of real-time data-driven assessment tools. This makes it difficult for educators and parents to track learning progress and adjust strategies accordingly. AI+AR serious games, however, leverage data analytics to continuously evaluate behavioural patterns and learning outcomes. Through dynamic adjustments in game difficulty and interaction modes, these systems offer highly personalized and responsive interventions, tailored to each child's needs.

Furthermore, the maintenance of engagement in conventional ASD interventions frequently necessitates repetitive training, which can result in diminished motivation. Conversely, game-based learning utilizes task-based rewards, virtual character interactions, and multi-sensory stimulation to enhance engagement and sustain attention over extended periods. This gamified approach not only improves learning retention but also encourages ASD children to complete more complex cognitive and social tasks. Notwithstanding these advantages, large-scale implementation of AI+AR serious games still faces challenges. Initial difficulties with AR-based interaction mechanics for some children with ASD may indicate a requirement for further interface optimization and interaction model refinement to better align with their cognitive characteristics. Furthermore, a significant area for future research is the integration of AI+AR serious games with traditional intervention methods, with the potential to create a more holistic ASD intervention framework by combining game-based training with real-world social skill development, leveraging the strengths of both approaches to maximize learning outcomes.

16.4.3 Challenges and Limitations of AR-Based Serious Games

The integration of AI and data-driven technologies within the domain of ASD education has given rise to significant concerns regarding data privacy and security. ASD interventions require the collection of behavioural data, emotional responses, and learning progress, thus giving rise to critical questions surrounding the personalization of learning while preventing unauthorized data usage and the emergence of security vulnerabilities. Current research emphasizes the anonymization of data, parental consent, and compliance with privacy regulations such as the General Data Protection Regulation (GDPR), with the objective of ensuring secure data management. However, achieving an optimal balance between privacy protection and effective data utilization remains a significant challenge. Additionally, AI-based behavioural analysis systems may be affected by data bias, which limits the adaptability of personalized recommendation systems. To address this, future research must focus on developing fair, transparent, and unbiased AI frameworks to mitigate potential ethical risks. Despite the promising applications of AI+AR technologies in ASD education, hardware costs and technical complexity continue to hinder large-scale adoption. The expense of current AR devices, such as head-mounted displays and tablets, poses a significant barrier to their widespread adoption by families and schools.

Furthermore, the complexity of these devices can create a learning curve for children with ASD, potentially hindering their ability to adapt to game-based learning environments. To facilitate broader adoption, future efforts should focus on designing lightweight, affordable, and user-friendly AR educational platforms. Additionally, for underfunded ASD education institutions, the development of cost-effective yet scalable AI+AR solutions remains an important research direction.

Despite the evidence of successful learning outcomes in experimental settings, there are several challenges to the real-world implementation of AI+AR serious games. One such challenge is the training of teachers and therapists. At present, most ASD educators are not familiar with AR interaction design and AI-based adaptive learning systems, thus making professional training programmes essential for effective classroom integration. Furthermore, the integration of AI+AR-based serious games into existing curricula and therapy programmes requires careful consideration of policy frameworks, resource allocation, and measurable learning outcomes. Addressing these challenges is pivotal to ensure the successful adoption of AI+AR interventions in ASD education. Another critical factor influencing the widespread adoption of AI+AR serious games is social acceptance. Concerns have been expressed by parents and educators that over-reliance on digital learning may have a negative impact on real-world social skill development in ASD children. To address this, future research should explore strategies for combining AI+AR interactive learning with real-world social skill training. The integration of game-based learning with face-to-face interactions has the potential to facilitate the development of transferable skills that extend beyond virtual environments and into everyday social contexts for children with ASD.

16.5 Conclusion and Prospective

This study examined the application of AI+AR-based serious games in ASD education, exploring their effectiveness from multiple perspectives, including game design frameworks, interaction experience optimization, comparative analysis of learning models, and assessment-feedback mechanisms. The findings indicated that AI+AR serious games provide personalized learning environments, real-time feedback systems, and immersive interactive experiences, leading to notable improvements in cognitive development, social interaction, and emotional regulation in children with ASD.

In comparison to conventional ASD intervention methods, AI+AR-integrated educational models exhibit superior adaptability to individual requirements, enhanced engagement through gamified learning, and a more sustainable intervention approach. Leveraging AI-driven adaptive systems, these games can dynamically adjust learning tasks based on ASD children's behavioural responses, cognitive levels, and emotional states, ensuring a tailored and responsive educational experience. Nevertheless, despite their significant potential, AI+AR serious games encounter several challenges in large-scale implementation. These challenges encompass data privacy concerns, hardware costs, teacher training requirements, and the necessity for long-term intervention evaluation. Furthermore, ethical considerations pertaining to AI-driven personalization, including algorithmic bias and transparency in data processing, necessitate further research to ensure the responsible integration of these technologies.

In order to optimize the potential of AI+AR-based serious games for ASD education, future research and development should concentrate on four key areas. Firstly, there is a necessity for technological advancements and accessibility. AI+AR educational games must become more lightweight, cost-effective, and computationally efficient. Efficient, ensuring smooth operation on affordable hardware. Secondly, there is a requirement for further optimization of AR interaction designs to allow high-quality augmented reality experiences without the need for head-mounted displays. Exploration of gesture-based interactions on mobile devices and haptic-audio feedback mechanisms to enhance accessibility is recommended.

Secondly, in the context of Long-Term Effectiveness Evaluation, the majority of current studies focus on short-term experimental observations, with a paucity of evidence regarding long-term impacts on the cognitive, emotional, and social development of children with ASD. It is therefore recommended that future research employs longitudinal study designs, tracking the learning progress of children with ASD over months or years, in order to validate the sustainability of AI+AR interventions.

Thirdly, advancements in personalized learning strategies: prevailing AI adaptation models primarily employ rule-based mechanisms and are limited by the capacity of machine learning algorithms. It is therefore recommended that future studies integrate deep learning and reinforcement learning techniques to create highly adaptive AI-driven learning paths. The incorporation of biometric feedback technologies (e.g. EEG-based brain activity monitoring and heart rate analysis) could enable real-time emotional regulation, thereby further enhancing adaptive learning experiences.

Finally, the scalability and global implementation of AI+AR-based serious games should be assessed in a variety of cultural, linguistic, and educational contexts to evaluate their adaptability. Future studies should explore the most effective means of integrating these technologies into existing ASD education frameworks, including special education schools, therapy centers, and home-based learning environments. Enhancing teacher training programs, parental monitoring platforms, and user-friendly interfaces will be crucial for ensuring seamless adoption.

Acknowledge This work was supported by the Public Welfare Application Research Project of the Huzhou Science and Technology Bureau (No. 2022GY01), titled 'Research and Clinical Validation of New AI-Guided Language Assistance Intervention Methods for Children with Autism.'

References

Abd El-Sattar, H. K. H. (2025). Future Metaverse-based education to promote daily living activities in learners with autism using immersive technologies. *Spring*. https://doi.org/10.1007/s10639-024-12844-3

Abd-Elrazaq, A., Abuelezz, I., & Hassan, A. (2022). Artificial intelligence-driven serious games in health care: Scoping review. *JMIR Serious Games*. https://doi.org/10.2196/39840

Adako, O. P., & Adeusi, O. C. (2024). Revolutionizing autism education: Harnessing AI for tailored skill development in social, emotional, and independent learning domains. *Bonview Press*. https://doi.org/10.47852/bonviewJCCE42023414

Ahmad, W., Raj, R., & Shokeen, R. (2025). Reshaping special education: Strategic use of artificial intelligence. *IGI Global*. https://doi.org/10.4018/979-8-3693-5538-1.ch001

Almurashi, H., Bouaziz, R., Alharthi, W., & Al-Sarem, M. (2022). Augmented reality, serious games and picture exchange communication system for people with ASD: Systematic literature review and future directions. *MDPI Sensors*. https://doi.org/10.3390/s22031250

Barua, P. D., Vicnesh, J., Gururajan, R., & Oh, S. L. (2022). Artificial intelligence-enabled personalized assistive tools to enhance education of children with neurodevelopmental disorders—A review. *International Journal of Environmental Research and Public Health*. https://doi.org/10.3390/ijerph19031192

Caruso, F., Peretti, S., Santa Barletta, V., & Pino, M. C. (2023). *Recommendations for developing immersive virtual reality serious game for autism: Insights from a systematic literature review*. IEEE Xplore.

Carvalho, A. P., Braz, C. S., & dos Santos, S. M. (2024). Serious games for children with autism Spectrum disorder: A systematic literature review. *International Journal of Human-Computer Interaction*. https://doi.org/10.1080/10447318.2023.2194051

Chaidi, I., Pergantis, P., Drigas, A., & Karagiannidis, C. (2024). Gaming platforms for people with ASD. MDPI Journal of Intelligence. DOI: 10.3390/jintelligence12120122.

De Carvalho, A. P., Braz, C. S., & Dos Santos, S. M. (2024). Serious games for children with autism spectrum disorder: A systematic literature review. *International Journal of Human-Computer Interaction*. https://doi.org/10.1080/10447318.2023.2194051

Guilbaud, P., Sanders, C., & Hirsch, M. J. (2022). The greater good: Exploring the use of serious game. In *Virtual reality and artificial intelligence to elicit Prosocial behaviors and strengthen cognitive abilities of youth*. Springer. https://doi.org/10.1007/978-3-031-05939-1_29

Habibi, F., Sedaghatshoar, S., Attar, T., & Shokoohi, M. (2025). Revolutionizing education and therapy for students with autism spectrum disorder: A scoping review of AI-driven tools, technologies, and ethical implications. *Spring*. https://doi.org/10.1007/s43681-024-00608-1

Honorato, N., Soltiyeva, A., & Oliveira, W. (2024). Gameful strategies in the education of autistic children: A systematic literature review, scientometric analysis, and future research roadmap. *Spring*. https://doi.org/10.1186/s40561-024-00309-6

Kotsi, S., Handrinou, S., Iatraki, G., & Soulis, S. G. (2025). A review of artificial intelligence interventions for students with autism Spectrum disorder[J]. *MDPI Disabilities, 5*(1), 7. https://doi.org/10.3390/disabilities5010007.16

Lamnai, A., & Elmhouti, A. (2025). Artificial intelligence in educational serious games: Implications and innovations. *IGI Global*. https://doi.org/10.4018/979-8-3693-8965-2.ch012

Lan, L., Li, K., & Li, D. (2025). Exploring the application of AI in the education of children with autism: A public health perspective. *Frontiers in Psychiatry*. https://doi.org/10.3389/fpsyt.2024.1521926

Lyu, Y., Liu, D., An, P., Tong, X., & Zhang, H. (2024). EMooly: Supporting Autistic Children in Collaborative Social-Emotional Learning with Caregiver Participation through Interactive AI-infused and AR Activities. https://www.jeffjianzhao.com/papers/emooly.pdf

Mihova, P., Stankova, M., & Andonov, F. (2022). The use of serious games for developing social and communication skills in children with autism spectrum disorders. *Spring*. https://doi.org/10.1007/978-3-031-11170-9_7

Mitsea, E., Drigas, A., & Skianis, C. (2025). A systematic review of serious games in the era of artificial intelligence, immersive technologies, the Metaverse, and Neurotechnologies: Transformation and cognitive benefits. *MDPI Electronics*. https://doi.org/10.3390/electronics14040649

Paneru, B. (2024). The Nexus of AR/VR, Large Language Models, UI/UX, and Robotics Technologies in Enhancing Learning and Social Interaction for Children: A Systematic Review. arXiv. https://doi.org/10.48550/arXiv.2409.18162.

Sarker, S., Linkon, A. H. M., & Bappy, F. H. (2021). Improving joint attention in children with autism: A VR-AR enabled game approach. *ResearchGate*. 10.349748347

Sideraki, A., & Rassias, M. (2023). Using artificial intelligence and game theory to enhance executive function development in people with ASD: Strategic interventions and applications. *ResearchGate*.

Stasolla, F., Curcio, E., Passaro, A., Di Gioia, M., & Zullo, A. (2025). Exploring the combination of serious games, social interactions, and virtual reality in adolescents with ASD: A scoping review. *MDPI Technologies*. https://doi.org/10.3390/technologies13020076

Zhao, W., Xu, S., Zhang, Y., Li, D., Zhu, C., & Wang, K. (2024). The application of extended reality in treating children with autism Spectrum disorder. *Spring*. https://doi.org/10.1007/s12264-024-01190-6

Chapter 17
The Use of AI Tools by Persons with Determination in Higher Education: A Case Study of Media Students at the University of Sharjah

Thouraya Snoussi, Mohamed Abdulzaher, Omer Jawad Al Ali, Nadeen Selim, and Dalia Hassan

Abstract Inclusive education allows for equitable, accessible learning for all students, including students with determination. This study analyses how AI tools support "students with determination" in digital media design and radio/television programs at the University of Sharjah. We used two 75-min focus group discussions (n = 12) to investigate students' uses, perceived advantages, and challenges when using AI tools. Participants mentioned they had used ChatGPT for ideation and script writing, Canva and Runway ML for rapid visual prototyping, and Otter.ai for transcription of lectures. Participants believed that using these applications sped up task completion by 40%, enhanced creativity, and boosted academic independence. However, participants reported a steep learning curve, occasional technical glitches, and premium-feature costs were considered barriers. Students were curious and expressed a desire to pursue structured training on AI tools, institutional licensing of tools, and expanding options of personalization (e.g., Adaptivity recommendations) for each of the tools. The findings illustrate how AI tools can change approaches to accessibility in learning and instructional design while providing personalized scaffolding. However, we must intentionally strike a balance between implementing AI in the classroom and ensuring students acquire foundational skills for their development. This research study offers timely information for educators and policymakers who aim to develop inclusive post-secondary learning environments through the implementation of AI.

T. Snoussi (✉)
National Defense College, Abu Dhabi, UAE
e-mail: thouraya.snoussi@ndc.ac.ae

M. Abdulzaher · O. J. Al Ali
Department of Mass Communication, College of Communication, University of Sharjah (UAE), Sharjah, UAE

N. Selim · D. Hassan
College of Mass Communication, Umm Al Quwain University, Umm Al Quwain, UAE

M. Abed et al. (eds.), *Metaverse and Artificial Intelligence in Education for a Sustainable Society*, Future Education and Learning Spaces,
https://doi.org/10.1007/978-981-95-8852-7_17

Keywords Artificial Intelligence · Persons with determination · Digital media · ChatGPT · Otter · Education

17.1 Introduction

Generative AI has the potential to improve educational decision-making through analytics and recommendations while also presenting a risk of perpetuating inequities based on dataset bias, automating decision-making, and development processes that do not account for the needs of students with determination (Zhao et al., 2025; Almufareh et al., 2024). This research explores how the students in the Digital Media Design and Radio & Television programs at the University of Sharjah utilize AI tools in their creative work, and whether these technologies have created a more equitable learning experience for students with determination.

17.2 Research Gap and Questions

The current study aims to address the existing gap in research on the role of artificial intelligence in supporting students with determination in the United Arab Emirates. It focuses specifically on students enrolled in the Digital Media Design and Radio and Television programs at the University of Sharjah, investigating how AI tools are employed to enhance accessibility, learning experiences, and academic performance.

Two research questions were formulated as follows:

RQ1: How do students with determination in the Digital Media Design and Radio and Television programs at the University of Sharjah utilize AI tools to support their learning?

RQ2: What are the perceived benefits and challenges of using AI technologies among students with determination in these programs?

This study is guided by two complementary frameworks: the Technology Acceptance Model (TAM) and the Social Model of Disability. The Technology Acceptance Model provides insight into how students with determination at the University of Sharjah perceive, adopt, and engage with artificial intelligence tools in their educational journey. In parallel, the Social Model of Disability shifts the focus from individual impairments to the societal and environmental barriers that limit participation and inclusion. From this perspective, the effective use of AI tools can be seen as a means of removing obstacles within the learning environment and fostering greater accessibility and equity.

Table 17.1 Study sample characteristics

T	Focus group (Digital Media Design)		Focus group (Radio &TV)
No	Gender	No	Gender
P1 DMD	Female	P1 R&TV	Male
P2 DMD	Female	P2 R&TV	Male
P3 DMD	Male	P3 R&TV	Male
P4 DMD	Male	P4 R&TV	Male
P5 DMD	Male	P5 R&TV	Female
P6 DMD	Male	P6 R&TV	Female
	2 F &4 M		2F &4M

17.3 Research Methodology

This study adopted an exploratory qualitative design, employing semi-structured focus-group discussions to generate in-depth insights into how students with determination engage with AI tools in media programs.

17.3.1 Participants

Twelve students from the Department of Mass Communication at the University of Sharjah participated in this study. Six were enrolled in the Digital Media Design program and six in the Radio & Television program. Each group comprised two females and four males, and all participants self-identified as having a disability ("determination"). Participants were purposefully recruited via faculty referrals and email invitations to ensure balanced representation across both programs (Table 17.1).

17.3.2 Data Collection

Data were collected exclusively through two semi-structured focus-group discussions, held on 24 February and 16 April 2025. Each session lasted 1 hour and 15 minutes and was guided by a discussion protocol developed directly from the study's two research questions:

1. Uses of AI vs. traditional tools in media design
2. Advantages and limitations of AI in content creation
3. Future directions for AI integration in media curricula

This guide was pilot tested with two student volunteers to refine question phrasing and ensure comprehensive coverage of each theme. All sessions were audio-recorded using digital voice recorders and transcribed verbatim via Sonix.ai; any passages flagged as unclear were manually verified against the original recordings to guarantee transcription accuracy.

17.3.3 Data Analysis

MAXQDA v.2024 was used to analyze verbatim transcripts using a predetermined codebook consisting of four main categories (AI Tools Use, Perceived Benefits, Perceived Constraints, Expectations/Involvement). Two researchers double-coded the whole dataset and then evaluated inter-coder reliability on a 10 % random sample in order to reach raw agreement of 92 %; any discrepancies in coding were reconciled and settled through discussion. The frequencies of codes were summarized to provide an indication of common patterns and then following thematic summaries were made based on the two research questions in this study (Table 17.2).

The coding framework is designed to investigate both how and why students with determination have engaged with AI tools in their Digital Media Design and Radio

Table 17.2 Inductive codes for the qualitative analysis

Research question	Main code	Subcodes
RQ1: How do students with determination in the Digital Media Design and Radio and Television programs at the University of Sharjah utilize AI tools to support their learning?	Usage of AI Tools	Tool selection like Adobe Photoshop, After Effects, InDesign, Dreamweaver, Canva, Remove.bg, Runway ML, Otter, ChatGPT, Fotor AI…etc
		Frequency of use
		Type of support needed
RQ2: What are the perceived benefits and challenges of using AI technologies among students with determination in these programs?	Perceived Benefits of AI	Increased independence
		Enhanced engagement with learning material
		Personalization of learning experiences
	Perceived Limitations of AI	Increased independence
		Enhanced engagement with learning material
		Personalization of learning experiences
	Expectations and Involvement	Desire for AI training
		Involvement in AI policy development

and Television programs. For RQ1, we look at how they engaged with the tools themselves: what applications they used -whether it be Photoshop or ChatGPT-, how often they relied on these tools, and the areas (e.g. writing, design, and research) in which they believe their studies are supported by AI. RQ2 explores students' perspectives on the kinds of benefits they receive (e.g. increased independence, greater engagement, and individualization), the downsides to their learning experiences (e.g. questions of reliability or ethics), and their hopes for AI moving forward (e.g. requests for more training, inclusion in AI policy for the institution).

17.3.4 Reliability and Validity

To ensure reliability, we assessed inter-coder consistency by having two analysts independently code the full data set and then comparing their results, achieving over 90 % agreement; all coding decisions and codebook revisions were recorded in detailed audit trails within MAXQDA. For validity, we established credibility through peer debriefing after each coding cycle and maintained reflexive memos that tied every analytic choice back to the original verbatim excerpts, while transferability was supported by providing rich descriptions of participant demographics, context, and data-collection procedures so that readers can judge applicability to other settings.

17.4 Findings

Study Findings The findings from this study provide valuable insights into how students with determination in the Digital Media Design and Radio and Television programs at the University of Sharjah use AI tools, the benefits they perceive, and the challenges they face.

17.4.1 Findings of Digital Media Design Student's Focus Group

Use of AI Tools

Students with determination shared that they felt a major difference in their learning journey once they added AI tools to their design workflow. P1 DMD, who has both hearing and speech challenges, said that while using their design AI interface, the sophisticated design combinations became simpler to do, "help with design, and save time." Rather than a regulated process and complex steps, the design AI made the process acceptable for P1 DMD. P3 DMD—who has hearing and vision limitations—said the traditional software was taxing his eyes and slowing down his work. He felt that using AI helped him facilitate his work, reduce the number of seals, and produce polished results at a faster rate compared to traditional tools. P4 DMD was the most amazing story in the group. He is completely deaf. He found traditional tools cumbersome and inaccessible. When he used various AI applications, he said, "they made me feel that learning was much easier and less boring," and these applications rekindled his motivation to approach advanced techniques. In each story, it was evident (the impact) AI helped lift restrictions and sparked motivation, transforming what was once thought of as too much into an empowering opportunity to be creative and develop (Matre & Cameron, 2024; McCarthy & Yan, 2023).

Perceived Benefits

Students in the Digital Media Design program were enthusiastic about a few AI tools like Canva, Otter.ai and Google Live Transcribe, indicating that these innovative ways to work creatively significantly improved parts of their journeys through design projects. AI tools helped students engage with information in a structured world, and, in some cases, what used to take weeks of design work, was sorted out in minutes with the help of tools like otter.ai or just using zaps along the way. Knowledge creation also sped up so rapidly, that novice designers finished their assignment at speeds that matched higher skilled designers. For example, one student said that AI "makes the design process a whole lot easier to organize visual files," and another student commented about templates, that "polished logos are instantaneously created." In terms of sense of autonomy, using AI tools did more for their confidence, as learners who were committed to getting assignments done reported feeling more confident to be able to complete assignments, like a genuine creator, without relying on fellow classmates, or an instructor. This was motivationally inspiring to their engagement with the learning and design process.

Perceived Challenges

While students noted many advantages, they also noted having some struggles. The learning curve associated with certain AI tools was one of the main struggles we talked about, particularly for those with no former experience with AI at all. P4 DMD shared with us, "Learning to use AI tools took adjustment. I had to figure out how to incorporate it into my own everyday practice and some of the directions were vague." It took some range of effort for some students to transition from a traditional design tool to an AI-enhanced tool with a full understanding of the tool's capabilities and how to incorporate the tool in their individual workflow (Khan, 2024).

In addition, while the students embraced the time-conserving factors of AI tools, some students expressed concern that they felt too dependent on the technology (Zhou & Zhang, 2025). P2 DMD, for example, cautioned, "AI makes things easier, but I worry that having dependence on AI, stifles our ability to design by not doing manual labour and develop the skills technically." This acknowledgement provides an opportunity to stress balanced integration strategies for AI that support students with persistence while also viewing the value of foundational design skills.

Future Outlook

Students expect ongoing improvements to AI and are calling for its comprehensive integration and formal instruction within their coursework. They clearly expressed a request for training—"I want more training on AI, so I can start using these tools to their potential," stated one student—which would allow them to advance beyond basic functionality. The students' optimism regarding the future of AI was universal, and learners expect these technologies, once better developed, to become vital to their future practice ("AI will just get better and will be an important part of our future work"). Overall, these findings indicate AI's essential role in providing usability, autonomy, and creativity for students with determination but also indicate the need to balance AI proficiency with core design competencies.

17.4.2 Findings of R&TV Students Focus Group

The focus group discussions with students enrolled in the Radio and Television program at the University of Sharjah revealed valuable insights into the integration of AI tools in their academic work. These findings underscore how AI tools are enhancing students' learning, creativity, and independence, while also highlighting the challenges they face and their outlook on the future.

Use of AI Tools:

AI tools are playing a pivotal role in supporting students in their Radio and Television studies. Students appreciate how these tools simplify tasks and make complex processes more manageable. P1 R&TV, for example, explained that AI helps in extracting main ideas and key points from selected topics, stating, "ChatGPT has helped me, and my colleagues understand our assignments and projects more easily through its clear explanations." This sentiment was echoed by several students, who indicated that AI tools—especially ChatGPT—were instrumental in brainstorming creative ideas, improving their work on video and radio presentations, and simplifying the writing process (Alsahli et al., 2025; Ayala, 2023).

Students with determination, such as P2 R&TV, who use a hearing aid, particularly benefited from AI tools. He noted, "AI tools like speech-to-text apps [Otter.ai and Google Live Transcribe] help me follow conversations and lectures more easily." P2 R&TV's experience highlights how AI applications, especially speech-to-text tools, enable students with hearing impairments to stay fully engaged in academic discussions, thereby promoting inclusivity and accessibility in the learning environment.

Additionally, P3 R&TV mentioned how AI helps him speed up his work: "ChatGPT helps me generate new ideas. It helps me understand information faster and stay organized." This reflects the efficiency that AI brings to students' workflows, supporting both idea generation and content organization (Botchu et al., 2023).

Perceived Benefits:

Students studying Radio & Television commented that AI tools substantially increased creativity, efficiency, and autonomy (Abduljabbar et al., 2024). One student ("P4 R&TV") described an instance when new ways of communicating were realized, and increasing clarity in idea expression was improved via apps like Canva, and applications that recognize speech and convert it to text like Otter.ai. Another student described how AI tools provided students with the ability to review lectures and discussions independently and related that AI made "learning so much easier: for him, and felt it was easier to rhythm his practice and concentrate on performance." AI increased personal confidence for students, and students did not feel as reliant on their peers or teachers because they were completing assignments not expecting to rely on others. Students who shared themselves as having almost no technical knowledge said how they did not find tools like ChatGPT "take very much management and that there have been little things to review," demonstrating that even with almost no technical knowledge, students could utilize AI because of functional user interfaces.

Perceived Challenges:

While students found AI tools to be highly beneficial, several challenges were also identified. One of the primary difficulties mentioned was the occasional ineffectiveness of certain AI tools (Yun et al., 2025; Strielkowski et al., 2024; Malmstrom et al., 2023). P2 R&TV noted that while AI generally works well, "Sometimes it's not very effective," suggesting that although AI is valuable, its accuracy and reliability can sometimes be inconsistent. Similarly, P6 R&TV observed that AI tools did not always function properly, sharing, "Last time I used AI, it didn't work properly twice." These experiences highlight that AI tools are not foolproof and that students may encounter technical issues from time to time.

Another challenge, raised by P5 R&TV, concerned the cost of premium features in AI applications: "The only challenge is when certain AI tools require payment for advanced features." This financial barrier can be particularly limiting for students who do not have access to paid subscriptions, thereby restricting their ability to take full advantage of AI capabilities (Eziamaka et al., 2024).

Future Outlook:

Students maintained a positive disposition as to the outlook of the use of AI in their studies and future occupation (Alshurideh et al., 2025). They saw expanding the number of specialized applications of AI will enable the delegation of multiple individual tasks and hinted at various tools they were using with one student saying, "There are so many AI tools, many for different kinds of tasks," which indicated appreciation for the variety of tools. Students commented on AI contributing to independent and creative engagement—"AI helps me stay independent, creative, and engaged with my work"—and they anticipated that familiarity with AI leads to improved efficiency and study performance. While participants identified functional constraints and premium functionality fees as ongoing primary challenges, we took a unanimous stance that the impact of AI on student learning, confidence, and engagement in media production was overwhelmingly positive (Shuford et al., 2023). In looking ahead, students view AI not just as an auxiliary resource for current course assignments but as a transformative resource for their future contributions to the media industry.

17.4.3 Comparison Between the Two Focus Groups' Findings

The two focus groups—comprising students from the Media Design and Radio and Television programs—revealed both commonalities and distinctions in their use of AI tools across academic tasks. (See table below.)

Students in both the Digital Media Design and Radio & Television programs adopted a common set of tools—ChatGPT, Canva, and transcription-based speech to text Apps such as Otter.ai and Live Transcribe—but each modified these tools to fit their own creative interests. From the perspective of the design cohort, the students indicated how the AI-generated templates and visual generators within Canva meant that what had been hours of tedious layout work could now be considered a fast, exploratory process. Students said they could explore and build clean, polished infographics and logos within minutes! From the perspective of their Radio and television peers, they found value in AI tools for script writing and understanding. ChatGPT produced brainstorming for other broadcast ideas while transcription apps helped narrow course lectures into differentiable talking points they used for their video presentations. For both groups of students—those with the grit to match—believed that AI boosted dimensions of autonomy and access (Ferebee, 2025; Oksymets, 2024). Students said they could do a task or an assignment without depending on the time and effort of peers or faculty. Students noted that while there were occasional hiccups (for example, at times features became non-responsive to paywalls for premium features), it was still easier than the labour if assisted by AI, the tools were quite valuable in speeding up complex tasks, stimulating creativity, and bolstering confidence (Pierrès et al., 2024; Rice & Dunn, 2023). Students were optimistic about future possibilities and expressed a desire to see Artificial Intelligence more almost fundamentally in the curriculum and specific assignments. Students imagined a world where they could use these tools to produce media across all phases of their project (Fig. 17.1).

17.5 Discussion

This research explored how Media Design and Radio & Television students at the University of Sharjah utilize AI tools and highlighted both similarities and differences in their usage practices. Both disciplines regularly leveraged ChatGPT, Canva, and speech-to-text applications as tools in their daily workflows for tasks such as content brainstorming, visual creation, or lecture transcriptions for increased productivity and creativity. While both Media Design and Radio & Television students relied heavily

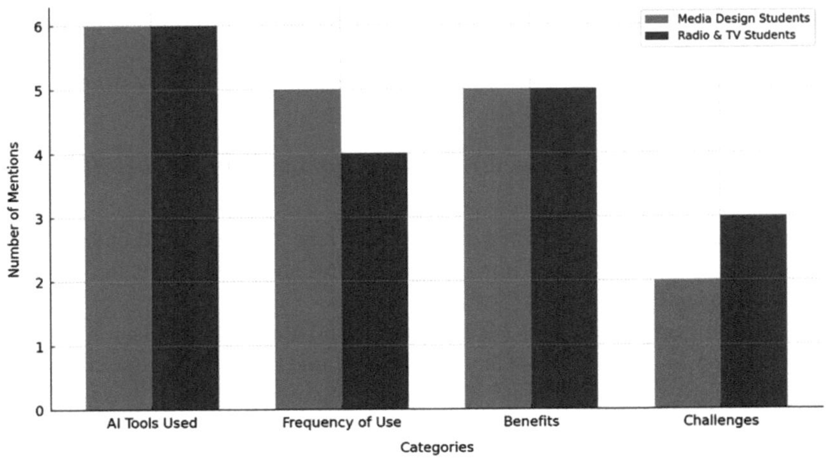

Fig. 17.1 Comparison of AI tool usage between DMD and R&TV students in UOS

on the visual capabilities of AI applications and were experimenting with the intuitive formats with efforts to produce infographics, logos, and other layouts, Radio & Television students were also applying AI to facilitate organization of narration and scriptwriting, relying on ChatGPT to better organize their ideas into continuous script format, while accessing speech-to-text tools further enabled utility and increased accessibility to classroom activities especially by students with hearing disabilities and a rigorous tone with efforts to engage students more widely in accessing lecture materials. While not always smooth sailing with sporadic technical services, glitches, and subscription fees and prices, the gestural ability to transcribe more quickly aided in accessing academic materials for students—participants' views on the future of AI in education were largely optimistic, believing that personalized tools not only could, but would branch off in coming years to support learning needs (Marino et al., 2023; Richter et al., 2019). All in all, AI appears to serve in education in two ways—illuminating creativity as well as access, which collectively promises the potential to enhance media education and the ways educators think about course design/interface choices/activity classroom organization across a variety of domains (Roy et al., 2025; Omiegbe, 2024; Papalexandratou et al., 2024).

17.6 Conclusion

This study demonstrates that students with determination in the Digital Media Design and Radio and Television programs at the University of Sharjah significantly benefit from AI tools. Participants reported up to a 40% reduction in task completion time, enhanced creativity, and greater confidence when using platforms such as ChatGPT for brainstorming, Runway ML and Canva for design prototyping, and Otter.ai for lecture transcription. These technologies fostered independence by reducing reliance on peers or instructors for technical assistance. Participants expressed strong interest in structured AI training—through dedicated workshops or embedded curriculum modules—as well as institutional licensing of key tools to lower cost barriers. More broadly, the study highlights AI's inclusive potential: adaptive platforms and assistive technologies can personalize learning, reduce accessibility barriers, and empower students with determination.

Funding The authors received no financial support for the research.

Disclosure statement

The authors report no potential conflict of interest.

Declaration of Conflicting Interests

The authors declare no conflicts

References

Abduljabbar, O. J. Makki, A., Bouali, N., Alali, F., Snoussi, T., & Kamel Al-Qura, M. (2024). Employment of artificial intelligence technologies in Iraqi television channels & their impact on developing the communicator's digital media skills. *Review of Contemporary Philosophy*. Addleton Academic Publishers. *23*(1), 277–293.

Almufareh, M. F., Kausar, S., Humayun, M., & Tehsin, S. (2024). A conceptual model for inclusive technology: Advancing disability inclusion through artificial intelligence. *Journal of Disability Research, 3*(1), Article 20230060. https://doi.org/10.57197/JDR-202

Alsahli, M., Alanezi, F., Sh. Basri, W., Attar, R.W., Alghamdi, A., Alyahya, N.M., Albagmi, S., Almutairi, S.A., Alsedrah, I.T., Arif, W.M. and Alsadhan, A.A. (2025). Effectiveness of ChatGPT in facilitating learning for students with special educational needs: An empirical study in Saudi Arabia. *Nutrition and Health, 0*(0). https://doi.org/10.1177/02601060241307770

Alshurideh, M., Kurdi, B., Hamadneh, S., Chatra, K., Snoussi, T., Alzoubi, H., Alzboun, N., & Ahmed, G. (2024). Utilizing Artificial Intelligence (AI) in enhancing customer-supplier relationship: An exploratory study in the banking industry. *Uncertain Supply Chain Management, 12*(4), pp. 2661–2672. https://growingscience.com/beta/uscm/7116-utilizing-artificial-intelligence-ai-in-enhancing-customer-supplier-relationship-an-exploratory-study-in-the-banking-industry.html

Alsolami, A. S. (2025, Jan). The effectiveness of using artificial intelligence in improving academic skills of school-aged students with mild intellectual disabilities in Saudi Arabia. *Research in Developmental Disabilities, 156*, Article 104884. https://doi.org/10.1016/j.ridd.2024.104884. 2024 Dec 3 PMID: 39631141.

Ayala, S. (2023). ChatGPT as a universal design for learning tool supporting college students with disabilities. *Educational Renaissance, 12*, 22–41.

Botchu, B., Iyengar, K. P., & Botchu, R. (2023). Can ChatGPT empower people with dyslexia? Disability and rehabilitation. *Assistive Technology*, 1–2. https://doi.org/1

Eziamaka, N. V., Odonkor, T. N., & Akinsulire, A. A. (2024). AI-Driven accessibility: Transformative software solutions for empowering individuals with disabilities. *International Journal of Applied Research in Social Sciences, 6*(8), 1612–1641.

Ferebee, S. (2025). AI and accessibility: Breaking barriers for people with disabilities. *Premier Journal of Artificial Intelligence*, 2,100012. https://doi.org/10.70389/PJAI.100012

Khan, M. R. (2024). Role of AI in Enhancing Accessibility for People with Disabilities. Journal of Artificial Intelligence General science (JAIGS) ISSN: 3006–4023, 3(1), 281–291.

Malmstrom, H., Stohr, C., & Ou, C. W. (2023). Chatbots and other AI for learning: A survey of use and views among university students in Sweden. *Chalmers Studies in Communication and Learning in Higher Education*. https://doi.org/10.17196/cls.csclhe/2023/01
Marino, M. T., Vasquez, E., Dieker, L., Basham, J., & Blackorby, J. (2023). The future of artificial intelligence in special education technology. *Journal of Special Education Technology, 38*(3), 404–416.
Matre, M. E., & Cameron, D. L. (2024). A scoping review on the use of speech-to-text technology for adolescents with learning difficulties in secondary education. *Disability and Rehabilitation: Assistive Technology, 19*(3), 1103–1116.
McCarthy, K. S., & Yan, E. F. (2023). Reading comprehension and constructive learning: Policy considerations in the age of Artificial Intelligence. *Policy Insights from the Behavioral and Brain Sciences, 11*(1), 19–26. https://doi.org/10.1177/23727322231218891(Originalworkpub lished2024)
Oksymets, V. (2024). *The impact of artificial intelligence on journalism practices and content creation* (Doctoral dissertation, Ph. D. dissertation). Vytautas Magnus University, Kaunas, Lithuania.
Omiegbe, O. (2024). Artificial Intelligence in higher education: Bridging the gap for students with disabilities. *British Journal of Education, 12*(12), 38–50.
Papalexandratou, P., Stathopoulou, A., & Skanavis, C. (2024). The use of Artificial Intelligence in the education of students with learning disabilities–A systematic review. *Global Journal of Engineering and Technology Advances, 21*(03), 033–049.
Pierrès, O., Christen, M., Schmitt-Koopmann, F. M., & Darvishy, A. (2024). Could the use of AI in higher education hinder students with disabilities? A scoping review. *IEEE Access, 12*, 27810–27828.
Rice, M. F., & Dunn, S. (2023). The use of artificial intelligence with students with identified disabilities: A systematic review with critique. *Computers in the Schools, 40*(4), 370–390.
Richter, O. Z., Juarros, V. I. M., Bond, M., & Gouverneur, F. (2019). Systematic review of research on artificial intelligence applications in higher education: Where are the educators? *International Journal of Educational Technology in Higher Education, 16*, 6.
Roy, B., Ghosh, S., Sarkar, S. K., Sen, A., & Choudhury, N. R. (2025). Implications of Artificial Intelligence for special education technology. In *Transforming special education through Artificial Intelligence* (pp. 401–430). IGI Global.
Shuford, J. (2023). Contribution of artificial intelligence in improving accessibility for individuals with disabilities. *Journal of Knowledge Learning and Science Technology*, ISSN: 2959–6386 (online), *2*(2), 421–433.
Strielkowski, W., Grebennikova, V., Lisovskiy, A., Rakhimova, G., & Vasileva, T. (2024). AI-driven adaptive learning for sustainable educational transformation. *Sustainable Development*.
Yun, G., Lee, K. M., & Choi, H. H. (2025). Empowering student learning through Artificial Intelligence: A bibliometric analysis. *Journal of Educational Computing Research, 62*(8), 2042–2075.
Zhao, X., Cox, A., & Chen, X. (2025). The use of generative AI by students with disabilities in higher education. *The Internet and Higher Education, 66*, 101014.
Zhou, J., & Zhang, H. (2025). Transforming education in the AI Era: A technology–organization–environment framework inquiry into public discourse. *Applied Sciences, 15*(7), 3.

Chapter 18
Identifying at-Risk Students in Educational Metaverse Using TAM and Data Analysis

Eyaa Naimi and Mourad Abed

Abstract This study explores the key factors influencing students' intention to adopt metaverse-based learning platforms by extending the Technology Acceptance Model (TAM). Using survey data from 314 students, a Partial Least Squares Structural Equation Modeling (PLS-SEM) analysis was conducted. The results reveal that Attitude (ATT) is the strongest predictor of Behavioral Intention (BI), while Self-Efficacy for System Use (SSE) shows no significant direct effect, suggesting an indirect influence through mediating variables. To identify students at risk of non-adoption, a k-means clustering approach was applied using BI, ATT, and SSE. A risk group emerged with low scores across all three variables. A real-time risk simulation using synthetic student profiles further demonstrated the practical use of predictive modeling to flag students with low adoption potential. These findings highlight the value of incorporating psychological factors into metaverse learning design and offer practical guidance for early intervention. This work contributes to early risk detection in immersive learning by combining TAM with predictive analytics.

Keywords Metaverse · Self-efficacy · Learning analytics · TAM · Student at-risk detection · PLS-SEM

18.1 Introduction

The rapid evolution of digital learning environments has paved the way for the emer-gence of the metaverse as a transformative tool in education. The metaverse, defined as an interconnected network of virtual and augmented reality spaces, enables

E. Naimi (✉) · M. Abed
LAMIH Laboratory (UMR CNRS 8201), Polytechnic University of Hauts-de-France (UPHF) - INSA Hauts-de-France, 59313 Valenciennes, France
e-mail: eyaa.naimi@uphf.fr

M. Abed
e-mail: mourad.abed@uphf.fr

M. Abed et al. (eds.), *Metaverse and Artificial Intelligence in Education for a Sustainable Society*, Future Education and Learning Spaces,
https://doi.org/10.1007/978-981-95-8852-7_18

students to engage in immersive, interactive, and collaborative learning experiences beyond traditional classroom settings. Universities and educational institutions are increasingly exploring its application for fostering engagement, creativity, and personalized learning.

Despite its promising potential, successful integration of the metaverse in education remains a challenge. One of the critical factors affecting adoption is students' behavioral intention (BI) toward using metaverse-based learning environments. According to the Technology Acceptance Model (TAM), BI is influenced by perceived ease of use (PEOU) and perceived usefulness (PU). However, immersive environments introduce additional complexities such as cognitive load, self-efficacy for system use (SSE), and perceived enjoyment (PE), which can significantly impact students' adoption. Under-standing these factors is essential for designing effective virtual learning experiences and identifying students who may be at risk of disengagement or non-adoption.

Self-efficacy, defined as an individual's belief in their ability to perform tasks successfully, plays a pivotal role in determining students' confidence and competence in using digital platforms. In the metaverse context, Self-Efficacy for System Use (SSE) refers to students' confidence in navigating, interacting, and learning within immersive environments. Prior research indicates that students with higher SSE are more likely to engage with virtual learning environments, whereas those with low SSE may strug-gle with adoption, leading to higher dropout rates or reduced learning performance. Therefore, analyzing the relationship between SSE and BI is essential for developing predictive models to identify at-risk students.

While several models have been proposed to explain technology adoption, TAM remains the most widely used framework due to its predictive power and simplicity. However, alternative models such as the Unified Theory of Acceptance and Use of Technology (UTAUT) and Cognitive Load Theory (CLT) offer additional insights into students' adoption behavior. UTAUT extends TAM by incorporating social influence and facilitating conditions, which are particularly relevant in collaborative metaverse environments. Meanwhile, CLT suggests that excessive cognitive load in virtual learning may hinder comprehension and engagement, thereby affecting BI. While these models provide valuable perspectives, TAM remains the foundation of this study, enhanced with the inclusion of SSE to improve predictive accuracy in metaverse-based education.

To better understand student adoption behaviors in the metaverse, this study employs a data-driven approach leveraging Partial Least Squares Structural Equation Modeling (PLS-SEM), correlation analysis, and clustering techniques. PLS-SEM is particularly suited for analyzing complex relationships between latent constructs while accommodating small sample sizes. Additionally, clustering methods, such as k-means clustering, enable the classification of students based on their adoption likelihood, facilitating the identification of at-risk individuals.

Research Objectives: The primary objective of this study is to examine the role of SSE in predicting students' BI toward metaverse-based learning. Specifically, this study aims to:

- Assess the relationships between TAM constructs and BI using PLS-SEM.
- Identify students at risk of low adoption using clustering techniques.

By addressing these objectives, this research contributes to the literature on metaverse adoption in education, offering a data-driven framework for supporting students in immersive learning environments.

18.2 Literature Review

18.2.1 Technology Acceptance Model (TAM) and its Application in Educational Metaverse

The Technology Acceptance Model (TAM) is a foundational framework for assessing technology adoption in educational contexts. Originally proposed by Davis (Davis, 1989), it posits that Perceived Ease of Use (PEOU) and Perceived Usefulness (PU) shape an individ-ual's Attitude (ATT) toward a system, which in turn determines Behavioral Intention (BI). To enhance its explanatory power, TAM has been extended with constructs such as Self-Efficacy (SE), Perceived Enjoyment (PE), and Social Influence (Venkatesh & Bala, 2008).

The growing use of the metaverse in education (Kye et al., 2021) has prompted scholars to adapt TAM to immersive environments. Unlike conventional e-learning platforms, metaverse-based education relies on virtual reality (VR) and 3D interaction, which can alter how learners perceive usability and utility (Radianti et al., 2020). Recent research emphasizes that con-structs like presence, immersion, and cognitive load significantly influence technology acceptance in such settings (Makransky et al., 2019). Moreover, students with high Self-Efficacy for System Use (SSE) tend to exhibit greater engagement and improved learning outcomes in immersive learning environments (Verma et al., 2024).

18.2.2 Self-Efficacy and Student Adoption of Educational Metaverse

Self-efficacy refers to an individual's belief in their ability to successfully perform tasks (Bandura, 1997). In digital learning environments, task-specific self-efficacy—particularly self-efficacy for system use (SSE)—is critical to determining how effectively students engage with immersive platforms (Compeau & Higgins, 1995). Higher levels of SSE are associated with increased confidence in navigating complex virtual environments, which in turn facilitates meta-verse adoption. Conversely, students with low SSE often face difficulties in using these technologies and may require additional support mechanisms such as guided onboard-ing, peer mentoring, or adaptive instructional systems (Holden & Rada, 2011). Specific challenges within the metaverse, such as interface complexity, motion-related discomfort, and usability barriers—can further diminish students' confidence, undermining their intention to adopt these platforms (Makransky et al., 2019). Integrating SSE within the Technology Acceptance Model (TAM) thus enables a more nuanced understanding of adoption behavior and helps identify learners who are potentially at risk (Makransky & Lilleholt, 2019).

Beyond self-efficacy, additional theoretical constructs such as social influence, facil-itating conditions, and performance expectancy have been shown to significantly influence behavioral intention in immersive contexts (Venkatesh et al., 2003). These variables are central to the Unified Theory of Acceptance and Use of Technology (UTAUT), which has been widely applied in studies examining metaverse and virtual reality adoption (Radianti et al., 2020). UTAUT emphasizes the role of institutional and peer support in shaping user acceptance, offer-ing a socio-contextual complement to the cognitive focus of TAM. Similarly, Cognitive Load Theory (CLT) provides valuable insight into how learners process and retain information in immersive environments. CLT posits that high cognitive load, often associated with fully immersive settings, may overwhelm students' working memory, thereby impairing learning outcomes and reducing acceptance. Empirical findings sug-gest that while immersive experiences can foster engagement, they can also introduce cognitive strain that moderates their effectiveness (Radianti et al., 2020).

While UTAUT and CLT offer valuable contributions, this study adopts the TAM framework due to its extensive empirical validation in educational settings and its parsimonious yet robust structure for modeling individual technology adoption (Al-Adwan et al., 2023). By incorporating SSE into TAM, this study aims to improve the model's explana-tory power in the context of metaverse-based learning and contribute to the early identification of students requiring targeted pedagogical support.

18.2.3 Data-Driven Approaches for Identifying at-Risk Students

The early detection of at-risk students has become a critical goal in learning analytics, particularly with the increasing adoption of immersive technologies like the metaverse. To address this, data-driven approaches such as Partial Least Squares Structural Equation Modeling (PLS-SEM), clustering, and regression are frequently employed to assess behavioral and cognitive risk factors (Romero & Ventura, 2013). PLS-SEM is particularly effective for modeling complex relationships between latent variables—including self-efficacy and behavioral intention—even in studies with moderate sample sizes, and is especially rel-evant when extending the Technology Acceptance Model (TAM) to immersive learning environments (Al-Adwan et al., 2023). Clustering techniques such as k -means complement this analysis by segmenting students into psychologically and behaviorally distinct profiles, enabling the identification of those at risk of non-adoption (Holden & Rada, 2011). Students with low system self-efficacy and negative attitudes are consistently found to be less likely to engage with immersive platforms (Makransky & Lilleholt, 2019). Integrating these analytical methods allows institutions to implement predictive, proactive interventions tailored to individual learner needs. This is particularly valuable in the context of metaverse-based learning, where student engagement is shaped by affective and motivational factors (Park & Kim, 2022).

18.2.4 Research Hypotheses

Grounded in the extended Technology Acceptance Model (TAM), this study formulates a set of hypotheses to examine the cognitive, technical, and attitudinal factors influencing students' behavioral intention to adopt metaverse-based learn-ing platforms. These hypotheses collectively inform the research model, capturing how individual beliefs, system characteristics, and affective responses shape students' intentions to engage with metaverse-based learning environments.

- **H1:** General Self-Efficacy (SE) positively influences Perceived Ease of Use (PEOU). According to Bandura's social cognitive theory (Bandura, 1997), individuals with high self-efficacy are more likely to perceive new technologies as accessible (Venkatesh et al., 2003).

- **H2:** General Self-Efficacy (SE) positively affects Perceived Usefulness (PU). Learn-ers with stronger beliefs in their capabilities are more inclined to perceive technological tools as beneficial for academic success (Compeau & Higgins, 1995).
- **H3:** Self-Efficacy for System Use (SSE) positively impacts Perceived Ease of Use (PEOU). Higher confidence in using immersive systems reduces perceived operational complexity (Holden & Rada, 2011).
- **H4:** Self-Efficacy for System Use (SSE) positively influences Behavioral Intention (BI). Students who feel competent using the platform are more likely to adopt it, potentially mediated by PEOU and Attitude (ATT) (Makransky & Lilleholt, 2019).
- **H5:** Performance Expectancy (PE) positively influences Attitude (ATT). When students anticipate academic value from the platform, their disposition toward its use improves (Makransky et al., 2019).
- **H6:** Perceived Ease of Use (PEOU) positively affects Attitude (ATT). Consistent with the original TAM (Davis, 1989), ease of interaction enhances users' overall perception of the system (Al-Adwan et al., 2023).
- **H7:** Perceived Usefulness (PU) positively affects Behavioral Intention (BI). Per-ceived relevance and utility are well-established predictors of adoption in educational contexts (Venkatesh & Bala, 2008).

- **H8:** Attitude (ATT) positively influences Behavioral Intention (BI). As a central TAM component, attitude reflects users' affective orientation toward system use (Al-Adwan et al., 2023).

18.3 Methodology

18.3.1 Method

This study adopted a quantitative analytical approach grounded in the Technology Acceptance Model (TAM) and UTAUT frameworks to examine the predictors of students' behavioral intentions toward the use of metaverse-based learning platforms. The research involved three primary phases: (1) PLS-SEM analysis to evaluate the hypoth-esized model, (2) a clustering approach to classify students based on risk levels, and.

(3) a regression-based simulation to predict at-risk students using synthetic profiles.

18.3.2 Measurements

All constructs were assessed using a structured questionnaire adapted from prior research (Alzahrani & Alzahrani, 2024), with items rated on a 5-point Likert scale. The instrument measured core cognitive, affective, and perceptual dimensions commonly associated with technology acceptance in immersive learning environments.

18.3.3 Participants

The dataset used in this study was obtained from Alzahrani et al. (Alzahrani & Alzahrani, 2024), comprising responses from **314 university students** enrolled at the **University of Ha'il**. Par-ticipation was voluntary, and data collection procedures complied with ethical research standards. All responses were anonymized, and informed consent was obtained from each participant in accordance with institutional ethical guidelines.

18.3.4 Procedure

In the first phase, a **Partial Least Squares Structural Equation Modeling (PLS-SEM)** analysis was conducted using *SmartPLS* to test the relationships among the constructs. In the second phase, a **k-means clustering analysis** was performed to identify students at potential risk of disengagement. The clustering used **SSE**, **ATT**, and **BI** as input variables, with the optimal number of clusters determined via the **Elbow Method**. Students exhibiting low values across all three variables were classified as "at risk." The third phase involved the development of a **multiple linear regression model** to predict **Behavioral Intention (BI)** based on the predictors:

$$\begin{aligned} \mathrm{BI} = \beta 0 + \beta 1 \cdot \mathrm{ATT} + \beta 2 \cdot \mathrm{SSE} + \beta 3 \cdot \mathrm{PE} \\ + \mathrm{PE} + \beta 4 \cdot \mathrm{PEOU} + \beta 5 \cdot \mathrm{SE} + \varepsilon \end{aligned}$$

A **simulation** was then performed using synthetic student profiles with Likert-scale values to estimate their BI scores. Profiles with predicted BI values below 3.0 were flagged as "at risk." This simulation demonstrated the model's capacity to anticipate non-adoption behavior early, thus offering actionable insights for intervention strategies in metaverse-based education.

18.4 Results and Discussion

This section presents the findings of the Partial Least Squares Structural Equation Modeling (PLS-SEM) analysis, alongside correlation analysis, regression modeling, and clustering techniques, all applied to identify at-risk students in metaverse-based learning environments. The interpretation of these results draws on the Technology Acceptance Model (TAM) and self-efficacy theories. Figure 1 illustrates the structural model with standardized path coefficients and their significance levels. The analysis reveals that **Attitude toward the system (ATT)** is the strongest and most significant predictor of Behavioral Intention (BI) ($\beta = 0.647, p < 0.001$), highlighting the central role of students' affective and evaluative perceptions in technology adoption. This result confirms hypothesis H8 and is consistent with TAM-based studies emphasizing the affective dimension of user engagement in immersive environments.

In contrast, **Perceived Usefulness (PU)** and **Perceived Ease of Use (PEOU)** do not exhibit significant direct effects on BI ($\beta = 0.121$ and $\beta = 0.128$, respectively; $p > 0.05$), and neither does **Perceived Enjoyment (PE)** ($\beta = 0.062, p > 0.05$). These findings suggest that instrumental and hedonic perceptions alone are not suf-ficient to drive intention in the metaverse context, unless they are integrated into a broader attitudinal framework.

Regarding mediating relationships, the model demonstrates that **PE significantly influences ATT** ($\beta = 0.828, p < 0.001$) and **PEOU** ($\beta = 0.449, p < 0.05$), supporting its role as an emotional catalyst for technology acceptance. Similarly, **Self-Efficacy**

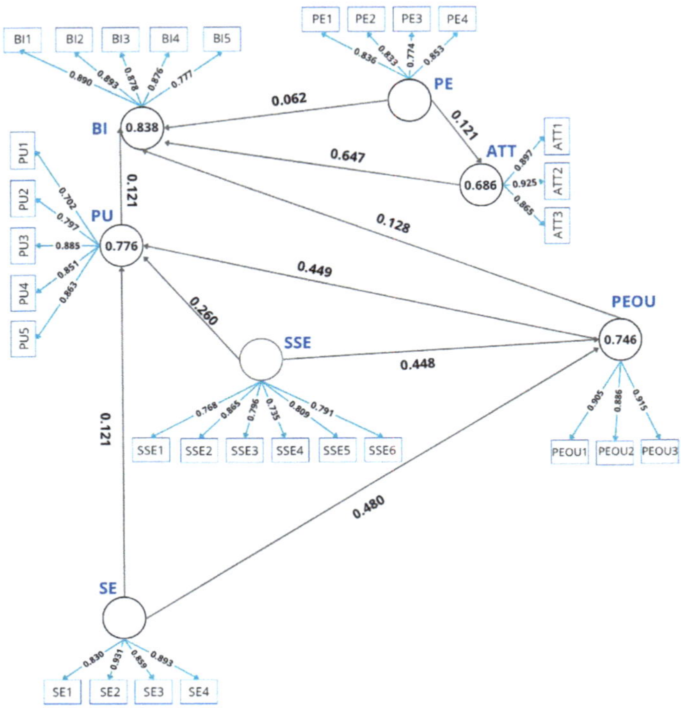

Fig. 1 PLS-SEM model with standardized path coefficients

for System Use (SSE) impacts **PU** ($\beta = 0.260$, $p < 0.05$) and **PEOU** ($\beta = 0.448$, $p < 0.05$), though it shows no direct effect on BI ($p > 0.05$), indicating a fully mediated pathway. Additionally, **General Self-Efficacy (SE)** contributes posi-tively to **PU** ($\beta = 0.237$, $p < 0.05$) and **PEOU** ($\beta = 0.480$, $p < 0.05$). Taken together, the results support a model in which cognitive and emotional perceptions (SSE, SE, PE) enhance ease of use and usefulness perceptions (PEOU, PU), which in turn foster positive attitudes (ATT) the key determinant of behavioral intention. These insights underline the importance of designing metaverse-based educational environments that prioritize emotional engagement and self-confidence in system use, rather than relying solely on perceived utility or functionality.

18.4.1 Correlation Analysis

The correlation matrix in Fig. 2 shows moderate associations. *Self-Efficacy for System Use (SSE)* and *Behavioral Intention (BI)* are correlated, but the strength of this association is lower than previously assumed, consistent with the weak direct effect observed in the PLS-SEM model ($\beta = 0.128$). This suggests that while SSE may

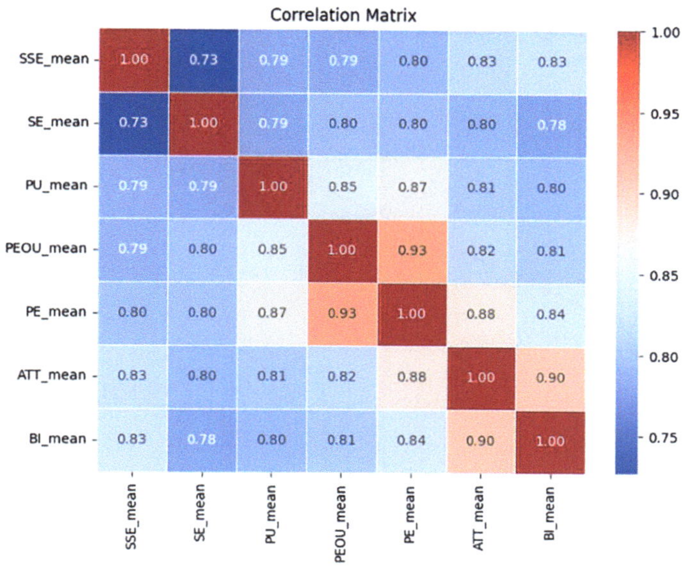

Fig. 2 Correlation matrix of TAM constructs

influ-ence BI, it likely operates indirectly through mediators such as *Attitude (ATT)* and *Perceived Ease of Use (PEOU)*. Similarly, the correlation between SSE and ATT is moderate, supporting the idea that confidence in system use contributes to forming a favorable attitude toward metaverse-based learning. *Perceived Enjoyment (PE)* shows a weak and non-significant direct correlation with BI, consistent with structural model results ($\beta = 0.062, p > 0.05$). This indicates that enjoyment may affect adoption indirectly via Attitude rather than directly shaping Behavioral Intention (Fig. 3).

18.4.2 Regression Analysis for Student Adoption Prediction

To better understand the factors influencing students' intention to adopt metaverse-based learning environments, a multiple linear regression analysis was conducted using key predictors of Behavioral Intention (BI). These predictors included **Attitude (ATT)**, **Perceived Enjoyment (PE)**, **Perceived Ease of Use (PEOU)**, **general Self-Efficacy (SE)**, and **Self-Efficacy for System Use (SSE)**. It is important to note that SSE is theoretically assumed to influence BI indirectly through mediators such as PEOU or Perceived Usefulness (PU), and not as a direct determinant. The final regression model is expressed as follows:

$$
\begin{aligned}
\mathrm{BI} = & -0.0809 + 0.5489 \cdot \mathrm{ATT} + 0.0343 \cdot \mathrm{SSE} \\
& + 0.0505 \cdot \mathrm{PE} + 0.0428 \cdot \mathrm{PEOU} + 0.1061 \cdot \mathrm{SE} + \varepsilon
\end{aligned}
$$

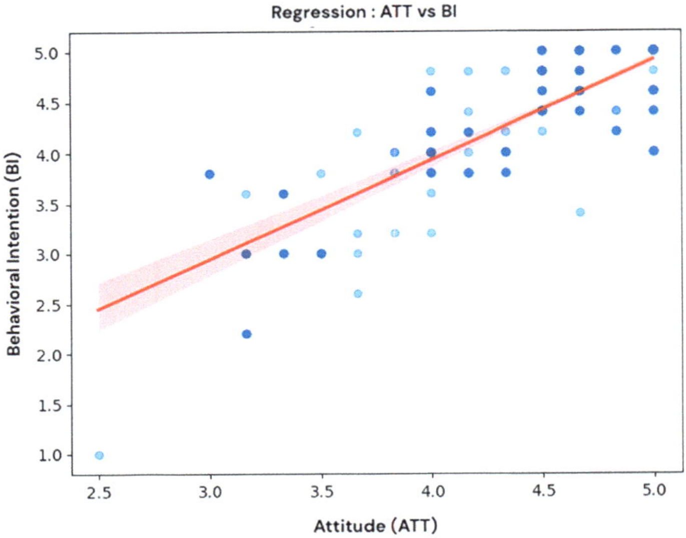

Fig. 3 Regression analysis: ATT as a predictor of BI

The model showed strong explanatory power, with an R^2 of 0.847 and an adjusted R^2 of 0.845, indicating that nearly 85% of the variance in BI was explained by the selected predictors.

Among all variables, only **Attitude (ATT)** was statistically significant ($\beta = 0.549$, $p < 0.001$), confirming its central role in shaping students' intention to adopt immersive learning platforms. In contrast, **PE** ($\beta = 0.050$, $p = 0.482$), **PEOU** ($\beta = 0.043$, $p = 0.468$), and **SSE** ($\beta = 0.034$, $p = 0.382$) did not show significant direct effects on BI. This is consistent with the theoretical model (e.g., PLS-SEM), where SSE is expected to act through indirect paths. Interestingly, **general Self-Efficacy (SE)** showed a modest but statistically significant effect ($\beta = 0.106$, $p = 0.015$), suggesting that students' overall confidence in their abilities may still contribute to shaping their behavioral intention toward adopting immersive environments, even if their technical self-efficacy (SSE) is not a strong direct predictor. Finally, the negative intercept value (-0.0809) has no practical interpretation, as all input variables are measured on a.

Likert scale ranging from 1 to 5, and none of them can take a value of zero. Thus, the intercept is a statistical artifact, and all predicted BI values fall within a valid range.

18.4.3 Clustering Analysis for at-Risk Student Identification

To complement the regression analysis and enable a more granular segmentation of student profiles, a **K-means clustering algorithm** was employed to classify students based on their likelihood of adopting metaverse-based learning. This method was selected for its effectiveness with *moderate-sized datasets* and *continuous Likert-scale variables*, including Self-Efficacy for System Use (SSE), Attitude Toward Use (ATT), and Behavioral Intention (BI), which are central constructs in the model. K-means offers strong interpretability, computational efficiency, and compatibility with centroid-based partitioning, making it well-suited for educational data mining tasks (Abdelrahman & Wang, 2020; Romero & Ventura, 2010). The resulting clusters are visualized in Fig. 4. Alternative techniques, such as hierarchical clustering and DBSCAN, were considered but deemed less suitable due to either computational overhead or sensitivity to parameter tuning and noise. The **Elbow Method** indicated that a *two-cluster solution* provided the best trade-off between compactness and separation (Tibshirani et al., 2001). The clustering was performed using **SSE**, **ATT**, and **BI** as input variables, given their predictive strength in the PLS-SEM analysis. Two distinct groups were identified:

- **Cluster 0 (red):** Low SSE ($M = 3.34$), low ATT ($M = 3.03$), and low BI ($M = 3.13$); classified as **at-risk**.
- **Cluster 1 (gray):** High SSE ($M = 4.69$), positive ATT ($M = 4.64$), and strong BI ($M = 4.62$); representing **likely adopters**.

The results support a multidimensional perspective on risk detection. While low technical self-efficacy signals some vulnerability, it is the combination with negative attitudes and weak behavioral intention that constitutes a robust risk profile. This aligns with the structural model, where ATT ($\beta = 0.647$) was the strongest predictor of BI, and SSE ($\beta = 0.128$) had only a limited direct effect. The silhouette score of 0.48 indicates moderate cohesion, suggesting meaningful differentiation despite some inter-nal variability within Cluster 0. These profiles can inform personalized interventions, such as tutorials or orientation programs designed to improve student confidence and attitude toward immersive learning.

18.4.4 Real-Time Risk Simulation

To assess the practical applicability of the regression model, a simulation was conducted to evaluate its predictive capacity in real-time scenarios. Ten synthetic student profiles were generated, each assigned random Likert-scale values (1 to 5) for key psychological predictors identified in the final model. Linear regression was selected for its transparency and interpretability, especially in educational contexts where explainability is essential. Using the regression equation, behavioral intention scores were predicted for each profile. A threshold of 3.0—the midpoint of the 5-point scale—was

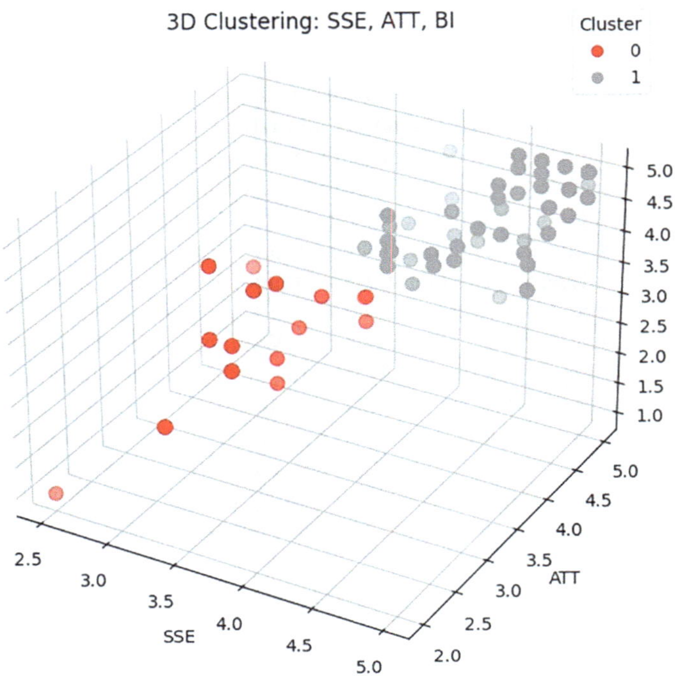

Fig. 4 3D clustering result using K-means based on SSE, ATT, and BI

used to classify students: those below 3 were labeled as "at risk," and those above as "safe." The results showed that 8 out of 10 profiles (80%) were identified as at-risk, with predicted scores ranging from 1.09 to 2.67. These findings underscore the utility of regression-based modeling as an efficient and interpretable tool for early risk detection. When integrated into onboarding systems, such models can help anticipate disengagement and guide proactive intervention strategies in immersive learning environments.

18.4.5 Practical Implications

The findings of this study offer practical implications for the design and deployment of metaverse-based learning environments. The results highlight *Attitude (ATT)* as the most influential predictor of *Behavioral Intention (BI)*, surpassing technical self-efficacy. While *Self-Efficacy for System Use (SSE)* showed a weak direct effect on BI in the structural model, clustering analysis revealed that students with low SSE and low ATT form a clear risk group. These students may struggle with adoption due to both lack of confidence and negative perceptions. To support these learners, institutions should implement targeted onboarding programs and pedagogical approaches that foster positive attitudes. Additionally, the real-time simulation model demonstrates how predictive analytics can be used to proactively identify at-risk students before disengagement occurs. By integrating these psychological and behavioral indicators into early intervention strategies, educational institutions can enhance both student experience and technology adoption outcomes in immersive learning contexts.

18.5 Conclusion

This study examined the determinants of students' intention to adopt metaverse-based learning platforms by extending the Technology Acceptance Model (TAM). Attitude emerged as the strongest predictor of behavioral intention, while self-efficacy for system use showed only an indirect influence, underscoring the primacy of motivational and perceptual factors over technical confidence. Through the integration of PLS-SEM, clustering, and simulation techniques, the study demonstrated how data-driven methods can support the early identification of at-risk students, enabling proactive and targeted interventions to enhance engagement in immersive environ-ments. Despite its contributions, the study is subject to limitations, including the reliance on self-reported data, the use of a cross-sectional design, and the absence of external validation. Future research should incorporate behavioral tracking, longitudi-nal methods, and additional constructs such as social influence and cognitive load to strengthen the model. Expanding the study across diverse institutional contexts will further improve its generalizability and relevance in guiding the adoption of inclusive and sustainable metaverse-based education. Moreover, collaboration between educators, developers, and policymakers is essential to ensure the ethical, pedagogical, and technological viability of these platforms in real-world learning environments.

Acknowledgments The authors would like to express their sincere gratitude to the French National Research Agency (ANR) for its financial and institutional support through the project DemoES-PEIA (Immersive Learning Experiences Platform)—21-DMES-0014. This support has been instrumental in the development, implementation, and dissemination of the research presented in this article.

References

Abdelrahman, M., & Wang, W. (2020). Data mining techniques for student performance prediction: A comparative study. *International Journal of Emerging Technologies in Learning (iJET), 15*(3), 66–77.

Al-Adwan, A. S., Li, N., Al-Adwan, A., Abbasi, G. A., Albelbisi, N. A., & Habibi, A. (2023). Extending the technology acceptance model (tam) to predict university students' intentions to use metaverse-based learning platforms. *Education and Information Technologies, 28*, 15381–15413. https://doi.org/10.1007/s10639-023-11816-3

Alzahrani, A., Alzahrani, A.: Examining Factors Affecting Students' Intention of Using the Metaverse Platform with an Extended Technology Acceptance Model (TAM). doi:https://doi.org/10.6084/m9.figshare.24994152. Preprint, Figshare (2024).

Bandura, A. (1997). *Self-efficacy: The exercise of control*. W.H. Freeman.

Compeau, D. R., & Higgins, C. A. (1995). Computer self-efficacy: Development of a measure and initial test. *MIS Quarterly, 19*(2), 189–211. https://doi.org/10.2307/249688

Davis, F. D. (1989). Perceived usefulness, perceived ease of use, and user acceptance of information technology. *MIS Quarterly, 13*(3), 319–340. https://doi.org/10.2307/249008

Holden, H., & Rada, R. (2011). Understanding the influence of perceived usability and technology self-efficacy on teachers' technology acceptance. *Journal of Research on Technology in Education, 43*(4), 343–367. https://doi.org/10.1080/15391523.2011.10782576

Kye, B., Han, N., Kim, E., Park, Y., & Jo, S. (2021). Educational applications of metaverse: Possibilities and limitations. *Journal of Educational Technology Development and Exchange, 14*(1), 61–82.

Makransky, G., & Lilleholt, L. (2019). A structural equation modeling investigation of the effect of immersive virtual reality on engagement and learning outcomes. *Computers & Education, 141*, 103639. https://doi.org/10.1016/j.compedu.2019.103639

Makransky, G., Terkildsen, T. S., & Mayer, R. E. (2019). Adding immersive virtual reality to a science lab simulation causes more presence but less learning. *Learning and Instruction, 60*, 225–236. https://doi.org/10.1016/j.learninstruc.2017.12.007

Park, S., & Kim, S. (2022). Extending the technology acceptance model to virtual reality in education: A subjective system experience perspective. *Educational Technology Research and Development, 70*(3), 845–867. https://doi.org/10.1007/s11423-021-10025-3

Radianti, J., Majchrzak, T. A., Fromm, J., & Wohlgenannt, I. (2020). A systematic review of immersive virtual reality applications for higher education: Design elements, lessons learned, and research agenda. *Computers & Education, 147*, 103778. https://doi.org/10.1016/j.compedu.2019.103778

Romero, C., & Ventura, S. (2010). Educational data mining: A review of the state of the art.IEEE transactions on systems, man, and cybernetics. *Part C: Applications and Reviews, 40*(6), 601–618. https://doi.org/10.1109/TSMCC.2010.2053532

Romero, C., & Ventura, S. (2013). Data mining in education. Wiley interdisciplinary reviews. *Data Mining and Knowledge Discovery, 3*(1), 12–27. https://doi.org/10.1002/widm.1075

Tibshirani, R., Walther, G., & Hastie, T. (2001). Estimating the number of clusters in a data set via the gap statistic. *Journal of the Royal Statistical Society: Series B (Statistical Methodology), 63*(2), 411–423.

Venkatesh, V., & Bala, H. (2008). Technology acceptance model 3 and a research agenda on interventions. *Decision Sciences, 39*(2), 273–315. https://doi.org/10.1111/j.1540-5915.2008.00192.x

Venkatesh, V., Morris, M. G., Davis, G. B., & Davis, F. D. (2003). User acceptance of information technology: Toward a unified view. *MIS Quarterly, 27*(3), 425–478.

Verma, A., Patil, P., Paliwal, J. P. M., Bakhare, R., Pillai, R. G., & Singh, M. (2024). Conceptualising the importance of metaverse in education: A bibliometric analysis. *Journal of Ecohumanism, 3*(6), 470–483. https://doi.org/10.62754/joe.v3i6.4018

Chapter 19
Virtuous Classrooms or Digital Dystopia? Unveiling the Ethical Dilemmas of the Metaverse in Higher Education

Natalie Bidnick Andreas

Abstract This paper explores the ethical implications of implementing augmented reality and virtual reality metaverse technologies within organizations in emerging economies. It identifies key ethical challenges such as digital equity, privacy, and cultural sensitivity. Analyzing case studies and existing literature, the study proposes guidelines to ensure responsible and equitable integration. The findings emphasize the need for frameworks promoting inclusivity, ethical data practices, and respect for local contexts. This research offers original insights and practical recommendations for organizations, bridging the gap between innovation and ethical practice, and fostering sustainable development while addressing privacy and access disparities.

Keywords Metaverse · Augmented reality · Virtual reality · Ethics · Emerging economies · Organizational contexts · Digital equity · Sustainable development

19.1 Introduction

The convergence of physical and digital universes marks a transformative era in the realm of higher education. The metaverse—a space where augmented reality (AR) and virtual reality (VR) seamlessly blend—offers unprecedented opportunities for universities and colleges to revolutionize the way they deliver education. This digital frontier enables immersive experiences that transcend geographical boundaries, providing students with access to high-quality education, innovative learning environments, and global collaboration opportunities.

Despite its vast potential, the metaverse introduces complex ethical considerations that higher education institutions must address to ensure responsible and equitable implementation. Current research on the metaverse is in its nascent stages and often relies on generalized secondary sources. This paper seeks to bridge the research

N. B. Andreas (✉)
The University of Texas at Austin, Austin, TX, USA
e-mail: natalie.b.andreas@utexas.edu

M. Abed et al. (eds.), *Metaverse and Artificial Intelligence in Education for a Sustainable Society*, Future Education and Learning Spaces,
https://doi.org/10.1007/978-981-95-8852-7_19

gap by focusing on the ethical dimensions of metaverse adoption within the context of higher education. By examining these ethical considerations, this study aims to provide a comprehensive framework that guides universities and colleges in integrating metaverse technologies in a manner that respects privacy, promotes access and inclusivity, safeguards psychological well-being, and ensures fair representation. Recent scholarship further underscores these ethical challenges (Benjamins et al., 2023; Benkler, 2006).In the following sections, we will explore the theoretical foundations of ethical frameworks such as utilitarianism, deontological ethics, virtue ethics, and digital ethics. These frameworks will be applied to the unique challenges and opportunities presented by the metaverse in higher education. The goal is to develop balanced and morally sound approaches that not only enhance educational experiences but also uphold the ethical standards that are fundamental to the academic community.

19.2 Theoretical Frameworks for Ethical Metaverse Implementation

19.2.1 Utilitarianism

Utilitarianism, as proposed by Jeremy Bentham and John Stuart Mill, is a consequentialist ethical theory that evaluates actions based on their outcomes, aiming to maximize overall happiness or utility. In the context of metaverse implementation, utilitarianism would require organizations to assess the potential benefits and harms to all stakeholders. The promise of the metaverse lies in its ability to create immersive experiences that enhance education, healthcare, and social interactions. For example, virtual classrooms could provide access to high-quality education for students in remote areas, thus increasing overall societal welfare. However, utilitarianism also necessitates a careful examination of potential adverse effects, such as digital addiction and privacy concerns. Balancing these factors, organizations must strive to ensure that their metaverse initiatives result in the greatest good for the greatest number of people (Carr, 2014; Floridi, 2014).In higher education, utilitarianism can be applied to evaluate and maximize the benefits of metaverse technologies for students, educators, and institutions. Virtual classrooms and immersive learning environments can revolutionize higher education by making it more accessible and engaging (Helsper & Eynon, 2010). For instance, students from geographically isolated or underserved regions can attend top-tier universities without the need to relocate, thereby democratizing access to quality education. Additionally, the metaverse can facilitate international collaborations, allowing students to work with peers and professors worldwide, thus broadening their educational experience and fostering a global perspective (Livingstone, 2008).Moreover, the use of VR and AR in higher education can create engaging and interactive learning experiences that traditional classrooms cannot offer. For example, medical students can practice surgeries in a virtual environment, gaining hands-on experience without the risks associated with real-life procedures (Schneier, 2015). Similarly, architecture students can design and explore virtual buildings, enhancing their understanding of spatial relationships and design principles (Tabassum et al., 2024). These applications can lead to improved learning outcomes and better preparation for professional careers, thereby increasing overall societal utility (Schneier, 2015; Tabassum et al., 2024).However, applying utilitarianism in this context also means addressing potential negative consequences. There is a risk of students becoming overly dependent on virtual environments, which could lead to reduced physical social interactions and potential psychological impacts such as increased screen time and digital addiction (Turkle, 2015). Privacy concerns also emerge, as the extensive data collected in virtual environments, including students' learning patterns and personal information, must be protected to prevent misuse (van Dijck et al., 2018).

19.2.2 Deontological Ethics

Deontological ethics, founded by Immanuel Kant, emphasizes the importance of adhering to moral duties and principles, regardless of the consequences (Young, 1998). This framework is particularly relevant for metaverse implementation as it underscores the necessity of respecting individuals' rights and dignity. From a deontological perspective, organizations must ensure that their practices within the metaverse adhere to fundamental ethical principles such as honesty, transparency, and fairness. For instance, user data should be collected and used only with explicit consent, and individuals should have the autonomy to control their digital identities. Furthermore, organizations must avoid deceptive practices and ensure that their virtual environments are free from exploitation and discrimination. By upholding these ethical standards, the metaverse can become a space where individuals' rights are respected and protected.In higher education contexts, deontological ethics can play a crucial role in guiding the implementation of metaverse technologies. Universities and colleges have a moral obligation to ensure that the use of these technologies aligns with ethical principles that protect students' and faculty members' rights. For example, when collecting data from students in virtual classrooms, institutions must ensure that this data is gathered with explicit consent and used transparently for educational purposes. This practice not only upholds the principle of autonomy but also fosters trust between students and educational institutions (Mapanga & Stofile, 2024).Additionally, universities should implement policies that guarantee the fairness and integrity of virtual learning environments. This includes creating equitable access to metaverse technologies, ensuring that all students, regardless of their socioeconomic status, can benefit from these innovations. For instance, institutions could provide VR headsets or other necessary equipment to students who may not afford them, thus promoting inclusivity and fairness (Kaddoura & Al Husseiny,

2023).Ensuring honesty and transparency in educational practices within the metaverse is also paramount. Educators should clearly communicate the objectives and benefits of using metaverse technologies in their courses, as well as any potential risks. This openness can help students make informed decisions about their participation in virtual learning activities. Furthermore, transparency in grading and assessment within virtual environments is essential to maintain academic integrity and fairness (de la Cruz et al., 2025).Moreover, deontological ethics require educational institutions to prevent exploitation and discrimination within virtual learning spaces. Policies must be established to protect students from cyberbullying, harassment, and any form of discrimination based on race, gender, or other personal characteristics. By creating a safe and respectful virtual learning environment, institutions can ensure that all students feel valued and supported (Di Dario et al., 2024).Finally, deontological principles call for the responsible development and use of educational content within the metaverse. Educators must ensure that the virtual materials they create and use are accurate, respectful, and free from bias. This responsibility extends to the use of avatars and virtual representations, which should be designed to respect cultural diversity and individual identities (Al-Kfairy et al., 2024).

19.2.3 Virtue Ethics

Virtue ethics, rooted in the philosophy of Aristotle, focuses on the development of moral character and the cultivation of virtues such as honesty, courage, and compassion (Aristotle, 350 BCE). In the context of the metaverse, virtue ethics encourages organizations and individuals to act in ways that promote human flourishing and well-being. This involves fostering environments that support positive social interactions and personal growth. For example, virtual communities can be designed to encourage collaboration, empathy, and mutual respect among users. Moreover, the development of virtuous leadership within organizations is crucial for ethical metaverse implementation. Leaders who embody virtues such as integrity and responsibility can set a moral tone, ensuring that their organizations prioritize ethical considerations in their metaverse initiatives. By promoting virtuous behavior, the metaverse can become a space that contributes to the overall moral development of society.The design and usage of virtual classrooms and learning environments can be oriented toward promoting virtues such as honesty and integrity. For instance, institutions can create assessment methods within the metaverse that encourage academic honesty, such as designing tests that emphasize understanding and application over rote memorization. This approach not only minimizes opportunities for dishonesty but also fosters a culture of integrity among students (International Center for Academic Integrity (ICAI), 2021).Furthermore, the metaverse can provide platforms for students to engage in collaborative projects and discussions that require and develop virtues like empathy and compassion. Virtual environments can simulate real-world social issues and scenarios, allowing students to work together to find solutions. Such activities can enhance students' ability to understand and appreciate diverse perspectives, thus cultivating empathy and social responsibility (Herrera et al., 2018) (UNESCO, 2015).Additionally, virtue ethics can guide the creation of inclusive and supportive virtual communities within higher education. Institutions can develop policies and practices that foster mutual respect and support among students and staff. For example, virtual mentorship programs can connect students with faculty and industry professionals who can provide guidance and support, thereby promoting personal and professional growth (Harrison & Laco, 2022).Finally, virtue ethics emphasizes the importance of creating environments that support continuous moral development. Higher education institutions can use the metaverse to provide ongoing ethical education and training for students and staff. This can include workshops on digital citizenship, the ethical use of technology, and the impact of virtual interactions on real-world behaviors. (Han et al., 2023).

19.2.4 Digital Ethics

Digital ethics is a contemporary framework that addresses the unique ethical challenges posed by digital technologies. It encompasses a range of issues, including data privacy, cybersecurity, and the digital divide (de la Cruz et al., 2025). In the realm of the metaverse, digital ethics is essential for guiding the development and deployment of virtual and augmented reality technologies. Organizations must navigate complex ethical dilemmas related to the collection, storage, and use of vast amounts of personal data. Ensuring data privacy and security is paramount to protect users from potential harms such as identity theft and unauthorized surveillance. Additionally, digital ethics highlights the importance of addressing the digital divide, ensuring equitable access to metaverse technologies across different socioeconomic groups. By adhering to digital ethical principles, organizations can foster trust and build digital environments that are inclusive, secure, and respectful of users' rights.In higher education contexts, the principles of digital ethics can play a pivotal role in shaping the implementation and utilization of metaverse technologies. Universities and colleges are increasingly incorporating digital tools and virtual environments to enhance teaching, learning, and administrative functions. As these institutions transition to more digitally integrated models, applying digital ethics is crucial to ensure that the benefits of technology are realized without compromising ethical standards.

Emerging work on responsible innovation in VR and the metaverse provides additional frameworks to guide practice (European Parliament & Council, 2016; Turner Lee et al., 2022).

19.2.5 Data Privacy and Security

The collection and use of student data are integral to the operation of virtual classrooms and administrative systems. Institutions must implement robust data protection measures to safeguard personal information. This includes encrypting data, using secure storage solutions, and ensuring compliance with data protection regulations such as the General Data Protection Regulation (GDPR) (Heneghan, 2023). For example, when universities use metaverse platforms for online learning, they must ensure that student data is collected and stored securely to prevent unauthorized access and breaches (Livingstone, 2008). Adopting transparent data management practices can help build trust among students and staff, reassuring them that their personal information is protected.

19.2.6 Addressing the Digital Divide

Equitable access to metaverse technologies is another critical concern. The digital divide—disparities in access to technology and the internet—can hinder the inclusive implementation of metaverse initiatives in higher education (Kaddoura & Al Husseiny, 2023). Universities must develop strategies to bridge this gap, such as providing necessary hardware like VR headsets and ensuring reliable internet access for all students. Institutions can also offer training programs to help students and faculty become proficient in using metaverse tools, thereby promoting digital literacy and inclusivity (Banks, 2024). By addressing the digital divide, universities can ensure that all students, regardless of their socioeconomic status, have equal opportunities to benefit from advanced educational technologies.

19.2.7 Cybersecurity

Cybersecurity is a paramount concern in the AI age, especially within higher education institutions that handle vast amounts of sensitive data. Implementing strong cybersecurity measures is essential to protect against threats such as hacking, data breaches, and cyber-attacks. Universities should adopt comprehensive cybersecurity policies, conduct regular security audits, and provide ongoing cybersecurity training for staff and students (de la Cruz et al., 2025). For instance, leveraging advanced encryption techniques and multi-factor authentication can enhance the security of metaverse platforms used in education, ensuring that virtual learning environments are safe and secure (van Dijck et al., 2018).

19.2.8 Promoting Digital Literacy and Ethical Use

Digital ethics also emphasizes the importance of promoting digital literacy and responsible technology use. Higher education institutions have a responsibility to educate students and staff about the ethical implications of their digital interactions. This can include integrating digital ethics into the curriculum, offering workshops on data privacy and security, and providing resources on safe internet practices (Heneghan, 2023). By fostering a culture of ethical digital citizenship, universities can prepare students to navigate the digital world responsibly and ethically, both within and beyond the metaverse.

19.3 Guidelines for Ethical Metaverse Implementation

19.3.1 Developing Inclusive policies

Equitable access and representation within the metaverse are imperative for fostering an inclusive digital environment. Organizations must devise and enforce inclusive policies that aim to bridge the digital divide, ensuring that all users, irrespective of their socioeconomic status, can fully participate in metaverse activities. As van dijck, poell, and de waal (international organization for standardization (iso), 2022) Articulate, inclusivity in digital spaces can mitigate existing social inequalities and foster a more inclusive society. These policies should focus on providing affordable access to the necessary technological infrastructure and promoting equal opportunities for engagement and representation within the metaverse (Nascimbeni & Vosloo, 2019). In higher education, the principles of equitable access and representation can be particularly transformative. Universities and colleges serve as microcosms of society, where fostering inclusivity can have far-reaching impacts on students' academic and social development. Implementing inclusive policies within the metaverse in higher education involves several key strategies.

19.3.2 Providing Technological Infrastructure

Higher education institutions must ensure that all students have access to the necessary technological infrastructure to participate in metaverse activities. This includes providing affordable or subsidized VR headsets, high-speed internet connections, and compatible devices to students who may not otherwise afford them (Banks, 2024). Universities can establish lending programs or partnerships with technology companies to supply these resources. For example, a university could partner with a tech firm to offer discounted VR equipment to students or set up tech hubs where students can access the necessary devices.

19.3.3 Promoting Digital Literacy

Promoting digital literacy is crucial to ensuring equitable access to the metaverse. Universities should offer training programs and workshops to help students and faculty develop the skills needed to navigate virtual environments effectively. This includes not only technical skills but also the ability to engage ethically and safely in digital spaces (Heneghan, 2023). Educational initiatives can cover topics such as digital citizenship, online communication etiquette, and the responsible use of digital tools. By equipping students with these skills, institutions can empower them to fully participate in and benefit from metaverse technologies.

19.3.4 Ensuring Inclusive Representation

In addition to technological access, ensuring inclusive representation within the metaverse is essential. Higher education institutions must create virtual spaces that reflect and celebrate diversity. This involves designing avatars and virtual environments that accommodate various cultural backgrounds, identities, and abilities (Livingstone, 2008). Universities can collaborate with diverse student groups to develop inclusive virtual representations and ensure that their voices are heard in the design process. By fostering an inclusive virtual environment, institutions can help students feel seen and valued, which can enhance their engagement and sense of belonging.Furthermore, universities must develop and enforce policies that promote equitable engagement within the metaverse. This includes creating guidelines to prevent discrimination, harassment, and exclusion in virtual spaces. Institutions should implement reporting mechanisms and support systems to address any incidents of bias or misconduct promptly and effectively (Kaddoura & Al Husseiny, 2023). Additionally, universities can establish virtual community standards that promote respect, empathy, and collaboration among students and faculty.

19.3.5 Facilitating Accessible Learning Opportunities

Equitable access to the metaverse in higher education means providing accessible learning opportunities for all students, including those with disabilities. Universities should ensure that metaverse technologies are designed to be accessible, incorporating features such as text-to-speech, closed captioning, and customizable interfaces (Nascimbeni & Vosloo, 2019). Institutions can also offer specialized support services to assist students with disabilities in navigating virtual learning environments. By prioritizing accessibility, universities can create inclusive educational experiences that cater to the diverse needs of their student populations.

19.3.6 Enhancing Data Protection Measures

Addressing privacy and data security concerns is paramount for the ethical implementation of the metaverse. Organizations must implement robust data protection measures that comply with international standards, such as the General Data Protection Regulation (GDPR). These measures include the use of encryption, anonymization, and secure data storage practices to safeguard personal data from breaches and unauthorized access. As Floridi (Floridi, 2014) emphasizes, the ethical management of personal data is crucial for maintaining user trust and preventing potential harms associated with data misuse. Furthermore, organizations should establish transparent data governance frameworks to ensure accountability and ethical handling of user data (Nascimbeni & Vosloo, 2019).Universities must ensure that their virtual learning environments and administrative systems within the metaverse are equipped with advanced encryption technologies to protect data in transit and at rest. For instance, when students participate in virtual classes or submit assignments through metaverse platforms, their data should be encrypted to prevent unauthorized access (Heneghan, 2023). Anonymization techniques can further protect student privacy by ensuring that personal identifiers are removed from datasets used for research or analytics (van Dijck et al., 2018).

Compliance with International Standards Higher education institutions should also comply with international data protection regulations, such as the GDPR, to ensure that they are meeting high standards of privacy and security (Nascimbeni & Vosloo, 2019). This compliance includes obtaining explicit consent from students and staff before collecting and using their data, as well as providing them with clear information about how their data will be used and protected. By adhering to these regulations, universities can build trust with their stakeholders and demonstrate their commitment to ethical data management.Transparent data governance frameworks are essential for accountability and ethical handling of user data in the metaverse (Nascimbeni & Vosloo, 2019).

19.3.7 Addressing the Risks of Data Breaches and Unauthorized Access

Preventing data breaches and unauthorized access is a critical aspect of data security in higher education. Universities should conduct regular security audits and vulnerability assessments to identify and address potential risks in their virtual environments (Livingstone, 2008). Implementing multi-factor authentication and access controls can also enhance security by ensuring that only authorized individuals can access sensitive information (van Dijck et al., 2018). In the event of a data breach, institutions must have a response plan in place to mitigate the impact, notify affected individuals, and take corrective actions to prevent future incidents.

19.3.8 Educating Students and Staff on Data Privacy and Security

Finally, education and awareness are key components of data security in higher education. Universities should provide training and resources to help students and staff understand the importance of data privacy and how to protect their personal information in the metaverse (Heneghan, 2023). Workshops, online courses, and informational materials can cover topics such as safe internet practices, recognizing phishing attempts, and using secure passwords. Digital literacy programs should be comprehensive, encompassing not only technical skills but also critical thinking and ethical awareness (Nascimbeni & Vosloo, 2019).

19.4 Conclusion

The ethical implementation of metaverse technologies in emerging economies necessitates a multifaceted approach that meticulously addresses privacy, access, psychological well-being, and representation. By adhering to rigorous ethical principles and guidelines, organizations can effectively harness the transformative potential of the metaverse while ensuring its benefits are equitably distributed across diverse societal segments.

However, achieving this vision demands a concerted and proactive engagement from all relevant stakeholders, including policymakers, technology developers, and end-users. Policymakers must craft and enforce comprehensive regulations that safeguard user data and promote equitable access to metaverse technologies. Technology developers are tasked with the critical responsibility of designing and deploying solutions that prioritize user safety, inclusivity, and ethical data management. Concurrently, end-users must be educated and empowered to navigate the metaverse responsibly, fostering a culture of ethical digital citizenship.The successful realization of an ethically sound metaverse requires immediate, collaborative action and sustained commitment from all parties involved. This collective endeavor presents a unique opportunity to shape a digital future where technology serves humanity's best interests and where ethical considerations are integrally embedded within the fabric of innovation.

References

Al-Kfairy, M., Alrabaee, S., & Alfandi, O. (2024, November). Ethical pathways in VR and the metaverse: Frameworks for responsible innovation. In *2024 2nd International Conference on Intelligent Metaverse Technologies & Applications (iMETA)* (pp. 9–17). IEEE. https://doi.org/10.1109/IMETA62882.2024.10807903

Banks, S. (2024, February 29). *Getting started with data governance*. EDUCAUSE Review. https://er.educause.edu/articles/2024/2/getting-started-with-data-governance
Benjamins, R., Rubio Viñuela, Y., & Alonso, C. (2023). Social and ethical challenges of the metaverse. *AI and Ethics, 3*, 689–697.
Benkler, Y. (2006). *The wealth of networks: How social production transforms markets and freedom*. Yale University Press.
Carr, N. (2014). *The glass cage: How our computers are changing us*. W. W. Norton & Company.
Díaz de la Cruz, C., Fernández Fernández, J. L., & Villegas-Galaviz, C. (2025). Model of ethical analysis of digital technologies: Towards true digital humanism. AI & Society. https://doi.org/10.1007/s00146-025-02330-w
Di Dario, D., Pentangelo, V., Colella, M. I., Palomba, F., & Gravino, C. (2024, June). Collecting and implementing ethical guidelines for emotion recognition in an educational metaverse. In *Adjunct proceedings of the 32nd ACM conference on user modeling, adaptation and personalization* (pp. 9–17). *ACM*. https://doi.org/10.1145/3631700.3665232
European Parliament & Council. (2016). Regulation (EU) 2016/679 of 27 April 2016 on the protection of natural persons with regard to the processing of personal data and on the free movement of such data (General Data Protection Regulation). *Official Journal of the European Union, L 119*, 1–88. EUR-Lex.
Floridi, L. (2014). *The fourth revolution: How the Infosphere is reshaping human reality*. Oxford University Press.
Gündüz, N., & Sincar, M. (2024). Metaethics in higher education institutions: Is the metaverse the second forbidden fruit of humanity? *International Journal of Contemporary Educational Research, 11*(2), 186–203. https://doi.org/10.52380/ijcer.2024.11.2.578
Han, E., Miller, M. R., DeVeaux, C., Jun, H., Nowak, K. L., Hancock, J. T., Ram, N., & Bailenson, J. N. (2023). People, places, and time: A large-scale, longitudinal study of transformed avatars and environmental context in group interaction in the metaverse. *Journal of Computer-Mediated Communication, 28*(2). https://doi.org/10.1093/jcmc/zmac031
Harrison, T., & Laco, D. (2022). Where's the character education in online higher education? Constructivism, virtue ethics and roles of online educators. *E-Learning and Digital Media, 19*(6), 555–573. https://doi.org/10.1177/20427530221104885
Helsper, E. J., & Eynon, R. (2010). Digital natives: Where is the evidence? *British Educational Research Journal, 36*(3), 503–520.
Heneghan, L. (2023). 5 ways to shape an inclusive and equitable metaverse. *World Economic Forum.*. https://www.weforum.org/stories/2023/01/5-ways-shape-inclusive-metaverse-davos2023/
Herrera, F., Bailenson, J. N., Weisz, E., Ogle, E., & Zaki, J. (2018). Building long-term empathy: A large-scale comparison of traditional and virtual-reality perspective-taking. *PLoS One, 13*(10), e0204494. https://doi.org/10.1371/journal.pone.0204494
International Center for Academic Integrity (ICAI). (2021). *The fundamental values of academic integrity* (3rd ed.). International Center for Academic Integrity.
International Organization for Standardization (ISO). (2022). ISO/IEC 27001:2022 Information security, cybersecurity and privacy protection—Information security management systems—Requirements. ISO.
Kaddoura, S., & Al Husseiny, F. (2023). The rising trend of Metaverse in education: Challenges, opportunities, and ethical considerations. *PeerJ Computer Science, 9*, e1252. https://doi.org/10.7717/peerj-cs.1252
Livingstone, S. (2008). Internet literacy: Young people's negotiation of new online opportunities. In T. McPherson (Ed.), Digital Youth, Innovation, and the Unexpected (pp. 101–122). MIT Press.
Mapanga, A., & Stofile, R. (2024). Ethical dimensions of metaverse in business education in the global South: A thematic content analysis. *Journal of Economic and Social Development, 11*(1), 206–220.
Nascimbeni, F., & Vosloo, S. (2019). *Digital literacy for children: Exploring definitions and frameworks* (Scoping Paper). UNICEF Office of Global Insight and Policy.

Schneier, B. (2015). *Data and goliath: The hidden battles to collect your data and control your world*. W. W. Norton & Company.

Tabassum, A., Elmahjub, E., & Qadir, J. (2024). Ethics and regulation in metaverse: Risks, current approaches, and way forward. In S. K. Sharma, B. Dwivedi, & M. Rana (Eds.), Understanding the Metaverse: Applications, Challenges, and the Future (pp. 269–292). Springer.

Turkle, S. (2015). *Alone together: Why we expect more from technology and less from each other*. Basic Books.

Turner Lee, N., Ray, R., Lai, S., & Tanner, B. (2022, September 6). Ensuring equitable access to AR/VR in higher education. *Brookings Institution—TechTank*. https://www.brookings.edu/articles/ensuring-equitable-access-to-ar-vr-in-higher-education/

UNESCO. (2015). *Global citizenship education: Topics and learning objectives*. https://unesdoc.unesco.org/ark:/48223/pf0000232993

van Dijck, J., Poell, T., & de Waal, M. (2018). *The platform society: Public values in a connective world*. Oxford University Press.

Young, K. (1998). Internet addiction: The emergence of a new clinical disorder. *CyberPsychology & Behavior, 1*(3), 237–244.

Chapter 20
Artificial Intelligence and Student: What Training for an Ethical Use?

Vanessa Marescot, Laura Wallard, and Céline Faure

Abstract The focus of the article is a training module for students on GAI and it presents case study feedback. The first session was used to gather materials for exploratory research. GAI made great advances in the last couple of years and its use is widespread. The rise of GAI has shaken the academic world through the relationship to learning and assessment. It is necessary to train students and support them to use GAI ethically. In this sense, a training module was created with the aim of developing competence: Integrating GAI tools into my student practices. Designed in an interdisciplinary way, it brings together 14 stakeholders from a variety of different fields. The first session is a face-to-face kick-off meeting promoting exchanges between students. The students were tasked with the production of a series of materials intended to facilitate the collection of their preconceptions and beliefs. In this initial year of the program, 70 students participated. The exploratory analysis of students' production shows a collective awareness and critical thinking when specifically asked to reflect on it.

Keywords GAI · Students training · Ethical use · Exploratory research · Qualitative method · Module polytechnique · e-ForIA project

---

The module is part of the eFor-IA project led by the *DNum* (UPHF) and co-financed by the *Conseil Régional Hauts-de France.*

V. Marescot (✉)
LARSH (Laboratoire de recherche en Sciences Humaines), DeVisu département, Université Polytechnique Hauts-de-France, Valenciennes, France
e-mail: vanessa.marescot@uphf.fr

L. Wallard
LAMIH (Laboratoire d'Automatique, de Mécanique, d'Informatique Industrielles et Humaines), CNRS, UMR 8201, Université Polytechnique Hauts-de-France, Valenciennes, France
e-mail: laura.wallard@uphf.fr

C. Faure
Celulle Ingénierie Pédagogique et TICE, Université Polytechnique Hauts-de-France, Valenciennes, France
e-mail: celine.faure@uphf.fr

M. Abed et al. (eds.), *Metaverse and Artificial Intelligence in Education for a Sustainable Society*, Future Education and Learning Spaces,
https://doi.org/10.1007/978-981-95-8852-7_20

20.1 Introduction

Artificial intelligence (AI), and more specifically generative AI (GAI), has become ubiquitous and has penetrated all spheres of society such as education and learning, culture, and research. GAI is mainly used to generate text and images for personal and professional purposes. Indeed, since the launch of ChatGPT by OpenAI in November 2022, the platform alone has been used by more than 200 million people every week.

However, although these technologies offer many advantages, they also present many challenges, particularly in the academic world by changing the link between learning and assessment of learners. Indeed, usage studies show that by 2023, more than 60% of students will use GAI in their academic practices, with performance expectations related to the completion of learning activities or assignments to be submitted, and to increase their productivity (Meyer & Piché, 2024). Moreover, students' use of AI impacts directly the relationship to knowledge, the thinking skills or the activities implemented by the teacher (Agbon, 2024; Lepage & Roy, 2023; Meyer, 2025). Indeed, GAI reinforces the evolution of traditional relationship to knowledge by offering easily structured information. This evolution raises questions about memorization and ability to integrate this information, but also about reflection and critical thinking of the learner (Siemens et al., 2022).

In this context, the e-ForIA project was born, supported by the *Hauts-de-France* Region and hosted by the *Université Polytechnique Hauts-de-France* (UPHF). The target audience of this project is students, but the project aims to reach them in two ways. First indirectly, by informing and even training teachers about AI. It will enable them to integrate pedagogical activities that encourage students not only to use AI in an informed way, but also to analyze AI productions. Then the project creates a training program specifically designed for students: this is the module studied in this article.

Firstly, the article presents a theoretical overview of GAI impact in pedagogy. Then, it presents the module through the particularities of *Modules Polytechniques* and the learning design. It also analyses the first session which enabled researchers to collect students' preconceptions. Finally, it concludes with a few perspectives.

20.2 Theoretical Overview

20.2.1 AI in Education Opportunities

The development of AI over the last several decades has opened up a wide range of applications in the field of education, serving learners, teachers, and institutions (Holmes & Tuomi, 2022). These authors propose a taxonomy of AI in Education (AIED) organized into three distinct and overlapping categories. Student-focused AIED includes tools specifically designed to support students, such as Intelligent Tutoring Systems (ITS), AI to support learners with disabilities, chatbots, AI-assisted apps (e.g., mathematics, text-to-speech, language learning). More than interfaces for teachers included in previous systems, teacher-focused AIED includes tools designed to support teachers in their tasks: smart curation of learning materials, classroom monitoring, AI Teaching Assistant (including assessment assistant). For institutions, AI technologies can support the administrative and management functions of educational institutions: admissions (e.g., student selection), course-planning/ scheduling/ timetabling, identifying dropouts, and students at risk.

All these examples emphasize that AI has a large increasing role in education, particularly for personalized teaching systems "with growing evidence of their effectiveness for improving learning" (Khosravi et al., 2022). AIED allows the creation of an interface designed to deliver a quality learning experience (Khosravi et al., 2022) with adaptive learning (Romero et al., 2023).

Generative AI (GAI) emerged in the 2015s to generate text and images for personal and professional purposes. These advances went unnoticed by the general public until the launch of the freely accessible ChatGPT (OpenAI), and the democratization of image generation tools such as DAll-E and Midjourney. However, with the rise of GAI, particularly with conversational agents based on large language models such as ChatGPT, education is facing a major shift. These AI apps have shaken the academic world through the relationship to knowledge and assessment. GAI allows students to provide productions to be used as proof of learning, breach of the tacit contract between the teacher ("referent") and the student ("referee") on which the assessment is based (Nizet, 2025).

20.2.2 Didactic Triangle's Evolution

The relationship to knowledge is "the relationship to the world, to others and to oneself of a subject confronted with the need to learn" (Charlot, 1997; Meyer, 2025). It is an (organized) set of relationships that links a subject with everything that has to do with learning and knowledge (Meyer, 2025). The development of the Internet and digital technology at the turn of the millennium had already changed this relationship to knowledge: knowledge could be reached in your pocket (Serres, 2012). GAI represents a further turning point: there is no longer any need to search for information—simply ask the conversational agent and it will provide you with an oracle-like answer.

The pedagogical triangle introduced by Houssaye (Houssaye, 1988) represents the pedagogical space with three poles: Teacher, Knowledge, and Learner. It has been reshaped by the introduction of a fourth pole Group (Faerber, 2003) or even by the inclusion of technologies in the center of the tetrahedron thus formed (Meyer, 2025).

The place of GAI in the educational triangle remains an open research question. Indeed, GAI intervenes at different levels in the Knowledge pole (Allouche, 2024):

production and/or extraction of knowledge, critical distancing, IME[1] and training critical thinking, support for scientific research, data processing, etc. Furthermore, GAI impacts the other poles too (Allouche, 2024) such as pedagogical engineering assistance, assessment, AI literacy, adapted and personalized learning paths. Many of these innovations seem to have advantages, but the use of data and the replacement of production by possible copy and paste raise ethical questions.

20.2.3 Ethical Use of IA

AI will change the world of work. This means a rethink of education to adapt to new job skills (Kennel & Burger-Helmchen, 2023). With AI more and more used in the academic world, it becomes crucial to learn to use these tools ethically and effectively, while maintaining a critical approach (Kennel & Burger-Helmchen, 2023). Indeed, while AI cannot be ethical on its own, it does require that it be used in an ethical way (Collet, 2023).

First, there is a need for clear, consistent, and collegial guidelines on the topic of AI integration in education, in higher education (Tremblay Chevalier et al., 2023). Consequently, numerous academic institutions have established AI use charters. This is also the case at UPHF, where a charter is currently being drafted and will be voted on in July 2025.

On the other hand, teachers must adapt their assessment methods and promote academic integrity in the context of these emerging technologies. It is important to ensure that AI remains a tool for learning and not a substitute. This is why understanding these impacts and adopting appropriate/adapted and ethical pedagogical strategies for the use of GAI is essential. However, even in 2024, teachers use GAI much less than students (Goudey et al., 2023).

To educate in and through AI, it is therefore necessary to train teachers and support them in integrating it into their teaching practices. Lot of training for teachers became available in 2024: for instance, two MOOCs on the French platform Fun Mooc. At UPHF, the e-ForIA project has created a series of technical training courses to help teachers get started with AI, as well as webinars and reflection workshops to think about the impact of AI on learning and assessment. However, the time required for teachers to be available for training, and therefore the time required to take a step back, demonstrates the importance of developing training for students (Many et al., 2024). Céci et al. (2023) also point to the necessity to cultivate the capacity of learners to act in this new digital era of AI. They consider students as "digital citizens", who need to develop their agency and critical regulation of their practices.

In this sense, the polytechnic module was created, targeting the skill: Integrating GAI tools into student practices.

[1] Information and media Education.

20.3 Module Design

20.3.1 PRéLUDE and Individualized Path

The demographic evolution, in conjunction with the implementation of French national policies in the 1960s, gave rise to a period of substantial university population expansion. Successive waves of massification have resulted in a heterogeneous composition of the student population. It is characterized by diversity in terms of demographic characteristics, educational backgrounds, and other factors (Duguet et al., 2016; Rossignol-Brunet et al., 2022). Therefore, student success has been a major concern in French higher education for several decades.[2]

Although a variety of factors contribute to student success, research has demonstrated that teachers' posture and teaching methodologies play a substantial role in student failure (Annoot et al., 2019; De Clercq et al., 2025). From this perspective, numerous French reports have emphasized the necessity of a pedagogical and digital transformation in teaching (Bertrand, 2014; Filâtre, 2017).

A variety of ministerial calls for projects have been initiated to assist universities in the much-needed transformation of teacher practices. These calls for projects[3] are incentive instruments for transforming universities to solve these public policy problems (Mocquet, 2021). A project called PRéLUDE has been developed by two universities in northern France,[4] which have collaborated to offer this innovative program.

In order to enhance student success, the objectives of the initiative are to provide students with the opportunity to design their own curricular trajectory and thereby access a diverse range of courses. This diversification will be achieved through modularization, and by providing students with support in the development of their career paths. PRéLUDE is a pedagogical/training model that involves the design of courses following a competency-based approach. This approach is modeled after a methodology developed by Jacques Tardif (Poumay et al., 2017). The program is designed to allow students to customize their academic trajectory by leveraging a curated selection of competencies from a catalog of available courses.

---

[2] *Parcours Réussite en Licence Universitaire à Développement Expérientiel*: Experiential Development University Degree Success Course—winner of PIA 3 wave 2 in 2018—*Nouveau Cursus Universitaire* (University New curriculum).

[3] The French government is allocating resources to a series of initiatives aimed at modernizing education and cultivating innovation. These investments prioritize the development of digital learning tools, the training of educators in innovative pedagogical practices, and the support of experimental projects within academic institutions. Initiatives such as the Programme d'Investissements d'Avenir (PIA) and France 2030 (https://anr.fr/en/france-2030/france-2030/) fund programs like Nouveaux Cursus à l'Université (University New curriculum) and Territoires Numériques Éducatifs (Digital Educational Territories). These programs aim to enhance student engagement, promote academic success, and align educational offerings with contemporary societal and economic challenges.

[4] The *Université Polytechnique Hauts-de-France* (UPHF), and *Université Catholique de Lille* (UCL)

Both institutions have developed their own catalog. The institution of higher education referenced in this article is the *Université Polytechnique Hauts-de-France* (UPHF). The catalog encompasses two types of courses. First, students must select courses designated as *Modules d'Ouvertures*, which enable them to discover new cultural and sporting disciplines, or to prepare for the world of work. On the other hand, *Modules Polytechniques* embody the vision of the strategic project. One of these subjects is the focus of the present article.

20.3.2 Module Specifications

A *Module Polytechnique* (MP) is a learning course of 36 hours and 4 ECTS credits. It has to be co-designed by a team of teachers from the two core disciplines (Humanities—Science and Technology) and from at least two faculties of the university. The desired approach is an original blend of different disciplinary resources. A MP must be described by a competency accorded to Tardif's model, and must aim at its development.

Teachers are also encouraged to integrate Student-centered pedagogy. Also, MP must respect hybrid learning modalities (minimum 20 h asynchronous lecture class, maximum 16 h face-to-face tutorials class). The schedule is adapted module by module, depending on the skills and related activities. Face-to-face sessions take place on Fridays, a day normally reserved for this purpose in all degree programs.

Asynchronous remote learning modules are encouraged to enable students like apprentices to follow them despite the absence of flexibility in their schedules.

20.3.3 Learning Outcomes

The MP "Artificial Intelligence (AI) and me" target the competency: integrate generative AI tools into students' practices. To achieve this competency properly, they must develop four essential components: to adopt an ethical and reflective posture, to be aware of the benefits and limitations of using AI, to project themselves into the professional world and to keep their knowledge up to date. Six learning outcomes are intended, students must be able to:

- Explain how GAI tools work.
- Choose the right tool for the activity.
- Write relevant and effective prompts (Analyze and evaluate the relevance of the response).
- Analyze their own use of GAI.
- Identify different uses of GAI in the professional world.
- Develop a critical approach to GAI (legal and ethical, societal, sovereignty, ecological impact, status of information).

20.3.4 Interdisciplinary

The course created goes far beyond the requirement of the specification to cross two disciplines and two faculties. Indeed, it is the first module to involve members of the three faculties of the university (INSA, ISH, IUT) and several university services: the University Library, Careers Advisory Service, Digital Teaching Support Service and Teaching Support Service. It allows 14 contributors to work in synergy on the topic from very different fields: 8 professors or assistant professors (computer science (3), digital art, neuroscience, information and communication sciences, management sciences, foreign language), 3 educational engineers, a professional integration manager, university library staff, and a social/environmental issues project manager.

Therefore, it allows the program to embrace reflections from Science and Technology and from Humanities and Social Sciences through employment and ethical perspectives. The number of contributors and the range of disciplines represented present a considerable challenge; nevertheless, such interdisciplinarity is essential for the development of critical thinking skills.

20.3.5 Hybrid Learning

The learning scenario was based on Lebrun's IMAIP model, which proposes 5 components to support the depth of the student learning process: information, motivation, activities, interaction, and production (Lebrun et al., 2011). Table 1 presents these five components and the module design related.

Salmon's model (2012) asserts that e-learning is inseparable from the digital environment and the social interactions it generates. Both help to build confidence and better commitment in participants' learning. In this model, e-learning needs to create the role of "e-moderator" ensuring the running of online activities and the quality of exchanges. In this case, the module manager is the e-moderator, and his role targets two of the five stages defined by Salmon's model: access/motivation and information sharing. Indeed, he ensures that participants can connect, welcomes them, tutors, and encourages the use of resources by sending a weekly plan of what must be done.

20.4 First Session, First Feedback

The module was conducted from February to May 2025, during a period of 11 weeks. Consequently, the article does not offer an evaluation of the course; rather, it provides feedback on the course and exploratory research based on the deliverables available in February, i.e., from the first session. One objective of the session was to collect data on student use of AI and preconceptions. These outputs were to be used by the

Table 1 Module design through IMAIP's model

Component of the learning process	Description	Module design
Information	Resources, knowledge, and their materials	Videos, PDF
Motivation	Meaningful context environment promoting engagement	Activities rooted in student's practice e-moderation (Salmon) Kick-off session
Activities	Activities for resources related to the appropriation and development of higher-level skills (analysis, synthesis, evaluation, critical thinking...)	Quiz Tutorials class (AI use case)
Interaction	Interactivity in various resources Interactions between students and teachers	Interactive videos including quiz Tutorials class
Production	Learning outcomes Personal or collective construction Assessment materials	Assessment on implementation and self-analysis Reflexive production

teachers involved to gain insight into the profile of the two groups of 35 students ($n = 70$, Bachelor 2 to Master 2, from different study fields). These productions could subsequently be utilized for exploratory purposes.

20.4.1 Learning Design

The first session is organized as a face-to-face kick-off meeting promoting exchanges between students. The session is designed to get them to talk about how they use AI, identify their preconceptions, and introduce the module. This first session is based on the pedagogical method known as feedback from experience, also known as the experiential method. This pedagogical method is based on the principle of learning under real-life conditions (Delabre, 2023). It therefore draws on learners' experiences and real-life experiences to quantify and characterize their prior knowledge and understanding.

After an interactive quiz targeting their expectations, four stages are planned:

- an ice-breaker that allows students to express their previous experiences with GAI, positives and negatives,
- a mapping of uses classified in four categories: study, hobbies, professional world, and daily life,
- a world-café organized in three rounds collecting their conceptions about the impact of AI in three fields: education, employment, and society. Each round

allows them to reflect about the contributions, limitations, and issues of AI in each field sequentially,
- a discussion around the question: What does a human need in order to live in a world with AI, what kinds of learning?

Each stage is collaborative: after a short amount of time of self-reflection, students must discuss in groups and the class debriefs with the teacher. This learning design enables the teachers to collect precious knowledge of what students think about GAI before starting the module. Next, the paper focuses on two elements through the eyes of these students. The last activity (the discussion) allows to describe the skills needed by humans in the era of AI (4.2). And the materials gathered from the world café were analyzed and Sect. 4.3 presents the issues related to the use of AI in the three areas studied.

20.4.2 Humans in the Era of AI

This activity is organized with a one-pair-share method. It enables the collection of 17 skills needed for this new era, from the students' perspective. 16 are presented in Table 2 and organized through the classic distinction: hard-skills and soft-skills (which are independent).

Elements collected in the hard-skills column show the need for technical proficiencies. They emphasize AI expertise, computer literacy, and comprehension of underlying mechanisms. These competencies enable individuals to adapt to new business requirements. Concurrently, transversal competencies (soft skills) stress the necessity of developing a critical, ethical, and adaptive approach. This approach

Table 2 Humans' skills needed for AI era

Hard-Skills	Soft-Skills
Maintain advanced knowledge	Adaptability
Possess fundamental computer literacy	Maintain critical perspective
Comprehend operational mechanisms	Demonstrate versatility
Undergo training for enhanced efficiency	Receive training (benefits/limitations/implications) in developing perspective/ethical considerations
Cultivate versatility in AI platform utilization	Conduct personalized monitoring
Understand AI functionality [black box]	Maintain meta-awareness of personal usage
Develop AI-adapted competencies for improved performance	Adopt ethical and deontological approach
Address challenges of business 4.0 and digital transformation in business	Maintain critical approach to daily utilization

promotes versatility, information monitoring, and metacognitive reflection on AI usage.

This analysis demonstrates students' awareness and demand of training to optimize efficiency in AI technology utilization, as well as to cultivate an ethical and critical approach to this ever-evolving technology. This awareness is stressed by the 18th skills collected. Students reveal the importance to respect rules at both the state level and individual levels, underscoring the necessity for the establishment of such guidelines.

20.4.3 AI-Related Issues for Education

The group work revealed that the students have a great deal of awareness of the issues surrounding the use of AI in education, employment, and society. This section focuses on education and training. All the issues collected have been gathered by meaning and organized in a mind map (Fig. 1).

Students express concerns about risks related to misinformation and loss of critical thinking, emphasizing the importance of source verification and maintaining open-mindedness. They question the impact of AI on learning and cognition, particularly regarding knowledge validation, educational quality, and potential effects on intelligence, memory, and creativity. They also fear a lack of empathy in teaching. AI dependency and social isolation are significant concerns, with concerns about addiction and loss of social connections. Students raise issues regarding the regulation and ethics of AI in education. These issues include limitations on the use of AI, the ethical implications of its use, and the control exercised by AI designers.

These elements are echoed when the subject is employment and society. Firstly, students emphasize that the integration of AI into the work environment can lead to a loss of skills through the overuse of AI. At the same time, they underscore

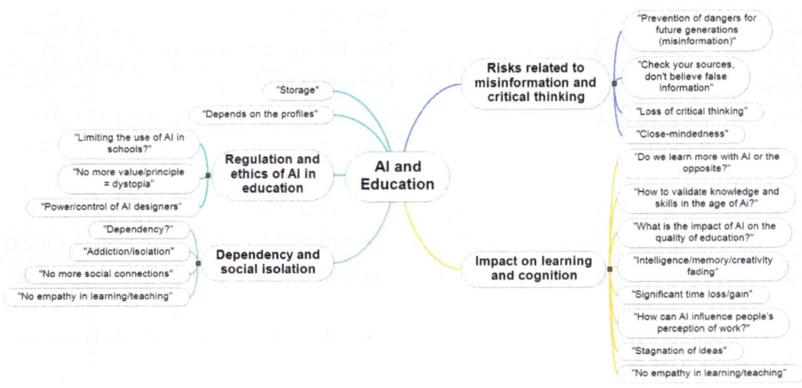

Fig. 1 Mind map (authors)–Issues related to education

the challenge of the workforce' inadequate qualifications, which requires constant updating of knowledge about generative AI, training in its applications, and the associated risks. However, they raise concerns regarding excessive reliance on these technologies. On the other hand, they are concerned about the transformation of human relationships in the workplace, which may result in the dissolution of specific interpersonal interactions. However, students recognize the prospects for enhancing professional well-being through the automation or delegation of tasks.

This dual awareness of contributions and limitations is pervasive throughout the issues collected. Students demonstrate remarkable foresight and ask themselves the appropriate questions to develop targeted skill.

The analysis of the students' production during this first session shows a collective awareness and critical thinking when specifically asked to reflect on it. The module has an important breeding ground for critical thinking.

20.5 Conclusion

The objective of the *Module Polytechnique*: "Artificial Intelligence (AI) and me: integrating generative AI tools into my practices" is to assist students in developing a critical mind and a more ethical use of GAI. To achieve this, the first session aimed to highlight their use of AI in order to identify their preconceptions through interactive activities. This first session revealed that the students possess a substantial degree of awareness regarding the issues surrounding the use of AI in education, employment, and society. Students express concerns about risks related to misinformation and loss of critical thinking. They have underscored the significance of verifying sources of information and maintaining an openness to diverse perspectives.

However, the notion of critical thinking and the operationality of its development comes with new challenges and limitations, and particularly with the use of GAI. It supposes interdisciplinarity but cannot consist in the development of fragmented micro-skills, or be reduced to a juxtaposition of courses designed to train it (Petit, 2022). The module was designed in order to embrace the potentiality of several fields. This cannot have happened without the orchestration of the project manager and the work on the mediatization of educational resources of educational engineers. From a pragmatic point of view, an evaluation questionnaire aimed at continuous improvement is being deployed to prepare for the following year.

Research on GAI is therefore a field of study that mobilizes many research areas and disciplines in order to notably analyze the pedagogical implications and best practices for integrating these tools into learning environments offering new learning opportunities. Regardless of this module, it will be necessary to evaluate these effects on the development of students' skill and on the development of a real sense of perspective on their practices.

References

Agbon, G. (2024). *L'intelligence artificielle générative: savoir quand l'utiliser plutôt que comment.* The Conversation.

Allouche E. (2024, November 29). IA générative et ingénierie pédagogique: De la conception à l'évaluation [présentation]. *Éducation, numérique et recherche.* Consulté le 25 février 2025 à l'adresse https://doi.org/10.58079/12sfj

Annoot, E., Bobineau, C., Daverne-Bailly, C., Dubois, E., Piot, T., & Vari, J. (2019). *Politiques, pratiques et dispositifs d'aide à la réussite pour les étudiants des premiers cycles à l'université: Bilan et perspectives.* Conseil national d'évaluation du système scolaire.

Bertrand, C. (2014). *Soutenir la transformation pédagogique dans l'enseignement supérieur—Rapport à Mme Simone Bonnafous.* Ministère de l'Enseignement Supérieur et de la Recherche. https://www.vie-publique.fr/rapport/34320-soutenir-la-transformation-pedagogique-dans-lenseignement-superieur

Céci J.F., Heiser L., Romero M. (2023). Le dispositif 5J5IA, un exemple de régulation critique de l'IA en éducation. *Canopé. Enseigner et apprendre à l'ere de l'IA-Acculturation, intégration et usages créatifs de l'IA en éducation Livre blanc, hal-04032083v2.*

Charlot, B. (1997). *Du rapport au savoir.* Anthropos.

Collet, P. (2023, December). Une IA peut-elle être éthique ? p 32 de l'IA: Aux frontières de l'intelligence? Eds. Savoir(s), n°47, Université de Strasbourg.

De Clercq, M., Perret, C., & Constans, A. (2025). Les réussites dans l'enseignement supérieur: Fondements conceptuels pour une approche tridimensionnelle. *Carrefours de l'Education, 60,* 1–31.

Delabre, U. (2023). Les expériences de cours comme pédagogie active pour améliorer la motivation et la compréhension des étudiants lors des cours à l'Université: comparaison avec d'autres pédagogies. *Études & Pédagogies.*https://doi.org/10.20870/eep.2023.7699

Duguet, A., Le Mener, M., & Morlaix, S. (2016). Les déterminants de la réussite à l'université. Quels apports de la recherche en éducation ? Quelles perspectives de recherche ? *Spirale-Revue de recherches en éducation*, Supplément électronique au n°57.

Faerber, R. (2003). Groupements, processus pédagogiques et quelques contraintes liés à un environnement virtuel d'apprentissage. *Environnements Informatiques pour l'Apprentissage Humain, 2003*, 199–210. https://edutice.archives-ouvertes.fr/edutice00000137/

Filâtre, D. (2017). Réformer le premier cycle de l'enseignement superieur et améliorer la réussite des etudiants.

Goudey A., Loupiac P., Quinio B. (2023). Regards croisés sur les IA Génératives dans l'Enseignement Supérieur en Gestion: Panorama des pratiques et perspectives—FNEGE

Holmes, W., & Tuomi, I. (2022). State of the art and practice in AI in education. *European Journal of Education, 57*(4), 542–570. https://doi.org/10.1111/ejed.12533

Houssaye J. (1988). *Le triangle pédagogique. Théorie et pratiques de l'éducation scolaire*, Peter Lang, Berne, 2000 (3e Éd., 1re Éd.)

Kennel, S. & Burger-Helmchen, T. (2023, December). Enseignement et IA génératives: apprendre à vivre ensemble p 22 de l'IA: aux frontières de l'intelligence? Eds. Savoir(s), n°47, Université de Strasbourg.

Khosravi, H., Shum, S. B., Chen, G., Conati, C., Tsai, Y.-S., Kay, J., Knight, S., Martinez-Maldonado, R., Sadiq, S., & Gašević, D. (2022). Explainable artificial intelligence in education. *Computers and Education: Artificial Intelligence, 3,* 100074. https://doi.org/10.1016/j.caeai.2022.100074

Lebrun, M., Smidts, D., & Bricoult, G. (2011). *Comment construire un dispositif de formation ?: Guide pratique à l'usage des enseignants, des formateurs, des concepteurs pédagogiques* (1er édition). De Boeck Supérieur.

Lepage, A., & Roy, N. (2023). Une recension des écrits de 1970 à 2022 sur les rôles de l'enseignant et de l'intelligence artificielle dans le domaine de l'IA en éducation. *Médiations Et médiatisations, 16*, 9–29. https://doi.org/10.52358/mm.vi16.304

Many, H., Shvetsova, M., & Forestier, G. (2024). Transformation numérique: comment enseigner (avec) l'IA générative dans l'enseignement supérieur ? *Études & Pédagogies. https://.* https://doi.org/10.20870/eep.2024.8100

Meyer, F. (2025, février 4). Repenser l'enseignement à l'ère de l'IA: vers un nouveau paradigme pédagogique ? [Webinaire].

Meyer, F., & Piché, S. (2024) Portrait des pratiques et préoccupations entourant les IAG en contexte académique: perspectives étudiantes à l'Université de Sheerbrooke—équipe « Apprivoiser les IA »—présentation 16 février 2024.

Mocquet, B. (2021). Manager l'innovation du Sup': entre perception et injonction. *Management des technologies organisationnelles, 12*, 83–100. https://doi.org/10.3917/mto.012.0083

Nizet, I. (2025, février 27). L'évaluation au temps de l'IA générative: Quels défis nous attendent ?

Petit, L. (2022). La rencontre de l'Intelligence artificielle (IA) et de l'esprit critique (EC): Nouveaux enjeux? nouvelle formation? *Communication, Technologies et Développement*, (12), Article 12. https://doi.org/10.4000/ctd.8256

Poumay, M., Tardif, J., & Georges, F. (2017). *Organiser la formation à partir des compétences.* Un pari gagnant pour l'apprentissage dans le supérieur.

Romero, M., Heiser, L., Lepage, A., Gagnebien, A., Bonjour, A., Lagarrigue, A., Palaude, A., Boulord, C., Gagneur, C.-A., Mercier, C., Caucheteux, C., Guidoni-Stoltz, D., Tressols, F., Henry, J., Alexandre, F., Céci, J.-F., Camponovo, J., Fouché, L., Métral, J.-F., Borgne, Y.-A. L. (2023). *Enseigner et apprendre à l'ère de l'intelligence artificielle: Vol. Livre blanc.* Canopé. https://hal.science/hal-04013223

Rossignol-Brunet, M., Frouillou, L., Couto, M.P., & Bugeja-Bloch, F. (2022). Ce que masquent les « nouveaux publics étudiants »: Les enjeux de la troisième massification de l'enseignement supérieur français. *Lien social et Politiques, 89*, 57–82.

Salmon, G. (2012). *E-moderating, the key to online teaching and learning* (3d éd ed.). Routledge.

Serres, M. (2012). *Petite poucette* (Vol. 125). Le pommier.

Siemens, G., Marmolejo-Ramos, F., Gabriel, F., Medeiros, K., Marrone, R., Joksimovic, S., & de Laat, M. (2022). Human and artificial cognition. *Computers and Education: Artificial Intelligence, 3*, 100107. https://doi.org/10.1016/j.caeai.2022.100107

Tremblay Chevalier, I., Poirier, J., & Bernier, F. (2023). Pour une utilisation juste, éthique et responsable de l'intelligence artificielle: Se donner les moyens de s'adapter. *Apprendre et enseigner aujourd'hui, 13*(1), 21–24. https://doi.org/10.7202/1107538ar

MIX
Papier aus verantwortungsvollen Quellen
Paper from responsible sources
FSC® C105338

If you have any concerns about our products,
you can contact us on
ProductSafety@springernature.com

In case Publisher is established outside the EU,
the EU authorized representative is:
Springer Nature Customer Service Center GmbH
Europaplatz 3, 69115 Heidelberg, Germany

Printed by Libri Plureos GmbH
in Hamburg, Germany